ST JOHN OF T...

Colin Thompson has been Faculty Lecturer in Sp... ...of Oxford and Fellow and Tutor in Spanish at St Catherine's Colle... ...ce 1989. He specializes in the literature of the Golden Age of Spain (the sixte... ...h and seventeenth centuries) and has published widely in this area. He has written an earlier study of St John of the Cross and a book on Fray Luis de León, and has lectured on these writers in the USA, Ireland, Italy and Spain.

He was born in Exeter and spent his school years in Alfreton (Derbyshire), Clacton and Colchester (Essex), before going up to Oxford to read Modern Languages, then Theology. He was ordained in 1971 and is a minister of the United Reformed Church, which he has served in a number of capacities, and has a particular interest in liturgy and hymnody. After completing his doctoral and post-doctoral studies in Oxford he moved to the University of Sussex, where he was University Chaplain for 11 years.

For Charles and Carolyn

ST JOHN OF THE CROSS

Songs in the Night

COLIN THOMPSON

First published in Great Britain in 2002
in hardback

Society for Promoting Christian Knowledge
36 Causton Street
London SW1P 4ST

Re-issued in paperback 2008

British Library Cataloguing-in-Publication Data
A catalogue record for this book is available from the British Library

ISBN 978–0–281–06007–8

1 3 5 7 9 10 8 6 4 2

Typeset by Kenneth Burnley, Wirral, Cheshire
Printed in Great Britain by Ashford Colour Press

Produced on paper from sustainable forests

Contents

Acknowledgements

I began to imagine this book, appropriately enough, in Ávila. During 1991–92 I received many invitations to speak at conferences commemorating the quatercentenary of San Juan's death. It seemed to me that both the work I had prepared for them and the different perspectives of the many speakers I heard might be the starting-point for a fuller exploration of the poet and the mystic than my doctoral thesis 20 years earlier had allowed. So, late one evening in that mystical city, I found myself saying to a friend that I was going to write another book on San Juan, without having been aware that such a thought was in my mind.

A book like this cannot be written in a hurry, nor without help. I would like to thank the Rockefeller Foundation for the month's residence it granted me at the Villa Serbelloni, Bellagio, in February 1994, where the first exploratory drafts of some of the chapters were sketched out in the most beautiful and congenial of surroundings. I would also like to thank St Catherine's and St Anne's Colleges, Oxford, as well as the University of Oxford, for the periods of sabbatical leave in the autumn and winter of 1993–94 and the spring of 1999, without which it would have been impossible to prepare the ground for it, and bring the task to fruition.

I am grateful to many colleagues who have supported and encouraged me: to Professor Luce López-Baralt of the University of Puerto Rico, and Professor Terry O'Reilly of University College, Cork, my fellow-seekers; and to Eric Southworth, Ronald Truman, and my colleagues in the Sub-Faculty of Spanish in Oxford, who have listened to my work in progress and have commented helpfully on it. I am especially grateful to Professor Richard Parish, of St Catherine's, who read through my final draft and with characteristic incision suggested many improvements.

My final word of thanks must go to the Order of Discalced Carmelites, who have kept alive the tradition founded by Santa Teresa and San Juan, and who live by their teaching, rather than peer in, as I do, from a safe and worldly distance. In particular, I would like to thank Steven Payne OCD for his comments, many of which have been incorporated. I owe an especial debt to Iain Matthew OCD, whose doctoral thesis I had the privilege of examining, and from whom, as these pages will show, I have learnt far more than ever he could have learnt from me.

COLIN THOMPSON

A Note on References and Translations

REFERENCES

The following short titles are used for the poems, to distinguish them from their commentaries:

'Cántico'	'Cántico espiritual' poem.
'Noche'	'Noche oscura' poem.
'Llama'	'Llama de amor viva' poem.

References to the prose commentaries are as follows:

C	*Cántico espiritual,* both redactions
CA	*Cántico* commentary, first redaction.
CB	*Cántico* commentary, second redaction.
S	*Subida del monte Carmelo.*
N	*Noche oscura del alma.*
L	*Llama de amor viva,* second redaction.

In the cases of CA, CB, and L, the reference is given by chapter and paragraph, e.g. CB 39.3. I use the CA order for the 'Cántico', and CB for the *Cántico,* but because of the way CB rearranges the order of stanzas, the CB commentaries on CA verses are often different in numbering (e.g. CA 19 = CB 28). A list of the changes to the verses between the two redactions will be found on p. 113 (n. 26). CA, CB, N and L are also used to refer to individual verses of the three poems above, following standard practice. The context should make it clear that in such cases the poem, not the first redaction of the commentary, is meant.

For S and N, references are given to book, chapter, and paragraph, e.g. S 2.13; N 2.9.7.

Biblical references are given according to the Vulgate (Vg); where these differ by number (in the case of many of the Psalms) or by verse, the Authorized Version (AV) reference is given in square brackets. Where San Juan's Spanish version of the Latin is more or less identical with the AV the English is not normally given, but where the AV has a different reading from the Vg, this is noted.

TRANSLATIONS

Translations are my own, unless otherwise indicated. They tend towards the literal, so that something of the underlying Spanish style is preserved. I have used the feminine pronoun for the soul, not so much reflecting Spanish 'alma' as her nature and role as the female lover. I have generally capitalized 'Beloved' when in San Juan's mind this refers to the divine (male) lover.

Abbreviations

BAC	*Biblioteca de autores cristianos*
BH	*Bulletin Hispanique*
BHR	*Bibliothèque d'Humanisme et de Renaissance*
BHS	*Bulletin of Hispanic Studies*
CSIC	Centro Superior de Investigaciones Científicas
EphCarm	*Ephemerides Carmeliticae*
FMLS	*Forum for Modern Language Studies*
JHR	*Journal of Historical Research*
MLR	*The Modern Language Review*
NRFE	*Nueva Revista de Filología Española*
RFE	*Revista de Filología Española*
PL	Patrologia Latina, ed. by J. P. Migne, 221 vols (Tournai, 1844–64)
SCM	Student Christian Movement
SJC	*San Juan de la Cruz*
SPCK	Society for the Promotion of Christian Knowledge
Actas	Edited by A. García Simón, *Actas del congreso internacional sanjuanista*, 3 vols (Valladolid: Junta de Castilla y León, 1993)
Aspectos históricos	Edited by José Vicente Rodríguez, *Aspectos históricos de San Juan de la Cruz*, (Ávila: Institución 'Gran Duque de Alba', 1990)
El sol a medianoche	Edited by Luce López Baralt and Lorenzo Piera, *El sol a medianoche* (Madrid: Trotta, 1996)
Experiencia y pensamiento	Edited by Federico Ruiz, *Experiencia y pensamiento en San Juan de la Cruz* (Madrid: Espiritualidad, 1990)
Introducción a San Juan de la Cruz	Edited by Salvador Ros and others, *Introducción a la lectura de San Juan de la Cruz* (Valladolid: Junta de Castilla y León, 1991)
'Juan de la Cruz, espíritu de llama'	Edited by Otger Steggink, *'Juan de la Cruz, espíritu de llama'* (Kampen: Kok Pharos, 1991)
Obras (FL)	Fray Luis de León, *Obras completas castellanas*, edited by Félix García, 2 vols, 4th edn (Madrid: BAC, 1957)

Obras (SJ)	San Juan de la Cruz, *Obras completas*, edited by Lucinio Ruano de la Iglesia, 11th edn (Madrid: BAC, 1982)
Obras (ST)	Santa Teresa de Jesús, *Obras completas de Teresa de Jesús*, edited by Efrén de la Madre de Dios and Otger Steggink, 2nd edn (Madird: BAC, 1967)
Presencia	Edited by Juan Paredes Núñez, *Presencia de San Juan de la Cruz* (Granada: Universidad de Granada, 1993)

1

Introduction

Souls are not SPANIARDS too; one freindly flood
Of BAPTISM blends them all into a blood.
(Richard Crashaw, 'An Apologie')

I came upon San Juan de la Cruz, by a 'dichosa ventura', a happy chance, as a schoolboy studying an anthology of Spanish poetry.[1] He is a saint and Doctor of the Roman Catholic Church, a mystic, a poet, a theologian, a teacher of the way to joyful union with God through the painful processes of self-denial, detachment and prayer. People react to many of these categories. They may feel antagonistic towards the Church and her saints. They may suspect that mysticism and its claims of union with God are fantasies, forms of infantile dependence or sexual sublimation. They may be moved by beautiful love poetry but be put off when they are told it is about God and the soul. It is easy to treat San Juan as a curiosity. This has been done as much by those who have edited all humanity out of him in order to turn him into an inaccessible model of saintly perfection, as by those who have adopted a particular theory or critical stance to explain his writings in reductionist ways.

It is time for a new study of him in English. Like other mystical writers, he has become unexpectedly popular since I wrote my doctoral thesis on him a quarter of a century ago. A great deal has been written about him since then, but most of it, with a few notable exceptions, by scholars in the Spanish-speaking world. In particular, the quatercentenary of his death in 1991 produced large numbers of articles and books, many of which shed new light on particular aspects of his writing. This book has three main objectives. The first is to familiarize readers at the start of the new millennium with the work of San Juan, the second to assist them to interpret what they read. The third is to attempt to hold together San Juan as a poet and San Juan as a spiritual teacher, biblical exegete and theologian, through a study of the point of union between them, his use of language, which is quite unlike that of any of his contemporaries, whether in poetry or prose.[2] This last aim reflects a commitment on my part to an eirenic, ecumenical approach to San Juan in particular and to the varieties of human knowing in general. I approach these objectives with fear and trembling, hoping that an outsider, British by nationality and Reformed by religion, may bring San Juan closer to the English-speaking world, and offer a different perspective from the Spanish-speaking one.

This book therefore attempts a revaluation of the figure of San Juan. It does not advance any sensational new thesis or announce major discoveries. I have used the academic training I have received, and brought to the task as much intellectual rigour as I can muster, but I cannot pretend to be wholly objective, since my own encounter with San Juan is bound to have affected me. I have always appreciated the remark attributed to Auden, that we should not ask 'When did you last read a book?' but 'When were you last read by a book?' In reading San Juan, we may find ourselves and our own values being read by him. Despite the gap of 400 years and the intellectual and cultural distances between us, I have sometimes found San Juan to be sharply contemporary and thought-provoking. The powerful currents of religion and sexual love, usually perceived as pulling in opposite directions, are impossible to avoid in reading him, but approached with sensitivity and care he will question many of our preconceptions about them.

A survey of the ways English and Spanish readers have judged him in the past will provide an introduction to my account. In his study of the relationship between Spanish and English poetry in the seventeenth century, José Ángel Valente writes: 'El lector de ambas poesías [. . .] percibe en ellas demasiadas notas comunes para no sospechar – independientemente del complicado mecanismo de fijación de influencias – que existe entre ambas más de un vínculo soterrado',[3] 'The reader of both [. . .] becomes aware of too many aspects they have in common not to suspect that, independently of the complicated business of identifying influences, there exists between them a number of buried connections.' He notes, for example, how important the writings of Santa Teresa were to the poet and Catholic convert Richard Crashaw (1612/13–49). The surprising popularity in England among Anglican and Puritan readers, as well as Recusants, of Spanish devotional works of the sixteenth and early seventeenth centuries – Fray Luis de Granada being the most obvious case – has often been noted. But one name consistently impresses by its absence, that of San Juan de la Cruz.

Valente's point about hidden correspondences strikes me when I read the poetry of England's greatest religious lyricist, George Herbert (1593–1633). A community of ideas and imagery exists between them, yet it is most unlikely that Herbert read San Juan. Here, for example, are a few stanzas from 'The Search', set alongside passages from the 'Cántico espiritual':

Whither, O, whither art thou fled, My Lord, my Love?	¿Adónde te escondiste, Amado, y me dexaste con gemido? Como el ciervo huyste [. . .]
I sent a sigh to seek thee out, Deep drawn in pain, Winged like an arrow: but my scout Returns in vain.	Mas, ¿cómo perseveras, ¡oh vida!, no viviendo donde vives, y haziendo por que mueras las flechas que recives de lo que del Amado en ti concives.

Where is my God? What hidden place
Conceals thee still?
What covert dare eclipse thy face?
Is it thy will?

O let not that of anything;
Let rather brass,
Or steel, or mountains be thy ring,
And I will pass.

Since then my grief must be as large,
As is thy space,
Thy distance from me; see my charge,
Lord, see my case.[4]

Buscando mis amores
yré por esos montes y riberas;
ni cogeré las flores
ni temeré las fieras,
y passaré los fuertes y fronteras.

Descubre tu presencia,
y máteme tu vista y hermosura;
mira que la dolencia
de amor, que no se cura
sino con la presencia y la figura.[5]

The stress on divine hiddenness and fleeing, the sighing and the pain experienced, the determination to seek out the hidden God, the images of the arrow of desire and of mountains to be passed, the grief and the wish to see, are common to both poems. To them one might add the presence of the Augustinian 'pregunta a las criaturas' couched in terms of an address to fields below and starry fields above in both poems (Herbert, lines 5–15, San Juan, stanza 4). In another famous poem, 'Prayer (I)', Herbert uses exactly the same technique for his definition of prayer as San Juan uses in his poem for the definition of the 'Amado' (CA 13–14):

Mi Amado, las montañas,
los valles solitarios nemorosos,
las ínsulas estrañas,
los ríos sonorosos,
el silvo de los ayres amorosos;

la noche sosegada
en par de los levantes del aurora,
la música callada,
la soledad sonora,
la cena que recrea y enamora.[6]

My Beloved, the mountains,
lonely, wooded valleys,
strange islands,
resounding rivers,
the whistling of the loving breezes;

calm night,
before the rising of the dawn,
silent music,
resonant solitude,
the supper which recreates and brings love.

Prayer the Church's banquet, angels' age,
God's breath in man returning to his birth,
The soul in paraphrase, heart in pilgrimage,
The Christian plummet sounding heav'n and earth;
Engine against th'Almighty, sinners' tower,
Reversèd thunder, Christ-side-piercing spear,

The six-days' world transposing in an hour,
A kind of tune, which all things hear and fear;
Softness, and peace, and joy, and love, and bliss,
Exalted manna, gladness of the best,
Heaven in ordinary, man well dressed,
The milky way, the bird of Paradise,
Church-bells beyond the stars heard, the soul's blood,
The land of spices; something understood.[7]

Herbert's poem shares the same grammatical structure: a noun subject, no copulative verb, a series of complements defining the subject, expressed in rich, strange and varied imagery, though Herbert's is more obviously drawn from religious language. The chief difference is that Herbert makes his barest utterance – 'something understood', the confession of ineffability – form the climax of the poem, whereas San Juan characteristically alternates across his poem between the kind of sensuous imagery we have just noted, and a more unadorned, uncertain discourse, found, for example, in the onomatopoeic 'un no sé qué que quedan balbuciendo', 'and I know not what that they are stammering' of C 7, or at greater length in CA 37:

Allí me mostrarías	There you would show me
aquello que mi alma pretendía,	what my soul was seeking,
y luego me darías	and then you would give me
allí tú, vida mía,	there, you, my life,
aquello que me diste el otro día.[8]	what you gave me the other day.

It is as though none of the images can capture the inexpressible reality of Herbert's prayer or San Juan's Beloved, yet together they convey beauty and mystery.

The connections are not limited to San Juan's poetry. Herbert's 'The Windows' makes a similar point, about preachers needing to live their doctrine rather than express it pleasingly in sermons, to that made at greater length by San Juan, in:

Doctrine and life, colours and light, in one
When they combine and mingle, bring
A strong regard and aw: but speech alone
Doth vanish like a flaring thing,
And in the ear, not conscience ring. (p. 58)

San Juan takes a firm view of the proper relationship between the two extremes in the Renaissance debate about the purpose of literature, pleasure and profit (the Horatian *delectare* and *prodesse*). The third book of the *Subida* is devoted to the active night of the spirit; that is, to breaking dependence on spiritual practices and habits which have become ends in themselves rather than steps on the road to union with God.[9] Like Herbert, he proposes a distinction between outward delight in the spoken truth and its inward appropriation. One kind of preacher has a lofty style and uses fine language to press home his doctrine, but the effects of such preaching are limited to pleasing the senses and the mind of the listener, with very little effect on the will, which for San Juan, working within an Aristotelian–Thomist framework, is the seat of motivation and therefore of choice between good and evil:

> porque comúnmente se queda tan floja y remisa [la voluntad] como antes para obrar, aunque haya dicho maravillosas cosas maravillosamente dichas, que sólo sirven para deleitar el oído [. . .]; mas el espíritu [. . .] no sale de sus quicios más que antes, no teniendo la voz virtud para resucitar al muerto de su sepultura (S 3.45.4).

> for it [the will] generally remains as weak and wayward as it was before as far as actions go, even if he [the preacher] has said wonderful things wonderfully said, which only serve to delight the hearing . . . while the spirit . . . does not leave its natural bounds any more than it previously did, the voice having no power to raise the dead from the grave.

The other kind of preacher is the one whose life reflects more nearly the sermon he preaches, 'por bajo que sea su estilo y poca su retórica y su doctrina común, porque del espíritu vivo se pega el calor', 'however lowly his style, poor his rhetoric and ordinary his teaching, because heat takes hold from a living spirit'. The effect of the first sort on the sermon-taster (a term San Juan would have liked) is short-lasting, is limited to appreciation of outward skills, and bears little practical fruit, whereas the second matches teaching to life and takes root in the life of the listener.[10]

What kind of 'vínculo soterrado' is one dealing with here? There is a clue – no more than that – in a late medieval work we know San Juan to have read and which was probably familiar to Herbert, the pseudo-Augustinian *Soliloquia*, popular in the sixteenth century, which believed it to be by Augustine and which included it among his works. Rosamund Tuve notes that Herbert owned Augustine's works and was familiar with at least one pseudo-Augustinian opuscule, the *Meditationes*, usually printed with the *Soliloquia*.[11] San Juan quotes from the *Soliloquia* – one of his few non-biblical sources – a number of times.[12] There are several echoes of the *Soliloquia* in the 'Cántico' poem, but it comes as something of a shock to discover there the germ of its first words, as of Herbert's 'The Search': 'Ubi es absconditus, pulcher quem desidero?' – '¿Adónde te escondiste/Amado?'[13] When reading poetry and devotional literature of this period, we need to bear in mind that we are dealing with a common tradition which goes back into biblical and patristic times and is present in the liturgy, as Tuve has shown in her reading of Herbert's poem 'The Sacrifice'. We may therefore expect to find connections between writers who cannot have known each other's work but who drew freely on this tradition.

In his study of the English mystical tradition, Dom David Knowles asserts of the spiritual literature produced by sixteenth-century Spanish writers: 'there was a lag of several decades before this movement reached the exiled English Catholics in France and the Low Countries'.[14] We should recall that there was a potential English-speaking readership for San Juan, among the Catholic exiles in Europe (mostly France and the Low Countries). Fr Augustine Baker (1575–1641) is most frequently cited as evidence of the influence of San Juan on English recusant writers. He certainly read the *Subida del monte Carmelo* (probably in French translation), though Knowles judges him deficient in his understanding of San Juan, particularly in respect of the nature of infused contemplation and the workings of divine grace (pp. 155, 183).

English readers encountered San Juan for the first time in their own language only in the middle of the nineteenth century, in striking contrast to the works of Santa Teresa de Ávila.[15] Whereas San Juan's works were translated into French, Italian and Latin at a relatively early date, no English translation appeared until 1864. Other English readers – and there were some, like the Anglican divines and writers William Law and Jeremy Taylor – had to be content with the French or Latin versions.[16] His first actual appearance in English translation came in 1856, in a popular anthology of mysticism edited by the Congregationalist Robert Alfred Vaughan (1823–57), who is said to have learnt Spanish (among other languages) for the purpose.[17] Vaughan's assessment is predictable, the civilized Englishman observing with horrified fascination the peculiarities of more benighted nations. His comment about both Teresa and John being 'supremely concerned to enforce the doctrine of blind obedience to ecclesiastical superiors' (II, p. 125) sets the tone. He continues: 'The piety of John is altogether of the Romanist type. In his doctrine of humility, truth is not to be considered, but expediency – that is, an edifying display of self-vilification' (II, p. 151). Vaughan finds him guilty of Quietism (p. 157), attacks his use of the Bible as 'most irrelevant' (p. 159), and concludes: 'This resurrection to a supersensuous serenity, wherein divine powers supersede your own, is a mere imagination – a change of words; the old hallucination of the mystic' (p. 160). Yet he damns with faint praise: 'It is impossible not to recognise a certain grandeur in such a man. Miserably mistaken as he was, he is genuine throughout as a mystic and ascetic [. . .] Let, then, a melancholy admiration be the meed of John' (p. 161). The enlightened and superior tones of this self-confident voice from the mid-nineteenth century were soon seriously to be challenged themselves, from a very different source – Darwin's *The Origin of Species* (1859).

San Juan's complete works received their first English translation by David Lewis in two volumes in 1864, with a preface by Cardinal Wiseman. Lewis's translation was based on the texts printed in volume XXVII of the *Biblioteca de autores cristianos* of 1853 (edited by Manuel de Rivadeneira), which itself went back to the 1703 Seville edition of San Juan's works, deficient by the standards of modern editorial practice. Lewis, who had been an Anglican curate under Newman at the University Church of St Mary the Virgin in Oxford, was received into the Roman Catholic Church on 30 May 1846, the year after Newman's conversion, and undertook his translation at the request of one of the best-known Catholic priests of the nineteenth century, Father Faber (1814–1863).[18] It therefore owes its existence to a group of these early converts. The second edition (1891) was revised by the Carmelite historian Benedict Zimmerman, and was probably timed to coincide with the tercentenary of San Juan's death. The *Ascent* and the *Dark Night* both went into revised editions (1906, 1908), but the fourth edition of the *Complete Works* (1916) marked a departure, because Zimmerman was able to use the first critical Spanish edition of the new century, that of Gerardo de San Juan de la Cruz (Toledo, 1912–14). In a prefatory note, the publisher explained that he had acquired the rights to its English translation. Whereas in Lewis's original translation San Juan's 'noche oscura del alma' had been rendered 'obscure night of the soul', from Zimmerman's 1891 revision onwards it has been the 'dark night of the soul', the one phrase of San Juan's which has passed into common usage in the English language, though increasingly as a synonym for any experience of testing or depression, in a way which would have puzzled its originator.[19]

It cannot be said that the works of San Juan, once published in English, reached more than a small Catholic readership. Boyce has suggested, rightly, that the atmosphere was not conducive in a predominantly Protestant country (p. 101). Yet interest in mystical literature was maintained, even increased, in the wake of Vaughan's anthology. The early years of the twentieth century in particular were marked by several notable works on mysticism and mystical writers. One thinks of William James's chapter 'Mysticism' in *The Varieties of Religious Experience*, the published version of his Gifford Lectures of 1901–2, with its generally favourable account of Santa Teresa and San Juan from a philosophical and psychological point of view; of Baron von Hügel's work on St Catherine of Genoa (1908), and Evelyn Underhill's influential *Mysticism* of 1911, also much reprinted.[20] Boyce writes: 'John of the Cross would seem to hold pride of place among those who influenced her thought' (p. 102). But the single most important step forward came in 1935, with the publication of the translation by the pioneering scholar of Spanish mysticism in England, E. Allison Peers (1891–1952).[21] It was through Peers's translation that T. S. Eliot read San Juan, and through this reading that we owe the presence of San Juan in the *Four Quartets*. Peers based his translation on the new critical edition of San Juan edited by Silverio de Santa Teresa (Burgos, 1929–31). He criticizes his predecessors for their omissions, paraphrases and failure to translate San Juan's biblical quotations accurately: the consequence, he supposes, of suspicion of vernacular translations of the Bible in the Roman Catholic Church. In his preface, Peers explains that because of the inaccuracy of earlier Spanish editions, English readers could never be sure 'whether in any particular passage, they are face to face with the Saint's own words, with a translator's free paraphrase of them or with a gloss made by some later copyist or early editor in the supposed interests of orthodoxy' (p. xvi). For the first time in an English translation, Peers provides introductory material intended to guide the reader through the intricacies of the text, and, as far as I am aware, was the first non-Roman Catholic to bring the complete works of San Juan sympathetically to the notice of the reading public. Peers's translation, still in print more than half a century later, was followed by a series of studies on the Spanish mystics. He, more than anyone else in the twentieth century, brought San Juan out of the cloister, and began a process whereby he is more widely read in English at the start of the twenty-first than ever before. Since Peers, one major new translation, that of Kieran Kavanaugh and Otilio Rodríguez, has appeared (1964), thoroughly revised in 1991 to coincide with the quatercentenary of San Juan's death.[22] It is written in a clearer, more modern style than Peers's now somewhat archaic prose, but it too has brought increasing numbers of English-speaking readers to San Juan for the first time.

Biographies of San Juan have followed a similar trajectory. The four most significant twentieth-century examples, those of Jean Baruzi, Bruno de Jésus-Marie, Silverio de Santa Teresa and Crisógono de Jesús, date from the 1920s, 1930s and 1940s.[23] Baruzi's work was a pioneer in the field, the first major study of San Juan to move beyond the limits of traditional Carmelite orthodoxy and hagiography, and therefore not well received in some quarters. The others followed the proclamation of San Juan as a Doctor of the Church in 1926, two centuries after his canonization, but also constituted a response to Baruzi. Crisógono, widely regarded as the most talented of the three Carmelites, showed himself able to question some of the more fanciful legendary accretions, at the same time as preserving the best of his seventeenth-century sources. The most popular English biographies, those of Allison Peers and Gerald Brenan, are heavily dependent on these Spanish and French originals.[24]

In his preface to the 1864 translation, Cardinal Wiseman made hardly any reference to the poetry, except to observe that each of San Juan's works was prefaced by a poem, which in the case of the *Noche oscura* 'forms not merely an introduction, but an argument rather, to a full dissertation on mystical science' (p. xxxii). He was nearer the mark when he added that the commentary to the *Obscure Night* is 'rich upon only one line' of the poem. Vaughan's anthology merely noted: 'Sundry verses head the work as texts', and gave the Spanish text of the first verse of the 'Noche oscura', with what was probably his own translation (II, p. 152), perhaps the first ever to appear in print in English.

To understand the reception of San Juan's poetry in English one must first look to North America. In his three-volume *History of Spanish Literature*, George Ticknor distinguished the prose writings from the poetry.[25] The former, he asserted, are 'treatises which have given him much reputation for a mystical eloquence that sometimes rises to the sublime, and sometimes is lost in the unintelligible', while the latter, 'of which a little is printed in the many editions of his works, is of the same general character, but marked by great felicity and richness of phraseology'.[26] The English poet Arthur Symons (1865–1945) produced translations of some of San Juan's poems, together with a short literary analysis.[27] He contends that pure lyric poetry 'cannot be found in Spanish literature outside the mystics' (p. 543) and describes San Juan's poetry as 'a metaphysical fire, a sort of white heat in which the abstract, the almost negative, becomes ecstatically released by the senses' (p. 544). Though his translations are faulty and dull (he described them as being as literal as he could make them, maintaining the metre and rhyme scheme of the Spanish), he nevertheless shows some appreciation for the originals. The 'Cántico' he describes as 'almost ludicrous in the liveliness of its natural images':

> there is an abandonment to all the sensations of love, which seems to me to exceed, and on their own ground, in directness and intensity of spiritual and passionate longing, most of what has been written by the love-poets of all ages. These lines, so full of rich and strange beauty, ache with desire and all the subtlety of desire [. . .] this monk can give lessons to lovers. (p. 546)

While Symons's judgement is too effusive for modern taste, his use of the term 'metaphysical' is surprising, given that San Juan has not usually been linked with the English metaphysical poets. Nevertheless, his article brought San Juan's poetry to the attention of an educated reading public in a way which the Lewis–Zimmerman translations did not. Almost a century after Ticknor, Aubrey Bell's assessment had altered little in 1938: 'We discover a basis of scholasticism and a Castilian core of concreteness in his poetry and in his prose, difficult rather than obscure and built around a kernel of song.' But Bell rates the poetry highly, writing of

> the incomparable lyrics of San Juan and Luis de León, which soar heavenward yet remain substantial and concrete. For one brief period in the lovely flowering of prose and verse in the hands of the mystic writers the Castilian genius may seem to have reached its perfect expression.[28]

Allison Peers, too, praised the poetry:

> In these lyrics there is a passion more vibrant and moving than can anywhere else be found in Castilian literature [. . .] The white heat of the author's emotion is luminous, but the shades gather round him when he attempts to explain his meaning in prose, and what intelligibility is found in the commentaries is a reflection from his verse.[29]

Peers's translations of the poems appeared as a separate volume in 1947, alongside the Spanish text – the first time the poetry as a whole, in isolation from the treatises, was made accessible to an English readership. The fact that it was reprinted the following year suggests that it proved popular.[30] In his preface Peers made specific mention of the first scholarly study of the poetry this century by a Spanish scholar, Dámaso Alonso, noting particularly its emphasis on the technical skill of San Juan as a poet.[31] But his translations were quickly eclipsed by Roy Campbell's, which, despite attempts by other scholars and poets, remain the best-known version in English of San Juan's poetry.[32] Campbell's translations retain the form and versification of the *lira*, and stay as true as possible to the feel of the Spanish, even if the English is sometimes archaic and he has to resort to some padding and paraphase. Many others have risen to the challenge, especially of the 'Noche oscura', which has become a kind of test piece for aspiring translators.[33] After Allison Peers, and with the advantage of writing elegantly about the poetry as such, Gerald Brenan (1894–1987) has probably done more than anyone else to make San Juan's verse known:

> It is not possible to give in a short space any idea of the intoxicating effect these poems produce or the manner by which this has been attained. But the rocket-like soaring and bursting associated with the lyrical impulse, the sense of flight and thrill and ecstasy which Juan de la Cruz's two great poems display have never been equalled by anyone else.[34]

Despite such praise, it has tended to be San Juan's prose which has found its way into twentieth-century English poetry. That is the case with Eliot, as I have suggested elsewhere.[35] Elizabeth Jennings, for example, has a prose-poem entitled 'Teresa of Avila', from her collection *A Sense of the World* (1958) and another, 'John of the Cross', from *Song for a Birth or a Death* (1961). The former is a meditation on Teresa's famous analogy of prayer as the Four Waters (*Vida*, pp. 11–22); the latter begins with images of emptiness, space and darkness, the deprivation of the senses, the urge to communicate what cannot be described, the flame which comes in the darkness and which is not produced from within but given, received. In this poem she charts the principal stages in the journey of the soul as San Juan depicts them in his prose commentaries, but I cannot find any echo of the poems as such. The imagery is either her own creation – 'Fingers not touching, crushing cool leaves', as she imagines the withdrawal of the senses from pleasure – or taken directly from the treatises, as in her fourth of the six stanzas:

> Flame, then, firm – not the inward flame of passion, urgent, wanting appeasement, close to the senses and sighing through them: but a pure light pouring through windows, flooding the glass but leaving the glass unaltered.[36]

The image of the sun streaming through the window, popular in medieval devotional literature, is one of San Juan's favourite analogies.[37]

The pages Elizabeth Jennings devotes to San Juan in *Every Changing Shape* are among the most thoughtful yet written on the subject of the relationship between the poetry and the prose of San Juan, even if I cannot entirely agree with the sharp distinction she makes between them.[38] In comparison with the prose, she writes, 'his poems [. . .] are personal not didactic, a drawing together not an analysis. They are, as it were, the overflow of a vision, the expression of a consummation [. . .] In his poems St John is not concerned to teach but to assert, not to warn but to invite [. . .] The poems arrive, the commentaries only approximate' (pp. 65–6). She points to the fact that his stress on inexpressibility needs to be qualified by the existence of the poetry itself: 'The mystic, by simply attempting to express his vision in poetic language, is asserting implicitly that such language is a fit medium to contain that vision' (p. 70). Likewise, she is right to stress that his work embodies both the negative and the affirmative ways of the Western mystical tradition: if 'St John really believed that sensible images were of little use in the attainment of direct union with God, why did he himself try to express that union in poetic terms?' (p. 65).

San Juan's poetry continues to influence contemporary British verse. Geoffrey Hill (b. 1932) has used Spanish *cancionero* and Golden Age poetry as models for new writing.[39] His inspiration was J. M. Cohen's anthology *The Penguin Book of Spanish Verse*, first published in 1956, which gave literal English translations of a wide range of Spanish poetry at the foot of each page, and in which San Juan's 'Noche oscura', 'Llama de amor viva' and 'Vivo sin vivir en mí' appear.[40] He also read Brenan's *The Literature of the Spanish People* and R. O. Jones's volume *The Golden Age: Prose and Poetry* in *A Literary History of Spain*, from which he took the epigraph for his first version of 'The Pentecost Castle': 'San Juan de la Cruz sang, as he danced holding in his arms an image of the infant Jesus snatched from a crib, the words of an old love song:

> Si amores me han de matar
> agora tienen lugar.'[41]

There are echoes of San Juan throughout 'The Pentecost Castle', in lines like 'when I cried out you/made no reply', recalling the opening of the 'Cántico'; in the use of the imagery of the 'caza de amor' and the night; and more generally of erotic language to represent divine love.[42] Most recently, in section XI of his collection *Station Island* (1984), the Irish poet Seamus Heaney includes a version of 'Que bien sé yo la fonte', having been given as a penance the task of translating something by Juan de la Cruz.[43]

Spanish attitudes towards San Juan have also been coloured by ideological considerations, but of different kinds from the English. During the nineteenth century the alternation of conservative and liberal governments and the fluctuating fortunes of the religious Orders affected his standing considerably, not least because it depended largely on Carmelite scholarship. While the centenaries of the first Discalced male foundation at Duruelo (1568) in 1668 and 1768 had been purely internal affairs, by 1868 the Carmelite Order was beginning to recover from the problems of the 1830s and 1840s.[44] The Church itself mirrored that larger division of national life into conservative and liberal camps, and many of the bishops and clergy, including the two Carmelites most active in the renewal of the Order, were Carlist sympathizers. Between 1868 and 1891 14 Discalced *conventos de frailes* were restored, though Segovia became the focus for the tercentennial celebrations, in the absence of re-foundations in Fontiveros and Úbeda, where San Juan was born and where he died. Two new biographies of San Juan appeared in 1875, Francisco María Martínez Marín's *Compendio histórico de la vida* [. . .] *del Doctor San Juan de la Cruz* (Cuenca: Gómez) and Manuel Muñoz Garnica's *San Juan de la Cruz: Ensayo histórico* (Jaén: Rubio). They were followed by another, the Discalced Carmelite Gregorio de Santa Salomé's *Vida del extático Padre San Juan de la Cruz* (Madrid: Asilo de Huérfanos del S.C. de Jesús) in 1884. Three editions of the *Obras completas* appeared; Rivadeneira's, for the *Biblioteca de autores españoles* (1853), with a prologue by Pi y Margall; Ortí y Lara's two-volume edition (Madrid, 1872); and a four-volume edition (Barcelona, 1883). The respective prologues of Pi y Margall and Ortí y Lara reflect the two Spains of the period: Pi's is influenced by the philosophy of Krause, adopts a Republican, socialist stance, sees San Juan as unique but believes that modern philosophy has rendered his beliefs obsolete; Ortí argues back from a neo-Thomist, royalist and conservative position. A journal entitled *San Juan de la Cruz* appeared briefly in 1890–91; when San Juan's chapters on images and religious devotions in the third book of the *Subida* were treated as crypto-Protestant by an anonymous Protestant writer, this drew a firm riposte from Eulogio de San José in its second volume, while the *Revista Popular* of 1891 presented San Juan as 'modelo y maestro' of all 'antiprotestantes y antiliberales verdaderos', 'the model and master of all true anti-Protestants and anti-liberals'.

Juan Bosco San Román's researches have also painted a vivid picture of the many and varied celebrations for the tercentenary of San Juan's death in Spain. Santa Teresa's, in 1882, had no doubt prompted thought as to how to celebrate her collaborator's. The Bishop of Avila exhorted the faithful to follow San Juan's teaching as a corrective against modern materialism, pitting his humility against the sensuality of the age and his prayer against its dissipation. In the parish church of San Cebrián in Fontiveros there were novenas, and a great pilgrimage to the village took place, despite flooded roads. Confessions were heard through the night and souvenirs were sold. In Úbeda the Bishop was taken ill after confirming 5,000 people. There were special services, a pageant, a concert and fireworks. But the focus was in Segovia, where an organizing committee of 85 citizens raised money to feed the poor during the celebrations, an activity seen as beneficial to the depressed local economy. There were religious *fiestas* and pilgrimages to the shrine of San Juan, there was a solemn procession, a triduum and a novena, but also a literary competition, described as 'el homenaje civil y literario más importante que se le ha tributado nunca en España' (p. 218), 'the most important civil and literary tribute ever paid to him in Spain'. Menéndez y Pelayo was present, while the winning poem was printed several times. Since 1891, centennial celebrations have become increasingly important for generating new work on San Juan.

The argument between Unamuno and Ortega y Gasset, two of the leading Spanish thinkers of the earlier part of the twentieth century, about the place of the mystics in Spanish culture, may stand as a good example of the way conflicting nineteenth-century attitudes towards San Juan re-emerged, if in a new guise. Speaking of theology in his 1929 lecture, 'Defensa del teólogo frente al místico', Ortega says: 'Me parece transmitirnos mucho más cantidad de Dios, más atisbos y nociones sobre la divinidad, que todos los éxtasis juntos de todos los místicos' (V, p. 452); 'it seems to me to bring to us more about God, more glimpses and ideas of divinity, than all the ecstasies all the mystics have ever had'.[45] Though he admits that there have been intellectual mystics – he cites Plotinus, Meister Eckhart and Bergson – he complains: 'Mi objeción al misticismo es que de la visión mística no redunda beneficio alguno intelectual' (V, p. 452); 'my objection to mysticism is that no intellectual benefit at all is gained from mystical vision'. It reverses the direction of philosophy, which seeks to bring hidden truths to the surface, by submerging itself in hidden depths. Mystics lead you to the heights and cheerfully abandon you once you have reached them:

> Y el místico, tan locuaz antes, tan maestro del hablar, se torna taciturno en la hora decisiva o, lo que es peor [. . .], nos comunica del trasmundo noticias tan triviales, tan poco interesantes, que más bien desprestigian al más allá [. . .] El clásico del lenguaje se hace especialista del silencio' (V, p. 455; VII, p. 340)

> and the mystic, once so full of words, such a master of speech, becomes silent at the decisive moment or, worse still [. . .], communicates to us from the world beyond knowledge which is so trivial, of such scant

> interest, that it tends instead to give the beyond a bad name [. . .] The classic in language becomes a specialist in silence.

Interestingly, Ortega's views on mysticism almost exactly mirror the continuing divide between the aesthetic and the intellectual appreciation of San Juan. He can sense the beauty of the poetry, but, like Ticknor before him, finds no clear and compelling content to take the mind into new realms of knowledge. In 'Amor en Stendhal' (V, p. 581–2, 585) and in shorter references elsewhere (VII, p. 481; XII, p. 268), Ortega praises the beauty of San Juan's imagery – he is particularly struck by 'la soledad sonora' – but one gains the impression that for him the fine language is the happy by-product of a futile exercise.

Reacting sharply against Unamuno's opinion 'Si fuera imposible que un pueblo dé a Descartes y a San Juan de la Cruz, yo me quedaría con éste' (I, p. 129), 'If it were impossible for a people to produce both Descartes and San Juan de la Cruz, I would keep the latter', Ortega likens it to the way folk dances degenerate into 'una bárbara baraúnda', 'barbaric pandemonium': '¿Qué otra cosa es sino preferir a Descartes, el lindo frailecito de corazón incandescente que urde en su celda encajes de retórica extática?' (I, p. 129), 'What does this mean except to prefer the sweet little friar with his heart on fire, working the lace of his ecstatic rhetoric in his cell, to Descartes?' Unamuno's logic, moreover, implies that 'Como Juan de Yepes es superior a Descartes, es, en no pocas otras cosas, superior España a Europa', 'Since Juan de la Cruz is superior to Descartes, Spain is superior to Europe in a number of other respects.' Therein, perhaps, lies the conflict between the two men, in terms of the analysis they offered of the nation's problems and the remedies they proposed, in which Castile's understanding of itself and its relationship with Europe played so important a part. For Unamuno, as early as *En torno al casticismo* (1895), turning Menéndez y Pelayo's arguments against Calderón against their author and in favour of the Carmelite mystics, the issue was clear. In 'De mística y humanismo' he states baldly that 'El espíritu castellano [. . .] tomó por filosofía castiza la mística', 'the Castilian spirit [. . .] adopted mysticism as its own authentic national philosophy', seeking 'la fusión perfecta del saber, el sentir y el querer', 'the perfect fusion of knowledge, feeling and love'.[46] The mystics

> no construyeron filosofía propia inductiva ni abrieron los ojos al mundo para ser por él llevados a su motivo sinfónico, quisieron cerrarlos al exterior para abrirlos a la contemplación de las 'verdades desnudas', en noche oscura de fe, vacíos de aprehensiones, buscando en el hondón del alma, [. . .] en el castillo interior, la 'sustancia de los secretos', la ley viva del universo. (p. 103)

> did not construct their own inductive philosophy nor did they open their eyes to the world, to be transported by it to its principal theme; they desired to close them to the outside to open them to contemplation of 'bare truths', in the dark night of faith, empty of particular knowledge,

> searching in the depths of the soul, [. . .] in the inner castle, for the 'substance of secret things', the living law of the universe.

Their starting-point was self-knowledge, but though their method was not based on discursive reasoning, Spanish mysticism 'no cayó en el desprecio de la razón ni de la ciencia por abuso de ellas' (p. 104), 'did not lapse into scorn for reason or science through their abuse', but looked to 'ciencia pura, absoluta, final y contemplativa, visión de la divina Esencia por amor' (p. 105), 'a pure, absolute, final, contemplative science, the vision of the divine Essence through love'.

Unamuno's analysis, though questionable in certain aspects, such as his emphasis on San Juan's deliberate anti-Protestantism (p. 110), and the whole issue of *casticismo*, is based on a closer and more sympathetic reading of San Juan's texts than Ortega's: he can see beyond a superficial reading which might conclude that San Juan is anti-intellectual and a proponent of passivity and he has a feel for what the mystics are trying to say. Ortega gives the impression of never having got to grips with them, and contents himself with rather facile generalizations.

That kind of argument in Spain about the iconic status of San Juan now seems a world away. The final demise of the dictatorship, the coming of democracy, membership of the European Union, the long period of socialist government, the relative decline in the power and influence of the Catholic Church, the progressive secularization of Spanish society, have all marked Spanish perceptions of the place of Spain (not simply Castile) *vis-à-vis* its neighbours, and while it is entertaining to play the game of identifying national characteristics, the globalization of culture has modified at least some of them (witness the lamentable decline of that good old Spanish custom the *siesta*). San Juan de la Cruz, that warrior-mystic of the spirit of Castile, Machado's 'espíritu de llama', 'spirit of flame', has himself become an international figure. The critical interest he arouses has little to do with his status in that older Spain, and a great deal to do with understanding a man who seems to be writing twentieth-century poetry 400 years before its time, and with the journey he charts through the unknown regions of the human psyche.

Nevertheless, it is still hard for Spaniards to let go of the ideological baggage attaching to the figure of a Catholic mystic. A good example of this process can be seen in the case of Juan Goytisolo, whose novel *Las virtudes del pájaro solitario* (1988), which takes its title from an apparently lost treatise on the subject by the saint, rather surprisingly added him to the heterodox pantheon through which Goytisolo re-imagines the history of Spanish culture – the Arcipreste de Hita, Cervantes, Góngora, Quevedo, Blanco White. For the young Goytisolo, San Juan represented one of the many authors whose works were held up as shining examples of Catholic nationalist culture, which he saw as narrow, repressive, bigoted, life- and flesh-denying. Goytisolo's adoption of an Islamic counter-offensive to the official version of history led him to discover the poetry of the Sufis, and especially that of Jelaluddin Rumi (1207–73). When he looked again at San Juan, partly through the influence of Luce López-Baralt's comparative study *San Juan de la Cruz y el Islam*, he was astonished to find in him a kindred spirit to the Sufis.[47] Goytisolo's version of San Juan is an idiosyncratic construct, rewriting his imprisonment, for example, as the consequence of repressive Inquisitorial forces rather than of ecclesiastical politics and internal disputes within the Carmelite Order. But what liberates him for Goytisolo from the shackles of the past is that same combination of sensuality and spirituality which Goytisolo found in the Islamic mystics, and which has caused critics such difficulties.

Contrary to received opinion, the history of Spanish appreciation of San Juan as a poet does not begin with Menéndez y Pelayo's famous 'Discurso de entrada en la Real Academia Española' of 1881, entitled 'De la poesía mística'. His remarks on San Juan come at the climatic point of a survey of mystical poetry from the early Church onwards:

> Pero aun hay una poesía más angélica, celestial y divina, que ya no parece de este mundo, ni es posible medirla con criterios literarios, y eso que es más ardiente de pasión que ninguna poesía profana, y tan elegante y exquisita en la forma, y tan plástica y figurativa como los más sabrosos frutos del Renacimiento.[48]
>
> But there is an even more angelic, celestial and divine poetry, which no longer seems to be of this world, nor measurable by literary criteria, because it is more ardent in its passions than any profane poetry, and as elegant and exquisite in form and as crafted and figurative as the most appetizing fruits of the Renaissance.

He recognizes San Juan's quality as a poet, but is reluctant to analyse the technique of his art, preferring to attribute it to divine inspiration, as though it were sacred and therefore taboo.

It is true that some earlier critics had found San Juan's poetry hard to comprehend. In his *Teatro historica critica de la eloquentia espanola* of 1787 (II, p. 138), Antonio de Campagny (1787) complained about the carelessness and lack of intelligiblity of many of San Juan's lines.[49] But some 60 years later Antonio Gil y Zárate had a number of pertinent things to say about Spanish religious poetry in his *Manual de literatura*, in which he makes an interesting distinction between secular and religious poetry, the former dependent on classical models, 'la antigüedad materialista' (II, p. 135), 'materialist Antiquity', but the latter, though influenced by biblical language, more original: 'Aquí ya no podía haber imitación de los antiguos, y se abría un ameno campo a la originalidad' (II, p. 132), 'Here there was no possibility of imitating the ancients, and a pleasant space was opened up for originality.'[50] Whereas some religious poets indulged in an over-adorned style which now seems ridiculous, there were others who 'huyendo de semejantes absurdos, aplicaban a los asuntos místicos una poesía más alta y digna de su grande objeto' (II, p. 134), 'fleeing from such absurdities, brought to mystical things a loftier poetry, worthier of its great object'. Indeed,

> hallaron aquellos poetas en su corazón piadoso y en el amor divino que les inflamaba, una nueva fuente de entusiasmo, de donde corrieron con

> abundancia las ideas más sublimes, los afectos más tiernos y las expresiones más poéticas, dando todo esto a sus composiciones un giro enteramente nuevo y un carácter verdaderamente original (II, pp. 134–5).

> in their faithful hearts, and in the divine love which inflamed them, those poets found a new source of enthusiasm, from which there poured in abundance the sublimest ideas, the tenderest emotions and the most poetic expressions, which took their compositions in an entirely new direction and gave them a truly original nature.

For Gil y Zárate, Fray Luis de León 'brilla en primera línea' among 'estos autores celestes'. But of San Juan he writes:

> Pocas son la [*sic*] poesías que se conocen de este autor: la más notable es un *Diálogo entre el alma y Cristo su esposo*, imitación del *Cantar de los cantares,* en la que bajo la alusión de unos amores profanos y con expresiones de mayor ternura, canta el amor divino. A la manera de Fray Luis de León, hay en su versificación cierto abandono y descuido que manifiesta muy bien que el poeta se ha dejado arrastrar de la inspiración, cuidándose más bien de dar salida a los sentimientos de su alma, que de adornarlos con un lenguaje castigado y pretencioso: hay sin embargo, tal suavidad en este lenguaje, corre tan fácilmente, las expresiones son tan felices, las imágenes tan bellas, que toda la composición arrebata (II, p. 137).

> Few are the known poems of this author; the most notable is a *Dialogue between the soul and Christ her husband*, an imitation of the *Song of Songs*, in which he sings of divine love with expressions of the greatest tenderness through alluding to profane love. As with Fray Luis de León, there is in his poetry a certain slackness by which it is very evident that the poet has been carried away by inspiration, and is more concerned with finding an outlet for the sentiments of his soul than for adorning them in a language which is disciplined and striking. Nonetheless, there is such gentleness in his language, it runs so smoothly, its expressions are so felicitous, its images so lovely, that one is transported by the whole work.

The stress on inspiration is present, as later in Menéndez y Pelayo, but Gil y Zárate's perceptive remarks about San Juan's originality and its causes make him a better critic than his illustrious successor.

In both England and Spain the history of the reception of San Juan has been linked in general to changing attitudes towards the Catholic Church. But the two histories could hardly be more different. Whereas in Spain the Catholic Church and the Orders passed through crisis in the nineteenth century, again during the Republic, and enjoyed a long period of almost unchallenged influence and power following the Civil War, in England the Catholic minority slowly emerged from its ghetto during the second half of the nineteenth century, and by the end of the twentieth had entered mainstream English life. Ancient suspicions have largely died away, as the ecumenical movement has led to greater understanding between the different Christian confessions. San Juan could never have been used for ideological battles in England, as he was between Unamuno and Ortega in Spain, because he came from outside English culture, though the interest in him during the 1920s and 1930s does seem to be connected with a significant number of conversions among leading intellectuals and literary figures to Roman Catholicism during that period. At the start of the new millennium, the secular materialism of the West, which would have appalled the Bishop of Ávila of 1891, seems open to ideas of personal growth and individual spirituality, though suspicious of the formal practice of religion. This has given the mystics a certain cachet which the established churches and their rites lack. The difference between the quatercentennial celebrations and those 100 years earlier could hardly be more striking. Though local celebrations with a primarily religious focus continued to take place, national and international conferences, with an extraordinary range of speakers and topics, attracted greater attention. New work on textual criticism, biography and historical background, new general introductions and studies of individual works, continued to be produced, but not only by Spanish Catholic scholars or a few enthusiasts beyond. Contributions came from Christians outside the Roman Catholic Church and by members of other faiths, as well as from non-European perspectives. Psychology, aesthetics and ecology made their presence felt alongside more traditional doctrinal studies, but even the latter were affected by recent thinking, for example liberation theology and feminism.[51] That San Juan should have become the focus of international and multidisciplinary interest on this scale would have surprised his readers even as recently as a quarter of a century ago.

It is against such a changing background that I offer this study. I have chosen to follow, as far as that is feasible, the chronology of San Juan's own writing. For that reason I begin with his early life, education and vocation, as far as 1577, the year of his capture and imprisonment, out of which came his poetry. I am indebted to the excellent work that has been done in local and national archives by Spanish scholars, local historians and Carmelites alike, for their revision of the traditional hagiographical narrative of San Juan's life through documentary evidence, though I am certain that further discoveries will be made before the definitive biography can be written.[52] Nor do I wish to enter into the difficult area of the manuscript transmission of San Juan's works. New manuscripts will doubtless come to light, like the early MS of the second redaction of the *Cántico espiritual*, which caused such a stir at the Rome Symposium in April 1991.[53] I am not competent to argue in detail about the links with Islamic mysticism which have been studied by my colleague and friend Luce López-Baralt; again, I sense that more is hidden from us than has yet been revealed. Following my study of his poetry, I concentrate on the three commentaries he wrote on his most famous poems, in which he teaches the way to union with God. These difficult works take different routes towards that same goal, and in their complex language and structure, in dialogue with the Bible, reveal the true depth of San Juan's analysis of the self, its relations with the world, and its quest for meaning. Before concluding this analysis, I pause to consider his views about language.

I believe that San Juan should speak for himself before judgement is passed on him. But for the English-speaking world, a double act of translation is required, not simply from one language to another, but from one cast of mind and one cultural history to another. Not only San Juan's words but also his ideas have to be translated if sense is to be made of what he tried to articulate more than 400 years ago. It is too easy to fall into the kind of trap Ortega did, picking out particular expressions without understanding their context, or the precision of meaning attached to them, and go on to construct a mystic who is irrational, life-denying, passive and with an unhealthy desire for suffering. In every case San Juan deserves a more considered treatment. His analysis of the way human attachments and desires lead to possessiveness and ultimately vitiate freedom seems to me worth spelling out in an age devoted to acquisition. The use he makes of images of growth, especially that of the mother and child, makes clear what his more abstract analysis of mystical states sometimes does not: that he is concerned not, as some might think, with regression and repression, but with the discarding of infantile religion, with reaching a true measure of the self, and with countering any form of religious devotion which leads to a cult of spiritual possessiveness or of self-gratification.

Vaughan's comment about the irrelevance of the quotations San Juan claims as biblical authorities for his teaching, is understandable from the perspective of a mid-nineteenth-century scholar, but San Juan's exegeses are often subtle, and almost always related to the poetic image he is expounding through a common word or phrase. We may not always accept his procedure, but in artistic terms it is often illuminating, as biblical texts we would not expect to be related to one another are brought together to create new and fruitful combinations of meaning. That is exactly how he uses the images of the Song in his 'Cántico' poem: not in the same sequence as they are found in the Vulgate, but rearranged into fresh and surprising patterns, alongside images from other poetic worlds. Finally, in searching for a more integrated picture of San Juan I am also looking to a revaluation of his poetry as part of his spirituality, rather than as its antithesis. As many critics have observed, there appears to be a world of difference between the teaching on negation and detachment in commentaries and the richly sensuous imagery of the great *lira* poems. Elizabeth Jennings makes an important theological connection between poetry and Christianity: 'It is the Incarnation which explains and justifies St John's analogues of profane love.'[54] For all its spiritual flights, Christianity is a very earthed religion. It does not seek escape from physical reality so much as the encountering of the spiritual and the divine through body and matter, of which the Incarnation is the paradigm and from which the sacraments of the Church derive. San Juan's teaching leads in the end to a revaluation of the creation, as he moves from detachment, through reading the book of creation for signs of the Creator, to a vision of creation transformed through union with God.[55] The 'Cántico' poem in particular represents such a vision of the created world. Although some of its images stand for obstructive forces which are to be countered, the fact that it disrupts normal temporal and narrative sequence and juxtaposes apparently unconnected images means that as we read it we see the world as we have not seen it before, reordered through the breaking and remaking of poetic language. Its theology is found in its strangeness, its failure to be like pastoral or lyrical poetry of its age (or any other, till recently). Its paradoxes and puzzles, its discontinuities and sudden shifts, are a linguistic analogue of the impossible joining of the human and the divine in the Incarnation.

Spanish theologians and philosophers have, until recently, taken for granted a familiarity with Catholic tradition their English counterparts do not have. Spanish poets have read and admired San Juan, and written poetry in dialogue with his. It is no exaggeration to say that the twentieth century in Spain has witnessed the rediscovery of two of the greatest poets of the Golden Age, Góngora and San Juan: Lorca, Guillén, Salinas, Cernuda and Valente have demonstrated this amply.[56] Yet I hope that the analytical traditions of the English approach, coming to San Juan from the outside, may still have a contribution to make.

NOTES

1 I shall refer to him as Fray Juan when dealing with his life.

2 For an interesting account of the connections between theology and literature in San Juan (though from a Roman Catholic perspective) see George H. Tavard, *Poetry and Contemplation in St. John of the Cross* (Athens: Ohio University Press, 1988).

3 José Ángel Valente, 'Una nota sobre relaciones literarias hispano-inglesas en el siglo XVII', in *La piedra y el centro* (Madrid: Taurus, 1982), pp. 113–32 (pp. 113, 122).

4 Herbert, cited from *George Herbert and Henry Vaughan*, ed. Louis L. Martz, The Oxford Authors (Oxford: Oxford University Press, 1986), pp. 146–8. The theme of God's hiddenness is more explicit in lines 29–30: 'Where is my God? what hidden place/Conceals thee still?' Elizabeth Jennings, *Every Changing Shape* (London: André Deutsch, 1961; reprinted Manchester: Carcanet, 1996) also notes (p. 64) the likeness between the last verse of the 'Noche oscura' poem and Donne's 'The Exstasie' (lines 17–20).

5 Stanzas 1, 8, 3, 11, from *San Juan de la Cruz: Poesía*, ed. Domingo Ynduráin (Madrid: Cátedra, 1989), pp. 249–51.

6 Ynduráin, *San Juan*, p. 252.

7 Martz, ed., *George Herbert and Henry Vaughan*, p. 44. Martz describes Vaughan's 'Son-days' (pp. 303–4) as belonging to the mode of the Elizabethan definition-poem, characterized by 'a rapid sequence of analogies' (p. 506), and used by Sidney, Southwell, and notably Herbert, here, in 'Sin (1)' and at the start of his 'Sunday'. I am not aware of a similar tradition in Spanish literature of the period, though Garcilaso comes close in his 'Égloga primera', ll. 99–104, which shares several features with CA 13; see *Garcilaso de la Vega: Obra poética y textos en prosa*, ed. Bienvenido Morros (Barcelona: Crítica, 1995), p. 125.

8 Ynduráin, *San Juan*, p. 257. On this technique, see C. P. Thompson, *The Poet and the Mystic* (Oxford: Oxford University Press, 1977), pp. 87–8; *El poeta y el místico* (El Escorial: Swan, 1985), pp. 200–1.

9 See below, pp. 200–9.

10 San Juan here seems to be echoing early Christian suspicion of rhetoric as an art which could be practised to defend something (or someone) the speaker knew to be untrue (or guilty); see Domingo Ynduráin, *Humanismo y Renacimiento en España* (Madrid: Cátedra, 1994), pp. 41, 219, 223, 227–34, 287. He clearly takes Seneca's side, against Cicero. It is therefore ironic – perhaps deliberately so – that to make his point San Juan should use the highly rhetorical device of a double polyptoton and chiasmus – *dicho maravillosas* cosas *maravillosamente dichas* (my emphases).

11 Rosamund Tuve, *A Reading of George Herbert* (London: Faber & Faber, 1952), p. 206; on Herbert's use of the pseudo-Augustinian *Meditations*, see pp. 31, 45, 81. The Bodleian

Library has copies of the *Meditationes, Solioquia, & Manuale* printed in Antwerp, 1505 and 1557; and English translations of the three works printed in 1570, 1585 and 1591. For the *Soliloquia,* see *Liber soliloquiorum animae ad Deum* (PL 40, 863–98); I follow Migne, but have also consulted the English version, *The Soliloquies of St Augustine*, trans. L. M. F. G. (Edinburgh: Sands & Co, 1912), though this is scarcely the new and exact translation it claims to be. A. Wilmart, *Auteurs spirituels et textes dévots du Moyen Age latin* (Paris: Études Augustiniennes, 1971 [1932]), writes: 'Les faux *Soliloques*, lesquels paraissent dater du XIIIe siècle et ont été, dès lors, copiés abondamment' (p. 128, note 1), as Wilmart's list of MSS shows. It figures in St Teresa's reading, as Morel-Fatio observed; see 'Les lectures de Sainte Thérèse', *BH*, 10 (1908), pp. 17–67; especially pp. 47–8.

12 E.g. S 1.5.1; C 4.1; C 5.1.

13 PL 40, 865.

14 Dom David Knowles, *The English Mystical Tradition* (London: Burns & Oates, 1961), p. 152.

15 The Bodleian Library, for example, contains a number of editions of her works in translation, notably the versions by 'W.M.' (Antwerp, 1611), Sir Toby Matthews (Antwerp, 1642) and Woodhead (London, 1669 and 1671; reprinted, in abridged form, in 1757). For her presence in Crashaw, especially in his 'Hymne' addressed to her, see *The Poems of Richard Crashaw*, ed. L. C. Martin, 2nd edn (Oxford: Clarendon, 1957), pp. 317–21; for other poems on Teresa, see pp. 131–7, 322–7. George Eliot was familiar enough with the story of her *Life* to preface *Middlemarch* (1871–2) with a 'Prelude' which connects Teresa's youthful desire for martyrdom and her activity as a Reformer and Foundress with the story of Dorothea Casaubon and her search for a great enterprise.

16 See Martin Thornton, *English Spirituality* (London: SPCK, 1963), pp. 233–4, 254–6.

17 Robert Alfred Vaughan, ed., *Hours with the Mystics*, 2 vols (London: John W. Parker & Son), 1856; further edns, 1860, 1880. Eliot may have gleaned her story from Vaughan, where it is told in similar form (II, 128); Crashaw makes much of it in his 'Hymne'. On Vaughan, see *Dictionary of National Biography*, ed. Leslie Stephen, 63 vols (London: Smith, Elder, 1885–1900), LVIII, pp. 176–7.

18 See Philip Boyce, 'The influence of St John of the Cross in England', *Teresianum*, 42 (1991), pp. 97–121.

19 Vaughan's *Hours with the Mystics* had also used the title *The Obscure Night* to translate the *Noche* (II, p. 152).

20 Underhill refers to 'The Obscure Night', following the Arthur Symons translation of the poem (see below). Continuing interest in Catholic circles is shown by a copy of a limited edition entitled *The Song of the Soul*, trans. J. O'Connor (Capel-y-ffin, Abergavenny, 1927), signed Eric Gill, and now in Cambridge University Library (no. 45 of 150).

21 *The Complete Works of Saint John of the Cross*, trans. E. Allison Peers, 3 vols (London: Burns, Oates & Washbourne, 1934–5); repr., single volume (Anthony Clarke: Wheathampstead, 1974).

22 *The Collected Works of St John of the Cross*, trans. Kieran Kavanaugh and Otilio Rodríguez, revised edn. (Washington, DC: ICS, 1991).

23 Jean Baruzi, *Saint Jean de la Croix et le problème de l'expérience mystique* (Paris: Alcan, 1924; 2nd edn, 1931); Bruno de Jésus-Marie, *Saint Jean de la Croix* (Paris: Plon, 1929); Silverio de Santa Teresa, in *Obras de San Juan de la Cruz*, BMC, X–XIV (Burgos: El Monte Carmelo, 1929–31), X, pp. 7–113; Crisógono de Jesús, *Vida de San Juan de la Cruz* (Madrid: BAC, 1946).

24 E. Allison Peers, *Spirit of Flame: A Study of St. John of the Cross* (London: SCM Press, 1943); Gerald Brenan, *St. John of the Cross: His Life and Poetry* (Cambridge: Cambridge University Press, 1973).

25 Ticknor acknowledged his debt to two predecessors, the German Bouterwek (1766–1828), whose original text of 1804 was translated into English as *History of Spanish and Portuguese Literature* by Miss Thomasina Ross (London: Boosey, 1823), and the Swiss Sismondi (1773–1842), whose *De la littérature du midi de l'Europe* (Paris: Treuttel et Würtz, 1813) had its first English translation in 1823.

26 George Ticknor, *History of Spanish Literature*, 3 vols (London: John Murray, 1849), III, p. 164.
27 In 'The Poetry of Santa Teresa and San Juan de la Cruz', *The Contemporary Review*, 75 (1899), pp. 542–51.
28 Aubrey F. G. Bell, *Castilian Literature* (Oxford: Clarendon, 1938), pp. 99, 101.
29 From *Spain: A Companion to Spanish Studies*, 5th edn, ed. E. Allison Peers (London: Methuen, 1956 [1929]), p. 131.
30 *The Poems of St John of the Cross*, trans. E. Allison Peers (London: Burns & Oates, 1947).
31 Dámaso Alonso, *La poesía de San Juan de la Cruz* (Madrid: CSIC, 1942), coinciding with the quatercentenary of San Juan's birth. I follow the 4th edn (Madrid: Aguilar, 1966).
32 *Poems of St John of the Cross*, trans. Roy Campbell (Glasgow: Collins, 1979 [London: Harvill, 1951]).
33 See, for example, Edward Sarmiento, *Three Translations from St John of the Cross* (Ware: Carmel, 1976), pp. 1–2; Ann L. Mackenzie, 'Upon Two "Dark Nights": Allison Peers' Translations of "En una noche oscura"', *BHS*, 62 (1985), pp. 270–9. Mackenzie mentions the setting by the composer Sir Edmund Rubbra of the second Peers translation, probably made for the quatercentenary of the saint's birth (p. 271). Other composers who have set San Juan's words are Geoffrey Burgon and Jonathan Harvey.
34 Gerald Brenan, *The Literature of the Spanish People* (Penguin: Harmondsworth, 1963 [1951]), p. 156.
35 'La presencia de San Juan de la Cruz en la literatura del siglo XX: España e Inglaterra', in *El sol a medianoche*, ed. Luce López Baralt and Lorenzo Piera (Madrid: Trotta, 1996); pp. 189–203 (pp. 189–94).
36 From Elizabeth Jennings, *Collected Poems, 1967* (London: Macmillan, 1967), p. 100.
37 S 2.5.6; 14.9; 16.10; N 2.8.3–4; CB 26.17; L 3.77.
38 Pp. 62–71. Her study appeared independently of Jorge Guillén's important chapter on San Juan, 'Lenguaje insuficiente: San Juan de la Cruz o lo inefable místico', in *Lenguaje y poesía* (Cambridge, Mass.: Harvard University Press, 1961).
39 See my articles '"The Resonances of Words": Lope de Vega and Geoffrey Hill', *MLR*, 90 (1995), pp.55–70, and 'Translation and the Art of Poetry: *Cancionero* Poetry and Geoffrey Hill's "The Pentecost Castle" (1979)', *BHS*, 85 (1998), pp. 31–54.
40 See Henry Hart, *The Poetry of Geoffrey Hill* (Carbondale: Southern Illinois, 1986), p. 195.
41 R. O. Jones, *The Golden Age: Prose and Poetry* in *A Literary History of Spain* (London: Ernest Benn, 1971), pp. 87–8; see also *Agenda* 10.4–11.1 (Autumn–Winter 1972/3), p. 68. This text occurs in almost identical form in *Lírica española de tipo popular*, ed. Margit Frenk (Madrid: Cátedra, 1994), no. 300 (p. 150).
42 Geoffrey Hill, *Collected Poems* (Penguin: Harmondsworth, 1985), especially pp. 137–44.
43 See María Cristina Fumagalli, 'The Eternal Fountain of Poetic Imagination: Seamus Heaney's Translation of Juan de la Cruz's "Cantar de la alma que se huelga de conoscer a Dios por fee"', *Agenda*, 35 (no. 2), pp. 162–73. San Juan's verse has also influenced North American poets, such as Robert Lowell and Charles Simic.
44 See Juan Bosco San Román, 'El tercer centenario de la muerte de San Juan de la Cruz (1891) en España', *Teresianum*, 42 (1991), pp. 185–226. For details of the works of art and literature produced in celebration of the beatification and canonization of San Juan in Spain, Portugal and Mexico see Fernando Moreno Cuadro, 'El arte de las fiestas sanjuanistas' and Serafín Puerta Pérez, 'Manifestaciones literarias en las fiestas sanjuanistas', *SJC*, 15–16 (1995), pp. 9–104, 109–60.
45 All quotations from Ortega are from the *Obras completas*, 12 vols (Madrid, Revista de Occidente, Alianza: 1946–83).
46 Miguel de Unamuno, *En torno al casticismo*, 6th edn (Madrid: Espasa-Calpe, 1964), p. 102.
47 Luce López-Baralt, *San Juan de la Cruz y el Islam* (Mexico: El Colegio de Mexico, 1985).
48 Quoted from his *San Isidoro, Cervantes y otros estudios*, 3rd edn (Madrid: Espasa-Calpe, 1947), pp. 27–74 (p. 59).

49 Cited by Luce López-Baralt, *Asedios a lo indecible: San Juan de la Cruz canta al éxtasis transformante* (Madrid: Trotta, 1998), p. 140, from the prologue to *'Cántico espiritual' de San Juan de la Cruz*, ed. Cristóbal Cuevas (Mexico: Alhambra, 1985).

50 I cite from the only edition available to me, the one-volume 10th edition, revised and augmented, of what was originally a two-volume work (Madrid: Gaspar y Roig, 1862). I am grateful to Dr Andrew Ginger of Edinburgh University for alerting me to this work, which dates from the 1840s and was intended for university students and schoolchildren studying Spanish literature.

51 See Manuel Diego Sánchez, *San Juan de la Cruz: Bibliografía del IV Centenario de su muerte (1989–1993)* (Rome: Teresianum, 1993). Since 1993 many other articles and books have appeared.

52 For example, Luis Enrique Rodríguez-San Pedro Bezares, *La formación universitaria de Juan de la Cruz* (Valladolid: Junta de Castilla y León, 1992); Serafín de Tapia, 'El entorno morisco de San Juan de la Cruz', in *Aspectos históricos de San Juan de la Cruz* (Ávila: Institución 'Gran Duque de Alba', 1990), pp. 43–76; Alberto Marcos Martín, 'San Juan de la Cruz y su ambiente de pobreza' in *Actas del congreso internacional sanjuanista*, ed. A. García Simón, 3 vols (Valladolid: Junta de Castilla y León, 1993), II, pp. 143–84; and the many works of Carmelite scholars such as Teófanes Egido, Eulogio Pacho, Pablo María Garrido, Balbino Velasco Bayón, José Vicente Rodríguez and Otger Steggink.

53 See Eulogio Pacho, 'Nuevo manuscrito del "Cántico espiritual"', *El Monte Carmelo,* 99 (1991), pp. 243–71.

54 Jennings, *Every Changing Shape*, p. 70.

55 See my 'El mundo metafórico de San Juan', *Actas* I, pp. 75–93.

56 For Valente's use of San Juan, see Arthur Terry, 'Reading Valente: A Preface to *Tres lecciones de tinieblas*', in *Hispanic Studies in Honour of Geoffrey Ribbans, BHS* (Liverpool: Liverpool University Press, 1992), pp. 325–34; Juan Goytisolo, 'Palmera y mandrágora (Notas sobre la poética de José Ángel Valente)', in *El sol a medianoche*, pp. 205–11.

2

The Weaving

Hijo soy de un pobre tejedor.
I am the son of a poor weaver.
(San Juan de la Cruz)

The bell rang, summoning the friars to the Chapter House. The three candidates for the novitiate were led in by the novice-master and taken up to the Prior, who was seated before them. Their heads were already tonsured and on their feet they wore black, buckled shoes. Beside the Prior there lay folded the habits the novices would receive, and a stoup of holy water. He asked each in turn: 'What do you desire?' They answered: 'The mercy of God, the poverty of the Order and the company of the brethren.' He then explained to them the nature of the spiritual journey which they had begun as Carmelite novices. When the necessary questions had been asked, 12 in all, to ensure that there was no legal obstacle to proceeding, he spoke to them of the need for obedience, chastity and poverty. The novices replied that they would observe these, with the help of God and the prayers of the brethren. The Prior prayed: 'What God has begun in us may he bring to perfection in you.'

The ceremony continued with the symbolic divesting of lay garments, to represent the putting away of the 'old man', human nature in bondage to sin. The candidates knelt before the Prior as he sought the intercession of the Virgin Mary. As the tunic, embroidered with the cross, was placed on them, they were enjoined to put on the 'new man', human nature redeemed by Christ, to renounce worldly values and to walk in the way of the cross; as the girdle was tied around their waist they were reminded of Christ's words to Peter after the lakeside breakfast: 'When thou wast young, thou girdest thyself, and walkedst whither thou wouldest: but when thou shalt be old, thou shalt stretch forth thy hands, and another shall gird thee, and carry thee whither thou wouldest not' (John 21.18). As the scapular and cowl were placed over their shoulders they heard his words: 'For my yoke is easy, and my burden is light' (Matthew 11.30); and as they were vested in the white cloak they were joined to those whose robes were made 'white in the blood of the Lamb' (Revelation 7.14). Still kneeling, they were sprinkled with holy water and blessed by the Prior.

Now the friars began to chant the great hymn *Veni Creator Spiritus*, as they moved in procession to the church. Once there, each novice prostrated himself before the altar as the friars filed into their places. From one side of the altar the Prior spoke the concluding prayers and sprinkled the novices once more with holy water. They were raised from the ground and led to kiss the Prior's hands and cheek, in a sign of obedience and brotherly love, saying to him, 'Ora Deum pro me, pater', then to each of the friars according to the order of their profession, with the words 'Ora Deum pro me, frater.' They were then seated, and the Mass began.[1] The place was the Carmelite monastery of Santa Ana in Medina del Campo. The date was probably 24 February 1563. The Prior was Alonso Ruiz, and the novices Juan de Yepes, Rodrigo Nieto and Pedro de Orozco. Following the custom of the Carmelites of Castile, Juan de Yepes took the name of Juan de Santo Matía, in honour of the saint whose feast it was, St Matthias.[2] It is not the name by which we know him now. For us he is San Juan de la Cruz, St John of the Cross.

The story of his life has often been told before, but much of what has been read as biography in the past properly belongs to the genre of hagiography. His first biographers initiated the process in the seventeenth century, but its consequences may still be felt. Biographies in the modern sense were unknown to seventeenth-century authors, and even in our own time, whatever they may claim, they are not always objective historical accounts of a particular individual. They tend to present their subject in a particular light: a genius, a hero or heroine, maybe, or, if flawed, a rogue or a hypocrite. Different biographies of the same person may use the same historical evidence to construct strikingly contrasting personae, with controversial results. Three important lives of San Juan were written in the seventeenth century. José de Jesús María (Quiroga) OCD was exiled to Cuenca by the Discalced Carmelite authorities for publishing his *Historia de la vida y virtudes del Venerable Padre Fr. Juan de la Cruz* (Brussels: Jean Meerbeeck, 1628) without permission. Alonso de la Madre de Dios OCD left his *Vida, virtudes y milagros del Santo Padre Fray Juan de la Cruz* unpublished on his death in 1635, and only in 1989 did it see the light of day.[3] The most influential, though itself partially dependent on these earlier versions, was the semi-official *Historia del Venerable Padre Fr Juan de la Cruz* (Madrid: Diego Díaz de la Carrera, 1641), by Jerónimo de San José.[4] Curiously, the first book to be published containing any information about San Juan's life was a hagiographical account of his brother, Francisco de Yepes, who in old age acquired a degree of wealth and fame through possessing (and exploiting) a miracle-working relic of his younger brother. Six of the 16 chapters of José de Velasco's *Vida y virtudes del Venerable Varón Francisco de Yepes* deal with Juan.[5]

Hagiography, particularly of the baroque kind so popular in Spain for so long, is a recognizable literary genre and needs to be treated as such. It has its own ideology, which governs the presentation of its subject. At this period in Spain, it will expect the future saint, even if of poor and humble birth, to be of noble ancestry and untainted Christian blood, *limpieza de sangre*. It presumes that nobility of character is uniquely the property of the nobly born. Such a convention has a parallel in many of the short stories of the Golden Age: in two of the *Novelas ejemplares* of Cervantes, *La gitanilla* and *La ilustre fregona,* young women who attract the attention of young noblemen turn out not to be gipsy girls or scrubbing maids after all, while one critic has argued that another, *La fuerza de la sangre*, is actually based on a hagiographical model.[6] The hagiographer detects signs of the future saint from birth onwards: the story of his or her beginnings is read from the perspective of the end, so that the saint appears predestined to be such. This is particularly important in the case of San Juan, whose early biographers were all writing before his beatification or canonization with the aim of promoting his cause. In infancy and childhood narratives the pious imagination can have freer rein, while sayings and anecdotes assume exemplary significance. This tendency is already evident in the Apocryphal Gospels, which attempted to colour in the missing years of the childhood of Christ with accounts of sayings, actions and miracles which look forward to his redemptive death.[7] In a more secular, epic mode the great Spanish national hero, the Cid, will have stories invented about his precocious valour of which the *Poema de mio Cid* knows nothing. The birth of Amadis of Gaul, the hero of the most famous of all chivalric romances, is marked by a clear allusion to the tale of Moses in the bulrushes: the babe has been placed in a watertight ark which floats downstream to the sea, where he is rescued by a Scottish knight and brought up as his own son, even though the reason is to avoid the scandal brought about by an illegitimate birth from a secret love affair. However spurious such tales may be, they do bear witness to the belief still held, though now on genetic and environmental grounds, that the child is father to the man.

Patterns also become significant. Hagiographies look for parallels between the lives of saints and the life of Christ, so that the early biographers of San Juan, and even his recent ones, imply or even state that the poverty, exile, sufferings and death of Juan de la Cruz conform in a marvellous way to the life and death of Christ.[8] As a founder of what became a new religious Order, he is seen to be called to contemplation and solitude in his earliest years, and is characterized as a second Elijah.[9] However reliable or not the information these early writers give us about their subject is, what they choose to tell us undoubtedly reveals a great deal about their own concerns and interests.

These early manuscript and printed sources for the life of San Juan are problematical. Their concern is to project the life of a saint, in the hope that the beatification (and subsequently canonization) process of Fray Juan would reach a successful conclusion. They are based on the oral depositions of witnesses in the two-stage process which was begun in 1614, the year of Santa Teresa's beatification. Between 1614 and 1618 the Discalced Carmelite authorities gathered information about his life in the *proceso ordinario* or *informativo* from a large number of friars and nuns who had known him during his lifetime, completed by the *proceso apostólico* in 1627–28. The interviews followed a prescribed set of questions, an *interrogatorio*, which sought information about his noble Christian background, his writings, his virtues, miracles and saintly life.[10] That his cause was to prove more controversial than hers is clear from the fact that she was canonized by 1622, just 40 years after her death, and he only in 1726. One of the reasons for the delay may have been the existence of a strong local cult of Fray Juan and his relics in both Segovia and Úbeda. Urban VIII's decrees of 1625 and 1634 had banned cults which did not have the Church's permission, but because news of this took a long time to reach Segovia and Úbeda (they were suppressed in the two cities only in 1647–48) there was a delay in forwarding the case.[11] A new process was begun in 1649–51, which led to his beatification in 1675, canonization in 1726, and proclamation as a Doctor of the Church in 1926.

These depositions, especially the *proceso ordinario*, are immensely valuable, but must be treated with caution as historical documentation for a number of reasons. They recall events in some cases as much as 40 or 50 years earlier, with all the consequent distortions of memory. Sometimes they contradict one another, or may simply be repeating hearsay. The questions often suggest the answers required. Most of these depositions, but by no means all, have been published this century.[12] Other information comes from the writings of Teresa and from statements by Francisco not found in his biographer Velasco (though Francisco needed little enough encouragement to embroider). Very little comes from San Juan himself, who is said to have burnt many of his papers not long before his death.[13] In any case, except in his few surviving letters, he is a remarkably self-effacing writer, unlike Teresa.

Whether Christian believers or not, four centuries later we prefer saints earthed and human, and the baroque cult of sanctity, with its miracles and its macabre emphasis on relics, repels us. One example from the early biographies may serve as an illustration. On no fewer than three separate occasions during his childhood and youth, they tell us that Juan's life was endangered by water. Once, at the age of four, he was playing with other children by a pond in Fontiveros, overbalanced, fell in and disappeared. A beautiful lady stretched out her hand to him, but he did not wish to dirty it with mud from the bottom of the pond – an allusion to the Virgin Mary and his youthful devotion to her. Fortunately, a farmer arrived and pulled him out. A few years later, a monster arose from a river or pool in Medina and made as if to swallow him up; but he made the sign of the cross and it vanished. Francisco de Yepes, telling this story, attributes it to the devil's desire to put an end to the boy before he could become a powerful adversary. Again in Medina, Juan fell into a well at the hospital where he worked; also, according to Jerónimo de San José, through demonic intervention.[14]

What are we to make of this? We cannot be expected to believe that the young Juan de Yepes was so careless as to have been involved in three accidents involving water. While it is entirely credible that a child should fall into the water and be in danger of drowning, the emphasis on Marian protection, monsters and diabolic interference establishes the pattern of a devout, wonder-working exorcist which appealed to the baroque biographers but has little attraction for us, except as an historical curiosity. Our age wants facts and proofs, not received pieties, and is suspicious of interpretations which seem to twist them. About the early life of Juan de Yepes more can perhaps be said now with some certainty than ever before, because historical records have yielded valuable information. In the pages which follow, I shall try to differentiate the verifiable from the speculative and shall concentrate on four areas in which much scholarly work has been done: the poverty of his upbringing, the education he received, his entry into the Carmelite Order and his imprisonment in Toledo. But I do not simply present objective information. In Christian tradition, God chose to become incarnate in his Son in a distant corner of the Roman Empire at a particular moment, not in order to limit the extent of his self-bestowal but to give value to the local and the rooted by enabling them to become the place in which the universal is revealed. The particularities of history therefore have a significance in Christianity which lifts them out of the accidental and aleatory and attributes to them a necessary role in divine self-revelation.

In its own way, Juan's story is an example of this 'scandal of particularity'. He too was born in poverty and obscurity, yet the particular context of his life is important not so much because hearts may be warmed by the tale of a man who rose from the most unpromising beginnings to become one of the greatest poets of Spain and spiritual teachers of Western Christianity, but because that life is itself the raw material of the art he created and the theology and spirituality he taught. The Incarnation means that any time or place has the potential to become the locus of revelation. As Federico Ruiz has said, 'San Juan de la Cruz no es universal a pesar de sus particularidades de fe y de vocación, sino precisamente gracias a ellas', 'St John of the Cross is not universal in spite of the particularities of his faith and vocation but precisely because of them.'[15]

FONTIVEROS

How Juan de Yepes became San Juan de la Cruz is a story which begins in Fontiveros, a village a few miles north-east of what is now the main road from Ávila to Salamanca. Fontiveros lies high on the Castilian *meseta*, under a huge sky, with plains stretching around it almost as far as the eye can see. Distant mountain ranges can be glimpsed when the air is clear. The plain is dry and dusty for much of the year, and subject to fierce winds which whip up the dust and sting the eyes. But it is good agricultural land, and both grain and livestock flourish. The village seems archetypically Castilian in its introspection and its austerity. In the 1550s it had no more than 2,000 inhabitants; today, perhaps 1,400. A splendid parish church, the largest in the region, dedicated to St Cyprian, is its chief artistic glory, but it is as the place where Juan de Yepes was born that it is most famous.[16] A statue in the village square, erected in 1928, commemorates his birth, following his proclamation by Pius XI as a Doctor of the Church two years earlier.

The village lies at the western edge of the province of Ávila, bordering the province of Salamanca, in a region known as La Moraña, a name some scholars have associated with the existence there in times past of a sizeable *morisco* population.[17] Here, probably in 1542, Juan de Yepes was born.[18] In the parish church lie the remains of his father Gonzalo de Yepes, who died when Juan was a small child, and of an older brother, Luis, thought to have been a victim of famine.[19] His mother, born Catalina Álvarez, herself an orphan, lived on until the influenza epidemic (*catarro universal*) of 1580; his older brother Francisco, born around 1530, until 1607. The family earned a precarious living in the textile industry, as weavers of silk.

In its classic form, the story of how Gonzalo de Yepes met and fell in love with Catalina Álvarez in Fontiveros has great romantic appeal.[20] Gonzalo came from a well-to-do family of silk merchants from Yepes, in the province of Toledo. His father seems to have died when he was young, and nothing is known of his mother; if the family had been rich, Gonzalo's branch seems to have fallen on hard times. His job was to travel to and from Medina del Campo, one of the great trade centres of Europe, buying and selling silk fabrics. His route took him through Fontiveros, which had a small weaving industry, and where he lodged in the house where Catalina worked. They fell in love and were married. Since he was of noble birth and she was a poor orphan, his family disowned him and he settled with Catalina in Fontiveros to a life of poverty as a weaver. All this information comes from seventeenth-century versions of the family history and cannot be independently corroborated.

The dangers of building elaborate hypotheses on insecure foundations are well illustrated by the tendency among some scholars to stress the *converso* or *morisco* origins of Catalina de Yepes. While working in the grounds of his priory in Granada, Fray Juan is reported to have been greeted by a passer-by with the observation that he must be the son of 'labradores', workers of the land, to be so busily engaged. He replied that he was not: 'Hijo soy de un pobre tejedor', 'I am the son of a poor weaver.'[21] The remark, if accurately remembered, is not as innocent as it seems. 'Labradores' were thought of as *cristianos viejos*, as coming from pure Christian stock, untainted by Jewish or Moorish blood, whereas weaving was an occupation associated with *cristianos nuevos*. Was Catalina a *morisca*? Was this the stain on her reputation which caused the family of Gonzalo de Yepes to repudiate him on his marriage to her?

Recent historical research has shown that the *morisco* population of La Moraña has been overestimated, and in any case had suffered a process of acculturation which made *moriscos* increasingly indifferent to and ignorant of their own religious inheritance.[22] During Juan's childhood Inquisitorial pressure, always present, increased around Medina and Arévalo as a result of a suspected resistance group active in the area.[23] But mixed marriages were extremely rare, especially in the first third of the century, and out of the question between an old Christian of some family means and a poor *morisca*. The claim that Catalina and her family had friends who were *moriscos* is not borne out by examination of the 1565 records either, since none of the names mentioned in this connection appear there.[24] These factors strongly suggest that the stain of social inferiority and poverty was the true reason for the reaction of the Yepes family to Gonzalo's marriage, if the story has any truth.

The Yepes family in Fontiveros clearly belonged to the category of *pobres de solemnidad*, whose poverty was structural, rather than to the *pobres [en]vergonzantes*, who (like the squire in *Lazarillo de Tormes*) had once been prosperous but had fallen on hard times. The latter received the benefit of alms from the better-off and more nobly born, no doubt offered with an unspoken, 'There but for the grace of God go I', since they were believed to possess honour and good ancestry.[25] The status of the former was more precarious. They were permitted to beg, though the problem was serious enough for it to have been debated and made subject to legislation, in the familiar attempt to distinguish the deserving poor from the idle.[26] Local charities, where they existed, were vulnerable to fluctuations in the economic cycle caused by poor harvests, and their resources were severely strained by the sickness and epidemic which often followed these. In any case, in Fontiveros the two small hospitals of San Cebrián and La Concepción offered their charity to the transient rather than to the resident poor. There was a single *cofradía*, or guild, which did not engage in charitable work, and one convent, of Carmelite nuns. Juan's parents were both orphans, with no family connections in the area; the death of his father was an additional heavy blow. Local poll tax records (*padrones*) mention his mother, 'la de Yepes', from time to time, as a widowed head of household, taxed at the lowest possible rates. As a poor widow, her economic situation was desperate, as she struggled to bring up three small children with no family support or guaranteed income. There were many like her. The contrast with the family of Teresa of Ávila could scarcely be greater. Teresa was the eldest of ten children of her father's second marriage, all of whom survived into adulthood because the family was prosperous.

The records of the Archdiocese of Toledo prove that the 1540s were difficult years. Harvest levels were consistently below those of the 1530s and 1550s, while individual years could prove disastrous. A poor harvest triggered a rapid rise in the price of wheat and this in turn affected local industries, like the silk weavers of Fontiveros, who found that their market all but disappeared. Living at subsistence level and with no inherited resources, poor families quickly found themselves in serious hardship. For example, following the dreadful harvest of 1545 in Toledo, wheat prices rose, manufacturing declined, and by the following spring famine and deaths were being reported among workers in the silk trade, which was centred there. By April 1546 a census reckoned a quarter of the population of the city – 10,819 people – as poor.[27] In Fontiveros, the vicar-general of the diocese canvassed the idea of selling some of the treasures of the parish church to relieve the famine, but in the end the income from the local hospitals was applied instead.

Poverty and hunger drove Catalina and her two surviving children from Fontiveros. It was too small to offer sufficient work or charitable resources to cope with the numbers of people who were unable to earn a living. They moved first to Arévalo, then to Medina del Campo, where Catalina, Francisco and his wife Ana Izquierda (or Izquierdo) with their family were finally to settle.[28]

In doing so, they were joining the long procession of economic refugees through history, moving from place to place in search of a livelihood ever threatened by unemployment and famine. From the countryside they flocked into towns and cities, a process which had grown to enormous proportions in the second half of the twentieth century as the poor of the land sought work and food in great cities and settled in sprawling slums and shanty towns which bred violence and disease. It is an age-old pattern, witness the stories of Joseph and his brothers, or of Ruth, in the Hebrew scriptures.

Arévalo was larger than Fontiveros and possessed many fine buildings and churches; decayed signs of its splendid past may still be seen today. In the middle of the sixteenth century it was the centre of the Castilian wheat trade.[29] Catalina and her children lodged in the house of a weaver. Nothing is known about Juan's life here, but Francisco, according to his biographer, was growing up into a noisy, gregarious and work-shy young man, who passed half the night singing and dancing round the streets and often slept rough. The tale of his scrumping fruit belongs to a venerable tradition which stretches back at least to St Augustine, who concludes that he and his friends stole for the sheer pleasure of stealing, since the pears they took were hard and bitter to the taste (*Confessions* ii.4). Inevitably, for his life too is read from a hagiographical perspective, Francisco's life reached a moment of crisis and he was converted. Family life helped to settle him down, though he never held down any regular job and preferred to roam the streets engaged in charitable works or in search of spiritual conversation with clerics and friars. His relationship with his brother Juan seems to have remained close and warm.[30]

MEDINA DEL CAMPO

The family remained in Arévalo for three or four years (probably 1548–51), then moved on to Medina del Campo, best known now as an important railway junction. In the middle of the sixteenth century, until the national economic crisis of 1559–78, it was at the height of its prosperity as one of the great fairs, or trading and financial centres, of Western Europe, at the hub of an international communications network, and a natural magnet to the surrounding poor. A weekly mail service linked it with Seville, the centre of the lucrative trade with the Spanish colonies in America, and several printers were active there.[31] Like many other towns of the period, its resident population of some 20,000 consisted of a few influential noble families, important merchants and businessmen, a large number of craftsmen, and a lower class of farm labourers and shepherds, but it was augmented by a constant stream of visitors from all over the continent.[32] The impact on a family like the Yepes, used to life in a village or a small town, must have been considerable. For the first time in their lives they found themselves in a sophisticated urban culture, and everything that accompanied it, from prostitution to international banking facilities.

Medina boasted many charitable institutions founded on mercantile wealth: 13 hospitals and a number of guilds. There was some housing for poor widows, provision for the education of some poor boys, and from time to time the Council distributed money or wheat. In the census of 1561 Catalina is shown as living in an area of mixed economic population but with the greatest number of poor people (almost a third of the total), still a 'pobre de solemnidad', the proper object of Christian charity, especially as a widow. She lived off charity and a little work in the silk trade, as well as continuing with Francisco her own charitable work of rescuing and nursing abandoned babies and acting as godparents at their baptisms. But the move was successful: Catalina and Francisco remained there for the rest of their lives.

The rich had always been able to educate their children by engaging private tutors or by sending their sons to private schools. Girls, if educated at all, were taught at home or attended convent schools (the young Teresa is a case in point). The poor, as usual, were largely excluded.[33] However, from the late 1540s a movement had begun in Castile to found orphanage schools, in order to keep children off the streets and prevent them from begging or engaging in delinquency and petty crime. A royal provision of 1553 made statutes for these 'Colegios de los Niños de la Doctrina Cristiana', or *Doctrinas*, as they were popularly known, which had already begun to spring up in towns and cities, among them Medina, around 1550.[34] They provided an elementary education for orphan boys, who included those who had lost only one parent, teaching them elementary reading, writing and arithmetic as well as basic Christian doctrine, with the aim of preparing them for apprenticeship to a particular craft. The Medina *Doctrina* had been endowed soon after its foundation by Rodrigo de Dueñas, one of the most important businessmen of the reign of Charles V.[35] His will stipulated that four of the boys were to assist in the church of the Augustinian convent of La Magdalena, which he had founded, and to collect alms. Boys were also to act as attendants at burials, a useful source of revenue for the school, and a sign of prestige for the deceased: the more attendants, the more impressive the funeral.[36] To this school Juan de Yepes went, probably until he was 14; from it he received his first education, and engaged in the duties expected of him, serving the nuns from 7 to 11 a.m. in winter and 6 to 10 a.m. in summer, and occasionally also in the afternoons. He did not seem to be particularly gifted for a craft – Francisco mentions tailoring, carpentry, woodcarving and painting as those he tried,[37] though in later years he certainly used his practical skills in building. From here he was fortunate enough to be able to continue his education with the Jesuits, probably between 1559 and 1563.

Schools, though not part of the original Ignatian vision for the new Society, had quickly become part of the Jesuits' missionary enterprise, spread across Catholic Europe, and came to be seen as representing the best in contemporary educational theory and practice.[38] Cervantes has words of praise for them in the otherwise unflattering portrait of society in the first part of *El coloquio de los perros* (*The Dogs' Colloquy*), the last of his *Novelas ejemplares*.[39] The first school had begun in 1548 in Messina, Sicily, and from 1551 the Society was opening them at the rate of four or five a year. In December 1551 Ignatius's close companion Polanco had written to the Jesuit provincials of Spain and Portugal encouraging them to open similar schools. In fact, Jesuits had already started to teach in Medina, and for a time were lodged in the *Doctrina*; the school opened in its own buildings in 1553, once again thanks to the support of Rodrigo de Dueñas. It had some 160–170 pupils, consisting of novices, boys from rich families, and poor boys subsidized by their fees.[40] The Jesuit aim was to instil *pietas*, 'the development of character through the study of classical literature in preparation for a life of public service', the formation of the whole person rather than the simple acquisition of information.[41] In that sense, with their belief in human dignity and their theology of nature and grace in co-operation rather than conflict, they show affinities with the concerns of the great Renaissance humanists.

Juan de Yepes was not a boarder, and cannot have participated fully in the life of the school or have attended all the lessons. In order to pay the minimal fees required of poor pupils, but no doubt also to ease the family's burdens, he needed to earn money. He probably began to work at the Hospital de Nuestra Señora de la Concepción while still at the *Doctrina*, and it is generally accepted that the hospital's administrator c. 1555, Alonso Álvarez de Toledo, a highly respected citizen of Medina, arranged his entry into the Jesuit school.[42] Juan lived with the patients, helped with nursing duties and collected alms for the hospital, like good Mahudes, who, at the end of the *Coloquio* is engaged in this activity.[43] Alms were collected in the streets on Saturdays, during the fair among those engaged in commerce, on Sundays in churches and during August out in the fields among the harvesters, and later during the vintage.[44]

Maybe on these expeditions Juan heard some of the popular songs, traces of which can be found in his poetry.

Cervantes again provides a fictional parallel for the kind of hospital it was. The frame story of the *Coloquio*, *El casamiento engañoso* (*The deceitful marriage*), opens with a gaunt man leaving the Hospital de la Resurrección in Valladolid, having sweated out a serious illness – 'las bubas', the pox. Venereal disease was one of the scourges of the time, with no known cure.[45] The Medina hospital, popularly known as 'de las bubas', was one of the most successful institutions in the town, with 40–50 beds, and treated around 200 patients per year.[46] There must have been plenty of cases, given the cosmopolitan nature of Medina. One can only speculate about the effect of this on an adolescent boy. Did it, as Javierre suggests, mean that he knew everything about sex and the snares of pleasure? And is he right to draw so extreme an antithesis between 'el más exquisito poeta lírico de la lengua hispana, el futuro místico absorto en divinos coloquios', 'the most exquisite lyrical poet in the Spanish tongue, the future mystic absorbed in divine colloquies', and the youth who spent six years 'cuidando enfermos sifilíticos en un arrabal de la feria de Medina', 'looking after syphilitic patients in the outskirts of the fair of Medina'?[47] Juan can have had few illusions about his fellow-humans in the Medina hospital, and must have heard tales of their sexual exploits as well as their subsequent remorse and shame, as he tended his patients and watched many of them die.[48] His encounter with the dark side of human experience should not be underestimated: he is seriously misrepresented if, as a saint in the making, he is imagined to have led a sheltered and protected life, never exposed to human frailties and suffering, or to have sought escape from any possible contact with them. Born into poverty, familiar with disease and death, he was a young man with no privileges, who had to struggle to make his way in life.

Many of the teachers at the Jesuit school in Medina were recent university graduates, among them Juan Bonifacio, who was at the beginning of a career which would make him one of the foremost pedagogues of his age.[49] Boys followed the humanistic curriculum of grammar, rhetoric, Latin and Greek, those parts of classical literature thought compatible with Christianity receiving particular emphasis. They were encouraged to apply the knowledge they had gained, hence an 'exacting programme of lectures, complemented by a full array of drills, repetitions and disputations' was developed, through which students put into practice what they had been taught.[50] Each class consisted of a unit of work rather than a period of time, so that brighter boys progressed faster. The Jesuits also stressed the importance of physical exercise, decent food, recreation and holidays. For religious instruction the Jesuit schools in Spain used Juan de Ávila's catechism of 1527, *Doctrina cristiana que se canta*. Spiritual formation was encouraged by a daily examination of conscience, regular or daily Mass, Confession and the regular reception of Communion, occasional fasts and penances and some use of the liturgical Hours. Another notable feature of Jesuit education was the regular production of Latin plays, usually on biblical subjects, specially composed by teachers or pupils and the composition of other forms of academic exercise, such as Latin orations, disputations and poems. Jesuit drama has interested literary critics because of its relevance to the development of drama in Spain as a whole.[51] Juan must therefore have learnt Latin and studied grammar and rhetoric through extracts from the great classical writers, with complementary exercises in the practice of these skills. Undoubtedly this was where he gained his 'infraestructura humanística', his grounding in the humanities, the foundation on which he was later to build, both in Salamanca and in his own writing.[52] If, as seems probable, he also studied Nebrija's standard *Gramática castellana* of 1492, he would have received not only a thorough grounding in the Spanish language but also a familiarity with verse forms and figures of speech, the study of which occupies a considerable part of Nebrija's treatise.

Álvarez, recognizing Juan's talents, seems to have offered the young Juan immediate ordination and the post of chaplain to the Hospital. This he refused, so we are told by his friend Tomás Pérez de Molina many years later, on the grounds than he sought withdrawal from the world and an austerer lifestyle: 'deseaba apartarse más y apretarse más', 'he wanted to withdraw more and to be more restricted'.[53] Evidently more drawn to a contemplative than to an active life, more to prayer, silence and solitude than to involvement in ministry in a hospital or in the missionary zeal or educational innovations of the Jesuits, Juan's future was to lie elsewhere.

THE CARMELITES[54]

As befitted its size and prosperity, many religious Orders had houses in or around Medina – Dominicans, Premonstratensians, Trinitarians, Benedictines, Augustinians, Franciscans and Capuchins, and most recently, the Carmelites, together with the Society of Jesus.[55] To any of these Juan de Yepes might have turned, and to the last in particular, because he had been educated by them. The reasons for Juan's choice of the Carmelites are unclear; hagiographical tradition, typically, has him already conscious of his calling to be a monastic reformer.[56] But other reasons have been suggested. Did something of the fame of Diego de Rengifo, confessor to Charles V and founder of the Carmelite convent of Santa Ana in Medina as recently as 1557, reach him? Did he feel that a new foundation was more likely to observe the Rule than a well-established one? Some scholars have suggested that members of Juan's family on his father's side might have been Carmelites in Toledo, since the name Yepes is recorded among them; others doubt this, because it was not uncommon, nor should it be assumed that everyone who bore it was a relative.[57] In any case, Juan had scarcely known his father, who had died when he was a small child. It may be that he had childhood recollections or had been told family stories about the Carmelite nuns in Fontiveros. But the Carmelite Order had other attractions, which its full title – 'the Brothers of the Blessed Virgin Mary of Mount Carmel' – and history help to clarify. It held the Virgin in special veneration. Fray Juan's devotion to Mary is a constant theme among his early biographers and those who knew him, and even allowing for some exaggeration there is no reason to doubt this.[58]

Christian monasticism has followed two principal forms of life, the eremitical and the cenobitic. In the first, individuals follow their own spiritual journey, usually as hermits in remote, often wild or inaccessible places. Such a man is Paulo, at the start of

Tirso de Molina's powerful play *El condenado por desconfiado*, written in the 1620s; but unlike the ideal hermit, he is self-centred and arrogant, lacking the kind of spiritual discernment one might expect of those devoted to a life of solitary prayer amid the beauties of nature. Its origins, traditionally associated with St Anthony of Egypt, were inspired by an eremitical spirit which has remained a significant force in Eastern Christianity. Such 'going into the desert' represented a complete renunciation of the pleasures of civilized life in the late Roman Empire, but it appealed to many, especially once Christianity had been adopted as the religion of the state and began to lose its sense of offering a radical alternative to the values of society. The external, physical desert, scene of decisive moments in biblical narrative, like the wanderings of the children of Israel and the temptations of Christ, became the natural locus for an inward pilgrimage through the desert of withdrawal and detachment to the promised land of union with God.

The cenobitic form was based on the monastic community. Monks assembled in Choir for the divine Offices and ate and worked together. Instead of living alone in caves, they constructed buildings to house their communities and lived under a particular Rule, with brethren elected or appointed to the necessary administrative and practical positions required for the smooth organization of community life. Such monasteries could be found in towns and cities, and their occupants might well devote themselves, alongside prayer and study, to practical works of charity, like tending the sick or teaching the young. In the West, cenobitic monasticism became the dominant form, and even the Carthusians, who preserved the eremitical spirit to a greater extent than any other Order, lived in community. But the long debate about the respective merits of contemplative and active vocations continued within the Western Orders, the former keeping enclosure and concentrating on solitude, silence and prayer, the latter stressing a more outgoing form of spirituality.

By the beginning of the thirteenth century, during the precarious existence of the Crusader kingdom of Jerusalem, groups of hermits had settled in caves on Mount Carmel, a steep limestone ridge with many caves which dominates the modern port and bay of Haifa. Long before Christian hermits arrived it was a sacred place to Phoenicians, Egyptians, Greeks and Romans. When the Emperor Vespasian offered a sacrifice there at the end of the first century AD the historian Tacitus remarked: 'Carmel lies between Judaea and Syria; the same name is given to a mountain and a god. This god has neither statue nor temple; so willed the ancients; there is only an altar and worship.'[59] More significantly, for the Hebrew prophets the glory and majesty of Carmel is a metaphor for power and abundance, and its 'drying-up' a symbol of national disaster (see, for example, Isaiah 35.2, where it symbolizes the Messianic age, and Amos 1.2, where it introduces the divine judgement on Israel's transgressions). In the Song of Songs (7.5) it is used as a metaphor for the beauty of the Bride's head. Springtime on Carmel remains a glorious sight, with white and pink rock roses, yellow broom, the new leaves of the deciduous Tabor oak, the dark green of the evergreen Karmes oak, and the vivid magenta of the Judas trees. Its name means 'the hill of the vineyard of the Lord', and vines are still cultivated on its slopes.[60]

But above all, it is the place associated in biblical narrative with the momentous contest between Elijah and the 450 prophets of Baal (1 Kings 18.17–40). In Carmelite tradition, Elijah is the first of those who chose the ascetic or eremitical life, and the Carmelites, uniquely among the Orders, trace their spiritual ancestry back to a figure from the Hebrew scriptures. The contest is traditionally sited at Muhraqa, a high point on the ridge, above a spring, from which there are fine views of the Mediterranean Sea to the west and the Vale of Jezreel to the east. A Carmelite monastery built in 1868 commemorates it.[61] Elijah's victory is followed in the Bible by a strange event. He hears the sound of coming rain, breaking the two-year drought. He climbs to the crest of Carmel and orders his servant to look westwards. Six times he does so and sees nothing; but on the seventh he sees 'a little cloud [. . .] like a man's hand' (18.44), and the rains soon begin to pour down. The mysterious cloud, harbinger of refreshing rain, was for many centuries interpreted as a reference to the Virgin Mary, patroness of the Carmelites, and the new life she was to bring into the world. Early Carmelite writing makes an explicit connection between Elijah and Mary through this passage. Neither of these stories appears as such in the writings of San Juan, though his frequent use of the term 'sequedad', 'drought', for spiritual dryness may acquire fresh significance from association with the Elijah cycle, while towards the end of his longest poem, the 'Cántico espiritual', the lines 'Y luego a las subidas/ cabernas de la piedra nos yremos/ que están bien escondidas', 'and then we shall go to the lofty caverns of stone, which are well hidden' (CA 37), seem to recall the origins of the Order on Carmel. In any case, as we shall see, the figure of Elijah plays a part in San Juan's prose treatises.

Though Carmelite origins lay in eremitical monasticism, the Order had come to embrace a cenobitic style of life. Early in the thirteenth century Albert, Latin Patriarch of Jerusalem, invited the group of hermits who were living near Elijah's spring on Mount Carmel to build an oratory dedicated to the Virgin Mary and to choose from their own number a superior. By 1230 the church had been built, as a pilgrim guide of the period shows.[62] Though the Lateran Council of 1215, concerned about the proliferation of 'irregular' communities, had forbidden the foundation of any new Orders, the *formula vitae*, or Rule of the hermits of Carmel, was confirmed both by Pope Honorius IV in 1226 and Pope Gregory IX in 1229. In 1247 Pope Innocent IV produced an adaptation of the Rule of St Albert which became formative for the self-understanding of the later Carmelites. By then a westward movement was accelerating under the pressure of Muslim attacks on the Crusader kingdom, the fall of which in 1291 led to the abandonment of Carmel by all its hermits. Innocent IV's changes converted the hermits into a recognizable mendicant Order, living under its own Rule, which nonetheless retained a number of characteristics of its more eremitical past. Permission was given, for example, for hermitages to be built in the vicinity of monasteries, 'solares y sitios en los yermos', 'desert places'.[63] Friars were to have individual cells, for the sake of solitude, rather than sleeping in dormitories, were to remain in them or near them at all times, and to be engaged in constant prayer, save when other, necessary labours called. Seven years later, in 1254, Innocent granted the Carmelites authority to preach and to confess. The Second Council of Lyons in 1274 suppressed many newer religious groups, but gave the Carmelites a kind of interim permission to continue. Not until Boniface VIII's confirmation of their status in 1298, however, did their position become secure.

In the fifteenth century further significant changes took place without which the reform of the Order in the sixteenth cannot be understood. In the Bull *Romani Pontificis providentia* of 1432 Pope Eugenius IV had dispensed the Order from parts of its Rule, and this relaxation, or 'mitigation', followed by further dispensations by Pius II (1459) and Sixtus IV (1476), was the Rule by which Santa Teresa and San Juan first professed. One of the reasons for mitigation was that a mendicant lifestyle required greater freedom of movement than the 1247 Rule, with its insistence on living in as great a degree of enclosure as possible, allowed. Carmelites were now permitted to leave their cells and monasteries to engage in their apostolic work. At the same time, periods of silence were prescribed, from Compline to Prime, and excessive talking was discouraged at any other time. The diet was vegetarian, with a period of fasting from the Feast of the Exaltation of the Cross (14 September) until Easter (Sundays excepted). The emphasis on silence and on strict dietary rules are characteristic of hermits, and the aim of the mitigated Rule has been well described as 'un eremitismo interior', 'an inner eremiticism'.[64] Thus, although it had been necessary to abandon the strictly eremitical life of the hermits of Carmel, some of its elements had been preserved to create a reasonable compromise between faithfulness to its Eastern origins and flexibility in the face of Western conditions.

Such changes did not take place without protest. As early as 1274 Nicholas Gallicus, one of the early Priors-General, fought to preserve the eremitical life of the Order. The title of the work in which he did so, *Ignea sagitta*, pointedly alludes to the horses and chariots of fire associated with Elijah and Elisha (2 Kings 2.11, 6.17), the legendary founders of the Order:

> Quiero contaros ahora las alegrías de la vida solitaria. La hermosura de los elementos, y el cielo estrellado, los planetas ordenados en perfecta armonía, invitan a contemplar infinitas maravillas. Las aves del cielo, como si fuesen ángeles, nos regalan con melodiosas cadencias. Las montañas, como dice Isaías profeta, nos estrechan con dulzura y los cerros destilan leche y miel. Los montes con su boscaje hacen compañía, cual si fuesen hermanos conventuales y se unen a los salmos que decimos loando al Creador, como se acompaña la canción con el laúd. Mientras nosotros alabamos al Señor vegetan las raíces de los árboles, hundiéndose en el suelo; reverdecen las praderas; danzan a su manera, jubilosos, los arbustos, y se agita gozoso el ramaje de la arboleda, cual si batiese palmas al compás de nuestro canto. Flores de peregrina belleza, deliciosamente perfumadas, son la sonrisa en la adusta soledad. La luz callada de los astros marca el tiempo de cada jornada. Y hasta los zarzales y matojos dan sombra y brindan humildes presentes. Todas las criaturas, hermanas nuestras, se afanan en la soledad por llenar de caricias nuestros ojos, nuestros oídos y también nuestros sentimientos. En silencio clama su inefable belleza y convida a loar al admirable Creador.

> En la ciudad [. . .] no se oyen trinos de aves, sino vocerío y altercados de hombres y mujeres, gruñidos, relinchos y ladridos, de puercos, caballos y perros, que aturden los oídos. No se pisa la verde y suave alfombra de los prados, sino calles polvorientas o embarradas, ni se respira el aroma de flores campestres, sino el hedor pestilencial de la miseria interior.[65]

> I want to tell you of the joys of the solitary life. The beauty of the elements, the starry heavens and the planets ordered in perfect harmony, invite us to contemplate infinite wonders. The birds in the sky, like angels, delight us with their melodious cadences. The mountains, as the prophet Isaiah says, surround us sweetly and the hills drip with milk and honey. The wooded mountains, like conventual brethren, provide our company and join in the psalms we say in praise of the Creator, as a song accompanied on the lute. While we praise the Lord the roots of the trees grow, deep in the ground; the meadows grow green; in their own manner the bushes dance rejoicing and the foliage of the groves waves joyfully, as if clapping its hands to the rhythm of our song. Flowers of strange beauty and delightful fragrance smile in the austere solitude. The silent starlight measures the time of each day. Even the brambles and the brushwood provide shade and offer simple gifts. All our sisters the creatures strive in the solitude to fill our eyes, ears and feelings with their caresses. Their inexpressible beauty cries out in silence and invites us to praise the marvellous Creator.
>
> In the city [. . .] no birdsong is heard, only clamour and disputes of men and women, the grunting, neighing and barking of pigs, horses and dogs, which offend the ears. One cannot walk on the soft green carpet of the fields, but on dusty or muddy streets, nor can one breathe the fragrance of wild flowers, only the pestilential stench of inner destitution.

This moving and passionate defence has a number of remarkable features: its early date, its lyricism, the Franciscan spirit of its creation theology from the pen of a Carmelite, and the fact that it is not a literary *topos* but a cry from the heart of a man who wished to reverse the changes taking place within the Order of which he was the head. This tension between the two forms of monastic life, never entirely resolved, was to have fruitful results in the work of Santa Teresa and San Juan. By San Juan's time, the contrast between the simple pleasures of the countryside and the vice and corruption of the city and the court had become one of the great themes of Spanish Golden Age literature.[66] He probably never read these words, but the music of creation is heard in his 'Cántico' poem.

The Castilian Province of the Order, to which Santa Ana belonged, was relatively small and undistinguished, and Medina was only its seventh house. Its intellectual life had not flourished, either, though the foundation of the Carmelite College of San Andrés in Salamanca around 1480 opened the way for its more active participation in the life of one of Europe's greatest universities, and there is some evidence that this had borne fruit.[67] From 1532 onwards Carmelite students at Salamanca were obliged to reside in San Andrés, while from 1548 it was recognized as the centre of study for all the Spanish Provinces. However, a series of reforms in 1530–31 under the Generalship of Nicholas Audet, intended to lead to stricter observance of the Rule, had resulted in an exodus of friars, perhaps the majority, who were not prepared to accept them.[68] In her *Libro de fundaciones* Santa Teresa expresses her concern about the state of the Carmelite friars at the time of General Rubeo's visit early in 1567: 'Viendo [los frailes] ya tan pocos en esta provincia, que aun me parecía se ivan a acabar', '[The friars] were now so few in this province, I thought they were going to disappear.'[69] Her words, written barely four years after Fray Juan's profession, only increase surprise at his choice of Order. Scholars cannot agree whether or not the Carmelites in Medina provided further education in the arts; they may have done so.[70] In any case, within a year he was sent to Salamanca, to continue his education in one of Europe's greatest universities.

During his novitiate he must have studied the fundamental Carmelite text, the *Liber de institutione primorum monachorum in legi veteri exortorum et in nova perseverantium*. Copies of a Spanish translation belonged to the libraries of several monasteries, and it was printed in the *Speculum fratrum ordinis carmelitorum* (Venice, 1507). Though in all likelihood a work of the fourteenth century, it was believed until the seventeenth to be the primitive Rule of the Order composed around 400 by the Patriarch John XLIV of Jerusalem, and thus dating from the formative period of Western monasticism.[71] For Juan, as for his contemporaries, the *Liber* defined Carmelite life at its origins. It showed the eremitical life to have two modes: one, proper to human endeavour, to be pursued actively, with the assistance of grace, through the offering of a pure and sinless heart to God, made perfect in charity; the other, God's gift alone, of the power and sweetness of the divine presence within this life. This distinction between human activity and divine self-giving was to become fundamental for him, not in the sense of the traditional distinction between the active and contemplative lives *per se,* but as the co-existence within the contemplative life of elements which are within human control (such as ascetic practices) and those which are purely the initiative of divine grace. Whether he first found this contrast drawn in his study of the *Liber* is not known, but it was to become the basis of his innovative teaching on the active and passive dark nights of the soul.

Two other aspects of the *Liber* were to influence him. The first was the figure of Elijah, whose life and tribulations were given an allegorical reading. Its sense of continuity between the Hebrew scriptures and the New Testament is striking. Elijah becomes the hero and exemplar of the contemplative life, and Carmel, by metonymy, the community devoted to it. San Juan makes no distinction in terms of *auctoritas* between the two Testaments, citing the Old twice as often as the New, though always following the orthodox view that the former is fulfilled in the latter. The second was the status of the *Liber* itself as he perceived it. Since the reform of the Order initiated by Teresa of Ávila and extended at her instance by Fray Juan among the friars was based on a return to a life in conformity with its primitive Rule, the *Liber* must have played a significant part in how they envisaged such a life. As he studied it, Fray Juan cannot have been unaware of the gap between its intentions and their expression in the monastery of Santa Ana. It was not that the friars were corrupt or scandalous, but that they had become separated from their spiritual roots. It is interesting to note, therefore, that when Fray Juan began his studies at the Colegio de San Andrés in Salamanca, he apparently asked for and was given permission to observe the primitive Rule.[72] His vocational crisis when he dropped out of theological studies at Salamanca after only one year becomes the more poignant: having chosen the Carmelites perhaps because their eremitical inheritance made them the nearest Order to his ideal, the more he studied their traditions and lived among them, the less he felt he could be true to it. The Carthusians, on the other hand, had not compromised. Fray Juan might well have joined them, had not a meeting with an extraordinary Carmelite nun kept him within the Order yet changed his, and its, direction.

SALAMANCA[73]

By the time San Juan reached Salamanca, it was a city of 19,000 inhabitants, with an additional 5,000–7,000 students matriculating each year. Contrary to what might be supposed, far more students studied canon or civil law than theology, since it was the 'gateway to both clerical and secular careers'.[74] In 1555 only about 5 per cent of the students were members of religious Orders, again a surprisingly low figure. Like Fray Juan, they lived in colleges established by their Orders and followed a somewhat different regime from other students. Students were only permitted to leave San Andrés to attend lectures, and then only in pairs, properly attired and behaving as befitted religious. There may also have been additional classes in the Colegio, but once more scholars are in disagreement over their nature and extent.[75] San Andrés was small and poor, especially in comparison with the rich and influential *colegios mayores*, matriculating only ten to twelve students per year in the period of Fray Juan's studies (1564–68), and was often in receipt of grants from the University to enable it to provide adequately for them. But it was well regarded, partly because it provided confessions for students and partly for its work at the Hospital de Santa María la Blanca, mainly among patients with venereal diseases. Fray Juan's previous experience may have been put to use here, though no direct evidence for this survives.

The academic year ran from St Luke's Day (18 October) to the Nativity of the Blessed Virgin Mary (8 September), but holders of permanent Chairs (*cátedras de propiedad*) were not obliged to lecture after St John the Baptist (24 June) and could appoint substitutes over the summer months. Other Chairs (*catedrillas*) were held for periods of five years. Until 1641, all professors were elected by the student body, after open competition (*oposiciones*), with votes weighted according to the number of courses completed. What should have been a remarkably democratic system was nonetheless subject to internal political pressures and open to bribery and corruption. The Dominicans, from their magnificent college of San Esteban, valued their preeminence among the religious Orders at the University and held a near monopoly of the important theological Chairs. When these fell vacant they would organize the Dominican vote and do their best to ensure that their candidate was elected.[76]

New Statutes for the University had come into force in 1561, and, among other features, provided for each Chair to be visited five times a year in order to ascertain that the professor in question was lecturing on the required subject, had not been absent and did not dictate his material (this last provision being regularly disregarded). The records of these visitations, the *Libros de visitas de cátedras*, and of other documents in the University archives, have provided the first firm documentary evidence for Fray Juan's matriculation and information about the courses he was attending with his two Carmelite contemporaries, Rodrigo Nieto and Pedro de Orozco. He appears in the register of the University with his colleagues on 6 January 1565: members of religious Orders were matriculated *en bloc* at intervals, and would have begun their courses at the same time as everyone else, at the start of the academic year. Indeed, he was among those interviewed by the visitors on 20 December 1564 and recorded as attending the course on the *Súmulas* being given by Dr Pedro García Galarza. His first three years were spent following the prescribed Arts and Philosophy courses.

To gain credit for one year and pass on to the next, students were required to attend the lectures given by the appropriate established professors, and to have a notary certify that they had fulfilled this obligation over a period of six months. They also had to choose a *regente de curso*, a director of studies, within a month of matriculation. The timetable prescribed by the 1561 Statutes was very full. On winter mornings from 7.30 to 9 a lecture was given by the director of studies on the assigned topic, followed from 9 to 10 by a class. From 10 to 11 a.m. students attended the lecture given by their professor. Lunch was taken a good deal earlier than now. The afternoons from 2 to 5 were spent in revision, lessons, drills and exercises with the director. The summer timetable each year advanced the morning classes by an hour and placed the afternoon ones an hour later, perhaps to allow for a *siesta*. There were no classes on Sundays or major feasts, but on Saturdays from October to June students attended a session called *conclusiones* with the professor, which might last several hours.

Fray Juan and his colleagues seem to have chosen as their director of studies Pedro García, whose substitute during the summer was Hernando de Rueda. The first-year course, based on the *Organon* of Aristotle, began with Domingo Soto's *Súmulas*, the butt of humanist criticism for its bad Latin and sophistry.[77] It would nevertheless have provided a much fuller introduction to logic and dialectic, the parts of speech and the different forms of argument, than Fray Juan had yet received. On 2 December 1565 he matriculated for his second year, and is shown as having voted in an election to a five-year Chair at the end of the summer.[78] His director of studies was probably Hernando de Rueda, who had won Pedro García's *catedrilla* when it fell vacant the previous June. Logic (*Lógica magna*) was the principal element of the syllabus, and the professor was the Mercedarian Gaspar de Torres.[79] When lectures on Aristotle's *Logic* concluded, the course moved on to his *Physics*, with corresponding classes with Rueda. The timetable was similar to that of the first year, except that an additional hour of revision and practice with the professor took place between 1 and 2 in the afternoon.[80] Classes and lectures complemented one another, in the sense that they covered the same curriculum but at different times during the year.

The third year marked a change to philosophy. Fray Juan and his fellow-Carmelites matriculated together on 11 January 1567; his name appears in other documents during the year. There were two Chairs of Philosophy, Natural and Moral, and three *regentes;* he probably remained with Rueda. Both professors had recently retired and Miguel Francés and Diego Bravo occupied the respective Chairs as substitutes. The prescribed text was Aristotle's *Physics* for Natural Philosophy and his *Ethics* and *Politics* for Moral Philosophy, and students were able to vote for the precise areas to be covered in the lectures, to round off what they had been studying with their *regentes*. It seems to have been a bad year for the previously conscientious Rueda, as he was fined for beginning late and finishing early, for missing classes and using unauthorized substitutes. From 7.30 to 9 in the morning students did exercises in class; from 9 to 11 they attended first the Natural, then the Moral Philosophy lecture; between 1 and 2 in the afternoon there was a class on Physics; from 2 to 3 and 4 to 5 further exercises and revision, with a class in Natural Philosophy in between. On feast days there were study periods in the evening, and *conclusiones* continued on Saturday afternoons. The heavy emphasis on Aristotle must have left its mark on Fray Juan. When he quotes 'el Filósofo' in his works, as he often does, he means Aristotle and is making use of his university education, even if he does so primarily to enunciate a number of principles which underlie his analysis of the mystical journey.

Like the other Orders, the Carmelites had an internal system of *vivas* after graduation and ordination before candidates passed on to theology; Fray Juan was probably so examined after graduating as a Bachelor of Arts in the summer of 1567, though no records survive. He had already been ordained priest at the beginning of the summer of 1567, though we do not know the exact date, having been appointed 'prefect of students' for San Andrés by the Provincial Chapter held in Ávila in April of that year, a sign perhaps of the regard in which he was held as a student. He celebrated his first Mass in Medina that summer, no doubt with his proud family in attendance.[81] He matriculated on 1 January 1568 as a theologian, and once again several documentary records testify to his presence in Salamanca through the academic year.

The Church had long believed that knowledge of the biblical languages alone was insufficient for understanding the Bible and required the more formal and systematic doctrinal study of scholastic theology. Yet continuing tension between what the sixteenth century had come to call 'positive' theology (by which it meant study of the Bible, the Fathers, and devotional writing) and scholasticism at Salamanca is evident from a memorandum written by Gaspar de Torres for the governing council (*claustro*) of the University in May 1568, which nicely encapsulates the fears of an age which had witnessed the spread of Lutheranism in Germany and its battle-cry of *sola Scriptura* – scripture alone, untrammelled by the intricacies of scholasticism or the evasions of commentators. For Salamanca to keep itself free of error,

> conviene que se hevite la ocassión de donde tanto daño a venido en otras Universidades, que sin Theología Scholástica, sólo con lenguas, se an metido muchos a explicar la Scriptura e pretendido que todos la puedan oyr y tratar, de do vino el principal daño de Alemania.[82]

> it is necessary to avoid the reason which has led to so much harm in other universities, where by studying languages alone, without scholastic theology, many have become involved in expounding Scripture and have claimed that everyone can learn it and handle it, which was the main source of the trouble in Germany.

During Fray Juan's time at Salamanca, conflicts over the nature and authority of the Vulgate and of new versions of the Latin text, as well as of the originals, intensified and grew into open hostility between Hebraists and scholastics, which culminated in the arrest and imprisonment in 1572 of the three Salamanca Hebraists, Fray Luis de León, holder of the Durandus Chair, Gaspar de Grajal, substitute for the Chair of St Thomas, and Martínez de Cantalapiedra, who held the Chair of Hebrew.[83] The words of Torres may also have been aimed at the rival university of Alcalá, with its famous Trilingual College, though it was no longer the pioneering place it had been in the early days of its foundation by Cardinal Cisneros and the production of the Complutensian Polyglot Bible.

Such views did not always find favour with the student body. As early as 1560 theology students had asked to be taught more Hebrew, while in May 1568 they requested a greater emphasis on the teaching of scripture. The timetable attempted to accommodate their wishes, at the expense of clashes with other classes or lectures. Mornings began with Prime Chair of Theology lecture between 7.30 and 9, followed by a Latin Bible class for the next hour, and from 10 to 11 (or 4 to 5 p.m.), the Chair of St Thomas lecture. After lunch, from 2 to 3, students could attend lectures in the Chair of Durandus or Nominal Theology, from 3 to 4 the Vespers Chair, and from 4 to 5 the Scotus Chair. If they wanted to study Hebrew, classes took place between 10 and 11 a.m. or 1 to 2 p.m., with a Hebrew Bible class from 2 to 3. There is no direct evidence from the *Libros de visitas de cátedras* for the lectures and classes Fray Juan attended, or whether he took up any options, like Hebrew. The best guess is that he followed the same pattern as his companions from San Andrés, which would mean that he attended the lectures of the distinguished Dominicans Mancio de Corpus Christi in the Prime Chair, and Juan Gallo in the Chair of St Thomas, in the mornings, and those of Fray Luis, Juan de Guevara and Cristóbal Vela or Juan Gallo in the Durandus, Vespers and Scotus Chairs in the afternoons. It is not clear at what point he attended Grajal's lectures on the Latin Bible (Grajal was acting, until his arrest, as a semi-permanent substitute for the retired Gregorio Gallo). Major and minor disputations took place on lesser feast days, the former being carefully organized public events involving professors, the latter also students.

As far as the content of these lectures and classes was concerned, in the mornings he would have heard Mancio on simony and then the Incarnation, from *Summa* 3a.1–10; Grajal on Psalms 50–73 and the early chapters of Micah; and Juan Gallo in the Chair of St Thomas on creation and the three human faculties (1a. 63–83). In the afternoons, Luis de León was lecturing on faith from the third book of Durandus; Guevara on man, his acts and his end (1a 2ae. 1–9 or 10); Cristóbal Vela on the resurrection of the dead from Scotus (IV. dd. 43–4); if he attended any of Cantalapiedra's lectures, he would have heard him on Isaiah and perhaps Daniel. But there is no evidence in San Juan's works of any familiarity with Hebrew and it does not appear to influence his exegesis, which is always based on the Latin Bible. The possibility that one of the most important poets of the Golden Age attended lectures by another cannot be discounted; ironically enough, though both were among the greatest lovers and expositors of the Bible of that period, Fray Juan would have been listening to his Augustinian professor discourse upon the intricacies of medieval theology.[84]

Despite uncertainties about the detail, a fairly accurate picture in general terms of Fray Juan's four years at Salamanca emerges: a thorough grounding in grammar, rhetoric, logic and philosophy, followed by a year of scholastic theology and some biblical study. Since lectures on Aquinas were spread across several Chairs in a three-year cycle, his training in scholastic theology remained incomplete, though it was sufficient to enable him to use its methods as an analytical tool for his own treatises. We do not know if his love of the Song of Solomon had earlier been encouraged by lectures on that book given by the Professor of Semitic Languages in 1565–66, or if he attended Hernando de Aguilera's lectures on Copernican theory in the Chair of Astrology.[85] But whereas his two contemporaries went on to complete their theological studies over the next three years, Fray Juan's first year of theology was also his last, a year of crisis as he struggled with his Carmelite vocation and began seriously to consider leaving the Order for a stricter and more contemplative life among the Carthusians. Given the centrality of the Bible for his own writing, it might be thought that whatever doubts he had about studying at Salamanca would have been dispelled once he reached his fourth year. But perhaps the experience of Salamanca, with its crowded lecture halls and boisterous activity, affected him; perhaps he found the kind of theology he was learning arid and over-concerned with distinctions and definitions. Whatever the cause, his vocation to a life of prayer and austerity seems only to have been strengthened by his time there, at the same time as he became increasingly uncertain that his future lay in an Order which had abandoned the ideal of collective solitude for an urban apostolate. Otger Steggink touches the heart of the matter when he writes: 'Le tocó, particularmente en el estudio salmantino, vivir en su alma la crisis vocacional de los ermitaños carmelitas del siglo XIII, a su vuelta a Occidente', 'it fell to him, especially during his studies in Salamanca, to experience in his soul the vocational crisis of the thirteenth-century Carmelite hermits on their return to the West'.[86]

Two connected events must have sharpened his sense of unease, though in due course would bring about its resolution. The first was the visit of the Carmelite General Rubeo to Salamanca, probably in February 1567, as part of his long Visitation of all the Spanish Provinces, following the decision of the General Chapter in Rome in 1564 to accept Trent's proposals for reforming the monastic Orders. At San Andrés he met all its students, including Fray Juan, and was pleased by what he found. More significantly, when Fray Juan had returned to Medina del Campo to say his first Mass during the summer vacation he had met a nun who had been permitted to found a reformed house of Carmelite nuns, living by the primitive Rule of the Order, in cloistered poverty and devoted to prayer. Rubeo had been so impressed by what he heard from Teresa de Jesús and seen for himself in her first Discalced convent of San

José that he had authorized her to make new foundations in other places (27 April 1567), the first of which was in Medina in August 1567. Fray Juan learnt from Teresa de Jesús that the General had also authorized the foundation of two reformed houses for friars. Her own testimony is as much as we know about Fray Juan's inner conflicts:

> Poco después acertó a venir allí un padre de poca edad, que estava estudiando en Salamanca, y él fue con otro por compañero, el cual me dijo grandes cosas de la vida que este padre hacía. Llámase fray Juan de la Cruz. Yo alabé a nuestro Señor, y hablándole, contentóme mucho y supe de él cómo se quería también ir a los cartujos. Yo le dije lo que pretendía y le rogué mucho esperase hasta que el Señor nos diese monasterio, y el gran bien que sería, si havía de mejorarse, ser en su mesma Orden, y cuánto más serviría al Señor. El me dio la palabra de hacerlo con que no se tardase mucho. (*Fundaciones* 3.17)
>
> Soon afterwards there happened to come [to Medina] a young father, who was studying in Salamanca, along with a friend, who told me great things about the life this father led. He is called Fray Juan de la Cruz. I praised our Lord, and when I spoke to him I was favourably impressed and I discovered from him too how he wanted to join the Carthusians. I told him what I was trying to do and begged him to wait until the Lord provided us with a monastery, and how great a thing it would be for him to remain in his own Order if it was to be improved and how much more he would serve the Lord. He gave me his word to do so, as long as it was not too delayed.

Fray Juan agreed to postpone any decision about his future and to wait to see if Teresa's plan to extend her reform to the Carmelite friars might come to fruition. By the time he returned to Medina in the summer of 1568 the die was cast. He abandoned his studies in Salamanca and set out for a tiny hamlet called Duruelo, not far from Fontiveros, where the solemn inauguration of the first Discalced Carmelite priory took place on 28 November 1568. He arrived there at the beginning of October, with a workman, to begin to repair the tumbledown buildings, provided by a benefactor from Ávila, don Rafael Dávila Múxica, and prepare them for the foundation.[87] He marked the change by leaving behind the name under which he had professed – Juan de Santo Matía – and for the first time took the name by which we know him, Fray Juan de la Cruz. Two other friars joined him, Antonio de Jesús (Heredia), who was named Prior, and José de Cristo. According to Javierre, the former always coveted for himself the title of *primer descalzo*, the first Discalced friar and therefore founder of the Reform among the male Carmelites; but that honour properly belongs to Fray Juan.[88] Scarcely a thing do we know of their life there, for they seem to have agreed not to talk about it. Teresa paid them a visit at the end of 1569 and, though she praises their life, she asked them not to practise excessive mortifications – advice, she candidly adds, they took little notice of.[89] As Steggink aptly remarks, 'Al abismarse en Duruelo, busca y ensaya una vida de Cartujo carmelita', 'Burying himself in Duruelo, he both seeks and practises the life of a Carmelite Charterhouse.'[90] The little community moved in June 1570 to nearby Mancera de Abajo (Salamanca), having found the Duruelo site unsatisfactory. Fray Juan, who had been novice-master and sub-Prior since 1569, must have been especially gratified to have seen the first novices he had prepared make their professions in October 1570. From the beginning, the Reform began to attract recruits; that same month Fray Juan travelled to Pastrana to assist in building up the second male foundation there, partly because of Teresa's worries about its excesses.[91] In April 1571 he left Mancera to become Rector of the newly-established Discalced College in the university town of Alcalá de Henares, though a further visit to Pastrana was necessary to deal with the effect on the community of the extraordinary austerities of a female hermit who dressed as a man and who had been clothed as a Carmelite friar. In the early summer of the following year he took up new duties as vicar and confessor to the nuns of the Carmelite convent of la Encarnación in Ávila, where Teresa had become Prioress. He was to remain there for over five years, until he was forcibly removed. In this long period of collaboration between the two future saints surely lie the formative years of Carmelite mysticism.[92]

ARREST AND IMPRISONMENT

The story of Fray Juan's arrest, imprisonment and subsequent escape has been told many times, but to understand why his fellow-Carmelites should have taken such extreme steps against so gentle and humble a spirit requires more explanation than it usually receives. Its origins lie in wider conflicts of authority within the Order and the Church and between Church and State. Many of the Orders in Spain had been reformed in the later fifteenth and early sixteenth centuries, with the active support of Ferdinand and Isabella by Cardinal Cisneros; but not the Mercedarians, Trinitarians or Carmelites.[93] In 1560 Philip II began a campaign to reform these, planning to enforce observantism on them all under episcopal direction; since between 1486 and 1523 the Spanish Crown had won the right from Rome to appoint bishops, it was clear that he envisaged this process as falling ultimately under royal authority. Religious Orders were international organizations and their Generals and other leaders were as likely as not to be foreigners, so that Philip's desire to resist outside interference in national affairs is understandable from a political point of view. But his plan met with opposition from the Roman Curia and the Orders themselves. Rome, in the person of Cardinal Borromeo, supported the Tridentine policy of a general reform to be carried out by the hierarchies of each Order. For five years Philip and Rome argued, until Philip agreed to promulgate the Tridentine decrees (12 July 1564), and to permit the Carmelite General, Rubeo, to visit all the Spanish houses. But the death of Pius IV and the election of his successor, Pius V, who was thought to be more favourably disposed towards the Spanish Crown, raised Philip's hopes of gaining the outcome he desired. As Rubeo set out for Spain, in April 1566, the Spanish Crown gained what it had always sought – a reform under the Crown, to be overseen by 'ordinarios', appointed commissaries, themselves responsible to a 'Junta de reforma', or committee for reform, at court. Two separate reform processes were therefore under way, one with royal and the other with Papal support. A clash was inevitable. In addition, friars from the Andalusian Province, where Audet's earlier attempts to impose observantism had failed, were in a state of agitation and open defiance, preferring the king's reform to the General's, while the Calced majority was deeply suspicious of the reform movement Teresa and Juan had initiated. A period of conflict over the nature and extent of reform, and to whom the task should be entrusted, lasted for many years, and the imprisonment of Fray Juan is part of this larger picture.

When the royal commissaries, one from the diocese of Salamanca and two Dominicans, began their work in 1568, they discovered that Rubeo had preceded them. They returned to court for further instructions, set out again, and when Rubeo complained, came to a further halt. Philip's patience began to snap. In June 1568 he proposed dissolving the whole Carmelite Order in Spain and making its monasteries over to other, more compliant Orders. By the following summer the Pope had intervened to impose over the head of Philip a reform to be carried out internally, but under the supervision of apostolic visitors. The Visitor for Castile was the Dominican Pedro Fernández, of whom Teresa speaks highly.[94]

His visitation spread fear and anger among the Calced Carmelites, especially when the Provincial Chapter of September 1571 was informed that Discalced friars were to be sent into all unreformed houses to act as nuclei of reform, until the process was complete. In 1573 the new Papal nuncio Ormaneto renewed the Visitors' powers and sent Jerónimo Gracián, a rising young star among the Discalced friars, to deal with the continuing tensions in Andalusia. Disquiet among the Calced spread to the Province of Castile, its Provincial, Angel de Salazar, and Rubeo himself. A new Papal Brief of August 1574 terminated the Dominican Visitors' activities but named Gracián as apostolic visitor to both the Calced and Discalced of Andalusia, the latter of whom, with Teresa's support, began to agitate for a separate Discalced Province, fearing that the whole Reform might be jeopardized if they remained under Calced authority. However, by the time the Brief arrived, Rubeo had taken action against the Discalced at the Chapter General of Piacenza (May 1575), had ordered all Discalced friars living outside Castile to return to their original houses and face discipline, and had deprived them of all their offices. Teresa was confined to her convent of San José, under virtual house arrest. Jerónimo Tostado, who had been negotiating for the Calced in Rome since 1574, arrived in Spain in March 1576 with Rubeo's authority as Vicar General of all the Iberian Carmelites, to carry out this policy. The Piacenza measures were confirmed at the Provincial Chapter held in La Moraleja on 12 May.

As so often in wars, new alliances had come into play, so that it was no longer simply a conflict between royal and Papal authority. Rubeo had removed his early support for the Discalced, fearing for the unity of the Order. The nuncio, the king and Gracián were now allied against the General of the Order and the Pope, each side acting in accordance with legitimately granted authority. Ormaneto still favoured the Discalced and confirmed Gracián in his powers as Vicar General for Andalusia; he in turn, with the nuncio's support, called a Chapter of the Discalced at Almodóvar in September 1576, interpreted by Tostado as an act of open rebellion. The fate of the Discalced seemed sealed when Ormaneto died in June and the new nuncio, Sega, who was determined to bring them under the firm control of their Calced superiors, arrived in Spain at the end of August 1577. On 7 October 1577 Tostado came to the Encarnación in Ávila to supervise the election of a new Prioress, and read the nuns a letter warning them that if they elected one from outside their number, in contravention of the rules, they would be excommunicated. The atmosphere must have been extremely tense. When the votes were counted, Teresa de Jesús, still confined to San José and therefore not a member of the community, was found to have been elected by 54 votes to 39. The nuns who had voted for her were excluded from the convent and a new Prioress imposed – the so-called 'elección machucada', or overturned election.

Through all these troubles Fray Juan and his companion Fray Germán de Santo Matías had been living in a small house adjacent to the Encarnación, continuing their work as confessors to the nuns. They had already had a foretaste of the troubles to come. Early in 1576 the Carmelite Prior of Ávila had had them removed from their house and imprisoned in Medina on the grounds that Discalced friars were no longer to act as confessors to Calced nuns. Ormaneto had intervened, and to the chagrin of the Prior, had insisted on his returning them to their posts. Calced fury had nonetheless been aroused, and the Almodóvar Chapter, which Fray Juan had attended, had, perhaps as a precaution, relieved him of his post as vicar and confessor to the convent. But the nuns had petitioned for his return, and Ormaneto had overriden the Chapter's decision. Now Ormaneto was dead, and Fray Juan and Fray Germán were still living in the house by the convent as spiritual directors to the community.

They were powerless against the next onslaught. The Discalced appointment of Fray Juan as Prior of Mancera came too late. On the night of 2–3 December both friars were arrested by the Calced authorities and taken to the Calced priory in Ávila. Some later witnesses maintained that Fray Juan had managed to escape and return to his quarters to destroy papers which might have proved incriminating to those associated with the Reform, particularly Gracián and Teresa; some he is reported to have eaten, before Calced friars returned and recaptured him.[95] From Ávila they were hurriedly removed to different places, Fray Germán to La Moraleja, and Fray Juan by an indirect route, in order to avoid detection, to Toledo. The violence and secrecy had much to do with the fact that Tostado was acting *ultra vires*. He had been removed as Vicar General by the Royal Council a month earlier, but was in no mood to abandon his attempts at pacification of the Order, in which the silencing of one of the principal players, the *primer descalzo*, a 'gran pieza' ('real catch'), as Teresa wrote, was essential.[96] Gracián must have been next on the list.

Fray Juan's imprisonment was therefore not so much an act of spite or anger as the result of a conflict of jurisdiction between the Calced superiors of the Order, responsible to their General, and the dispositions of the former nuncio, which had not yet been revoked by Sega. Teresa and the Discalced believed that Fray Juan was resident at la Encarnación by the authority of the visitor Fernández, had been confirmed in the post by Ormaneto, and was under obedience to Gracián, whose powers were not removed by the new nuncio until July 1578, all of whom possessed a higher authority than the Provincial Chapter or Vicar General Tostado. So she wrote letters and made enquiries, worried to distraction about the fate of her 'little Seneca', as she called him, and unable to discover where he was being held. She feared for his life, since his constitution was not strong, and wrote to the king that she would rather he had been captured by the Moors, because they would treat him more mercifully – a fine comment on the state of Christian charity between the two branches of the same Order.[97] But the coming of the Christmas festivities delayed any responses, and Teresa's own health suffered at the same time when she lost the use of her left arm as a result of a bad fall.[98]

The Toledo Carmel occupied an impressive site below the Alcázar, partly carved into the rocks which fell away steeply to the waters of the River Tagus, hundreds of feet below. Today the site is occupied by gardens and walks. It was a large house, if not as large as earlier biographers have supposed.[99] In 1576, 42 friars belonged to it, only just over half of them resident, the remainder being absent for various reasons; by the end of the century it would become an important Carmelite centre for study and administration, with over 50 friars and some 20 students. There Fray Juan was imprisoned in a tiny, dark cell, which had previously served as the latrine for the adjacent guest room. He was fed on a diet of bread, water and sardines (with no fish on Mondays, Wednesdays or Fridays), never permitted a change of clothing, and once a week was taken out to be disciplined by the community for his stubborn rebelliousness. This is unlikely to have meant that each member took part in the whipping, as is often believed, and as Carlos Saura's film shows; probably one friar was deputed to do this.[100]

One can imagine something of the ordeal. Fray Juan was accustomed to privation and solitude, but of his own free choice. Attempts were apparently made to win him over from the Reform by promising him gifts and high office, while later witnesses claimed his greatest fear was that Teresa and the Discalced might come to believe that he had yielded to their promises and threats.[101] Fray Juan himself made only one clear reference to his experience, in his first surviving letter, written from Baeza on 6 July 1581 to Catalina de Jesús, lamenting the fact that he has not been able to return to Castile to see Madre Teresa: 'Después que me tragó aquella ballena y me vomitó en este extraño puerto nunca más merecí verla', 'After that whale swallowed me and vomited me up into this strange harbour I was never privileged to see her again'.[102] The metaphor from Jonah may be more pointed than it seems, because in the *Liber* Jonah is taken to be the second Old Testament Carmelite. In associating his experience with Jonah's in the belly of the whale he was imitating Elijah's sucessor, just as in N 2.6.1 he uses the same reference to describe the horrors of the passive night of the spirit, a 'sepulcro de oscura muerte', 'tomb of dark death', in which the soul lies awaiting resurrection. The letter occupies a mere 12 lines of text, yet the violent image and the pain expressed provide access to his feelings in a way the treatises never do. In its own way it is the mirror image of a poet of the last century, Antonio de Machado, Andalusian by birth but Castilian by adoption, whose poems written in Baeza evoke the Castilian landscape and his own sense of loss and desolation following the death of his young wife Leonor.

Fray Juan's ordeal has been paralleled many times. Fray Luis de León, imprisoned in solitary confinement by the Inquisition on Valladolid for almost five years, and released only a few months before San Juan himself was arrested, writes of a moment of deepest despair suddenly transformed into an experience of light and joy.[103] The case of the Beirut hostages John McCarthy and Brian Keenan is remarkably illuminating for understanding the kind of agonies through which he must have passed, even if their material deprivations must have been far greater than those of a friar already used to poverty and self-denial. Early in his captivity, while still in solitary confinement, McCarthy describes how from one moment to the next, blackest despair was changed into an overwhelming sense of goodness and joy on which he was able to draw in later times of anguish:

> One morning these fears became unbearable. I stood in my cell sinking into despair. I felt that I was literally sinking, being sucked down into a whirlpool. I was on my knees, gasping for air, drowning in hopelessness and helplessness. I thought that I was passing out. I could only think of one thing to say – 'Help me please, oh God, help me.' The next instant I was standing up, surrounded by a warm bright light. I was dancing, full of joy. In the space of a minute, despair had vanished, replaced by boundless optimism.
>
> What had happened? I had never had any great faith, despite a Church of England upbringing. But I felt that I had to give thanks. But to what?[104]

Keenan's account of his ordeal may shed light on the relationship between deprivation of sensory stimuli on the one hand and the creation of vivid mental images on the other:

> But wait. My eyes are almost burned by what I see. There's a bowl in front of me that wasn't there before. A brown button bowl and in it some apricots, some small oranges, some nuts, cherries, a banana. The fruits, the colours, mesmerize me in a quiet rapture that spins through my head. I am entranced by colour. I lift an orange into the flat filthy palm of my hand and feel and smell and lick it. The colour orange, the colour, the colour, my God the colour orange. Before me is a feast of colour. I feel myself begin to dance, slowly, I am intoxicated by colour. I feel the colour in a quiet somnambulant rage. Such wonder, such absolute wonder in such an insignificant fruit.
>
> I cannot, I will not eat this fruit. I sit in quiet joy, so complete, beyond the meaning of joy. My soul finds its own completeness in that bowl of colour. The forms of each fruit. The shape and curl and bend all so rich, so perfect. I want to bow before it, loving that blazing, roaring orange colour . . . Everything meeting in a moment of colour and of form, my rapture no longer an abstract euphoria. It is there in that tiny bowl, the world recreated in that broken bowl. I feel the smell of each fruit leaping into me and lifting me and carrying me away. I am drunk with something that I understand but cannot explain. I am filled with a sense of love. I am filled and satiated by it. What I have waited and longed for has without my knowing come to me, and taken all of me.

> For days I sit in a kind of dreamy lethargy, in part contemplation and in part worship . . . I focus all of my attention on that bowl of fruit. At times I lift and fondle the fruits, at times I rearrange them, but I cannot eat them. I cannot hold the ecstasy of the moment and its passionate intensity. It seems to drift slowly from me as the place in which I am being held comes back to remind me of where I am and of my condition. But my containment does not oppress me. I sit and look at the walls but now this room seems so expansive, it seems I can push the walls away from me.[105]

The sensuality of the imagery combined with the 'passionate intensity' of the language, the paradoxical statements, the religious awe, the inability to communicate, all are found in the poems Fray Juan wrote during his solitary confinement. For whatever the anguish through which he passed, out of his dark night there rose poetry, poetry of such beauty and grace that it is truly a resurrection. How he came to compose his songs in the night we do not know, but all the evidence suggests that when he escaped on a dark night between 10–12 August 1578, the first 31 stanzas of the first version of the 'Cántico', the ballads on the Trinity, the 'Fonte' and a Psalm paraphrase reached freedom with him.[106] Because his poems are his first word about his journey towards union with God, and because their unlimited horizons have their genesis in a claustrophobic cell, it is to them that we now turn.

NOTES

1 Based on the account by Otger Steggink, 'Arraigo de fray Juan de la Cruz en la Orden del Carmen', in '*Juan de la Cruz, espíritu de llama*', ed. Otger Steggink (Kampen: Kok Pharos, 1991), pp. 129–55 (pp. 134–5).

2 Luis Fernández Martín, 'El colegio de los jesuitas en Medina del Campo', '*Juan de la Cruz, espíritu de llama*', pp. 41–61, asserts that this was contrary to their custom (p. 61).

3 Ed. Fortunato Antolín (Madrid: Espiritualidad, 1989).

4 For earlier drafts of these lives, see *Primeras biografías y apologías de San Juan de la Cruz*, ed. Fortunato Antolín (Valladolid: Junta de Castilla y León, 1991).

5 First extant printed editions, Valladolid: Godínez de Milles, 1616; Jerónimo Murillo, 1617. On Francisco, see also Pablo María Garrido, 'Francisco de Yepes, hermano de San Juan de la Cruz: Un juglar "a lo divino"', '*Juan de la Cruz, espíritu de llama*', pp. 63–83. On the early biographies, see José Vicente Rodríguez, 'Historiografía sanjuanista', in *Aspectos históricos*, pp. 7–24 (pp. 10–11); Teófanes Egido, 'Contexto histórico de San Juan de la Cruz', *Experiencia y pensamiento en San Juan de la Cruz*, ed. Federico Ruiz (Madrid: Espiritualidad, 1990), pp. 335–77; Eulogio Pacho, 'Hagiografías y biografías de San Juan de la Cruz', *Actas* II, pp. 119–42.

6 See Alban K. Forcione, *Cervantes and the Humanist Vision: A Study of Four 'Exemplary Novels'* (Princeton: Princeton University Press, 1982), pp. 317–97.

7 A well-known example is Tchaikovsky's setting of such a legend, 'The Crown of Roses' (see *The Oxford Book of Carols*, ed. Percy Dearmer and others (London: Oxford University Press, 1928), no. 197).

8 The most recent is José María Javierre, *Juan de la Cruz: Un caso límite* (Salamanca: Sígueme, 1992). This massive work, popular, even journalistic in style, incorporates much recent scholarship but is often speculative, and lacks any references.

9 José Vicente Rodríguez, 'Historiografía sanjuanista', in *Aspectos históricos*, pp. 7–24 (p. 15).

10 Velasco relates how Catalina de Yepes appeared after her death to reveal to Francisco that his

father was of noble stock (Teófanes Egido, 'Los Yepes, una familia de pobres', *Aspectos históricos*, p. 30).

11 Fortunato Antolín, 'En torno al culto de San Juan de la Cruz en Segovia', *SJC*, 12 (1993), pp. 267–78.

12 See P. Silverio de Santa Teresa, *Obras de San Juan de la Cruz*, BMC, X–XIV (Burgos, 1929–31), especially I, pp. 347–441; IV, pp. 354–426; V.

13 See Federico Ruiz, ed., *Dios habla en la noche* (Madrid: Espiritualidad, 1990), p. 367; Crisógono de Jesús, *Vida y obras completas de San Juan de la Cruz*, 5th edn (Madrid: BAC, 1964), p. 331; Javierre, Juan, pp. 1108–9. The evidence comes from Fray Bartolomé de San Basilio in the *proceso informativo* at Jaén. Also, letters he had written to others, like the sisters in Granada, were apparently destroyed when Fray Diego de Evangelista was on the warpath collecting or fabricating evidence against Doria's 'enemies'; Javierre, *Juan*, p. 1072.

14 On these episodes, see José Vicente Rodríguez, 'Demonios y exorcismos, duendes y otras presencias diabólicas en la vida de San Juan de la Cruz', *Actas*, II, pp. 295–346 (pp. 302–5); also Crisógono, *Vida*, pp. 24–5, 29; Javierre, *Juan*, pp. 97–8, 126–7.

15 Federico Ruiz, 'Vida y experiencia carmelitana en los escritos de San Juan de la Cruz', in *Espíritu de llama*, pp. 673–86 (p. 686).

16 For population figures, see Marcos Martín, *Actas*, II, pp. 165–6; cf. Crisógono, *Vida*, p. 20, who gives 5,000. San Cebrián conserves its original twelfth-century naves; the chancel was rebuilt in the sixteenth century. In 1549 six priests served it, with two sacristans, who were also responsible for teaching basic Christian doctrine to the children of the parish. It was therefore more like a collegiate church, and its worship akin to that of a cathedral, including the reciting of the canonical hours; see Balbino Velasco Bayón, 'La villa de Fontiveros a mediados del siglo XVI', in '*Juan de la Cruz, espíritu de llama*', pp. 23–39.

17 Especially F. Gómez Menor Fuentes, *El linaje familiar de Santa Teresa y de San Juan de la Cruz* (Toledo: Gráficas Cervantes, 1970).

18 Some scholars have argued for 1540, a date more in keeping with the chronology given by Velasco, who places the death of Gonzalo de Yepes in 1540 or 1541; notably Pablo María Garrido, '*Juan de la Cruz, espíritu de llama*', pp. 63–83 (p. 67) and 'La biografía de San Juan de la Cruz: Nuevas precisiones y correcciones', *SJC*, 13 (1994), pp. 33–71 (pp. 34–7).

19 Crisógono, *Vida*, pp. 22, 25; Javierre, *Juan*, pp. 83, 95.

20 Crisógono, *Vida*, pp. 21–23.

21 Teófanes Egido, *Experiencia y pensamiento*, pp. 341–4; Crisógono, *Vida*, p. 230; Javierre, *Juan*, pp. 79–80.

22 There were probably nearer 20,000 in Castile, rather than the figure of a quarter of a million sometimes cited, and tax registers for 1565 show, for example, a mere 13 households listed in Medina, though 109 in Arévalo; see Serafín de Tapia, 'El entorno morisco de San Juan de la Cruz en tierras castellanas', *Aspectos históricos*, pp. 43–76.

23 There is no connection between this group and the 'mancebo de Arévalo', who worked in Aragón and Granada, sometimes mentioned as a possible link between San Juan and Islam; see Luce López-Baralt, *San Juan de la Cruz y el Islam*, pp. 285–304.

24 Cf. J. Jiménez Lozano, in his introduction to *San Juan de la Cruz. Poesía completa* (Madrid: Taurus, 1983), p. 21.

25 Priority for those who had fallen on hard times over those who had always been poor dates back at least as far as the *Siete Partidas* of Alfonso X ('El Sabio'), Partida I, Título XXIII, Ley VII; see *Las siete partidas del rey don Alfonso el Sabio*, 3 vols (Madrid: Imprenta Real, 1807), I, p. 492. On the historical background, see Marcos Martín, *Actas*, II, pp. 143–84.

26 Marcos Martín, *Actas*, II, p. 160.

27 Marcos Martín, *Actas*, II, pp. 146–52. In Fontiveros, the harvests of 1539, 1542 and 1545 were 42.3 per cent, 61.4 per cent and 27.9 per cent respectively of the mean for the 1540s, and a decline from the preceding year of 54.5 per cent, 66.8 per cent and 40.9 per cent.

28 Only one of the eight children of Francisca and Ana survived childhood, and she became a Cistercian nun in Olmedo; Garrido, '*Juan de la Cruz, espíritu de llama*', p. 68.

29 David E. Vassberg, *Land and Society in Golden Age Castile*, Cambridge Iberian and Latin

American Studies (Cambridge: Cambridge University Press, 1984), p. 186.

30 Marcos Martín, *Actas*, II, pp. 169–75; but see Teófanes Egido, 'El hermano de San Juan de la Cruz: reliquias y testamento', *Actas*, II, pp. 483–92, who notes that we only have Francisco's word, via Velasco, for this (p. 484).

31 For printers, see Juan Delgado Casado, *Diccionario de impresores españoles (siglos XV–XVII)*, 2 vols (Madrid: Arcos, 1996), who gives the following names and dates of activity: Pedro de Castro (1541–50), Diego Fernández de Córdoba (1550–52), Adrián Ghemart (1550–52), Guillermo de Millis (1551–55), Francisco del Canto (1551–90), Mateo del Canto (1555–68) (I, pp. 116–19, 131–3, 224–6, 273–4, 459–61).

32 On population, figures differ. Crisógono gives 30,000 (*Vida*, p. 28), Javierre 16,000 (*Juan*, p. 117), Velasco Bayón, 'El colegio de Carmelitas de Santa Ana de Medina', *Espíritu de llama*, pp. 111–27 (p. 111), 20,000.

33 On levels of literacy in the period, see Sara T. Nalle, 'Literacy and Culture in Early Modern Castile', *Past and Present*, 125 (1989), pp. 65–96; for details on the Ávila area and interesting comparisons by occupation, gender and date, Serafín de Tapia, 'Las primeras letras y el analfabetismo en Castilla. Siglo XVI', *Actas*, II, pp. 185–220.

34 On the 'doctrinas', see Egido, 'Contexto histórico de San Juan de la Cruz', *Experiencia y pensamiento*, pp. 353–6; 'Los Yepes', *Aspectos históricos*, pp. 39–41; Marcos Martín, *Actas*, II, pp. 176–80; Serafín de Tapia, *Actas*, II, pp. 190–4.

35 Luis Fernández Martín, 'El colegio de los jesuitas de Medina del Campo', '*Juan de la Cruz, espíritu de llama*', pp. 41–61 (p. 45).

36 On the presence of *niños de la doctrina* at funerals, see Carlos M. N. Eire, *From Madrid to Purgatory: The Art and Craft of Dying in Sixteenth-Century Spain* (Cambridge: Cambridge University Press, 1995), pp. 145–6.

37 Crisógono, *Vida*, p. 31.

38 On Jesuit education, see John W. O'Malley, *The First Jesuits* (Cambridge, Mass: Harvard University Press, 1993), especially, pp. 200–42. They seem to have arisen out of the provision in the Jesuit *Formula* for colleges in university centres to train future members of the Society, seven of which had been founded by 1544, but expanded when it became clear that there was a ready market for education of young men in general, only a few of whom would join the Society.

39 Miguel de Cervantes, *Novelas ejemplares*, ed. Harry Sieber, 2 vols (Madrid: Cátedra, 1986), II, p. 316.

40 Figures from Fernández Martín, '*Juan de la Cruz, espíritu de llama*', p. 51; see also Marcos Martín, *Actas*, II, p. 183. Crisógono's figure of 40 (*Vida*, p. 37), must refer to a core of novices and paying pupils.

41 O'Malley, *The First Jesuits*, p. 90.

42 On the hospital and its administrator, see Marcos Martín, *Actas*, II, pp. 180–3.

43 It is interesting to note that a month's hospital service was one of the tests for Jesuit novices (O'Malley, *The First Jesuits*, p. 172), which suggests that the young Juan may at one stage have been thought of as a possible recruit.

44 Ruiz (ed.), *Dios habla en la noche*, p. 56.

45 See Jon Arrizabalaga, John Henderson and Roger French, *The Great Pox: The French Disease in Renaissance Europe* (New Haven: Yale University Press, 1996).

46 On the Hospital and Juan's education with the Jesuits, see Marcos Martín, *Actas*, II, pp. 180–3; Egido, 'Contexto histórico', *Experiencia y pensamiento*, pp. 357–60.

47 Javierre, *Juan*, pp. 135–6.

48 Perhaps his words in S 3.22 reflect something of this early experience.

49 His *Christiani pueri institutio,* published at Salamanca in 1575, shows the influence of the great Spanish humanist scholar and educationalist, Juan Vives, and was followed by *De sapiente fructuoso* (Burgos, 1589). See F. Olmedo, *Juan Bonifacio 1538–1606 y la cultura literaria del Siglo de Oro* (Santander: Sociedad de Menéndez Pelayo, 1939); Fernández Martín, '*Juan de la Cruz, espíritu de llama*', pp. 55–60.

50 O'Malley, *The First Jesuits*, p. 118.

51 For an outline and further bibliography, see Melveena McKenrick, *Theatre in Spain:*

1490–1700 (Cambridge: Cambridge University Press, 1989), pp. 50–2, 276.

52 Egido, 'Contexto histórico', *Experiencia y pensamiento*, p. 360.

53 Otger Steggink, 'Fray Juan de la Cruz, carmelita contemplativo: vida y magisterio', *Actas* II, p. 251 and 'Arraigo de fray Juan de la Cruz en la Orden del Carmel', '*Juan de la Cruz, espíritu de llama*', p. 130.

54 For the history of the Order, see Joachim Smet, *The Carmelites: A History of the Brothers of Our Lady of Mount Carmel*, 5 vols (Darien, IL: The Carmelite Press, 1988).

55 Steggink, 'Arraigo', '*Juan de la Cruz, espíritu de llama*', p. 130.

56 See, for example, Jerónimo de San José, in *BMC*, 14, p. 415; Crisógono, *Vida*, p. 43.

57 Steggink, 'Arraigo', '*Juan de la Cruz, espíritu de llama*', p. 131.

58 For a survey of these and other factors offered in explanation of Juan's choice, see Ronald Cueto, 'A Quest for Order in a Poet-Saint's Choice of Order', in *Essays and Poems Presented to Daniel Huws* (Aberystwyth: National University of Wales, 1994), pp. 329–50.

59 *Histories*, ii.78; quoted in J. Murphy-O'Connor, *The Holy Land* (Oxford: Oxford University Press, 1986), p. 297; on Carmel, see pp. 297–301.

60 For the flora of Carmel, see F. Nigel Hepper, *Illustrated Encyclopedia of Bible Plants* (London: InterVarsity Press, 1992), pp. 24–5.

61 Murphy-O'Connor, *The Holy Land*, p. 300.

62 Ruiz, ed., *Dios habla en la noche*, p. 57.

63 Steggink, 'Fray Juan', *Actas* II, pp. 251–69 (p. 254).

64 Steggink, 'Arraigo', '*Juan de la Cruz, espíritu de llama*', pp. 138–9; 'Fray Juan', *Actas* II, p. 255.

65 Quoted from Velasco Bayón, *Historia del Carmelo español*, 2 vols (Rome: Institutum Carmelitanum, 1992), I, p. 61. See 'Nicholas of France, *sagitta ignea*', ed. Adrianus Staring, *Carmelus*, 9 (1962), 237–307.

66 Notably Antonio de Guevara's *Menosprecio de corte y alabanza de aldea* of 1539.

67 For distinguished alumni of San Andrés, see Pablo María Garrido, 'El solar carmelitano de San Juan de la Cruz', '*Juan de la Cruz, espíritu de llama*', pp. 85–109 (pp. 97–9), and Velasco Bayón, 'Fray Juan de Santo Matía en Salamanca', *Espíritu de llama*, pp. 157–3 (pp. 161–2, 166).

68 Steggink, 'Fray Juan', *Actas*, II, pp. 260–1.

69 *Obras completas de Santa Teresa de Jesús*, ed. Efrén de la Madre de Dios and Otger Steggink, 2nd edn (Madrid: BAC, 1967); Santa Teresa de Jesús, *Libro de fundaciones* 2.5, *Obras* (ST) (p. 520).

70 On the *colegio* associated with the Medina house, see Bayón, 'El colegio', '*Juan de la Cruz, espíritu de llama*', pp. 116–24; Vicente Muñoz Delgado, 'Filosofía, teología y humanidades en la Universidad de Salamanca durante los estudios de San Juan de la Cruz (1564–1568)', '*Juan de la Cruz, espíritu de llama*', pp. 175–211 (p. 177); Pablo María Garrido, 'El convento carmelita de Santa Ana de Medina del Campo: Presencia e irradiación sanjuanistas', *SJC*, 9 (1993), pp. 9–26; also 'La biografía de San Juan de la Cruz: Nuevas precisiones y correcciones', *SJC*, 13 (1994) pp. 40–2.

71 I follow the Spanish translation, *Liber de la Institución*, by an anonymous Discalced Carmelite (Ávila: Vda. de Sigirano, 1959). For a study of the *Liber*, see Steggink, 'Arraigo', '*Juan de la Cruz, espíritu de llama*', pp. 129–55 (pp. 140–9).

72 Javierre, *Juan*, p. 204; Ruiz, ed., *Dios habla en la noche*, p. 80; Steggink, 'Fray Juan', *Actas*, II, p. 258.

73 I am indebted here to Luis Enrique Rodríguez-San Pedro Bezares, *La formación universitaria de Juan de la Cruz* (Valladolid: Junta de Castilla y León, 1992), and to V. Muñoz Delgado, 'Filosofía, teología y humanidades', '*Juan de la Cruz, espíritu de llama*', pp. 175–211.

74 Richard L. Kagan, *Students and Society in Early Modern Spain* (Baltimore: Johns Hopkins, 1974), p. 212; Kagan's tables of matriculation by faculty, p. 250, are very revealing. See also pp. xxii, 136–8, 160, 164–7, 188–90, 196.

75 Velasco Bayón, 'Fray Juan de Santo Matía en Salamanca', '*Juan de la Cruz, espíritu de llama*', pp. 157–73 (pp. 162, 169–70).

76 This was partly the cause of Dominican hostility to Fray Luis de León; see my *The Strife of*

Tongues (Cambridge: Cambridge University Press, 1988), pp. 5, 51.

77 Muñoz Delgado, 'Filosofía', '*Juan de la Cruz, espíritu de llama*', pp. 181–2.

78 Rodríguez-San Pedro Bezares, *La formación universitaria*, p. 35, gives 2.12.1566, but this must be a misprint.

79 See Guillermo Vázquez Núñez, 'Fray Gaspar de Torres', in *Mercedarios ilustres* (Madrid: Revista Estudios, 1966), pp. 281–9.

80 I give winter times; summer times continued to be adjusted each year, as explained.

81 Velasco Bayón, '*Juan de la Cruz, espíritu de llama*', pp. 171–2.

82 Quoted from Rodríguez-San Pedro Bezares, *La formación universitaria*, p. 88.

83 Thompson, *The Strife of Tongues*, pp. 36–51.

84 For an attempt to draw parallels between them, see Francisco García Lorca, *La escondida senda: de fray Luis a San Juan* (Madrid: Castalia, 1972).

85 The teaching of Copernicus at Salamanca is well established, and seems to lie behind a passage in L 4.4, 'al modo que al movimiento de la tierra se mueven todas las cosas materiales que hay en ella', 'in the same way that as earth moves so all material objects on it move', censored and changed in 1618 *ed. princeps*. On the possible influences of Copernican thought on San Juan, see José Luis Sánchez Lora, *San Juan de la Cruz en la revolución copernicana* (Madrid: Espiritualidad, 1992).

86 Steggink, 'Fray Juan', *Actas*, II, p. 259.

87 *Fundaciones* 13.2.

88 Javierre, *Juan*, pp. 236, 292–3, 758. On the history of the Reform, see Smet, *The Carmelites*, II, pp. 40–131.

89 *Fundaciones* 14.12.

90 Steggink, 'Arraigo', '*Juan de la Cruz, espíritu de llama*', p. 151.

91 Javierre, *Juan*, pp. 335–9.

92 Javierre, *Juan*, p. 392.

93 See José García Oro, *La reforma de los religiosos españoles en tiempo de los Reyes Católicos* (Valladolid: Instituto "Isabel la Católica", 1969); for this dispute, see his 'Observantes, recoletos, descalzos: La monarquía católica y el reformismo religioso del siglo XVI', in *Actas*, II, 53–97, and Otger Steggink, 'Dos corrientes de reforma en el Carmelo español del siglo XVI: La observancia y la descalcez, frente a la "Reforma del rey"', *Aspectos históricos*, pp. 117–42.

94 *Fundaciones* 28.6.

95 Crisógono, *Vida*, pp. 117–18; compare Steggink, 'Dos corrientes', *Aspectos históricos*, p. 137. Javierre, *Juan*, p. 539, discounts it.

96 Letter 214, to the Archbishop of Évora, 16 January 1578; *Obras* (ST), p. 888.

97 'Tuviera por mejor que estuvieran entre moros, porque quizá tuvieran más piadad'; letter 208, to Philip II, 4 December 1577; *Obras* (ST), p. 880.

98 Javierre, *Juan*, p. 546.

99 Crisógono, *Vida*, p. 120, gives 80 friars, Alain Cugno, *Saint John of the Cross: The Life and Thought of a Christian Mystic* (London: Burns & Oates, 1982), p. 46, 800; but see J. Carlos Vizuete Mendoza, 'La prisión de San Juan de la Cruz: El convento del Carmen de Toledo en 1577 y 1578', *Actas*, II, pp. 427–36.

100 For the 'disciplina circular', see Javierre, *Juan*, p. 556; Carlos Saura's film is *La noche oscura*, (Murcia: Mundografic, 1993) [video recording].

101 Steggink, 'Dos corrientes', *Aspectos históricos*, pp. 140–1.

102 *Obras* (ST), pp. 873–4.

103 Thompson, *The Strife of Tongues*, p. 72.

104 John McCarthy and Jill Morrell, *Some Other Rainbow*, Corgi Books (London: Transworld, 1993), p. 98.

105 Brian Keenan, *An Evil Cradling* (London: Arrow, 1993), pp. 68–9.

106 The best guide to the chronology of the poems remains Eulogio de la Virgen del Carmen [Pacho], *San Juan de la Cruz y sus escritos* (Madrid: Cristiandad, 1969), pp. 99–150.

3

Songs in the Night (1)

This ring the Bridegroom did for none provide
But for his Bride.
(Henry Vaughan, *Silex Scintillans*, 1650)

San Juan's writing activity has three principal phases, which shade into each other. His poetry, begun in prison, was virtually completed by 1584, when it appears in the Sanlúcar MS, by far the most important of the early MSS, and with annotations in the hand of San Juan himself.[1] Meanwhile, he began to prepare his substantial prose commentaries on the greatest of his songs in the night, as the impulse to lyrical creation gave way to the desire to chart the journey of the soul in a more analytical manner. The third period was devoted to the revision of the *Cántico* and *Llama* commentaries, the former to a considerable degree, including changes in the order of the verses.

Inevitably, the 'Noche', 'Cántico' and 'Llama', written in the *lira* metre associated with a more cultivated Renaissance style, have received the greatest critical attention and acclaim.[2] But San Juan wrote other poems: a series of nine *romances* (ballads) on the Trinity, a number of popular *glosas*, a psalm paraphrase, and two which combine popular and lyrical elements, the 'Pastorcico' and the 'Fonte'. These occupy a significant space between the poetic intensity of the *liras* and the dense arguments of his prose commentaries. That he also used traditional Spanish metres is entirely consistent with the spirit of the Golden Age; the most difficult of all its poets, Luis de Góngora, moved freely between the two extremes.[3]

Both kinds of poetry need attention if we are to gauge the full measure of San Juan's achievement as a poet. There are many points of stylistic and thematic connection between them, though critics have preferred to dwell on the differences. The ballads on the Trinity, for example, provide a wider narrative and doctrinal framework for San Juan's whole poetic enterprise, and link the passionate and sensuous encounter of the two lovers in the *liras* with the divine Trinity's embrace of all humanity through use of the same fundamental image, the marriage. The *glosas* follow a tradition in which the same paradoxical language was used for erotic and spiritual love alike. The paraphrase of Psalm 136 [137] provides a good example of the way San Juan handles biblical poetry. The 'Pastorcico' illustrates the confluence of the language of profane love in pastoral guise with more religious imagery, while the more symbolic language of the 'Fonte' is rooted in Trinitarian, biblical and liturgical texts. It is with these poems that we begin.

THE ROMANCES SOBRE EL EVANGELIO 'IN PRINCIPIO ERAT VERBUM'

The *romance* is the most traditional of all Spanish verse forms. It dates at least as far back as the middle of the fourteenth century and has evolved across the centuries into the twenty-first, preserving old forms and responding to new currents of thought and taste. Originally anonymous and chanted or sung, the advent of printed collections of ballads fixed the texts, and named authors began to write them. In print they tended to be written down in octosyllabic lines, with their distinguishing feature, assonantal rhyme, occuring at the end of the even lines. Cycles of ballads, usually about epic or legendary characters, like the Cid, formed an important part of the tradition. It has often been said that the ballad's survival in Spanish-speaking countries and communities is a unique phenomenon, and that Spain was the only country in Western Europe where the cultivated classes of the Renaissance did not reject the traditional ballad as crude and unsophisticated. Educated Spanish poets never turned their back on older, popular traditions in their desire to create new and often highly complex poetic structures:

> The acceptance by the court of Ferdinand and Isabella, and by the cultured classes generally, of the ballads as part of the national literary tradition was to have notable consequences for the history of Golden Age literature generally. This phenomenon, like the acceptance of popular lyric poetry – religious and secular – reveals how far away general literary taste in Spain in the time of Ferdinand and Isabella was from the literary standards of the Italian humanists, who had regarded popular literature as barbaric – and trivial as well.[4]

Of all Spanish poetic forms, the ballad is the one most rooted in Spanish culture and of the most enduring appeal.

Ballads in fact constitute the largest metrical form in San Juan's poetic output (compare the 264 lines of his *liras* and roughly the same number in the *glosas*), but have received the least critical attention, probably because of their more limited artistic appeal.[5] His cycle of nine ballads on the Prologue to St John's Gospel are described in the Sanlúcar MS as 'acerca de la Santísima Trinidad', 'about the Most Holy Trinity'. In the 'Epistola missoria' to his *Moralia* on the book of Job, one of the most influential of all early biblical commentaries and widely read in the sixteenth century, St Gregory the Great (c. 540–604) had written that scripture was 'fluvius [. . .] planus et altus, in quo et agnus ambulet, et elephas natet', like 'a river, shallow and deep, in which a lamb can walk and an elephant swim'.[6] Simpler souls could refresh themselves in it without danger, and scholars and philosophers could exercise their intellectual weight as they tested its profundity. At the end of every Mass the priest was required to recite quietly to himself the last Gospel, John 1.1–14, which San Juan certainly knew by heart. During his imprisonment, deprived of the sacraments, he perhaps found himself repeating these familiar words for his own comfort and devotion as he reflected on their meaning, reworking one of the most philosophical passages in the Gospels into a more accessible form. In any case, he was following a well-worn tradition of transposing biblical passages into a popular idiom, which continues to this day.[7]

Why did San Juan turn to the *romance*? The traditional Spanish ballad is primarily a narrative form. It tells its tales directly and simply, sometimes in direct speech and dialogue, often objectively, with little description and even less intrusion by the narrator to indicate how the audience is meant to respond. The story, in other words, must speak for itself and those who hear it formulate their own response. San Juan's ballads deal with the doctrines of the Trinity, Creation and the Incarnation. Yet he chooses to present them not in dogmatic or philosophical terms but in terms of *Heilsgeschichte*, the history of salvation, and in them he privileges the symbol of conjugal love, central to his *lira* poems, above all others. Though not as common in scripture as images of God as liberator of the oppressed or as lawgiver and judge (Exodus, the Prophets), it is prominent in Hosea and the Song of Songs, and is also found in the Gospels, Ephesians and Revelation. The bond this creates with the *liras* is never clearer than in the first ballad, where the relationship of Father and Son, 'como amado en el amante' (line 21), 'as beloved in the lover', is matched in the fifth verse of the 'Noche', 'amada en el amado transformada', 'lover transformed in the beloved'. The 'Noche', however, represents the union of the human lover with the divine Beloved, while the ballad marks the union of the divine Persons of Father and Son as a simile, since they cannot be lovers in any literal sense. The ballads reveal how the union of love between the divine Persons creates for the Son a bride in his image and likeness, 'ymagen' and 'semejança' (230, 237), leads him to seek her out in her tribulations, become one with her in human flesh (the point of difference between them, 233) and raise her to divinity. The implications of the use of nuptial imagery for San Juan's mystical thought are considerable. Instead of an ascent from darkness to light or from ignorance to knowledge, he charts a journey of love, in which these traditional antitheses will be reversed as God seeks the soul and the soul God in divine darkness and ignorance.

San Juan remains faithful to ballad style in his sequence, maintaining the same assonance in the common stressed *í* and unstressed *a* across its 310 lines, resulting in a degree of monotony at worst and a rather insistent, incantatory effect at best. Of the 155 assonating words in the sequence, only 21 are nouns; the rest are verbs, which Spanish morphology determines must be either imperfects or conditionals.[8] As in the old ballads, the tense chosen often appears to have more to do with the demands of assonance than with the sense of the passage. His style, too, is deliberately artless, with some use of the formulaic language typical of them ('desa manera dezía', 'he spoke in this way', 56, 228). But his ballads are more than simple paraphrases of the opening of the Gospel. They introduce references to other biblical passages and to liturgical and credal material, as they recount the story of the Incarnation as an act of Trinitarian love.

The first ballad, which assonates in 'ía' imperfect tenses throughout, explores the paradox of the opening words of the Gospel, which ascribe 'beginning' to the God who has no beginning, and proclaim the eternal begetting of the Word by the Father. Like the life of the Trinity itself, this act is governed by mutuality of loving, the theme of the whole sequence. But unlike the human lover of the 'Noche', who has to leave her house to be united with her Beloved, the divine Lovers of the Trinity are from all eternity one Lover possessed by one love, in 'un inefable nudo', 'an inexpressible knot' (39).[9] The language of love and the image of the knot play no part in the Johannine prologue; though love becomes important later in the Gospel, San Juan exceeds the bounds of strict paraphrase from the start. On the other hand, his paradoxes grow naturally out of John's: 'Él morava en el principio/y principio no tenía./Él era el mismo principio/por eso de él carecía', 'He lived in the beginning/And had no beginning./He was himself the beginning,/Therefore he had none'.

The second ballad initiates a dialogue which extends to the start of the fourth. Out of their mutual loving the Father addresses the Son in terms taken from the Nicene Creed and Hebrews 1.3: 'eres lumbre de mi lumbre', 'you are light of my light': 'eres mi sabiduría/figura de mi substancia', 'you are my wisdom,/the figure of my substance'. Though the Father's chief delight is the company of the Son (57–8), he loves all who are like him. Hence he announces his intention of giving him a Bride, who will share their companionship, the first use of the nuptial imagery which binds the life of the Trinity and the history of the Church in the *romances* to the journey of the individual soul in the *liras*. The Bride is humanity and, in the fourth and longest ballad, is given creation as a palace, divided into two storeys: the firmament below, earth, is the realm of the infinite multiplicity of creation ('differencias/infinitas'; 'infinite differences') and of human beings; and the firmament above, heaven, the dwelling-place of angels and beautified by the 'admirable pedrería', 'wondrous jewels' of the stars (107–10). Since the Prologue of John is itself a conscious reworking of the opening verses of the Hebrew scriptures, it is appropriate that the fourth ballad's first word, 'Hágase', 'Let it be done' (99), should echo the commands by which God creates the cosmos in the Genesis narrative.

Humanity is placed in this lower world, 'por ser en su compostura/algo de menor valía', 'being by creation/of somewhat lower worth' (117–18), a version of Psalm 8.6 as cited in Hebrews 2.7 ('Minuisti eum paulominus ab angelis', 'Thou madest him a little lower than the angels'). The world below and the angelic world above form 'un cuerpo/de la esposa', 'one body/of the bride' (121–2). The angels possess the Bridegroom in joy, while the lower creation is given faith and hope that it will be raised by him (125–34) through his descent as man to dwell with the human race, to eat and drink with it (Acts 10.41) and lift it to God (135–42). He will promise to remain with them to the end of the age (Matthew 28.20), when he will take all the faithful to himself (143–58), so that the Bride, whose head he is (149–50; Ephesians 5.23) 'dentro de Dios absorta/vida de Dios viviría', 'absorbed within God/will live the life of God' (165–6). This ballad is the most ambitious in scope of the sequence, the centre around which the others revolve. It narrates the story of God's actions in creation through the imperfect tense and the drama of salvation through the conditional, as if attempting to reconcile divine foreknowledge with human freedom, and it moves as freely from creation and Incarnation to eschatological fulfilment as it does through scripture.[10]

The fifth ballad expresses desire for the Incarnation largely through the voice of the Hebrew scriptures: the sighs and tears of the prophets longed for the Messiah (175–80); Isaiah asks for the One to come to be sent (16.1), for the heavens to be rent and for him to come down (64.1); for the heavens to drop down and water the earth so that it may produce flowers, not thorns (11.1, 45.8; part of the Advent liturgy but with echoes too of the parable of the sower). Others long to see and touch him, and walk with him (1 John 1.1–2). The sixth and shortest (18 lines) moves forward in biblical time to the Temple in Jerusalem, where the Holy Spirit reveals to old Simeon that he will not see death until he has seen the Lord's Anointed (Luke 2.25–6). Here San Juan departs from the chronology of the Gospels, where this event takes place after Christ's birth, imaginatively incorporating this promise with the others, so that the sequence may conclude with the Annunciation and the Nativity.

The seventh ballad returns to dialogue between the Father and the Son in heaven, as the Son prepares to assume humanity to rescue it from the heavy burden of the Mosaic Law (221–6). Three times in seven lines (237–43) the Father stresses the need for 'semejança', 'likeness', to create perfect love between lovers. Because humanity differs from divine simplicity of being through its subjection to the flesh (233–4), the Son must assume this (243–4) to achieve the desired likeness. The last 11 lines define his mission: to go forth into the world to bring it knowledge of the beauty and sweetness of God's sovereign power (255–8); to seek the Bride (259); to take upon his shoulders all her sufferings (260–2); to die for her (263–4); and to rescue her from the lake and bring her back to the Father (265–6). Following ballad tradition, no explanations for this are provided; there is no mention of sin, for example, original or personal. The image of the lake comes from the *Dies irae*, in which Christ is asked: 'libera animas omnium fidelium defunctorum de poenis inferni et de profundo lacu', 'rescue the souls of all the faithful departed from the pains of hell and from the deep lake', the lake of fire and brimstone of Revelation 20.10, into which the devil and all deceivers are cast.[11] The story of the Annunciation is simply told in the eighth ballad, with emphasis on Mary's obedience (270–2), the paradox of the One who only had a Father now also having a mother (279–80), and the Virginal Conception (281–4). But it returns to the Johannine prologue, for the last time in the sequence, as it describes how Christ is born not of man but of God (John 1.13), hence is both Son of God and Son of man (285–6).

The last ballad, which takes us to the stable in Bethlehem and the Lucan account of the birth (Luke 2.6–20), is undoubtedly the most charming, though not as unsophisticated as it seems. Because this baby is also the Word of God who has come to embrace his Bride, he appears paradoxically both as Mary's son and as a bridegroom coming from his chamber to her (Psalm 18.6 [19.5]), 'abraçado con su esposa/que en sus braços la traýa' (291–2), 'embracing his beloved,/for he held her in his arms'. She holds him in her arms as a baby; he embraces her in his as bridegroom of the human race. So his mother places her bridegroom-son in a manger 'entre unos animales/que a la sazón allí avía' (295–6), 'among some animals/there at the time'. San Juan is not concerned with a literal reading, which implies incest, but with using two intimate kinds of loving human relationship, mother and son and bridegroom and bride, to articulate the fundamental theological paradox of the divinity and humanity of the Son. His birth of Mary is also, through the Virginal Conception, the betrothal of humanity with divinity (299), celebrated by songs both human and angelic (297–300). But it is the final lines which, despite their apparent simplicity, most movingly and artfully draw the picture, as the infant cries and the mother is enraptured as she contemplates this wonderful exchange:

Pero Dios en el pesebre	But God in the manger
allí lloraua y gemía	there wept and cried;
que heran joyas: que la esposa	[his tears] jewels which the bride
al desposorio trayá	had brought to the betrothal.
Y la madre estaua en pasmo	And the mother was transported
el que tal trueque veía	to see such an exchange:
el llanto de el hombre en dios	human tears in God,
y en el hombre la alegría	and joy in human kind,
lo qual de el uno y de el otro	which used to be
tan ageno ser solía.[12]	quite alien to each other.

Nothing is said here which has not been said many times before about the mighty Maker of the worlds lying helpless in the manger. But the density of the conceit which turns the baby's tears into the Bride's jewels is as unusual as the paradox which provokes it, the baby betrothed through his mother to a humanity of which she is a part. The association of tear-drops with jewels through the common properties of shape, translucence, brilliance and precious value had become part of the neo-Petrarchan repertoire of the cultivated poet. But here the interpretation hangs on the image of the 'trueque', the 'exchange' of attributes, which is fundamental to metaphor itself but also to the theology of the poem, in which the divine assumes humanity so that humanity may rise to the divine. As the Virgin contemplates the crying child, she sees in her baby not only the vulnerable human tears she expects but also the impossible sight of God weeping. Since these divine tears are the sign that God has embraced humanity, they become tears of joy, the jewels the Bride wears in celebration of her betrothal, even though they are on the baby's cheeks, not her dress. That is the wonder of the exchange: jewels for tears, God for humanity. But they are not Mary's alone, because the Bride represents every faithful soul in the Church. Christ's infant tears, then, are her adornment, because divine nature has betrothed itself to humanity through Mary's obedience, though in due course the Word made flesh will shed tears more bitter and yet more precious for the salvation of all.

There are three good reasons why Iain Matthew is right to call these ballads the real prologue to all San Juan's writing, and Xavier Pikaza, the Gospel of San Juan de la

Cruz.[13] First, their story originates in the life of the Trinity, which 'rebosa', 'overflows' in Creation, Incarnation and Redemption. The journey of the individual soul to union, through betrothal and marriage, which the *lira* poems and their commentaries trace in their different ways, can only take place within this framework of divine self-bestowal and human reception, of which Mary is the first witness and in which the whole community of faith finds its direction. Second, the many biblical allusions beyond the Johannine text are more than merely illustrative or decorative. San Juan enables John's Prologue to gather to itself the witness of the whole Bible, as his own writing will. Third, the connections he makes between the two images of love, the Father and the Son for each other and the divine and human Bridegroom for the human Bride, show that each is implicated in the other in such a way that divine and human love can be spoken of in the same kind of language, inadequate though this will always be. For such reasons these neglected verses undergird San Juan's account of the soul's journey to God, whether expressed in the passionate imagery of his lyrical poems or the language of scripture so central to his commentaries. His other poems in popular metres, to which we now turn, will further illustrate the significance of the Trinity, the Bible and the language of love in his work, as well as serving to introduce the poetic language of the *liras* and the spiritual teaching of the commentaries.

THE POPULAR *GLOSAS*

The composition and singing of popular poetry was a feature of Carmelite tradition; in Ávila one can see the drum Teresa banged, no doubt enthusiastically, in processions, while she herself reports having written such poems as a result of ecstatic prayer.[14] Hers are more numerous and varied than San Juan's, since they include Christmas carols (*villancicos*) and pieces about the life of the Discalced, but they belong to the same tradition. For all the heights it reached, Carmelite spirituality was not afraid to use popular forms in which to express itself, mirroring in that respect the literary culture of the Golden Age. San Juan wrote five popular poems he entitled *coplas* or *glosas*, each based on an *estribillo*, a short text, often of independent origin, part of which acts as a refrain at the end of each verse. Their date of composition is uncertain, though two of them ('Sin arrimo y con arrimo' and 'Por toda la hermosura') do not appear in Sanlúcar and are therefore likely to have been composed after 1584. They were almost certainly intended to be sung to well-known tunes.

These five poems, to which may be added a fragment of a *villancico* long attributed to him, are of interest for a number of reasons.[15] Their *topoi*, their imagery and their characteristic paradoxes are rooted in the narrow range but great intensity of *cancionero* poetry, in which polyptoton, antithesis and oxymoron are used to convey the anguished suffering and contradictory emotions of the lover. The first *Cancionero espiritual* (Valladolid, 1549) showed that such language could be applied equally to spiritual love, and was followed by other collections of popular religious lyrics.[16] San Juan's *glosas* turn around four antitheses: knowing and not knowing, descent and ascent, life and death, light and darkness. 'Entréme donde no supe', 'I entered where I did not know', has as a refrain formed by a series of variants on the second and third line of the *estribillo*, 'y quedéme no sabiendo/toda ciencia tracendiendo', 'and I remained not knowing/transcending all knowledge'. Each verse explores one new idea: not knowing where I was, I understood great things (1); this was a secret knowledge (2);[17] my sense felt nothing, but my spirit understood by not understanding (3); to reach this state previous knowledge must be left behind (4); the higher you rise the less you know (5); this knowing and not knowing is so powerful that wise men cannot confute it (6); only by victory over the self can it be reached (7); it is 'un subido sentir/de la dibinal esencia', 'a sudden sensation/of the divine essence', granted by God (8). What San Juan describes is one of the fundamental principles of the mystical journey, that ordinary forms of knowledge are to be left behind and that the soul is to travel through unknown country on her way to God. The poem is a brief summary of his teaching in the first nine chapters of the second book of the *Subida*, the purging of the intellect by faith.

Its argument hinges on 'saber', knowing. It begins 'donde no supe', 'where I knew not', the famous 'nescivi' of Song 6.11, while the second verse's 'que me quedé balbuciendo' provides the other part of the equally famous onomatopoeic 'no sé qué que quedan balbuciendo', 'I know not what that they are stammering' of C 7. The indeterminacy of place, the unknown 'allí', 'there', of the first and fourth verses, is, like the 'allí' of the 'Cántico' (CA 35–6), nonetheless a place of revelation. The alliteration of 'paz' and 'piedad' in the second verse, reinforced by the chiastic 'sciencia perfecta' and 'profunda soledad', show San Juan's care in choice of words, while its emphasis on secrecy and solitude, and the ecstatic vocabulary of the next two verses ('embebido', 'absorto', 'ajenado', 'desfallesce'; 'intoxicated', 'absorbed', 'out of myself', 'fails') are widely found in his commentaries. But the fifth verse provides a more original touch through its paradox of an ascent which brings a diminution, not an increase, of knowledge. The explanation, 'que es la tenebrosa nuve/que a la noche esclarece', 'for this is the dark cloud/which illumines the night', is baffling unless one recalls the biblical pillar of cloud which gave light to the children of Israel by night (Exodus 14.19–20). Whereas in the natural world cloud at night only deepens the darkness, here the cloud is a sign of divine presence and sheds light beyond human knowing. In the sixth verse the power of this 'saber no sabiendo', 'knowing by not knowing', to confute the wise suggests the divine foolishness which confounds them (1 Corinthians 1.18–25). But the fact that this 'summo saber', 'highest knowing' (v. 7) transcends other forms of knowing should not be taken to mean that San Juan rejected all human striving after knowledge. Knowledge of God transcends finite creaturely capacities; it does not annihilate them. If the soul seeks purely human knowledge she will never find the fulfilment she longs for because it cannot bring her to God. Only God can do that; such 'summa sciencia', 'highest knowledge', is the 'obra de su clemencia', 'work of his mercy', as the last verse states.

'Vivo sin vivir en mí' applies a conventional paradox of secular love poetry, the lover who is alive because still in the body but dead because the love felt for the lady is not requited, to the soul's relationship with God, sometimes in direct address to him.[18] But unlike their secular analogues, life and death are here conceived of in literal terms, since death is the gateway to eternal life and the beatific vision. Without God, this life is nothing (1); it is a continual privation of life till I die (2); I suffer death while being alive (3); the more I live the more I die (4); the Blessed Sacrament is a cause of more pain than relief (5); the thought that I may lose you redoubles my pain and inspires fear (6); rescue me from this death and bring me to life (7); when will I be freed, so that I can truly say I am alive because I have passed beyond death? (8).

The first expression of the paradox recalls Galatians 2.20 ('Vivo autem, iam non ego, vivit vero in me Christus', 'nevertheless I live; yet not I, but Christ liveth in me'), where Paul distinguishes between life in the flesh (his) and life in the Spirit (Christ's), and Philippians 1.21 ('Mihi enim vivere Christus est, et mori lucrum', 'For to me to live is Christ, and to die is gain'), texts used a number of times in San Juan's commentaries.[19] They give rise to an extended polyptoton in which variants of 'vivir' occur 18 times, and 'muerte', 24, going far beyond '¡o vida!, no viviendo donde vives', 'o life, not living where you live' in C 8. The first three verses are variations on the paradox, defining and redefining it in terms of absence from God as privation of life. Halfway through the second verse statement gives way to direct address to God, which continues to the end. The comparison of the fish out of water finding relief in its death, described by Margaret Wilson as 'merely silly' (p. 39), fits the popular tone of the poem even if the sense is unclear: it seems to mean that the fish is bound to die, whereas I remain physically alive but find no relief, since I am out of my natural element, union with God. Verse 5 (the only one lacking a variant on 'vivir') speaks of the pain caused by contemplating God (i.e. the crucified and risen Christ) in the eucharistic species, which should alleviate, 'aliviar', the pain, as the fish finds 'alivio' in death, but only increases it because the poet cannot see God as he is. In the 'Fonte' the Eucharistic bread is a sign of presence, not absence, but this is a different kind of poem, not a meditation on faith but a complaint and a prayer for death to remove every veil between the soul and God. The sixth verse, with its fear of losing God, is one of the few places where San Juan ever broaches the topic, the most notable being in his description of the passive night of the spirit (N 2.6); his word, 'pavor', is a strong one.[20] By the end of the poem the terms of the paradox have shifted: whereas until this point 'vivo' has meant life in the body, which is a living death, the last line, 'vivo ya porque no muero', 'now I live because I do not die', looks to eternal life in heaven when death is past.

'Tras de un amoroso lance', 'After a loving encounter', belongs to the popular medieval tradition of the chase of love, based on metaphors derived from falconry. Typically, the falcon soars aloft to seize its larger prey, usually a 'garza' (heron or egret).[21] In secular terms, the man pursues the beautiful woman until he gains her. By the time San Juan came to write his poem, the popular *estribillo* he uses ('que le di a la caça alcance', 'that I reached my quarry') it was also applied to spiritual love.[22] The flight aloft is undertaken in the hope of at least catching sight of the lady, while 'alto' and its cognates had acquired by the Golden Age connotations of presumption. In one of the secular examples the paradox of an ascent which is a descent, apparently so original in San Juan's version, is already present:

cuanto más alto subía [el sacre],	The higher it [the falcon] rose,
tanto más bajo y rastrero	the lower and closer to the ground
se quedaba.[23]	it was.

San Juan's poem, in common with many others in the tradition, is written from the perspective of the first-person hunter soaring aloft to seize the divine prey. Unlike the secular versions, however, the quest is not a hopeless one, though it takes him into new territory. He has to fly out of sight to reach the divine catch, which love enables him to do (1); the further he rises the more dazzled he is; the conquest takes place in the darkness and love inspires the 'ciego y oscuro salto', 'blind and dark leap' which makes it (2). Then he flies so low that he is high enough to reach his prey (3), because hope of heaven is never disappointed (4). That hope, together with love's work, ensures a successful outcome to the hunt, and is the most distinctive element in San Juan's version. As one of the three theological virtues, hope plays a central part in the reordering of human memory and the reconstituting of the soul in the divine image in the *Subida-Noche,* while the paradox of an ascent which becomes a descent closely matches the insistence at the start of the *Cántico* on searching for God within the depths of the soul, not outside. The gloss takes a series of well-worn paradoxes and through them suggests that while the search for temporal love will inevitably end in frustration, eternal values survive human mutability. In that respect the lines 'esperança de cielo/tanto alcança quanto espera', 'hope of heaven/achieves all that it hopes for', in the last verse mark the poem's distance from its more conventional secular counterparts. Hoping to possess the woman does not lead to fulfilment; hope for God is sufficient to do so.[24]

'Sin arrimo y con arrimo' ('Without support and with support') reads like an anthology of San Juan's most characteristic ideas and images. Each of the three lines of the *estribillo* becomes in turn the closing line of each verse. The soul, 'desassida/de toda cosa criada', 'detached from every created thing', rises above herself to become 'arrimada', 'supported' in God. The paradox of the first line is straightforward enough: 'sin arrimo' represents detachment (from false reliance on the creatures), 'con arrimo' the divine support (which detachment enables the soul to experience). The opening lines also establish a further antithesis, 'sin luz y ascuras viviendo', 'living without light and in the darkness'. In secular contexts, the blindness of love is associated with Cupid, but San Juan's treatment of the theme owes nothing to this. The darkness the soul experiences becomes a metaphor for mortal life; her blindness is the consequence of the love which fills her with heavenly life in the way of faith. That too is a foundation of his spiritual teaching, especially at the start of the second book of the *Subida.* The power of love to transform good and ill alike into itself leads in the last verse to the image of fire:

Haze tal obra el amor	Love works in such a way
después que le conocí	since first I knew it
que si ay bien o mal en mí	that whether there be good or ill in me
todo lo haze de un sabor	it makes it all of one savour

y al alma transforma en sí	and transforms the soul into itself
y assí en su llama sabrosa	and so in its delightful flame
la qual en mí estoy sintiendo	which I am feeling within me
apriessa sin quedar cosa	quickly, with nothing remaining
todo me voy consumiendo.	I am being wholly consumed.

The transforming and consuming flame of love here is identical with the flame which consumes without pain of CA 38, the burning light which guides the lover to transformation in the Beloved in the 'Noche' and the living flame of love of the 'Llama'. In each case the image of fire, associated with themes of love and transformation, creates union out of separation. Whereas faith is the dark way by which the soul must travel (S 2.1–4), it is love which is unitive, able to create likeness between the unlike (S 1.4.3; 1.5.1), in consequence of the divine marriage with humanity.

The final *glosa*, 'Por toda la hermosura/nunca yo me perderé' ('For all the beauty/I shall never be lost'), takes as its refrain, in slightly varying guises, the third and fourth lines, 'sino por un no sé qué/que se alcança por ventura', 'save for something I know not what/which is gained by good fortune' (all the verses substitute 'se halla', 'is found', for 'se alcança'). Once again we meet the 'no sé qué' of C 7, while the 'ventura' which gains it suggests the 'dichosa ventura' which brings the lover through the night to the Beloved in the 'Noche'. But the controlling metaphor of the *glosa* is much more basic, food and eating, as it argues that the soul will never find solace in known pleasures, only in this unknown something. Thus, enjoyment of the finite only wearies the appetite (v. 1; S 1.6), while faith lifts the soul to discover this something (v. 2). Those touched by divine love find their tastes changed and desire the unknown, because the creatures can no longer offer satisfaction (vv. 3–4). Once the will has been touched by the divine it can never find satisfaction except in God (v. 5). But because divine beauty is so great that it can only be seen by faith, it can only be enjoyed 'solo sin forma y figura/sin hallar arrimo y pie', 'alone without form or figure/finding no stay nor foothold' (v. 6). Such enjoyment is above all earthly beauty (v. 7) and therefore the soul's 'cuydado', a word often used for the cares of love, is set 'en lo que está por ganar', 'on what is yet to be gained', rather than 'lo que tiene ganado', 'what is already gained' (v. 8). Nothing the senses can grasp, however 'subido', 'lofty', no 'gracia y hermosura', 'grace or beauty' they encompass, is worth losing oneself for; only this unknown something. San Juan is alluding to Christ's saying about gaining the whole world at the cost of one's soul (Mark 8.36), found also in the 'Cántico' (CA 17, 20). The rejection of grace and beauty seems to contradict its acceptance in CA 24, but San Juan's meaning is carefully delineated. There, the 'gracia y hermosura' of the soul is a divine gift, gratefully received. Here it applies only to sensual appreciation, from which the soul must become detached if she is to enter into more enduring joys. The same words in a different context can have radically different meanings for San Juan, and he can be easily misread if this is not grasped.

No one would claim that the *glosas* are great poems. But just as the ballads make fundamental Christian doctrines accessible by presenting them as a narrative of love, so the *glosas* show interesting links with the *lira* poems and encapsulate in a direct and popular way San Juan's teaching and its biblical grounding. But their language is nonetheless subversive. They take commonplace concepts, like the blindness of love and dying for love, but offer versions of them which are alien to secular poetry. They turn positive ideas like knowledge and light inside out, opening them out to new and unconventional readings. Just when one is tempted to think one is in familiar territory and let the attention slacken, San Juan has the disconcerting habit of reconfiguring it so that his readers may sense that they are standing on holy ground.

SUPER FLUMINA BABYLONIS

Psalm 136 [137] is one of the most poignant of the Psalms, dating from the Jewish exile in Babylon in the sixth century BC. It must have been a popular psalm in the sixteenth century, because a number of Spanish versions exist, including those by the Augustinians Luis de León and Malón de Chaide.[25] In the Vulgate, it consists of nine short verses, just over 100 words in all. Malón de Chaide's version runs to over 200 lines in 13-line *silvas*, the freest of the Spanish verse forms, so has about twice as many lines as the Vulgate does words.[26] His paraphrase is part of a larger work, a meditation on the story of the conversion of Mary Magdalene (Luke 7.36–50), which helps to explain the care he takes to establish its context. Having reached the point at which Mary, now repenting of her sins, stands weeping behind Jesus in the house of Simon the Pharisee, he compares her state in the exile of sin to the weeping of the children of Israel in exile in Babylon, with which the Psalm begins ('By the rivers of Babylon, there we sat down, yea, we wept'). About half his version imagines the exiles leaving the ruins of Jerusalem behind them, with tears and lamenting, as they approach the walls and towers of Babylon, 'do yace Semiramis sepultada' (line 84), 'where Semiramis lies buried', and see the fertile banks of the Euphrates through Renaissance eyes, 'cual la pinta la dulce primavera', 'as sweet spring paints it'. He compounds the already violent ending, with its blessing on those who dash the Babylonian children against the stones, by adding two other images of retribution: the cutting of their throats and the city being consumed in flames (ll. 202–8). To it he adds a paraphrase of Psalm 125 [126], with its promise that those who sow in tears shall reap in joy, in anticipation of the fruitful life of Mary following her conversion.

San Juan's paraphrase is much shorter: 62 lines in *romance*, assonating á-a.[27] It both follows the Vulgate text more closely and adopts a less grandiloquent and rhetorical tone than the Augustinian's. Unlike the original, to which in this respect Malón de Chaide remains faithful, it is written in the first person singular, not plural. The lament of a people in exile, 'sedimus et flevimus', becomes the lament of an individual in prison, 'me senté llorando', 'I sat down weeping' – at least, that is one possible interpretation. San Juan adapted the Psalm so that through it he could give voice to his own anguish through that of the Jewish exiles 2,000 years earlier. Deprived in prison of the sacraments and of community, he found himself repeating the words of the Psalm and put it into Spanish, because it so powerfully articulated and legitimized his own feelings. But the first person singular of a poem should always be treated with care. It may be a representative voice which speaks for any individual, as in many other

Psalms. The expression of a shared experience through an individual situation is characteristic of San Juan's biblical exegesis whenever he aligns the experience of biblical characters with the journey of the soul.[28]

Some of his additions are in their own way faithful to the feel of the Psalms: 'allí me senté llorando/allí la tierra regava' (3–4), 'there I sat weeping/there I watered the earth', repeats the same idea with a rhetorical variation, in imitation of the parallelisms of Hebrew verse. 'Dexé los traxes de fiesta/los de trabaxo tomava' (9–10), 'I put away my festive dress,/I put on working clothes', exemplifies the sensitivity to sound which is so notable a feature of San Juan's poetry, here through alliteration of 'tr', 't' and 'x' (modern 'j'). The longest (15–28) is full of characteristic expressions of the wound of love which causes longing for death, and the fire of love in which the speaker burns, both provoked by the memory of Zion and the hope remembering it brings. He also introduces a new image which has no biblical associations, the moth which is drawn to the flame and perishes in it.[29] From line 29 San Juan returns to the Vulgate, but omits its seventh verse, with its hint of divine vengeance.

But it is his treatment of violent imagery of the last verse which is the most striking, because unlike Malón de Chaide, he transforms it. He finds another biblical text with a more positive association for the image of stone in 1 Peter 2.4 (itself remembering Exodus 17.6 and 19.5–6), where Christ is the 'living stone' rejected by men but chosen by God. Through the hermeneutic principle of exegesis of one text by another, he is able to transform the dashing of the children's heads against the stones into a gentler prayer that all God's children will be gathered into Christ.[30] Like the change from a plural to a singular speaker, this alteration of a canonical text is illuminating. It suggests that San Juan reacted against a religion based on cruelty and fear, and that he was prepared to interpret difficult and violent passages in the Hebrew scriptures through Christian revelation. It thus implies, in a quite modern way, that particular texts can, and in this case must, be understood according to the Gospel as a whole. With his deep knowledge of the Bible he knew precisely where to look to find the solution.

THE *PASTORCICO*

The little shepherd boy is a familiar figure in *cancionero* poetry, usually as a term of endearment for the object of love. The pastoral literature of the Renaissance often explores the conflicting emotions associated with human love against an idyllic natural background. Though by the sixteenth century pastoral imagery was applied to both secular and sacred love, in approaching this poem one must also take into account the existence of a biblical pastoral tradition. The distinctive voice of the 'Pastorcico' comes from its participation in both. It is based on a secular model, but departs from it quite markedly, especially where at its climax it becomes biblical and liturgical.[31] The language of divine love is therefore not an extraneous intrusion, imposed upon the poem to negate the language of human love. It is perfectly natural to the subject in this context. Unlike so much of the religious art of the period, the poem does not dwell on the physical pain suffered by Christ the shepherd on the cross, but is suffused with a pervasive, controlled sadness. It is allusive rather than descriptive, which is why Margaret Wilson finds that despite its acknowledged charm it is too stylized to be convincing, its emotions borrowed rather than felt.[32] Dámaso Alonso described it as lacking the lyrical power of the mystical *liras*, which is true, but not relevant; it is not meant to be a mystical poem, and should not be so judged.[33]

The poem begins as if in secular mode: the shepherd is grieving, alone, thinking of his shepherdess, 'y el pecho del amor muy lastimado', 'and his breast sorely wounded by love', which acts as a kind of refrain to three of the four quatrains, the second being the exception, not because San Juan forgot but because, as other poems show, he is sensitive to the poetic effect of variation in repeated phrases. Whereas the secular model ends with the shepherd parted from his love in a foreign land, where he lies on the shore suffering because of her absence, San Juan's shepherd 'se dexa maltratar en tierra agena', 'allows himself to be ill-treated in a strange land' in the third verse, an active rather than passive victim, as he laments not for himself but for the one from whom he is now parted. Finally, 'a cavo de un gran rato', 'after a long time', he climbs a tree and dies with his arms outstretched upon it. This makes no secular sense at all. The point is not, as Margaret Wilson believes, that the allegory begins uncomfortably to surface, but that at the climax of the poem the sense of the whole is revealed, just as the discomfort provoked by the intrusion of directly Trinitarian and eucharistic language into the 'Fonte' poem completes its web of imagery and meaning. Terence O'Reilly has drawn attention to the need to read this poem (as indeed all San Juan's) in the context of the devotional literature of the period and mindful of the practice of *lectio divina*, that slow, meditative reading of scripture, often aloud, which encouraged the reader to experience and internalize the meaning of the text.[34] He notes how it diverges from the expectations of its secular model, in that the shepherd's sorrow is 'less self-centred' (p. 364) and more concerned with the object of his love, the 'bella pastora', than with expressing his own misery. This, he argues, relates to the theme of the *tristitia Christi*, which developed out of patristic commentaries on Christ's agony in the garden of Gethsemane ('Tristis est anima mea usque ad mortem', 'My soul is sorrowful unto death'; Matthew 26.38).

San Juan uses the language of pastoral love elsewhere, notably in the 'Cántico'. There, the Bride asks shepherds if they have seen her Beloved (C 2), loses her flock but is found by love (CA 17, 19–20). Many other verses hint at themes and landscapes which belong to pastoral literature, part of an exegetical tradition which read the Song of Songs as the pastoral eclogue *par excellence,* as Fray Luis de León clearly stated: 'Este Libro en su primer origen se escribió en metro, y es todo él una égloga pastoril, donde con palabras y lenguaje de pastores, hablan Salomón y su Esposa, y algunas veces sus compañeros, como si todos fuesen gente de aldea', 'this Book was originally written in verse, and it is all in the form of a pastoral eclogue, in which Solomon and his Bride, and sometimes their companions, speak in the language and words of shepherds, as if they were all village folk'.[35] A religious reading of the 'Pastorcico' naturally sees the shepherd as Christ and the shepherdess as the human soul. But the relationship presented as between two individual protagonists and intensified by the shepherd's death is paradigmatic of that between Christ and all Christians. In that sense the 'Pastorcico' is moving in the same world as the *romances*, narrating in another idiom the foundational Christian story on which every journey towards union with God is constructed, and without which the intensely lyrical world of the 'Cántico' and the 'Noche' could not be. But here the story represents not the wedding of divinity with humanity in the Incarnation, but the redemptive work of the cross, delicately and allusively handled.

The 'pastora' whom the shepherd loves, therefore, is the whole human race. The ill-treatment meted out to the shepherd in a strange country is the rejection and suffering experienced by the prophets and finally by the Son in his incarnate life on earth, of which Christ speaks in the parable of the wicked husbandmen and in his weeping over Jerusalem (Matthew 21.33–41; 23.37). The last verse reflects two texts from the Song, 'Dixi: ascendam in palmam, et apprehendam fructus eius', 'I said, I will go up to the palm tree, I will take hold of the boughs thereof' (7.8) and 'Sub arbore malo suscitavi te; ibi corrupta est mater tua', 'I raised thee up under the apple tree: there thy mother brought thee forth' (8.5; AV has a different translation), both of them texts long associated in exegetical tradition with the Crucifixion and Redemption, and the second part of the Holy Week liturgy. These in turn are linked with other texts associated with the open arms of Christ as a gesture of pleading with his children to follow him (Song 1.3; John 12.32).[36] The 'gran rato', 'long period', after which the shepherd ascends the tree, refers surely to the long ages during which God, the shepherd of Israel (Psalms 22 and 79 [23, 80]) sought his people before he sent his Son when the time was fulfilled (Galatians 4.4). The tree is the cross, as it has been since New Testament times (1 Peter 2.24), and as it is in CA 28 (CB 23):

Debaxo del mançano,	Underneath the apple-tree,
allí conmigo fuiste desposada;	there you were betrothed to me,
allí te di la mano,	there I gave you my hand,
y fuiste reparada	and you were restored
donde tu madre fuera violada.	where your mother was violated.

This is the clearest example in the 'Cántico' of a verse which needs to be understood with reference to traditional typology, which established a link between the tree in the Garden of Eden from which Eve, the mother of the human race, ate in disobedience with such fateful consequences, and the tree of the cross, where the Son of Mary, mother of all the faithful, in obedience regenerates the human race.[37] In devotional writing across many centuries Christ is portrayed as ascending the tree of the cross and reigning from it as if on a throne.[38] Likewise, eucharistic liturgies have often used phrases like 'he opened wide his arms for us on the cross', which helps to place the shepherd's action, 'do abrió sus braços vellos', 'where he opened his lovely arms'.[39] The refrain becomes progressively more poignant as it draws attention to the shepherd wounded by love, first in rejection, then suffering, and finally death, to drive home the lesson that this is the true work of love, against which all other loving must be measured.

Comparing the poem with its secular model or with Sebastián de Córdoba's rewriting of a passage from Garcilaso's second eclogue, in which Christ also appears as a wounded shepherd in a tree, contributes little to appreciating it. It ought to be understood as a devotional poem in its own right, not as a failed mystical poem, and its appeal lies in the way it seeks to make accessible and attractive the redemptive sacrifice of Christ, without which there would be no Christian mystical journey open to anyone. It creates its emotional impact not by depicting the injustice and violence of the scene but by drawing repeated attention to the self-giving love which inspires Christ's sacrifice, his willingness to bear it, the inward suffering which begins in Gethsemane and intensifies as he bears the sin of the world or experiences abandonment by the Father, acuter than any outward display of pain.[40] At each moment in his saving journey, where physical eyes see rejection, pain and death, the eye of faith is creatively centred on and nourished by love.

THE 'FONTE'

The poem 'Que bien sé yo la fonte que mana y corre', 'How well I know the fountain which flows and runs' (the 'Fonte'), bears the title 'Cantar del alma que se huelga de conocer a Dios por fe', 'Song of the soul which rejoices to know God by faith', and has generally been considered the best of San Juan's popular verses. Dámaso Alonso acknowledges that it has 'una gran hermosura y un encanto profundísimo', 'a great beauty and a most profound charm', though he stresses how different it is from the rest: 'una extraña composición que se aparta notablemente de todas las anteriores', 'a strange composition, notably different from all the earlier ones'.[41] Many critics have followed his judgement: Brenan calls it 'one of the most mysterious and beautiful' of San Juan's poems.[42] Margaret Wilson, however, has expressed serious reservations about it. While agreeing that the poem begins magnificently, she states: 'The pity is that it ends so drably.'[43] In particular, she notes a decline after the fifth verse: 'The verse becomes pedestrian, and the symbolism of the fountain first dwindles into a lame allegory of the formation of the Trinity, and is then uneasily linked with the idea of God's presence in the Sacrament' (p. 36). In order to enter into the poem's beauty and mystery, and to counter these criticisms, I propose a new reading of the poem, from a doctrinal, biblical and liturgical perspective, to reveal the intellectual and spiritual coherence which governs its flow and which can enhance our appreciation of it. It shows the same movement as the ballads from the infinite mystery of the Trinity to the physical and corporeal, but its climactic point is not the Incarnation but the Eucharist. It also is a profoundly biblical poem, like the ballads and the Psalm paraphrase, but in a more allusive and original manner.

Critical attention has hitherto centred largely on three areas: its relation to a more secular, popular poetic tradition; its use of the archaic, undiphthongized word 'fonte'; and the image of the fountain and its streams as a symbol for the complexities of Trinitarian theology across centuries of devotional writing. Alonso, whose pioneering study laid the foundations for a generation of criticism of San Juan's poetry, believed the poem's origin lay in a popular *villancico*, which survived wholly or in part in the first two lines and thereafter in the refrain (p. 99), and that the form 'fonte' was dictated by their assonantal pattern ('fonte', 'corre', 'noche'). He noted the pleonastic construction 'Que bien . . .', so characteristic of popular poetry, but concluded that the poem displayed a series of individual features from distinctive traditions, without being fully identifiable with any of them: Castilian (the theme of the fountain), western dialectal (the 'fonte'), the Galician–Portuguese *cancionero* (the form of two lines and *estribillo*), and learned Italianate poetry (the hendecasyllabic lines). Employing the form of Galician–Portuguese *canciones* but lacking their parallelisms and static lyricism, the *coplas* were 'una progresiva exposición teológica, que podría haber sido desarrollada doctrinalmente' (p. 102), 'a progressive theological exposition, which could have been developed doctrinally'.

Why did San Juan use 'fonte', archaic by the sixteenth century, in preference to the standard 'fuente'? It is tempting to think that he was recalling the name of his birthplace, Fontiveros, the first syllable of which preserves the older form, but more probably it is due to its resonance with popular poetry. One of the most famous of Spanish medieval *romances,* 'Fonte frida, fonte frida,/fonte frida y con amor', still well known at the end of the sixteenth century, tells the tale of a turtle dove who has lost her mate and who spurns the advances of another bird at the cold fountain.[44] Doves appear three times in the 'Cántico' poem, as a name for the Bride (CA 12), and in CA 33 as both 'palomica' (a reference to the dove which returned with an olive branch to Noah's ark) and 'tortolica', the same form as in the ballad, though in San Juan's poem she is reunited with her consort by green river-banks.[45]

Little interest has been shown in the development of the poem's argument, however, perhaps because it is not clear to most critics that it has a sustained one. Hatzfeld's study provides an outline of how the doctrinal exposition imagined by Alonso might have proceeded, by analysing the images it shares with the *lira* poems and San Juan's interpretations of them, especially the symbol of the dark night. He underlines its consistency with San Juan's teaching on possession and privation, but also notes the techniques of repetition and paradox through which the poetic effect is achieved. In particular, his analysis of its metrical qualities remains definitive.[46]

More particular attention has been given to the symbol of the fountain itself. Just as the fountain as a trysting-place for lovers is a commonplace of folk poetry, so God as the fountain of all being and the Godhead as the source from which the Persons of the Trinity flow are images used across many centuries of theological and devotional literature. Ricard drew attention to a chapter in Bernardino de Laredo's *Subida del Monte Sión*, a work which was read both by San Juan and Santa Teresa, though the image itself is so persistent that tracing a precise source is pointless.[47] The following expressions illustrate the closeness between Laredo and the poem, but cannot be taken to be more than a restatement of ideas in currency from the Fathers onwards: 'Del escondimiento oculto del secreto inaccesible de esta immensa y coeterna Majestad nasce *ab aeterno* una fuente de agua viva' (p. 150), 'a fountain of living water is born from all eternity from the hiddenness of the inaccesible secret of this immense, coeternal Majesty'; 'ni el entendimiento humano la puede jamás hallar, mas puede engolfarse en ella' (p. 151), 'nor can human understanding ever find it, but it can drown itself there'; 'el Hijo siempre nasce' (pp. 151–2), 'the Son is for ever born'; 'dos distintos ríos, de los cuales procede muy igualmente otro río de infinidad, es a saber, el

Espíritu Santo' (pp. 152–3), 'two different rivers, whence proceeds in all equality another river of infinity, that is, the Holy Spirit'; 'cuando ella [el ánima] llega a beber a la fuente', 'when [the soul] comes to drink at the fountain' (p. 153).[48]

The presence of the image in spiritual literature may be demonstrated from a work from which San Juan quotes in his prose commentaries, the treatise *De beatitudine*, which he ascribes to St Thomas Aquinas, though it is now regarded as spurious.[49] Of the soul's vision of the Trinity, the author writes: 'Item aperte videbit anima singula dona a fonte divino fluentia, non sic effluere tamquam ab ipso recedant, sicut rivus a fonte recedit; sed semper in ipso integraliter manent' (p. 709); 'the soul will clearly see each gift flowing from the divine fountain, not issuing forth so that they flow out of it, as a stream flows out of a fountain, but ever remaining within it in their entirety'. This comparison is followed immediately by another, based on how one light may be communicated to another without any diminution of itself. Commenting on the verse 'De torrente voluptatis tuae potabis eos' (Psalm 35.9), 'And thou shalt make them drink of the river of thy pleasures' (36.8), he adds: 'Fons vitae est Dei aeterna et immensa largitas, a qua fontis est gaudium sempiternum, nec sufficit semel aut bis aut millesies potare de isto fonte: ideo fidelis anima aeternam habebit in illo fonte quietem et beatissimam mansionem' (p. 712), 'the fountain of life is the immense and eternal abundance of God, from which comes the everlasting joy of the fountain, nor is it enough to drink once or twice or a thousand times from this fountain: hence the faithful soul will find in that fountain an eternal, peaceful and most blessed dwelling-place'. The writer is consciously referring to the next verse of the Psalm, 'Quoniam apud te est fons vitae', 'for with thee is the fountain of life', and some lines later emphasizes the 'claritas' of the face of Jesus Christ (p. 712), remembering the second part of that verse, 'Et in lumine tuo videbimus lumen' (35.10), 'in thy light shall we see light' (36.9). In that context, San Juan's line 'Su claridad nunca es escurecida', 'its brightness is never darkened', repeats the fountain-light association present in the Psalm and made explicit in *De beatitudine*.[50]

De beatitudine demonstrates clearly the weaving together of biblical texts and images associated with the fountain which San Juan inherited, though it may provide closer links with his own text, as the cluster of Trinitarian associations (fountain, clarity, light) suggests. But such elemental images as water and light are also found from the beginning to the end of scripture (quite literally from Genesis 1 to Revelation 22). In fact, the Bible itself holds together the secular and sacred meanings of the fountain, since a well is the locus of the courtship of Rebecca by Isaac (Genesis 24) and of Rachel by Jacob (Genesis 29), and it is at Jacob's well that Jesus has his memorable encounter with the woman of Samaria (John 4). Though such studies can enrich our understanding of the poem's background, I am not sure that they have brought us much closer to understanding how the poem works and holds together. To discover this, we have to look in another direction. Margaret Wilson's observations suggest that the poem is an uneasy compromise between a lyrical first half to which a doctrinal second half has been attached in a somewhat arbitrary fashion. It is difficult at first sight to understand how the procession of the Persons of the Trinity and the eucharistic climax grow out of the beginning and form an appropriate conclusion. Nor is it necessarily the case that to demonstrate that they do makes the 'Fonte' poem a better poem. But I should like to think that it makes it at least a more profound and coherent religious text.

Sometimes San Juan's biblical allusions are clear and specific (notably in the prose commentaries); at other times they form a background against which other images or ideas come to prominence. The 'Fonte' is a poem which depends on this second, more hidden familiarity with the Bible. Because the biblical substratum of the 'Fonte' has received little attention, the subtlety of the poem goes largely unnoticed. Domingo Ynduráin hints at this in his brief comments on the poem's relationship to the theme of the waters of love in popular poetry: the 'fonte frida' was a traditional meeting-place for lovers. He writes: 'Pero sin duda, la conexión doctrinal inmediata se establece con el agua de la samaritana', 'but the probable doctrinal link is made with the water of the Samaritan woman'.[51] He does not elaborate, but is surely correct, though the connection to which he alludes governs the artistic flow of the poem as much as it does its doctrinal sense.

Behind the 'Fonte' poem lie several passages from St John the Evangelist, whose whole Gospel is constructed around the same series of elemental images – light, darkness, water, bread – and on the base of a Trinitarian theology more developed than that of the Synoptic Gospels, precisely the combination which has worried even sensitive critics like Margaret Wilson. The Johannine texts in question are the visit of Nicodemus to Jesus by night in chapter 3, the encounter of Jesus at the well with the woman of Samaria in chapter 4, the living waters Jesus promises will well up within the believer (7.38), the discourse on the bread of life (6.48ff), and the Prologue (1). All but the penultimate are passages used a number of times by San Juan in his commentaries.[52] The Trinitarian theology of John is evident in all these places, but most of all in the Farewell Discourses of Jesus (chapters 14–17). Read against this Johannine background, the 'Fonte' poem acquires both its mysterious depth and its coherence.

The four words of the refrain, 'Aunque es de noche', endow night with that symbolic quality which is at one level entirely characteristic of the Gospel and at another of San Juan himself. Nicodemus comes to Jesus by night, knowing him to be a teacher sent from God, and is told that he must be born again of water and spirit. The whole poem could in one sense be imagined as the response of Nicodemus to the puzzling words Jesus speaks to him about the need to be born again of water and the Spirit: he has now identified the water, and in verse 8, the Holy Spirit. As so often in John's Gospel, narrative (3.1–4) is followed by discourse on the part of Jesus (3.5–21). The Nicodemus discourse concludes with darkness being equated with evil and light with truth, following the pattern established in the Gospel's prologue (1.4–9), while between it and the story of the woman of Samaria comes a passage which is based on the symbolism of water (3.22–6: the activity of John the Baptist and the dispute it causes; 3.27–36: discourse on the part of the Baptist, witnessing to the Christ and couched in Trinitarian terms).

A similar pattern can be seen in the story of the woman of Samaria, though here the discourse is in the form of a dialogue between the woman and Jesus (narrative, 4.1–6; dialogue, 4.6–26). This story turns into a dispute about the competing claims of Jews and Samaritans to knowledge of God.[53] It provides the missing link in the cluster of associations, because it adds the theme of knowledge to the imagery of light, darkness and water and the Trinitarian context, and accounts for the insistence on 'sé' and 'no sé' across the first nine verses. It is this close association of these elemental images with knowledge of the Trinity that lies at the heart of the poem. Jesus says to the woman: 'Si *scires* donum Dei, et quis est qui dicit tibi: Da mihi bibere, tu fortisan petisses ab eo, et dedisset tibi aquam vivam' (4.10), 'If *thou knewest* the gift of God, and who it is that saith to thee, Give me to drink; thou wouldest have asked of him, and he would have given thee living water.' Later, he says to her, as a Samaritan: 'Vos adoratis qui *nescitis*; nos adoramus quem *scimus*' (4.22), 'Ye worship *ye know not* what: *we know* what we worship'; and she replies: '*Scio* quia Messias venit' (4.25), '*I know* that Messias cometh' (my emphases). Set against this dialogue, another way of interpreting the opening line, 'Que bien sé yo la fonte que mana y corre', and all the other references to first-person knowledge, is as the statement of faith which the woman of Samaria would have made had she confessed her belief in Christ (in John her last words are 'Numquid ipse est Christus?' (4.29), 'Is not this the Christ?', whereas the other Samaritans she tells (4.39–42) are more positive in their response). The link between the poem and the Johannine story is further strengthened by the use of the epithet 'eterna' in the first verse, because Jesus tells the woman that for its drinker the water he will provide 'fiet in eo fons aquae salientis in vitam aeternam' (4.14), 'shall be in him a well of water springing up into everlasting life'.

The Johannine referent which lies behind the apparently arbitrary switch from the fountain to the bread which hides it is found in the discourse on the 'pan de vida', the 'living bread' of John 6.51 (one of the titles Jesus uses of himself, in 6.48). Like the place where the fountain flows out visibly from its unknown, hidden source, the living bread is another picture of the Incarnation, the physical form in which God made himself manifest through the Son. But there is a more particular connection with the sacrament of the Eucharist. St John's Gospel never mentions it directly, but the discourse on the bread of life (6.48–59) is profoundly eucharistic in sense. The deepest, unfathomable mysteries of the Trinity and the most basic and necessary nourishment for life – water and bread – are encompassed in a single span, centring on the Incarnate Christ, and represented in the movement of the poem. This same movement is represented in the Church's year, which celebrates the Feast of Corpus Christi, in thanksgiving for the gift of Christ in the eucharistic bread and wine, five days after Trinity Sunday, and reads this passage for the Gospel.[54] This is the feast dramatized in the *autos sacramentales*, short plays performed in the street for the feast of Corpus Christi, to similar theological effect. In Calderón's *La vida es sueño*, for example, the three Persons of the Trinity and the four created elements of water, earth, air and fire act out the whole drama of salvation from pre-existent chaos through Creation, Fall, Incarnation, Crucifixion, Resurrection and Ascension. But the climactic point is and must be bread – the sacred bread of the Host, displayed to the audience in the monstrance and accompanied by the *Tantum ergo* and the sound of *chirimías* (shawms), because it is in the eucharistic bread that the believer receives the Word made flesh, crucified, risen and ascended.

The paradoxical nature of the poem's discourse and the development of its imagery enable us to follow San Juan in discovering connections which carry the meaning forward, rather than lapses which undermine it. Broadly speaking, the structure of the poem represents a doctrinal progression: the paradox of the eternal fountain, hidden but known, dominates until the end of the second verse; in verses 3–6 the nature and work of the Trinity is alluded to through images of water and light; the begetting of the Word and the procession of the Spirit from the fountain are made specific in verses 7–8; and from verses 9–11 the eternal fountain of the Trinity, hidden but known, is seen and heard in the eucharistic bread. The first two lines of the poem contain no overt religious imagery, but a deeper meaning than the literal is hinted at by the epithet 'eterna' in the first verse and by the cumulative paradoxes of verses 2–5. The religious meaning becomes explicit thereafter, but shows its own progression, from the fathomless mysteries of the eternal Trinity to their revelation and grounding in the body of Christ, offered to satisfy not simply the 'yo' of the poem but the hunger and thirst of the whole creation. The bread of Eucharist, however, is but a foretaste on earth of the life of the Trinity, for which the speaker longs, just as in his account of the mystical journey San Juan understands unitive experiences in prayer to be but a foretaste of the beatific vision. This progressive structure is stylistically represented and complemented by the repetitions which link the different parts together, most obviously through the refrain and the rhymes, but also through the repeated 'sé que' (and in v. 2, 'no sé') running through the first eight stanzas. This anaphora concludes in verse 8, at which point San Juan repeats with only a slight variant the first line of the first verse, as if especially anxious to connect the eternal, hidden fountain of the poem so far with the new image of the bread of life. The variant may itself be significant: 'Aquella eterna fonte', 'that eternal fountain', now becomes 'Aquesta eterna fonte', 'this', suggesting it is now close at hand.

Despite its brevity, the poem is full of paradox, which is intended to ask the reader to ponder in what sense this is more than a poem about drinking at a fountain in the darkness. At the same time, it provides a number of clues, more of them and more explicitly than in the *lira* poems, which suggest that a literal reading is impossible. The opening lines seem straightforward enough: I know where the hidden fountain springs up ('mana') and flows, and can find my way to it even at night. But they contain a syntactical uncertainty about the relationship of the refrain to the lines which precede it, one which affects the sense of each verse of the poem. Is it that I know the fountain at night, or is it that it flows by night? The problem is acutest in the fifth verse, in which I know that all light proceeds from the fountain, 'aunque es de noche'. Is the paradox that I know this, but darkly; or is it that the fountain is the source of all light even by night; or both?

The first and second verses are puzzling, because they appear to undermine the opening statement by positing both a not knowing and a knowing: the eternal fountain is hidden, but I know where it springs up; I do not know its origin, since it has none, although I do know that everything originates from it. Because this is a poem, not a doctrinal exposition, San Juan does not spell out what he means, but his careful distinction between the unknown source or origin of the eternal fountain and its visible outflowing helps to resolve the paradox. The contrast is between the unknown hiddenness of the Godhead, far beyond all human thought (the fountain's 'origen'), a notion rooted in the traditions of negative theology, and the place where that same God makes himself known (its 'manida'), the Incarnate Christ, the second Person of the Trinity (v. 7) who will become the living bread (John 6.35) of the final three stanzas. The epithet 'eterna' marks the distinction and must be given its full weight. The second verse contrasts the uncreated Creator with the whole realm of created being which derives its life from him, a distinction fundamental to all San Juan's teaching.[55] It glosses John 1.3, 'All things were made through him, and without him was not anything made that was made.' In John, God creates everything through Christ, who in his divine nature is the eternal Word, the second Person of the Trinity, but who has assumed human nature and the mortal life of the creature. The paradox of knowing and not knowing, of unknown source and known spring, is resolved, but not in a trite or conventional way, because it is rooted in the paradox of the unknown Word made known flesh.

The third stanza initiates a sequence of four verses which define the fountain respectively in terms of its refreshing beauty, bottomless depths, unquenchable light and universal power, all seen against the insistent 'aunque es de noche'. Divine Beauty – 'No puede ser cosa tan bella', 'Nothing can be so beautiful' – is a theme beloved of San Juan and ultimately neo-Platonic and Augustinian (*Confessions* x.27; CA 35, and associated commentary in CB 36), but here connected with the image of the fountain, from which 'cielos y tierra beben', 'heavens and earth drink'. The unfathomable deep of the Godhead is a *topos* of ancient origin: the fountain flows out into a stream which has no bottom and which is unfordable. In the fifth verse, as we noted, the refrain's paradoxical role is at its sharpest: all light comes from the fountain, though it is night. San Juan here compresses a number of Johannine statements about light and darkness into a single antithesis to convey the paradox more powerfully: 'And the light shineth in darkness; and the darkness comprehended [extinguished] it not' (1.5); 'He was the true light, that lighteneth every man that cometh into the world' (1.9); and the Nicene Creed's proclamation of the Son as 'lumen de lumine', 'Light from Light'.

There is a surprising departure from Christian tradition in the sixth verse, where 'infiernos' drink at this fountain, which also waters 'cielos' and 'gentes'. The 'heavens' may represent a Pythagorean view of the different spheres, but probably reflect biblical usage: 'Caeli enarrant gloriam Dei', 'The heavens are telling the glory of God' (Psalm 18[19].2). While the 'gentes' may be the biblical Gentiles, this watering of 'hells' appears to go against the traditional view, based on the parable of Dives and Lazarus (Luke 16.19–31), that there is a great gulf fixed between heaven and hell which cannot be crossed. Dives, in hell, asks for Lazarus in heaven to be allowed to dip his finger in water to relieve his torment, and is told that this is impossible. Is San Juan suggesting an embryonic form of the doctrine of universalism, in which divine mercy reaches even hell? His only other reference to the parable (S 3.25.5) highlights the lack of charity of 'aquel epulón que comía cada día espléndidamente', 'that glutton who ate splendidly every day', in a passage which points to the moral consequences of greed. But there are other, less radical interpretations. San Juan has remarkably little to say about hell in his writings, but does use it sometimes as a vivid metaphor for the intense sufferings of the dark night of the spirit (N 2.6). Given the nocturnal refrain of the poem, the watering of hells to which it refers (and they are plural) may be the times of relief which occur in the heart of the darkness (N 2.7), or may also represent the traditional doctrine of the descent into hell, the harrowing of hell by Christ during his three days in the tomb and his freeing from its grip of the patriarchs and saints of the Hebrew scriptures. Or the expression may be purely hyperbolic, an arresting way of presenting the reader with the inclusiveness of divine mercy.[56]

The modern reader may feel that the poem would have been better if it had not become overtly Trinitarian in verses 7–8 and had been content to mark its meaning more subtly. But the last three verses restore the balance. It is impossible for a fountain to be hidden within bread in any literal reading, but both images can cohere in the same reality, Christ. He offers himself as both fountain and bread to 'the creatures' (San Juan's term for every created thing), which include the heavens, hells, peoples and earth of verse 6, and also ourselves, hence the first occurrence in the poem of the first person plural, 'darnos vida', 'to give us life', in verse 9. The refrain's meaning shifts again, this time and for the only time changing its wording: the conditional 'although' becomes the consecutive 'because'. This living bread/fountain is sufficient for all the needs of the creatures, '*aunque* a escuras/*porque* es de noche', '*though* in the dark/*because* it is night' (my emphases). The sense of the original refrain, 'aunque es de noche', has shifted forward into the verse, 'a escuras' replacing 'de noche'.[57] Why the change should occur here and not, for example, in the previous verse, where it would fit just as well, remains a mystery, except that the line which precedes it, 'y de esta agua se hartan, aunque a escuras', unites for the first time in a single line of the poem the two fundamental images of water and darkness.

Clearly San Juan wishes to draw our attention to these small changes. The creatures have their thirst satisfied in the dark because that is the condition of their being, both their creatureliness and (at least for humans) their sinfulness. We do not need to be too precise about the nature of that darkness; symbolic language is open-ended, and can be both personal and universal. But the last line returns to the 'aunque' form of the refrain and to the first person: I see the living fountain I desire in this living bread, in spite of the dimness of my vision, the burden of my sins, the seeing and the tasting which is but a glimpse and a foretaste in the darkness of what points me to the light no darkness can put out. The journey from the fountain of the unknown and hidden Father, from whom spring the Incarnate Son and the life-giving Spirit, is complete when Christ the Bread of Life is made present and visible in the Eucharist. The sacrament is the most physical and tangible sign of the divine mystery, and it is the act by which the life of God is received by the believer. The ending of the poem, therefore, is not anticlimactic or lame in any theological sense, for the eucharistic bread is the nearest and clearest token of the mystery of the Incarnation, the outflowing of the fountain, for timebound humans.[58]

I have argued that the theological coherence of the poem, rooted as it is in the Gospel of John, Trinitarian doctrine as expressed in the Nicene Creed, and the feast of Corpus Christi, is beyond dispute. But does San Juan display the same sensitivity to language in a poem full of popular echoes and symbolic discourse as he does in his greatest works? Perhaps not as strikingly, but there are signs of a close relationship between the use of language in the poem and the meaning the poet wishes to communicate. Take, for example, the relative clause defining the fountain, 'que mana y corre', 'which flows and runs'. What might be thought of as a straightforward example of *interpretatio*, in this case the use of two verbs of similar meaning for purely rhetorical purposes, becomes integral to the argument in verses 7–8, where the current becomes first a symbol for the begetting of the Son of the Father and then for the procession of the Spirit from both. The contradiction of a known 'manida' and an unknown 'origen' also resolves itself if we pay careful attention to the precise words San Juan uses. The fountain is hidden, but the poet knows where its 'manida' is, where it issues from the ground and becomes visible, as the eternal Word assumes flesh and is born among us. On the other hand, he is unable to say where the origin of this flow of water might be, its source deep below ground. That it is no ordinary fountain at once becomes apparent from the fact that, unlike any other, it has no point of origin and is itself the origin of everything (v. 2). The repetition of 'Aquella/Aquesta eterna fonte está ascondida/escondida' in the first and ninth verses makes a verbal connection between the symbols of water and night at the start of the poem and the new symbol of the living bread at its climax, while the *vivo/vida/viva/vida* polyptoton of verses 9 and 11 draws attention to the life-giving properties of the bread which is the other visible sign of the hidden fountain.[59] The brightness of the fountain and its nature as the source of 'toda luz', 'all light' in the darkness in verse 5 harks back to the paradox of 'todo origen' of the second verse, and anticipates the resolution of the tension between hiddenness and seeing found in the bread visible in the fountain by night at the end. The repeated first person 'sé', 'I know', ten times across the first eight verses in various forms ('bien sé yo', 'no lo sé', 'sé que', 'sé ser'), is transformed into 'yo la veo' ('I see it') immediately before the final refrain, indicating the journey from knowledge to seeing, though still darkly. The poem's voice is individual, but it embraces all created beings, as the second, third and sixth verses show in different ways, while the first person and third person plurals of the penultimate and antepenultimate verses underline this.

To appreciate the 'Fonte' poem, the reader needs to be aware of the Johannine dialogues between Jesus and Nicodemus, and Jesus and the woman of Samaria, as well as of Johannine symbolism in general, so pervasive an element in the poem. But they are not its sources, in the sense that San Juan is retelling their story. The poem is a creative fusing and rewriting of them, in which the search of Nicodemus at night is one and the same as the woman's thirst at the well, and in which both find resolution in the bread of life, who is also the light of the world and the living water. Bread, light, water and knowledge are all associated with Jesus in the Gospel. Just as the Prologue to John locates the revelation of Christ in the eternal life of God and the rest of his Gospel its working out in the particularity of first-century Palestine, so San Juan's poem begins by joining the God who is beyond origin with the revelation of his purpose in time through the distinction between the source and the flowing of the fountain. He then recalls Johannine figures like Nicodemus and the woman of Samaria, but by alluding to them indirectly and emphasizing instead the elemental images of night and water with which they are associated, universalizes them so that the poem becomes the confession of faith of any believer.

The biblical allusions are not, then, sources for the poem in the same way that John 1 is for the *romances*, but they are constantly present in the background. It is therefore a freer form of meditation on Johannine symbolism; free enough to depart from it in one important respect. For what is strikingly unJohannine but just as strikingly *sanjuanista* is that this darkness has redemptive power. It is not like the waste and void of Genesis 1.2, when 'darkness was upon the face of the waters', the first and most significant joining of the two images in the Hebrew Bible, where both darkness and water are associated with chaos and non-being. It is, above all, unlike the close association of darkness and night with wilful ignorance and evil on which the Gospel rests. At the moment when the darkness is at its deepest for Jesus, as Judas Iscariot leaves to betray him and he faces arrest and execution, John adds three simple words, ἦν δὲ νύξ, 'Erat autem nox' , 'And it was night' (13.30). He does not mean that it happened to be dark outside. He means that the powers of darkness, already foreshadowed in the Gospel prologue (1.5) have gathered their full strength and are about to seize their prey.

The reason for this is that the poem is also rooted in another, later tradition: the pseudo-Dionysian view of the necessary darkness of all human experience of God, not because God actually is darkness (he is light) but because human language and concepts can never express and are therefore always blinded by the radiance of divine glory. San Juan will develop the dazzling darkness of the pseudo-Dionysius into a more comprehensive symbol in the *Subida-Noche*), and has much to say about the limitations of language when applied to God.[60] San Juan's night is more as Henry Vaughan sees it in his poem 'The Night', another meditation on the visit of Nicodemus: 'Wise Nicodemus saw such light/As made him know his God by night.'[61] That is possible only because between the two St Johns there interposes a whole tradition of negative or apophatic theology, which does not so much reject language as use it to point to its own inadequacies. San Juan understands night to be blindness caused by dazzling light which human eyes are too weak to receive unmediated. It can therefore be posited of God, as it never could in St John's Gospel. With such an understanding, not only paradox but also antithesis is rescued from triviality: darkness becomes a form of light, a locus of revelation.

With its explicit references to divine omnipotence and to the procession of the Persons of the Trinity, the poem is clearly religious in meaning in a way the 'Noche', for example, is not. That lack of ambiguity explains why for many modern readers it falls short of San Juan at his best. Wherein, then, lies its appeal? The insistent repetition of the refrain, 5 syllables after two lines of 11, has something to do with it, providing the poem with a regular point of return as each new idea is explored, which is suddenly transformed in the penultimate verse by the change from 'aunque es de noche', 'though it is night', to 'porque es de noche', 'because it is night'. The effect of combining two elemental images, water and night, is a powerful one, especially as in Renaissance poetry fountains are normally associated with daylight encounters. The 'Noche oscura' is not San Juan's only night poem; the 'Fonte' is another, and points of correspondence between them are not hard to find. But whereas in the former the counterpoint is largely provided by images of light, fire and air playing against the darkness, the latter establishes it by water. It may be a more uneven poem, but it has unsuspected richness.

Although it may appear simple and elemental, it is paradoxical and profound. Occasionally its spiritual meaning rises to the surface, but for most of its course it sets up a series of associations between water, night and bread and weaves subtly-changing patterns out of them. It is not exactly mystical in the same sense as the 'Noche oscura': it is a confession of faith, the creed of the dark night, a religious poem, Johannine and Trinitarian, built out of allusions to the Gospel of John, yet using a repetitive form and images and paradoxes which also belong to popular poetry. The references to the eternal begetting of the Son and the eternal procession of the Holy Spirit from the Father and the Son in the seventh and eighth verses, however they are thought to affect the poem as poem, belong very firmly to the Johannine literature with which it is in dialogue and are not an extraneous insertion. It may therefore best be thought of as a meditation on the third and fourth chapters of John's Gospel, presented imaginatively as the first-person narrator assuming the voice of Nicodemus or the woman of Samaria as they move from doubt and searching in the Bible to faith in the poem. The overall effect, in spite of an element of didacticism in its Trinitarian theology, is profoundly moving. And the mystery of the Trinity is perhaps more tellingly grasped by the audience San Juan had in mind through his symbol of the fountain flowing in the darkness than ever it could be through the formal language of scholastic theology.

NOTES

1 Both Sanlúcar and the important, later Jaén MS, have been published in handsome facsimile editions, 2 vols (Madrid: Turner, 1991).

2 The *lira* is a five-line stanza introduced into Spanish by Garcilaso de la Vega, and named from the first line of his 'Oda ad Florem Gnidi', 'Si de mi baja lira', 'If from my lowly lyre'.

3 The Italianate metres introduced by Garcilaso were not considered to be rivals to popular forms; as Lázaro Carreter points out, *liras* and *romances* existed side by side in the *Romancero general* of 1600, which began 'la fecunda convivencia', that fruitful joining which is so notable a feature of the poetry of Lope de Vega and Góngora (*Actas*, I, p. 34).

4 P. E. Russell, in *Spain: A Companion to Spanish Studies*, ed. P. E. Russell (London: Methuen, 1973), p. 270.

5 For a positive evaluation of their theology and artfulness, see Xavier Pikaza, 'Amor de Dios y contemplación cristiana: Introducción a San Juan de la Cruz', *Actas*, III, pp. 51–96; George H. Tavard, *Poetry and Contemplation in St. John of the Cross* (Athens: Ohio University Press, 1988), pp. 19–29.

6 Santa Teresa, for example, mentions having read it in translation in her *Vida,* 5.8. For Gregory's text, see PL, 75, 515. Francis Quarles (1592–1644), 'On the Holy Scriptures', uses the image: 'The Scripture is a ford, wherein, 'tis said,/An elephant shall swim; a lamb may wade'; quoted from *Chapters into Verse*, 2 vols, ed. Robert Atwan and Laurance Wieder (Oxford and New York: Oxford University Press, 1993), II, no. 95.

7 For example, 'Before the world began', a gloss on John 1.1–14 by John Bell and Graham Maule, in *Rejoice and Sing* (Oxford: Oxford University Press, 1991), p. 180.

8 For the text, see *San Juan de la Cruz: Poesía*, ed. Domingo Ynduráin (Madrid: Cátedra, 1989), pp. 282–91. 'Compañía', 'día' and 'alegría' ('company', 'day', 'happiness') are the commonest nouns; the possessive pronoun 'mía' ('mine') occurs twice. Of the verbs, 'había', 'decía', 'vivía',

'poseía', 'tenía', 'nacía' and 'unía' ('had', 'said', 'lived', 'possessed', 'had', 'was born', 'united') are each used several times. Some assonances introduce a more difficult vocabulary, like the verb 'sublimaría' ('would raise to the heights', 98) and the nouns 'pedrería' ('jewellery', 110) and 'jerarquía' ('hierarchy', 114).

9 The image of the knot for the Trinity is ancient, as Celtic Christian art shows; see also the illustrations in Francisco Delicado's *La lozana andaluza* of 1528. Henry Vaughan uses 'the true Loves-knot' in 'The Knot' for the Virgin Mary, *George Herbert and Henry Vaughan*, ed. Louis L. Martz (Oxford: Oxford University Press, 1986), p. 379; Teresa's poem '¡Oh, Hermosura que excedéis' (*Obras completas de Santa Teresa de Jesús*, ed. Efrén de la Madre de Dios and Otger Steggink, 2nd edn (Madrid: BAC, 1967), p. 500), of the union of the soul with God.

10 CA 37 has the same imperfect/conditional rhyme scheme, to similar effect.

11 The *Soliloquia* also uses the image of rescuing 'de lacu miseriae' (p. 898).

12 I follow Sanlúcar rather than Ynduráin, whose text differs slightly.

13 'The Knowledge and Consciousness of Christ in the Light of the Writings of St John of the Cross', unpublished D. Phil. thesis, University of Oxford, p. 125; Pikaza, *Actas*, III, p. 53.

14 *Obras* (ST), p. 834; see my 'The Many Paradoxes of the Mystics', in *Homenaje a Eugenio Asensio* (Madrid: Gredos, 1988), pp. 471–88 (p. 477). On Carmelite poetry, see Emilio Orozco, 'Poesía tradicional carmelitana', in his *Poesía y mística* (Madrid: Guadarrama, 1959), pp. 115–79. At least one of Teresa's poems, 'Nada te turbe', has become popular through its use at Taizé; see also *Rejoice and Sing*, p. 548. For her poems, see *Obras*, pp. 499–512.

15 *Obras* (SJ), p. 41. For a generally well-balanced discussion of these poems, see Margaret Wilson, *San Juan de la Cruz: Poems* (London: Grant and Cutler, 1975), pp. 36–44; also Tavard, *Poetry and Contemplation*, pp. 8–13, 54–56, 159–173.

16 Wilson, *San Juan*, pp. 36–7; R. O. Jones, *The Golden Age: Prose and Poetry* (London: Ernest Benn, 1971), pp. 30, 115.

17 Neither Roy Campbell, *Poems of St John of the Cross* (Glasgow: Collins, 1979), p. 31, nor Ynduráin, *San Juan*, p. 264, punctuates this verse as Sanlúcar, and their texts are semantically obscure; cf. Sanlúcar, f. 212r.

18 Of the many examples of such poems, the closest parallel must be Santa Teresa's own gloss on the same words: vv. 3–8 of San Juan's are almost identical with hers, and it is not clear to which of them they should be attributed.

19 *Obras* (SJ), p. 950.

20 Sebastián de Covarrubias, *Tesoro de la lengua castellana* (1611), facsimile edn (Barcelona: Horta, 1943), p. 857, and *Diccionario de Autoridades*, 3 vols (Madrid: Gredos, 1984), III, p. 170, both define it from the Latin 'pavor' as 'temor con espanto o sobresalto', 'fear with terror or fright'.

21 Spanish 'garza', normally translated 'heron', is a non-specific word used for the various kinds of herons and egrets found in the Iberian peninsula, many of which are smaller than the familiar grey heron (*Ardea cinerea*) of Britain; see Keith Whinnom, *A Glossary of Spanish Bird-Names* (London: Tamesis, 1966), pp. 111–12. The 'garza' is described by Covarrubias as white and beautiful (Tesoro, p. 629), which suggests the egret rather than the heron; *Autoridades*, II, p. 30, includes grey herons as well. Both, like the poem, make the point that these birds fly so high that they are lost to sight.

22 See Francisco López Estrada, 'Volando en las alturas: Persecución de una imagen poética en San Juan de la Cruz', in *Presencia de San Juan de la Cruz*, ed. Juan Paredes Núñez (Granada: Universidad de Granada, 1993), pp. 265–89; Dámaso Alonso, 'La caza de amor es de altanería', in *Obras completas*, 10 vols (Madrid: Gredos, 1972–93), II, pp. 1057–75; also Thompson, 'The Many Paradoxes of the Mystics', pp. 481–4. The association of the 'garza' with the Virgin Mary is at least as old as the *Cantigas de Santa María* (López Estrada, pp. 269, 287).

23 By the sixteenth-century poet Diego Ramírez Pagán; López Estrada, 'Valando en las alturas', p. 275.

24 The thought is reminiscent of Abelard's lines in *O quanta qualia* about heaven, where desire and fulfilment are one – 'nor the thing prayed for falls short of the prayer'.

25 For a comparison between different versions, see Bryant L. Creel, *The Religious Poetry of Jorge de Montemayor* (London: Tamesis, 1981), pp. 132–65. On San Juan's version, see Tavard, *Poetry and Contemplation*, pp. 29–35.

26 The rhyme scheme is 7a, 7b, 11c, 7a, 7b, 11c, 7c, 7d, 7e, 7e, 11d, 7f, 11f (the *silva* permitted any combination of 7 and 11 syllables in any rhyming scheme). See *La conversión de la Magdalena*, ed. Félix García, 3 vols. Clásicos castellanos, 3rd edn (Madrid: Espasa-Calpe, 1957–59), II, pp. 217–24.

27 In Sanlúcar and Ynduráin; *Obras* (SJ) gives six additional lines.

28 See below, pp. 174–7.

29 For use of this image in a devotional context, see Santa Teresa, *Vida* 17.6, 18.14.

30 Also 1 Corinthians 10.4, where the rock from which the children of Israel drank fresh water in the wilderness is said to be Christ. See Terence O'Reilly, 'San Juan de la Cruz y la lectura de la Biblia: el *romance* "Encima de las corrientes"', in *Actas*, I, pp. 221–31.

31 For the model, see José M. Blecua, 'Los antecedentes del poema del *Pastorcico* de San Juan de la Cruz', *RFE*, 33 (1949), pp. 378–80; reprinted in his *Sobre poesía de la Edad de Oro* (Madrid: Gredos, 1970), pp. 96–9. For a different reading of this poem see Tavard, *Poetry and Contemplation*, pp. 173–176.

32 Wilson, *San Juan de la Cruz: Poems*, pp. 30–3.

33 Dámaso Alonso, *La poesía de san Juan de la Cruz* (Madrid: Aguilar, 1966), p. 44.

34 Terence O'Reilly, 'The literary and devotional context of the *Pastorcico*', *FMLS*, 18 (1982), pp. 363–70; reprinted in his *From Ignatius Loyola to John of the Cross* (Variorum, 1995), XIV.

35 Fray Luis de Léon, *Obras completas castellanas*, ed. Félix García, 2 vols, 4th edn (Madrid: BAC, 1957), I, p. 72.

36 See O'Reilly, '*Pastorcico*', pp. 366–7.

37 For discussion of San Juan's commentary on this verse, see below, pp. 176–7.

38 For example, the *Vexilla regis* of Venantius Fortunatus, whose image of God reigning from the tree derives from an old Latin translation of Psalm 95 [96].10, not attested in the Hebrew, Septuagint or Vulgate texts but known to the early Fathers; see *A Dictionary of Hymnology*, ed. John Julian (London: John Murray, 1892), p. 1220.

39 Preserved, for example, in the second Eucharistic Prayer of *The Sunday Missal* (1975), Eucharistic Prayer B of *Common Worship* of the Church of England (2000), and the First Thanksgiving in the *Service Book* of the United Reformed Church (1989).

40 For a powerful expression of this in Fray Luis de León's *De los nombres de Cristo*, see 'Rey de Dios', *Obras completas castellanas*, ed. Félix Garciá (Madrid: BAC, 1957), I, pp. 580–5.

41 Dámaso Alonso, *La poesía de San Juan de la Cruz*, pp. 170, 96. A number of different versions exist: Sanlúcar gives an eleven-stanza poem, while Jaén has ten. I follow Ynduráin. For translations, see *Poems of St John of the Cross*, trans. Roy Campbell (Glasgow: Collins, 1979 [1951]), pp. 44–7; also Seamus Heaney, above, p. 11.

42 *Saint John of the Cross*, p. 126.

43 Wilson, *San Juan de la Cruz: Poems*, p. 35.

44 One of the additional verses represented in the MS tradition connects faith and the dark night in a way characteristic of San Juan, but also alludes to the ballad: 'En esta noche oscura de esta vida,/que bien sé yo por fe la fonte frida/aunque es de noche'. It must be assumed to be a later composition. See *Obras* (SJ), p. 12.

45 The links between the ballad and the 'Cántico' have been studied by Marcel Bataillon, 'La tortolica de *Fontefrida* y del *Cantico espiritual*', *NRFE*, 7 (1953), pp. 291–306.

46 Helmut Hatzfeld, *Estudios literarios sobre mística española*, 2nd edn, Biblioteca románica hispánica (Madrid: Gredos, 1968), pp. 332–48. See also Tavard, *Poetry and Contemplation*, pp. 15–19. The most recent analysis, by Fernando Cantalapiedra, *Actas* I, pp. 373–85, is based on semiotic models, with a full complement of schemes and tables.

47 Robert Ricard, '"La Fonte" de Saint Jean de la Croix et un chapitre de Laredo', *BH*, 58 (1956), pp. 265–74.

48 For Laredo's text, see *Místicos franciscanos españoles*, 3 vols (Madrid: BAC, 1948–49), II, pp. 25–442.

49 Text in *S. Thomae Aquinatis: Opera omnia*, ed. Roberto Busa, S.I., 7 vols. (Stuttgart-Bad Cannstadt: Fromann-Holzboog, 1980), VII, pp. 709–14. San Juan uses the text cited in *De beatitudine* three times in the *Cántico* (CB 2.6, 26.1, 38.9); his reading of the opuscule is thought by some critics to have been the prime reason for his re-ordering of the stanzas of his 'Cántico' poem and consequent second redaction of the *Cántico* commentary, in which the closing stanzas refer to the beatific vision of the Trinity the soul enjoys everlastingly in heaven, rather than to the highest grade of union with God attainable in this life. It is also regarded as the main source for his teaching on the exchange of love which takes place between God and the soul; see below, pp. 179–82.

50 San Juan uses these psalm verses three times in CB – 2.6, 26.1, 38.9.

51 Ynduráin, *San Juan de la Cruz: Poesía*, p. 221.

52 See e.g. S 2.5.5; S 3.26.7; N 1.4.7; CB 12.3 (where John 4.14 and 7.39 are juxtaposed); L 1.1; CB 20–21.11; L 3.8.

53 The Vulgate uses 'fons' and 'puteus' interchangeably; I take 'fountain', 'spring' and 'well' to be variants of the same image. Samaritans accepted only the Torah (the first five books of the Hebrew scriptures) as canonical.

54 The suggestion of an implicit liturgical link in the poem comes from Jesús Castellano, 'La experiencia del misterio litúrgico en San Juan de la Cruz', in *Experiencia*, pp. 114–54; see pp. 124, 128, 151–2. He notes that if written in prison, it belongs to a time when San Juan was deprived of the Eucharist, and suggests links with the Bread of Life discourse and the Corpus Christi hymn 'Adoro te devote'. But he makes little of the liturgical connection, except to summarize: 'La Trinidad es fuente. La Eucaristía es pan vivo. El misterio de la salvación es profundo como la Trinidad. Y se hace cercano y sacramental como en la Eucaristía' (p. 152).

55 See S 2.8.3 below, p. 193.

56 San Juan does not always follow the obvious sense of scripture and is prepared to make accommodations in difficult passages, as we have seen in the Psalm paraphrase. He is also capable of stretching orthodoxy to its limits, not so much perhaps in his bold language about the transformation and deification of the soul in union with God, but in regarding the passive night of the spirit as the experience of purgatory already realized in this life, so that those who have passed through its terrors presumably go straight to heaven (N 2.6.6; 20.5). In such cases, the joys of heaven experienced, if fleetingly, in mystical union with the Fount of all being lead him to make such bold and merciful assertions.

57 The same phrase is twice used in the second stanza of the 'Noche oscura' poem and underlines the kinship between the two works.

58 San Juan may also have been thinking of John 19.34, where the blood and water flowing from the side of the crucified Christ have often been interpreted as sacramental signs.

59 Compare C 8, '¡oh vida! no viviendo donde vives', for a similar example.

60 See below, pp. 235–9.

61 *George Herbert and Henry Vaughan*, ed. Louis L. Martz (Oxford: Oxford University Press, 1986), p. 395.

4

Songs in the Night (2)

There is in God (some say)
A deep, but dazzling darkness; as men here
Say it is late and dusky, because they
See not all clear;
O for that night! where I in him
Might live invisible and dim.
(Henry Vaughan, *Silex Scintillans*, 1655)

Rarely has so small a body of writing been the subject of such consistent acclaim as San Juan's three *lira* poems. The 'Cántico' and the 'Noche', to which we now turn, both appear to tell a story; that is, the narrative of a love story is embedded in them, although it is not sequential in the way one expects such narrative of the period to be. The 'Noche', and the 'Llama' (which I study in the final chapter, for reasons which will become apparent there), are short poems of 40 and 24 lines; the 'Cántico', San Juan's longest single poem, has 200 lines in its final form. Each has a distinctive feel, but the 'Noche' and the 'Cántico' share another quality, a sense of otherness, of being like and yet unlike the love poetry of the age. It is in that respect more than any other that the question of the meaning of these poems asks to be raised.

The metaphor of erotic love is central to the 'Noche', but the language of the poem points beyond itself to a meaning which cannot be limited to its apparent literal sense. What kind of meaning that might be will also emerge from my discussion of the 'Cántico'. Rather than repeating what I and others have written elsewhere about their sources and stylistic techniques, I shall try to show how their dialogue with other literary traditions, and the poetic language created out of this encounter, themselves represent a fundamentally theological vision of creation and humanity.

THE 'NOCHE'[1]

In the 'Noche' a woman tells how she left her house at night, secretly and in disguise, to meet her lover and be united with him.[2] In the first four verses she narrates her journey – dark, dangerous, yet with a guiding light. We assume she arrives safely, though we do not witness their encounter. Instead, the fifth verse is addressed to the night which transformed them each into the other. The final three verses appear to describe their joyful rest after the ecstasy of love-making. The language and imagery of the poem suggest that it is a celebration of a purely human love. There are no words which point to a religious meaning. Read, however mistakenly, as a poem of erotic love, it succeeds brilliantly. It speaks of the mystery, wonder, tenderness and intimacy of a truly mutual relationship; it reveals sexual love as discovery, encounter, transformation, fulfilment. It is the complete opposite of the brutal and explicit treatment of sex in, say, *La Celestina*: sex as chase, possession, power. The poem does not attempt to describe sexual union, though the exclamations of the fifth verse testify to its joy. The language of the last three stanzas is physical, but in the most delicate way: mutual caressing against the background of the refreshing breezes of the night. Reciprocity governs the love-making: each is transformed into the other, each caresses the other, each rests on the other. At the end of the poem the woman's senses are suspended, all activity ceases and all cares are abandoned.

Of all San Juan's poems, then, the 'Noche' poses the question of meaning most sharply, because it is a beautiful poem of human love which appears to need no further explanation, certainly not the spiritual interpretation San Juan applies to it in his commentaries. For such reasons, critics have tended to find it the least convincing of his major poems as a piece of religious art. The strongest proponent of a purely human sense has been José Nieto, who has attacked all other critics for 'la pertinaz e insistente negación del *sentido obvio* y vivencial del poema' (p. 49), 'their stubborn and insistent denial of the *obvious* experiential *meaning* of the poem'.[3] He presumably means that since it contains no obviously religious language it cannot have a religious meaning. But the hermeneutical issues he identifies are common to all the *lira* poems. None of them is clearly or unambiguously religious: words like 'divino' or 'cristalina' in the 'Cántico' belong as much to secular as sacred traditions of poetic discourse. The 'Llama', as he himself notoriously recognizes, is susceptible of an obviously erotic interpretation, especially at the end of the first verse.[4] Only in San Juan's popular poems does a religious sense become explicit. But its absence should not lead us to adopt so polarized an attitude: it was a common exegetical principle that the literal sense of scripture had to be established firmly before any allegorical or mystical interpretations could be attached to it, as Luis de León clearly stated.[5] One should therefore expect the poem to have its own consistency as a metaphor, and to work as such, like the biblical Song itself.

It is not clear, therefore, why Nieto singles out the 'Noche' for different treatment. It is true that the distance between the poem and its commentary is greater than in the case of the *Cántico* or *Llama*. It is also true that the poem can be read as erotic verse of the highest order and does not demand a spiritual interpretation. As R. O. Jones wrote, 'unless we respond to the sexuality the poem must fail of its full effect'.[6] Critics may wish to disregard San Juan's explanations for any of these poems, on the grounds that authorial intention is a problematic guide, or that his subsequent rationalizations vitiate their lyrical beauty. But the 'palabra' of the poem – its stated meaning – is not as simple or obvious as Nieto maintains. Like the 'Pastorcico', the 'Fonte' and the other *liras*, its words have many resonances and are often in intertextual dialogue with traditions both of secular and spiritual love poetry. Like them, it is woven around a symbol which gives the poem openness and depth.

The narrative and stylistic techniques of the 'Noche' themselves suggest a meaning beyond that of a secular love poem of its age. There is an inherent mystery about it, which arises from the text itself, the story it tells and the language it uses, not from the imposition of extraneous interpretations, either in San Juan's own commentary or in the reader's mind. I fully agree with Luce López-Baralt when she writes that the complexities of the poem's meaning derive from 'razones estrictamente poéticas intrínsecas al poema exento', 'strictly poetic reasons intrinsic to the poem in itself'.[7] It asks for explanations which it does not provide; it creates uncertainties and does not resolve them.

The first of these surrounds the identity of the protagonists. The author is male, yet the voice of the poem is female. A male author recounting a sexual encounter from the female point of view is not uncommon in the traditions of *cancionero* poetry. No names are given; they are identified generically, as 'amado' and 'amada', 'beloved' and 'lover', as they are in the 'Cántico'. But in striking contrast to that poem, in the 'Noche' neither is described, nor does either speak of the other's beauty, nor is there any direct verbal communication between them. The woman speaks in the first person, except in the fifth stanza, when she seems to stand back from the action and observe herself in a more detached way, as 'amada' transformed in or into her lover.[8] While she dominates the narrative, the male figure remains entirely passive, awaiting her, then asleep (vv. 4, 6). Critics and translators have usually read the seventh verse as an exception, applying the words 'con su mano serena/en mi cuello hería/y todos mis sentidos suspendía', 'with his calm hand/he wounded my neck/and suspended all my senses' (v. 7), to the man, probably because it is reminiscent of Song 2.9 (though with a characteristic reversal of roles). Others have pointed out that this does not easily fit the grammar, which requires the subject of 'su mano' and of the verbs to be 'el ayre del almena', the breeze blowing from the battlements, an altogether more delicate image than that of the love-bruise.[9] Conversely, the possessive adjective in the second line of the verse, 'quando yo *sus* cavellos esparcía', 'when I stroked *his* hair', must refer to the Beloved's hair, which is why '*su* mano' could be *his* hand, as he responds to her caresses, rather than a metaphor for the breeze (my emphases). This reading is possible if the line 'el ayre del almena' is detached from the structure of the sentence which follows, and is read as a further definition of the breeze announced at the end of the previous verse. Strangeness of grammatical construction is a marked feature of San Juan's poetry, and it creates ambiguities. These are not the only mysteries. The solid architectural imagery of the first two stanzas, with the house and the staircase, gives way to the less physical, more paradoxical space of the illumined night through which the woman journeys (vv. 3–4) to 'quien yo bien me savía', 'he whom well I knew', and to her finding him 'en parte donde naide parecía', 'in a place where no one appeared'. Thus, when he might at last be expected to be identified he is only alluded to by a periphrastic expression with its roots in the Song ('quem diligit anima mea', 'he whom my soul loveth') and found in the 'Cántico' ('aquél que yo más quiero', 'he whom I love most', C 2). Equally, the locus of their union can only be defined negatively, as somewhere where no one else was present. This too is characteristic of the world of the 'Cántico', with its insistence on solitude for the lovers ('y no parezca nadie en la montiña', 'let no one appear on the mountain', CA 25; 'Que nadie lo mirava', 'For no one was looking', CA 39).

The sense of not being seen is already present at the start ('salí sin ser notada', 'I left without being noticed'), and in the third verse prepares the way for the meeting of the lovers: 'que naide me veýa/ni yo mirava cosa', 'for no one saw me/nor did I see anything'.[10] Likewise, the end of the poem dissolves into intangibility, this time through verbal forms: 'Quedéme y olbidéme', 'cessó todo, y dexéme/dexando mi cuydado/[. . .] olbidado', 'I stayed and I forgot myself', 'everything finished, and I left myself/leaving my care/[. . .] forgotten'. The journey through the night, therefore, leads to an undefined place where love is celebrated between two anonymous lovers. Only after the apostrophe to the night which joined the lovers does physical imagery return, with the caresses of the lovers in (or by) the breeze from the cedars and the battlements. This foregrounding of concrete and physical images against an otherwise largely unseen or indeterminate background is a notable feature of this poem.[11] They stand out against the dark background in a way many of those in the 'Cántico' do not – the house in the first verse, the stairway and the house in the second, the burning light in the heart in the third, the midday light in the fourth, the breezes from the cedars in the sixth and the series of physical images in the seventh; but above all, the lilies of the last line, the sudden appearance of which against the darkness gives them a power and a presence which is found nowhere else in Golden Age poetry.[12]

This brings us close to the heart of San Juan's gifts as a lyrical poet: his ability to take a word or an image in common use in the poetry of the period and make it shine as if freshly minted. We have seen something of the same process at work in his treatment of popular paradox, of which there is a particularly fine example in this poem, in the profound and original treatment given to the *topos* of light and darkness, or, more precisely, to the light shining in the darkness of John 1.5. The 'Noche' is a poem of the night, and nightscapes impose their own particular constraints, as they do in painting: one thinks of the brutal light of Goya's 'Los fusilamientos del 3 de mayo' or the play of light and shadow in El Greco's 'Adoration of the Shepherds'; of the need for there to be a point of light so that whatever needs to be seen against the surrounding darkness can become visible. Renaissance lyrical poetry, especially in the pastoral mode, is a poetry of daylight; Garcilaso's eclogues, for example, follow their classical models in spanning the period from sunrise to sunset. Nocturnal imagery usually evokes the splendour of the night sky (as in Fray Luis de León's famous 'Noche serena' ode), through a restricted stock of images: the moon, the stars, and the singing of the nightingale being the commonest. These are conspicuously absent from the 'Noche'; indeed, sun, moon and stars play little part in the *lira* poems and, where they do, their appearance is either unexpected (the heavens as a 'prado de verduras/de flores esmaltado', 'meadow of green/enamelled with flowers' (C 4), or paradoxical, as 'la luz de mediodía', 'the light of noon', here.

Where, then, is the point of light in the 'Noche' which illuminates the nightscape of the poem? In the first three verses San Juan constructs the atmosphere with great care, insisting through repetition and variation on the pervasiveness of the night: 'En una noche escura', 'sin ser notada', 'ascuras', 'a escuras', 'en la noche', 'en secreto', 'que naide me veía', 'ni yo mirava cosa', 'sin otra luz' ('On a dark night', 'without being noticed', 'in the dark' (twice), 'in the night', 'in secret', 'for no one saw me', 'nor did I look at anything', 'with no other light'). But all the time the character of the night is changing, as other definitions come into play. There is a sense of anxiety and danger in the first two verses, marked by 'con ansias', 'anxiously', and by the emphasis on secrecy and disguise, as if the speaker fears to be followed. But alongside it, almost from the beginning, is a sense of joy and a growing light to guide her. The narrative of the quest is twice interrupted by the exclamation '¡oh dichosa ventura!', 'o happy fortune!', in the same position (line 3) in the first two verses, anticipating some as yet unknown but joyful outcome.[13] The second verse begins by repeating the darkness motif but associates it with safety – 'ascuras y segura', 'in the dark and safely' – counterbalancing the anxiety of the first. It is not surprising, therefore, that by the start of the third verse the opening 'En una noche escura' has become 'en la noche dichosa', 'on the happy night', as the tone of fear and secrecy recedes and a dark night becomes the night of joy. This gradual transition prepares the way for the celebration of night's power to guide and to unite in the fourth and fifth verses, and its disappearance into the background in the caresses and peaceful rest of the last three verses, which contain no explicit mention of night at all.

This transition is also mirrored in the syntax of the first five verses. The first three are constructed almost entirely out of a series of adverbial phrases, in a way I have elsewhere identified as typical of sections of the 'Cántico':[14]

En una noche escura	On a dark night
con ansias en amores	with love's anxieties
sin ser notada	without being noticed
estando ya mi casa sosegada	my house being at rest
ascuras [= a oscuras]	in the dark
por la secreta escala	by the secret staircase
a escuras	in the dark
estando ya mi casa sosegada	my house being at rest
en la noche	in the night
en secreto	in secret
sin otra luz	with no other light
sino la que en el coraçón	except the one in the heart

Dámaso Alonso noted more than half a century ago the paucity of main verbs in long stretches of San Juan's poetry.[15] Indeed, in the first three verses of the 'Noche' there is only one, 'salí', 'I left', at the start of the fourth line of the first verse – exactly the same main verb and in almost the same position as the 'salí' at the start of the fifth line of the first verse of the 'Cántico'.[16] Otherwise, San Juan adopts the highly original technique of constructing the narrative of a journey out of disjointed phrases like these. That one scarcely notices is a testimony to the skilful way he handles it. But they have another function: to represent in the poem's syntax the difficulty of the journey which is its subject, made hesitatingly and with no clear view of the destination. Curiously, their repeated presence lends a kind of consistency to the verse, underlined by the fact that the first two verses share the same rhyming pattern ('-ura', '-ada'), while the '-ía' rhymes of the third are continued into the fourth. Fragmentation and coherence coexist, indicative of the breaking of traditional patterns at one level, but of remaking at another. Indeed, the syntactical contrast in the fourth verse could scarcely be greater: in place of the short phrases and absence of verbs comes a single overarching sentence, which begins with the theme of guidance foreshadowed at the end of the third verse, but moves on to the destination and the waiting Beloved. The fifth verse consists of three anaphoric apostrophes to the night, each defining a quality it possesses, and each longer than the preceding one. This verse is characterized by a series of internal rhymes and assonances which represent in the sound patterns of the poem the union the verse celebrates: 'guiaste/amable más que' across the first two lines and a series of '-ada' and '-ado' sounds in the second, fourth and fifth (my emphases):

¡*O noche*, que gui*aste*!	O night that guided!
¡*O noche* am*able más que* la albor*ada*!	O night more lovely than the dawn!
¡*O noche* que jun*taste*	O night that joined
am*ado* con am*ada,*	beloved with lover,
am*ada* en el am*ado* transfor*mada*!	lover transformed into the beloved.

Through the first four verses light gradually emerges to illuminate the nightscape and become the transforming night of the fifth. It appears first in the guise of the metaphorical flames of love, a topos of love poetry both sacred and profane: the speaker may journey 'con ansias' but her anxiety is 'en amores inflamada', 'inflamed in love'.[17] They reappear at the end of the third verse, in conjunction with light and guidance: 'sin otra luz y guía/sino la que en el coraçón ardía', 'with no other light or guide/than the one burning in my heart'. Now it becomes clear that the light which guides her through the darkness is the fire of love which sent her forth in the first place. Fire and light in Petrarchan tradition are usually associated with the passion the woman arouses and the dazzling beauty her presence displays. San Juan's treatment is different, however, since the fire of love becomes what it has been implicitly all along, the light which not only shines but burns within the lover to guide her through the darkness to the place of union. This inner, burning, guiding light expands through the fourth verse: 'Aquésta [luz] me guiava/más cierto que la luz del mediodía', 'That light guided me/more surely than the light of noon'. The hyperbole is extreme: this inner light is brighter than the burning light of the midday sun, the brightest term of comparison possible (and this from a poet who experienced its intensity in Spain).

Yet no sooner has it become clear that the light which illumines the journey through the night is an internal one which outshines the sun at the height of its powers than the poem makes a dramatic leap. The third verse introduces the light as 'guía', 'guide'; the fourth describes how the inner flames of love 'guiaba', 'guided' the lover to her goal.

When the fifth exclaims: '¡Oh noche que guiaste!', 'O night that guided', the very thing which at the start of the journey seemed to be the source of danger has become the means of safe arrival at the destination. San Juan's polyptoton ('guiaba', 'guiaste'), with its shift from an imperfect to a preterite tense, marks the night as having definitively achieved what until this moment has been credited to the guiding inner light. It seems that night, the time when it is most easy to lose one's way, is one and the same as the guiding light and the fire of love. Having introduced into the poem a vivid contrast between the secret, nocturnal world the woman travels through in safety and the inner light which shines with undiminished power in its midst to guide her steps, San Juan then erases the distinction at its heart. If this light is both inward and metaphorical yet belongs to the guiding night, must not the night itself, presented at the start in so tangible a way, as the woman leaves the house and descends the stairway, also be part of this same internal landscape? If it is not, how can it be illumined from within itself and act as guide? And in what sense can such a transformation be thought of as part of a poem which is straightforwardly and undeniably erotic? The poem poses too many questions and answers too few of them for it to fit into any simple category or be subject to a single interpretation. In fact, its revelation that both light and darkness belong to the inner world of the lover and that both symbolize her journey, from the moment of her setting forth to its successful conclusion, is entirely consistent with the broad outlines of San Juan's treatment of the night in his commentary, which takes each point on the trajectory of the soul, from her point of departure through danger and obstacle and sudden inflammations of love to the desired goal, as part of the single overriding symbol of the night.

The night becomes the principal protagonist of the poem as it leads the woman to her lover in the hesitant steps of the first three verses. Once its positive role has been established, it occupies the centre stage, first as guide (v. 4) then as the object of celebratory apostrophe, foreshadowed in the earlier exclamations of the first two verses ('¡oh dichosa ventura!'). Its work is then complete; it recedes into the background as the focus switches to the lovers. The final three verses are, in syntactical terms, a mirror image of the first three, in that the poem returns, if to a lesser extent, to the broken, hesitant phrases which characterized them:

En mi pecho	In my breast
allí	there
quando yo	when I
con su mano	with his hand
en mi cuello	on my neck
sobre el amado	upon the Beloved
entre las açucenas	among the lilies

There are more main verbs, though these indicate states, rather than actions, with the single exception of 'recliné me', 'I leant.' The static feel of these verses counterbalances the movement of the first three, offering a picture of lovers' rest after their union in the night.

Though the night is textually absent from the closing verses it remains the context in which the picture is drawn. If the first half of the poem sets a burning light in its midst by which its purpose and meaning are illumined, the last three verses belong not to the world of sight but of touch, and are the most physical of the entire poem. In his famous 'Ode to a Nightingale' Keats is able to picture by night the intense beauty of early May in England because the sounds and scents which reach him in the 'embalmèd darkness' enable him to imagine the lovely things he cannot see. San Juan achieves a similar effect through images of touch: the weight of the lover asleep on the woman's breast, her caresses, the breeze from the cedar trees which fan them (v. 6); the breeze from the battlements as she runs her fingers through his hair, and the wounding of her neck with its (or his) gentle hand, which brings her to ecstasy (v. 7); her face lying upon the Beloved. Only the mysterious image of the lilies where she abandons her cares belongs to the realm of the visual. The poetic effect of introducing an image otherwise alien to the language of the poem in the very last line, one which is all whiteness and perfume against the nightscape of the rest, is extraordinary. Apart from the darkness and the light of the midday sun, the only two natural images which prepare for the sudden appearance of the lilies are the 'pecho florido', the 'flowering breast' and the 'ventalle de cedros', the 'fanning of cedars' of verse 7. At the start the poem draws on architectural images ('casa', 'escala', 'almena'; 'house', 'ladder', 'battlements') and at the end, on physical and tactile ones ('pecho', 'cabellos', 'mano', 'cuello', 'rostro'; 'breast', 'hair', 'hand', 'neck', 'face'). In that respect it is quite unlike the 'Cántico' and more like the 'Llama', which also has images of wound, hand, touch, breast and breathing.

What kind of language, then, is this? Do the poem's sources shed any light on its perplexities? Its relationship to the biblical Song of Songs is less direct than in the case of the 'Cántico'. Some of its images belong to the orient – the cedars (of Lebanon; Song 1.16 [.17], 5.15, 8.9), the 'almenas' (not in the Song, though military imagery dominates in 6.9–12 [.10–13]) and 'açucenas' (Song 2.16, 6.1–2 [.2–3], 7.2; both words of Semitic origin). The blowing of the wind (4.16) and the caressing and wounding (4.9, 8.3) of the last three verses may also derive from the Song, though San Juan alters the original, as he does in the 'Cántico', so that the woman rests on the man as well as he on her bosom, and (in one reading) he wounds her, as opposed to being wounded by her (4.9, Vg only). But the whole poem grows out of two episodes in the Song, where the Bride twice leaves her house at night to search the city for her Beloved. On the first occasion she does not find him to begin with (3.1–3), but once she does will not let him go until she brings him into her mother's chamber (3.4). On the second occasion he knocks at the door of her house but is gone by the time she opens it, and the watchmen of the city wound her as she searches for him again (5.2–7).[18] From these episodes San Juan creates one single uninterrupted journey; there are no watchmen to wound the lover; the locus of union is vaguely defined, somewhere 'outside' the house.

There are other parallels. Ovid's account of the story of Pyramus and Thisbe describes Thisbe leaving her house at night:

Callida per tenebras versato cardine Thisbe
egreditur fallitque suos adopertaque vultum
pervenit ad tumulum dictaque sub arbore sedit.
Audacem faciebat amor.

Now Thisbe, carefully opening the door, steals out through the darkness, seen of none, and arrives duly at the tomb with her face well veiled and sits down under the trysting-tree. Love made her bold.[19]

Many of the same elements recur in the 'Noche', though the context is very different: the dark night, the leaving unobserved, the disguise, the arrival, the tree, and the boldness of love, implicit in San Juan's poem, where the initiative is taken by the woman. Perhaps this same passage lay behind a passage in Garcilaso's second eclogue, where cruel fate:

hizo que de mi choza saliese
por el silencio de la noche'scura [. . .]
Al pie d'un olmo hice allí mi asiento,
y acuérdome que ya con ella estuve
pasando allí la siesta al fresco viento.[20]

love made me leave my cabin
in the silence of the dark night [. . .]
At the foot of an elm there I sat down
and I remember how I was with her
spending the siesta there in the cool breeze.

In his rewriting of these words to give them a spiritual meaning Sebastián de Córdoba has Silvano, representing the sensual part of man, speak thus of Celia, the soul:

Esta [mi cruda suerte] me hizo, al fin, que me saliesse
por el silencio de la noche escura
a buscar un lugar donde muriesse,
   Y encaminando por mi desventura,
estos enfermos pies me conduxeron
sobre una torre de muy grande altura;
   Mis ojos en el lugar reconocieron
que alguna vez miré de allí contento
los favores de amor que se me dieron
   Allí entre dos almenas hize assiento,
y acuérdome que ya con ella estuve
las noches del verano al fresco viento.[21]

> [My harsh fortune] at last made me leave
> through the silence of the dark night
> to seek a place where I might die,
> and travelling along in my misfortune
> these sick feet led me
> up a very high tower;
> in that place my eyes recognized
> that once I gazed happily from there
> on the favours of love bestowed upon me.
> There between two battlements I sat down
> and remember how I was with her [Celia]
> on summer nights in the cool breeze.

Apart from the acknowledged debt to him at the beginning of the *Llama* commentary, this is the place San Juan comes closest to the *contrafacta* of Córdoba.[22] But it knows nothing of a night ablaze with light, the wounds of love's caresses, or lilies. Each of these images opens out on to a wider horizon.

The paradox of a night radiant with light has two important biblical forerunners.[23] The first is the 'columna ignis per noctem', the pillar of fire by night of Exodus 13.21–2, which went before the children of Israel to guide them by night in their wanderings through the wilderness. The second, like the poem, erases the antithesis: 'Et nox illumnatio mea in deliciis meis. Quia tenebrae non obscurabantur a te, et nox sicut dies illuminabitur; sicut tenebrae eius, ita et lumen eius', 'Even the night shall be light about me. Yea, the darkness hideth not from thee; but the night shineth as the day: the darkness and the light are both alike to thee' (Psalm 138.[139.]11–12). Both these passages find liturgical expression in the 'Exsultet', the proclamation sung at the Easter Vigil as Christ rises from the night of death to the dawn of Easter, in which the night of Holy Saturday becomes the *beata nox*, or 'noche dichosa', of a new Exodus which renews the whole creation and procures the salvation of the human race:

> Most blessed of all nights, chosen by God
> to see Christ rising from the dead!
>
> Of this night scripture says:
> 'The night will be clear as day:
> it will become my light, my joy.'
> [. . .]
> Night truly blessed when heaven is wedded to earth
> and man is reconciled with God![24]

By aligning the Lover's quest and its fulfilment with the great archetypes of biblical narrative, Exodus, death to resurrection, the poem can be seen participating in the journey every human soul is called to undertake.

Another biblical allusion is embedded in the poem. In verse 6, the Beloved rests on the lover's breast, caressing him; in the last verse, she leans her face against him. The gesture is reminiscent of the Beloved Disciple of John 13.23, 'Erat ergo recumbens unus ex discipulis eius in sinu Iesu, quem diligebat Iesus', 'Now there was leaning on Jesus' bosom one of his disciples, whom Jesus loved.' But here it is first reversed: he reclines on her. Such reversals of biblical images are not accidental.[25] The gesture follows immediately upon the transformation of the lovers each into the other. From that moment what can be attributed to the one can equally well be predicated of the other, because in union each becomes the other. San Juan's rewriting of the biblical image is intended to highlight this interchange, in which the Beloved Disciple becomes Christ and Christ the Beloved Disciple. In the last stanza, as the lover adopts the disciple's role, the mutuality of giving and receiving between the lovers is complete.

But most mysterious of all are the lilies in the final line. The Song has eight references to them. In their dialogue at the beginning of Chapter 2 the Bride calls herself 'lilium convallium', and the Bridegroom responds by calling her 'lilium inter spinas'. Twice she refers to him as feeding among the lilies (2.16; 6.2[.3]); on the second occasion she also speaks of his coming into his garden to gather lilies (6.1[.2]). Physical features of both lovers are also described in the same metaphor: she likens his lips to lilies (5.13), he likens her breasts to twin fawns feeding among lilies (4.5), and the Chorus likens her belly to a heap of wheat set round with lilies (7.2). Lilies therefore are associated with both protagonists and are mentioned by all the speakers. They have no fixed significance, but they are always associated with feeding or with physical features. Sometimes, as when the Bridegroom comes to gather lilies from his garden, they seem to indicate the consummation of love; at other times, their whiteness is a metaphor for breasts and belly and their fragrance for lips (sharply divergent from the Petrarchan tradition, in which lips are always red and associated with roses or carnations).

Ynduráin has pointed to the symbolic meaning of these flowers as defined by Covarrubias: 'es el açucena simbolo de la castidad por su blancura, y de la buena fama por su olor' (p. 215), 'by its whiteness the lily is a symbol of chastity and by its scent of good reputation'. Of all flowers it is the one most closely associated with the Virgin Mary and the Annunciation, and it is a Marian symbol found in several ancient Carmelite hymns, for example the 'Flos Carmeli', attributed to St Simon Stock (c. 1165–1265). Had San Juan reached this line in his commentary, he might have said something along those lines. If, following the Song, the Beloved feeding among the lilies or picking them in the garden is a metaphor for his caressing of her breasts or his possessing her, her cares of love are forgotten in fulfilment. But the truth of the matter is that the lilies in San Juan's poem have a mystery about them which goes beyond any sense they may have in the Song, and that mystery is incorporated into its final words. There is no real closure, only a new picture, compelling and strange, open to the imagination. San Juan's use of biblical and liturgical elements in the 'Noche', like the stylistic techniques we have analysed, represent the movement by which lover and Beloved, separated at the start by distance and darkness, become each other through a process of linguistic transformation. The strangeness of the language and the techniques San Juan uses, together with the puzzles of meaning embodied in the text, result in a rich and mysterious poem which cannot be reduced to a purely secular or sacred significance. Its art transcends the divide and gives value to both, as a love poem which is rooted in human experience yet which embraces the divine.

THE 'CÁNTICO'[26]

The 'Cántico' also tells a story, if a less coherent one, through its shifting perspectives of time and place. A cry of pain breaks in on the silence, addressed to an unseen, absent Beloved (1). It tells of a relationship which has been broken off, a wound left behind when he fled as a stag, a searching for him only to find him gone. There is no reply. In desperation, the speaker, identified only as 'Esposa', the Bride, asks some shepherds to tell the Beloved of her terrible grief if they should see him as they go about their work (2). In the ensuing silence (they remain deaf to her pleas) she announces her firm intention to go in search of her love, whatever the obstacles may be (3). For the third time she asks for news of him, now from the woods and meadows he himself has planted, to tell her if he has passed through them (4). For the first time there is a reply: the silence of the Beloved and of the shepherds is broken by the speech of inanimate nature. Its inhabitants, the creatures, tell her that he passed swiftly through their world and made them beautiful with a glance; but the swiftness of his passage implies that he has already gone (5).

This is an extraordinary beginning for a sixteenth-century poem. It treats of familiar subjects – love and its tribulations, in a familiar place – a pastoral landscape. But it cries out for explanation in its silences. The Beloved has vanished; but why? What kind of a world is this, in which inanimate woods, thickets and flowery meads reply when the Beloved and the shepherds have ignored her cries? Nature is often the passive witness, occasionally the active participant in the pastoral love poetry of the Renaissance, but never a speaker who intervenes so strangely.[27] And why, now that a reply has come, does this cause the Bride to burst into fresh expressions of grief?

The sixth verse is addressed once more to the Beloved. In her distress she calls on him to give himself to her, and to stop sending messengers, who only increase her pain by speaking of his many favours (7). She wonders how she can remain alive, pierced by arrows of love (8); turns to him again in anger, accusing him of failing to heal the wound he has caused and to carry off the spoils of her heart (9); and pleads for the sight of him, her only light (10). The messengers must surely be the elements of nature which have just spoken. But these stanzas move away from the external world to her inner state, suggesting that he is present to her inwardly, if only through the wound he has caused and the longing he arouses. The references to life, heart and eyes (vv. 8–10) and the imagery of the arrow of love and of her conception of something of the Beloved within herself (v. 8) give this a sharply physical expression.[28] Yet once again there is silence: the Beloved remains absent; no answers come.

She turns to the silvery waters of a fountain, desiring to see reflected in them 'de repente', 'suddenly', the very eyes of which she carries a sketch within herself. The periphrastic 'lo que del Amado', 'something of the Beloved' conceived within herself

(8) redefines itself as 'los ojos deseados/que tengo en mis entrañas dibuxados', 'the eyes I long for/which in my inmost self I have portrayed'. In the previous verse her wish was 'may my eyes see you'; now the terms are reversed: 'may I see your eyes'. To gaze upon the reflection of the Beloved in the water is a venerable literary topos.[29] But she is on the brink of a sudden and decisive change in her fortunes, because her next words reveal that not only has her wish been fulfilled but that what she most desired – to see her Beloved's eyes – has sent her suddenly into rapturous flight. Whatever other mysteries there have been in the poem, it is here that one first encounters that disconcerting shift in narrative from absence to presence without any explanation of how it has come about. The intermediate stages are suppressed: we pass straight from her expression of desire to her reaction when it has been fulfilled. The conditional 'si formases los ojos deseados', 'if you should form the eyes I long for', addressed to the fountain, becomes the imperative 'Apártalos', 'Take them away!' addressed to the Beloved, whose eyes, textually present only as the enclitic pronoun '-los', are too much for her to bear. The Beloved's self-revelation therefore takes place in the silence between two stanzas, and is not described, or cannot be.

Now he speaks for the first time in the poem, calling the Bride back from her ecstatic flight. In the first verse he had fled like a stag and she had borne the wound; now he appears as the stag who is himself wounded.[30] His sudden presence releases from the Bride a torrent of vivid and sensuous images which describe him across the next three verses (13–15), one per line, and which lack any main verb: mountains, wooded valleys, distant islands, sounding streams, whistling breezes, the calm night before the dawn rises, silent music, resonating solitude, the supper which revives and causes love.[31] She then describes the marriage bed, flowering, entwined with lions' caves, with purple linen, built in peace and crowned with a thousand golden shields. There is no logical sequence to the images, though they tend to move from plural forms to singular and from the world of nature to human artifice. The mystery of the poem increases. What is the relationship between the Beloved and the images she uses, given that the copulative verb is suppressed? Is he identical with them or like them? Does the order in which they come have significance? CA 13 partly uses the language of the Renaissance *locus amoenus*, with its woods, rivers and breezes; but the mountains and strange islands do not fit this. CA 14 is even more difficult: the first two images are natural (calm night before the dawn), then from human art (music, but paradoxically silent), a state (solitude, but resonant), and finally, human society (the supper which refreshes and increases love).

From CA 16–26 the poem shifts between past, present and future, sometimes pausing at a particular moment, at other times in dialogue between the lovers or addressing other persons. Young girls follow the Beloved's tracks, the touch of a spark and spiced wine, 'emissiones de bálsamo divino', 'outpourings of divine balsam', one of the few phrases in the poem with a possible religious sense (though 'divino' was frequently used to describe a woman's beauty in secular love poetry). The Bride then describes how she drank in the Beloved's wine-cellar, prompted perhaps by the 'adobado vino', 'spiced wine', of the previous verse, but when she emerged knew nothing and lost her flock. It was the place of their betrothal (18); now she has no other flock or office than loving him (19), and though her former companions will say that she has been lost, because she no longer appears on the common, she was lost in love and has been found (20). At 21 she addresses the Bridegroom again, describing garlands of flowers and emeralds they will make and twine in her hair; but at once returns to a past moment, when he became caught on a strand of her hair as he watched it fluttering on her neck, and was wounded in one of her eyes (22). Reference to his looking upon her continues through the next two verses: his eyes impressed grace upon her (23; another word with possible religious connotations) and he loved her even more. It is strange, therefore, that she asks him not to despise her because of her dark colour (24), since he has already given her grace and beauty. The address changes again: companions are asked to chase the vixen away from the flowering vine, while Bride and Beloved make a bouquet of roses in solitude (25). She calls on the north wind to cease and the south wind to blow through her garden so that its spices may flow and the Beloved come to feed among the flowers (26).

Now, for four verses, he speaks for the second time. He describes the Bride's entry into the garden and her resting in his embrace. He looks back to their betrothal (28) – a betrothal which earlier had happened in the wine-cellar (18), but which here occurs under the apple tree, where her mother had been violated. He calls on a host of creatures not to disturb the Bride's rest, secure behind the wall (29–30). As with 13–15, there is progression in the imagery, this time from the natural realm through human emotions to human artifice (music), but the images here seem to have negative connotations. In 31 the Bride appears to have awakened from the deep sleep the Bridegroom has just wished for her, and repeats a similar injunction to be left alone among the flowers and rose trees, addressed now to 'ninfas de Judea', 'nymphs of Judea', who are to stay outside and not cross the threshold. She turns to her dearest, 'Carillo', and asks him to do a number of puzzling things, though each recalls previous images: to hide, to look at the mountains, to say nothing, to look at the companies of her who goes by strange islands (32).

The Bridegroom speaks for the last time in 33–4, and the imagery changes. The Bride is now the dove who has returned with a branch and found her mate in solitude. In solitude she lived, there she has now made her nest, and there he guides her, himself wounded in solitude. When the Bride resumes, it is to close the poem looking towards a future in which they will travel deeper into nature and higher into mountain caves, to taste the juice of pomegranates (35–6). There he will show her what she desired and give her what he gave her 'el otro día' (37), 'the other day' (or 'yesterday'). That indefinable something is described in a final sequence of five images with no main verb: the breeze blowing, the nightingale singing, the graceful grove, the calm night, the flame which consumes but does not harm (38). The last verse returns to the past, and a series of imperfect tenses which are not easy to interpret after the futures and conditionals of the previous five verses. The fact that nobody was looking could be the answer to the prayer for solitude and no disturbance; but why Aminadab failed to appear is not explained, nor why, in a startling new image right at the end of the work, the cavalry should appear at the ending of the siege and descend to the waters (39).[32]

There is a narrative, of sorts, a movement from absence to presence, from abandonment to fulfilment, but quite unlike any found in the poetry of the age. It presents the reader with many puzzles and few clues as to their solution. In an earlier work I examined the poetic techniques San Juan uses in this poem to create so strange and beautiful a work of art, and I do not wish to go over that ground again.[33] Instead, I would like to approach the poem from a different perspective, to show how the language and the techniques it uses themselves mirror the subject it professes, the union of two lovers. I propose to follow the unity which emerges from the multiplicity of images and styles in the poem, to discover how through fusion of texts and traditions a unique poetic voice is created which rejoices in difference yet has a centre to which each separate component is related. In the end, I want to argue that this poetry is an integral part of San Juan's theological vision of the whole creation.[34] While remaining attentive to the language of the poem, in order to ask what kind of poem this is, I want to go beyond a critical approach concerned with identification of literary sources and analysis of rhetorical techniques. Like the 'Noche' but on a wider scale, the apparently fragmented narrative and language of the poem represent the movement from separation to union. But that movement is not something the critic imposes from without. It is inherent in the way San Juan handles language, which, as every critic of the Golden Age agrees, is unique for his time. For him, language cannot express the fulness of the truth but it can offer, through its disruption and reordering, glimpses of a transcendent reality beyond itself. In my earlier book I described how the stanzas are connected by repeated images (like mountains, flowers, water, air), syntactical structures (like the lack of any copulative verb in CA 13–15 or the long series of adverbial phrases), clusters of ideas (hiding, looking, beauty, solitude) and patterns of sound (alliteration, internal rhymes, repeated vowel sounds), all of which work to give the narrative fragments a sense of cohesion and act as points of stability amid the flux of images.[35] These ideas and images may be summarized as follows:

escondiste/escóndete/escondidas: 1, CA 32, 36
Amado/Amado: 1, 4, 8, CA 12–13, 17, 26–7, 35
salí/salía: 1, CA 17
ciervo/ciervos: 1, CA 12, 29
otero: 2, CA 12
amores/amorosos/enamora/amar/enamorada/amor/adamabas/adorar/amores:
  3, CA 13–14, 19–21, 23, 26
riberas: 3, CA 29, 33
montes, montañas, montiña, montañas, monte: 3, CA 13, 25, 32, 35
flores/florescidas/florescida/flores: 3, 4, CA 21, 25, 26, 31
passaré, passado: 4, 5
sotos/soto: 5, 38
mil gracias: 5, 7
hermosura: 5, CA 24, 35
llagan/llagado: 7, 9
muriendo/mueras: 7, 8

vida/viviendo/vives: 8
robado/robo/robaste: 9
ojos: 10, CA 11–12, 22–3
fuente/ríos/aguas/agua/aguas: CA 11, 13, 29, 35, 39
paloma/palomica/tortolica: CA 12, 33
aire: CA 12–13, 38
aspira, aspirar: CA 26, 38
valles: CA 13, 29
ínsulas estrañas: CA 13, 32
sonorosos/sonora: CA 13–14
soledad/soledad/a solas/soledad: CA 14, 34
noche/noches/noche: CA 14, 29, 38
leones: CA 15, 29
vino/bodega/beví: CA 16–17
ganado/ganado/ganada: CA 17, 19, 20
perdí/perdido/perdediza: CA 17, 20, 21
esposa/desposada/esposa: CA 18, 27–8, 30
cabello: CA 21–2
cuello: CA 22, 27
miraste/miravas/mirare/miraste/mirava: CA 22–4, 39
rosas/rosales: CA 25, 31
huerto/huerto: CA 26–7
entrado/entremos/entraremos: CA 27, 35, 36

The most noticeable among these are the different words for mountains and sources of water and the extended repetitions of words associated with flowers, solitude, love and looking.

What kind of a world is this? Looking first at the imagery of the poem, one observes that its natural landscapes occur in clustered groups. The first five stanzas have 'majadas', 'otero', 'montes', 'riberas', 'flores', 'bosques', 'espesuras', 'prado de verduras', 'flores', and 'sotos' ('sheepfolds', 'hill', 'mountains', 'banks', 'flowers', 'woods', 'thickets', 'meadow of green', 'flowers', 'groves'), before five stanzas of rhetorical complaint notably lacking in such imagery. Only when the fountain of CA 11 is addressed does another sequence begin, partly similar, partly different: 'otero', 'ayre', 'montañas', 'valles', 'ínsulas', 'ríos', 'ayres', 'noche', 'aurora' ('hill', 'breeze', 'mountains', 'valleys', 'islands', 'rivers', 'breezes', 'night', 'dawn'), to which a number of adjectives are attached. In this second sequence, too, birds and animals appear: the simile of the fleeing stag in the first verse is replaced by the Beloved imagining himself as a wounded stag and the Bride as a dove. Natural images then begin to give way to images from art: music (though silent), the reviving supper of love, the marriage bed with its carvings, fabrics and other decorations. Art, too, appears in the wine and the wine cellar of CA 16–17, but the appearance of 'bega', the fields by the river, in CA 17 returns to the more pastoral landscapes appropriate for the image of the shepherdess, the 'egido', or common land for grazing flocks. The flowers and emeralds of CA 21 mark a significant shift towards imagery of the human body, first the Bride's hair, then her neck, her eyes, his eyes, her dark skin.

From this point the world of nature reasserts is primacy: 'raposas', 'viña', 'rosas', 'montiña' (CA 25; 'vixen', 'vine', 'roses', 'mountain'); the opposing winds, 'cierço' and 'austro' ('north wind', 'south wind'), the 'huerto' ('garden') and its scented 'flores' (26–7). But in the garden physical images return, with the neck, arms and hand, and the mother's violation under the apple tree. CA 29 calls on creatures ('aves', 'leones, ciervos, gamos saltadores'; 'birds', 'lions', 'stags', 'leaping harts') and landscapes ('montes, valles, riberas,/aguas, ayres'; 'mountains', 'valleys', 'banks',/'waters', 'breezes') before passing to images from human art, especially the classical music of lyres and sirens' song (30). Perfumed flowers reappear in 31, and 'montañas' and 'ínsulas' (with the same adjective, 'estrañas' as in 13) in 32. The dove returns in 33, as both 'palomica' and 'tortolica', associated with her 'ramo', 'branch', as the biblical story requires, but also with the 'riberas verdes', 'green banks', where in the traditions of bestiaries she goes to mourn, but where in this poem she is reunited with her consort. 'Monte', 'collado', 'agua' and 'espesura' ('mountain', 'hill', 'water', 'thicket') mark 35; only 'collado' is a new image, but so are the 'subidas cabernas de la piedra', 'lofty caverns of stone' and the 'granadas', 'pomegranates', of 36. 37 lacks any such imagery, but its abstract 'aquello', 'that something', is transmuted into a whole series of images in 38, which define it, again with no copulative verb, as in CA 13–15. 'Ayre' returns; so does singing in a classical guise, except that it is birdsong ('el canto de la dulce filomena', 'the song of the sweet nightingale'), the 'soto', 'thicket', and 'noche', 'night'; but for the first time (unless the 'ardores' of CA 29 are counted) fire is seen, in the paradox of the 'llama que consume y no da pena', 'flame which consumes but without pain'. The final image of the poem, the cavalry descending 'a vista de las aguas', 'in sight of the waters', introduces for a last time water, the antithesis of fire.[36]

Images from nature and human art; images from biblical, classical and Renaissance traditions; images of wide landscapes, of mountains, woods and rivers, of plants and animals; images, many of which recur across the text; some of which point to the locus of the poem, others of which express the lovers' fear of disruptive elements and delight in each other's presence and beauty: all contribute to the creation of a world constituted of elements from the familiar world but arranged so that unexpected connections are made between them. In one sense, the fabric of the world is dismantled into its constituent parts, then rebuilt into new shapes. In another, a kind of unity is discernible between them, a new kind of world is created out of them as we read. It is the experience the poem represents that disrupts the normal vision of the world and provokes its rewriting. Language shines as if freshly created for that world, like language in the paradise of Eden. The wonder of the world can be sensed again, a world like Traherne's, where everything exists in bright immediacy before, as Wordsworth would later say, the child becomes an adult and weariness and cynicism exile 'the vision splendid', which fades 'into the common life of day'.[37] But in the 'Cántico' there is no such sense of loss. Here a world is gained as it is remade through the mutuality of love. Creation is affirmed, transfigured.

San Juan's use of rhyme also creates relationships between words to underpin significant linkages of meaning. Such are quiero/muero in 2, emphasizing the relationship between love and death most fully explored in 7–8; the movement from Amado/passado at the start (4), indicating absence, to Amado/vulnerado in 12, whose wounded presence marks a significant transition in the lover's quest; and camino/divino in CA 16, which is exactly the journey the lover is undertaking. After the frustrated 'salí' of the first verse, which yields no result, the rhyme salía/sabía in CA 17 makes going forth now lead to knowledge (or rather, that lack of knowing which is the prerequisite to finding true knowledge, the theme of CA 17–20). Hence, 'sciencia muy sabrosa', 'very enjoyable science', in CA 18 rhymes with 'Esposa', the one who has been taught it. Sometimes rhymes bring together similar words, like servicio/officio/exercicio in CA 19, to underline the Bride's emphatic assertion of her new devotion to the work of love. At other times they create contrasts: the common pasture, 'egido', of CA 20 is where people will say she is lost, 'me e perdido', because that is the locus of her former occupation, whereas the hallada/enamorada/ganada rhymes of its other three lines counterbalance this with a strong assertion of the relationship between finding, gaining and loving. Looking and loving are joined through miravas/adamavas (CA 23) and the importance of the 'huerto' as the place of union is highlighted by the rhymes Esposa/reposa and desseado/reclinado/Amado (CA 27): desire is fulfilled there, as the lover rests in the Beloved. The sense of love fulfilled is further enhanced by the palomica/tortolica of CA 33, who is associated with the rhymes tornado/desseado/hallado, linking desire with return and finding. The future tenses of CA 36, yremos/entraremos/gustaremos, create a dynamic series of interrelated actions which summarize the whole poem, from the journey of the opening stanzas to the entry into the garden and the coming enjoyment of the fruit of union. The caves where this will happen are subidas/escondidas, two important words in the lexis of San Juan, given his frequent use of images of ascent (often, paradoxically, in association with descent) and of hiddenness. These 'subidas/cabernas [. . . /] bien escondidas' are the only example in the poem of an enjambement which splits an epithet from its noun, yet its effect is to push the sense forward, to the hidden caverns. Finally, in at least two cases the rhymes combine antithetical elements: nido/querido/herido (CA 34) and filomena/serena/pena (CA 38) each create a relationship between two words with positive associations and one which introduces pain (even if in the latter case of a paradoxical kind).

Other sound patterns in the poem also create revealing effects. In CA 12, the lover's 'que voy de buelo' is countermanded by the Beloved's immediate response, 'buélvete'. Flight (movement away) is followed by return (movement towards), but the same consonantal and vocalic sounds, the alliterative 'v's, 'b's and 'l's and the 'ue' diphthongs, suggest that both movements are related. The aggressive 'raposas' of CA 25 are quickly followed by the restful 'reposa' of CA 27, a progression less easy to see in the second redaction (cf. CB 16, 22). Connections of this kind can also be found between poems, notably the 'lecho florido' of CA 15 and the 'pecho florido' of 'Noche' 6, both associated with love and with sleep.

Certain words and ideas, repeated at intervals across the poem, change their meaning as the narrative develops. We have already seen how the verb 'salir' 'to leave', occurs at the start for a search which brought no sight of the Beloved, but subsequently in connection with the lover's drinking of him in the wine cellar. But just as important is its counterpart, 'entrar', already implicit in 'la interior bodega' of CA 17, made explicit in the entrance of the Bride into the garden (CA 27), urged as entering the thicket in CA 35, and imagined as a future fruition of love in the lofty caverns of CA 36: 'allí nos entraremos', 'there we shall enter', one of the several places in the poem which answers the initial cry '¿adónde?', 'where?' (the others are CA 18 and 28). The three appearances of the word 'hermosura' also trace the journey of the lover. Beauty is first ascribed by the creatures to the Beloved's swift passage through the 'sotos' (5), the elements of creation where the lover sought him but found only traces of his presence. There it was consequential upon grace: 'Mil gracias derramando', 'Pouring down a thousand graces.' This same conjoining then becomes the gift of the Beloved to the lover, 'gracia y hermosura en mí dexaste' (CA 24), 'grace and beauty you left in me'. Finally, having moved from the grace and beauty of creation to the grace and beauty of the lover, with which her Beloved has now endowed her, beauty is predicated of him, and through him, of nature, as she looks forward to seeing 'en tu hermosura/al monte y al collado', 'in your beauty/the mountain and the hill'. Creation, lover and Beloved each possess beauty, but in ascending order, from effect to cause.

The way the theme of hiddenness develops across the poem is another important marker of meaning. It begins with the lover's desperate cry '¿Adónde te escondiste?', 'Where did you hide?' The sudden revelation of his presence is associated with his eyes (CA 11–12), losing and finding (CA 19–20) and looking (CA 22–4). But after her entry into the garden the Bride's language changes. No longer does she ask her absent Beloved where he hid, she appears to contradict herself by commanding him to hide: 'Escóndete, Carillo', 'Hide, my darling', before they ascend to the caverns of stone 'que están bien escondidas', 'which are well hidden'. The meaning of hiddenness cannot be fixed in the poem; it shifts from representing the pain of absence at the start to the intimate communion of the lovers in the closing stanzas, which must mean that everything that has happened between those two points has turned what was once a cry of pain into the source of great joy and fulfilment. Hence the same words have turned full circle in meaning.

Even those elements critics have found intrusive appear less so when examined more closely, because they do not exist in isolation. The sudden appearance of classical images in a largely biblical poem is more noticeable in CA, where the 'amenas liras/y canto de serenas', 'pleasant lyres/and sirens' song' of CA 30 are followed in CA 31 by the 'ninfas de Judea', so that three of the poem's four classical references occur in rapid succession (cf. CB 21, 18). The first two relate to music, while the 'canto de serenas' itself looks forward to 'el canto de la dulce filomena' in CA 38, the fourth of the classical references (though Cupid's arrows make an allusive appearance in 8). Earlier, music was one of the attributes of the Beloved, the 'música callada' of CA 14; we have already noted the syntactical parallel between CA 13–15 and CA 38. The lyres and sirens are a calming influence, though the nymphs are potentially disruptive, since they are commanded to keep their distance. The military image with which the poem so unexpectedly concludes, the ending of the siege and the horsemen's descent to the waters, also has precursors which connect it with the sleep of love – the marriage bed of CA 15, 'de mil escudos de oro coronado', 'crowned with a thousand shields of gold', and the potential attack on the Bride's slumber in her walled sanctuary in CA 29–30. One may justly conclude, therefore, that even where the images seem aleatory, they form part of patterns embedded in the text.

Of all the rhetorical tropes of repetition San Juan uses, polyptoton is the commonest:[38]

> escondiste/escóndete/escondidas: 1, CA 32, 36
> amores/amorosos/enamora/amar/enamorada/amor/adamabas/amores: 3, CA 13–14, 19–21, 23, 26
> flores/florescidas/florescida/flores: 3, 4, CA 21, 25, 26, 31
> muriendo/mueras: 7, 8
> vida/viviendo/vives: 8
> robado/robo/robaste: 9
> ganado/ganado/ganada: CA 17, 19, 20
> perdí/perdido/perdediza: CA 17, 20, 21
> miraste/miravas/mirare/miraste/mirava: CA 22–4, 39
> entrado/entremos/entraremos: CA 27, 35, 36
> soledad (four times)/a solas: CA 34

Many writers of the period used it – it is frequent in the early sonnets of Garcilaso, as a form of word-play – but none with quite such intensity as San Juan, perhaps because of its biblical pedigree: it is present, for example, in the opening words of the Song as he knew it, 'Osculetur me osculo oris sui', 'Let him kiss me with kisses of his mouth' (1.1). But he goes far beyond his contemporaries by placing four or five related words in close proximity. Why does he use it so consistently? One answer is that it draws attention to the insufficiency of language. In place of striving to find as many different ways as possible of saying the same thing, through the rapid flux of images or the puzzles posed by paradox, it marks the inability of language to express precisely what it means, reducing it to a frustrating dependence on one single word repeated in a variety of forms.

Both in the 'Noche' and in this poem San Juan uses the resources of language available to him to break and remake the familiar world, paralleling perhaps the breaking and remaking of habits, assumptions and desires which lies at the heart of San Juan's spiritual journey from an absent or distant God to union with a loving God. The same process can be seen if we turn to another much-debated issue, the poem's sources. I take as examples three very different areas, the biblical Song, popular *cancionero* poetry, and the devotional literature which nourished him. My prime concern is not to identify them but to ask what it means to read a poem which (depending on one's point of view) either shows a cavalier disregard for consistency of poetic diction by lumping together bits and pieces from various sources so that the joins show through, or has deliberately borrowed from as many as he could think of to give value to each but also to unite them for some larger purpose.

The Song of Songs has primacy of place among all the literary traditions in the poem, as scholars have consistently agreed. Many have identified the images which pass more or less directly from it into the 'Cántico'; others have noted how the poem imitates its biblical model in broader terms, through its frequent shifts of locations, times and speakers.[39] But San Juan's use of the Song in his 'Cántico' goes well beyond the practice of *imitatio* by the poets of his age, and for good reason. His view of the Bible as inspired and authoritative in all its parts, instead of limiting him, gave him the confidence to bring together texts from different books or (as with the Song) from different passages within the same book, so that the deeper sense of scripture could emerge through a process of mutual illumination. This is readily apparent in his commentaries, where, as we shall see in due course, he ranges so widely in his association of texts that modern readers are apt to suppose there is no connecting thread. But it marks his poetry too.

San Juan displays a remarkable sensitivity to the language of the Song in the Vulgate. Athalya Brenner, concerned principally with the literal poetic sense of the Hebrew text, points to the prevalence of parallelism, metre and rhythm, internal rhymes, refrains and recurrent expressions, similes and metaphors, repetitions of particular sounds, sound-play and word-play.[40] She writes of the lack of connectivity between verses and images (pp. 36–7), but of the way recurrent metaphors and symbols – the garden/vineyard/orchard, the gazelle, the dove, 'certain flowers, aromatics and perfumes, walls and fortifications' (pp. 15, 51–4) – provide points of linkage. Marcia Falk isolates four 'basic contexts' in the Song: '(a) the cultivated or habitable countryside; (b) the wild or remote natural landscape and its elements; (c) interior environments (houses, halls, rooms); (d) city streets'.[41] She further notes that the love monologues and dialogues take place largely in the countryside – pastures, groves, valleys, thickets, springtime blossom, rocks, hills, gardens, the shade of trees (pp. 139–40). San Juan reproduces all these stylistic features, metaphors and contexts (with the exception perhaps of city streets), in his own 'Cántico', as I have shown elsewhere.[42] Much of Spain shares more of a common topography with biblical Palestine than with the pastoral world imagined by English writers, and almost all the natural images of the 'Cántico' could be found there, even lions, which famously appear in the medieval epic *Poema de mio Cid* and in *Don Quijote*.[43] It is also possible that the apparent lack of continuity between some of the images in the poem may ultimately derive from an underlying Hebrew tendency to word-play. The Vulgate and other translations cannot reproduce the way Hebrew moves from one image to another because one Hebrew word may have several meanings, or because one word is played off against a similarly sounding one.[44]

Like the 'Noche', the 'Cántico' adopts a free approach to its biblical model, especially in the mutual exchange of attributes. The fleeing stag of the poem not only wounds the lover, which is the role of the watchmen in the Song, but then appears wounded himself. The biblical search for the Beloved through the city becomes the Bride's questioning of the natural elements. The lover desires to look into the

Beloved's eyes (CA 11); later, he looks upon her (CA 22–4). The lover in CA 26 calls on the south wind to blow through her garden, waiting for the Beloved to feed among its flowers; in CA 27 he describes her entry into what appears to be his garden, her penetration of his space. In CA 29–30 she calls on the creatures not to disturb his rest, reversing Song 2.7, where he adjures them to respect hers. By the time San Juan was writing, a whole series of *topoi* from the Song was part of the common inheritance of European literature. Though less frequent in occurrence than classical and Renaissance examples like the *locus amoenus*, *Beatus ille* or *Carpe diem*, motifs like the kisses of the mouth (1.1[.2]), 'Nigra sum, sed formosa' (1.4[.5]), 'I am black, but comely', the shepherd's noonday rest (1.6[.7]), 'quia amore langueo' (2.5), the end of winter and the coming of spring in the land (2.10–13) and the search through the city at night for the Beloved (3.1–3, 5.6–7) were reworked in the poetry of the sixteenth and seventeenth centuries as they had been for centuries before. Most influential of all was the *hortus conclusus* of 4.12, the garden walled around, an image used to represent a wide variety of ideas in secular and sacred art and literature, and memorably represented in the lover's entry into the garden in CA 27.[45]

What is the effect of this incorporation of so many features and images from the Song into a poem the title of which is itself the Spanish version of the Latin name of the book, 'Canticum'? The biblical poem begins with a kiss but ends with a renewed absence. San Juan's poem, in an exact reversal, begins with an absence and ends with the union of the lovers. According to Jewish tradition, the Song's last verse, 'Make haste, my beloved, and be thou like to a roe or a young hart upon the mountains of spice' (AV 8.14, which follows the Hebrew more closely than the Vg's 'Fuge dilecte mi') expresses the longing for the Messiah to return quickly. The last simile of the Hebrew Song, the stag hurrying upon the mountains, translated in the Vulgate as the stag fleeing, becomes the first simile of the 'Cántico', 'como el ciervo huiste', 'you fled like the stag'.[46] It is true that the simile of the stag also occurs in Song 2.9, but the mirror image of the Song offered by the beginning of the 'Cántico' is nonetheless striking. San Juan seems to have been writing his own Song, celebrating a fulfilment which the interpreters of the Hebrew Song regarded as yet to be achieved.

As with the lilies of the 'Noche', San Juan chooses a new image for the end of his poem, the cavalry descending to the waters, and a new character, 'Aminadab', whose sudden appearance and identity are unexplained. Reading the poem through the lens of the Song, one can see that how the two images connect: the verse which inspires this strange conclusion speaks of the soul's disturbance 'propter quadrigas Aminadab' (6.11; cf. AV, 'Or ever I was aware, my soul made me like the chariots of Amminadib', with marginal alternatives). The troops descend 'a vista de las aguas', 'in sight of the waters', perhaps alluding to Song 8.7, 'Aquae multa non potuerunt extinguere charitatem, nec flumina obruent illam', 'Many waters cannot quench love, neither can the floods drown it'. That solves the problem of how 'Aminadab', cavalry and waters come to be associated, but it creates another. Why is absence denoted by a textual presence?

The first line of the verse, 'Que nadie lo mirava . . .', 'For nobody was looking', takes up a theme more prominent in the 'Cántico' than in the Song. The biblical poem implies a great deal of mutual gazing by the lovers, but San Juan has reworked texts like 1.5 into a sequence of ideas which convey wider meanings. The creatures reply to the lover's question in CA 4 that they were beautified by the Beloved as he looked upon them, 'yéndolos mirando' (CA 5). Creation has been made lovely by the Beloved's glance; the lover has been transported into ecstasy by his eyes, having longed to see them (CA 11–12). Later, the extended polyptoton on 'mirar' (CA 22–4) has insisted that the mutual gaze of the lovers has been immensely fruitful. But whereas in neo-Platonic Petrarchan poetry eyes are the windows of the soul and in such gazing the spirits of lover and Beloved intermingle (an element of which survives in CA 10–12), here the look of the Beloved has effected a different result: 'gracia y hermosura en mí dexaste', 'you left grace and beauty in me'.[47] The desire of the lovers to be alone and unobserved in CA 34 and 39 seems to fulfil CA 25's 'Y no parezca nadie en la montiña', 'Let no one appear on the mountain', even if the locus has moved to lower ground. The 'lo' these absent people are not observing in the final stanza seems to refer back to the 'aquello' of CA 37, the inexpressible something bestowed on the lover by the Beloved, and the five images which picture it in CA 38. The lovers may now look upon one another, which they could not do at the start; but no one else is to observe this; except, of course, the reader of the poem, who sees the representation of the 'lo' and the 'aquello' through its language. The 'Cántico' and 'Noche' do not provide the kind of closure one might expect. In both, the union of the lovers takes place, yet in both a further perspective opens out at the end through new images. As poetry, the text ends when the poet has said all he can; once he absents himself from his text, he opens the door to the reader's presence. San Juan reads the imagistic world of the Song as a whole and gives it a different sense of direction. But to make the physical absence of onlookers the subject of textual presence creates a strange sense of closure.

From these examples, it is clear that the 'Cántico' exercises an unusual freedom with respect to its model. Images from one verse in the Song attract others from other verses and poetic traditions; images clustered together in the Song are broken up and scattered across the poem, where they collide with ones more familiar to a European readership; contexts and speakers are changed and identities exchanged. Sudden tense changes across the poem sugggest a world in which time does not have the same meaning as in the everyday world; space, direction and perspective are in a state of constant flux and do not exist in the same dimensions as ours. There is not one *locus amoenus*, but several, each both like and unlike the stylized Arcadian landscapes of Renaissance pastoral, yet each seems to refer to the same journey through the same space.[48] San Juan's assimilation and recreation of the Song is largely responsible for a poetic narrative unlike that of any other poem of the period.

But the poem also speaks through the voices of other poetic traditions, in association rather than competition with each other. Of these, *cancionero* poetry has received the least critical attention. One senses its influence in San Juan's *coplas* and *glosas*, as in the only surviving *villancico* (carol) attributed to him:

Del Verbo divino la Virgen preñada viene de camino; ¡si le dais posada!	Pregnant with the divine Word the Virgin is coming by; oh that you give her lodging!

But there are echoes of its images, paradoxes and motifs throughout the 'Cántico'.[49]

The plural 'amores', as in 'Buscando mis amores' (C 3), 'Seeking my loves', to describe the object of the lover's attention is common across *cancionero* poetry. The address of the Beloved by the affectionate diminutive 'Carillo', 'Dearest' (CA 32; Alín 171, 364, 430–1) or the use of the periphrastic 'aquel que yo más quería', 'him whom most I loved' (C2; Alín 173; Frenk 95) are also well represented. Other diminutive forms are frequent, such as 'palomica', 'little dove' (CA 33; Frenk 493) and 'pastorcico', 'little shepherd' (the 'Pastorcico' poem; Alín 584, 680; Frenk 223, 279). The association of love with wounding, suffering and death is commonplace (C2, 6–9; Alín 179, 222, 513; Frenk 28, 87, 152–3, 299). Sometimes this is associated with birds and animals, notably the 'ciervo del monte', 'stag of the mountain', which is 'ferido', 'wounded' (C 1, CA 12; Frenk 26, 37, 51) or the 'garza', 'egret' ('Tras de un amoroso lance'; Alín 188). The reference to dark and fair skin, another topos of *cancionero* poetry, finds place in the 'Cántico' (CA 24; Alín 209, 637, 791, 842; Frenk 198, 599), though here San Juan's inspiration is mainly the Song (1.5). Sometimes the association is pastoral:

Aunque soy morena,	Though I am dark,
blanca yo nací;	I was born white;
guardando el ganado	keeping my flock
la color perdí	I lost my colour.
(Frenk, 196)	

Flowers, roses, vines, gardens, green branches, nightingales, fountains (often in the archaic 'fonte' form), mountains (including the form 'montiña', as CA 25), shepherds, rivers, riverbanks, breezes, even frontiers (C 3, Frenk, 285) and doves ('palomicas', CA 33) are landscapes and creatures these brief verses share with the 'Cántico' in their intense expressions of the many states of love; dark nights and dawn provide times (CA 14, 38; Alín 306, 590, 595, 822; Frenk 220, 224, 365, 368; 20, 25, 171, 222, 360, 362, 364, 622). In one such poem, night is associated with fear (Frenk 212; compare CA 29's 'miedos de las noches', 'night-time fears' and Song 3.8's 'timores nocturnos'); in another (Alín 212), 'clara estaba la noche/más que el sole', 'the night was brighter/than the sun', a topos San Juan uses in the fourth stanza of the 'Noche' poem, though it too has biblical origins (Psalm 139[138].11–12).

Even more telling are the recurrent motifs. The love caused by the presence of the Beloved within the soul (CA 12, 28) occurs in *cancionero* poetry in expressions like 'quiérola en el alma' and 'tengo a mi querida/dentro del alma' (Alín 214, 638), 'I love her in my soul', 'I have my beloved within my soul', while desire for the Beloved to manifest himself to cure the sickness of love in the added stanza (CB 11) can be found in the question '¿para qué le llaman cura/si es la misma enfermedad?' (Alín 734, though in a text of Góngora), 'why do they call it cure/if it is the sickness itself?' The 'mil gracias' and 'un no sé qué' of C5 and 7 also belong to *cancionero* language ('tengo gracias más de mil', 'un no sé qué' (Alín 204, 665). The image of imprisonment through a strand of hair, which derives from Song 4.9, can be found in 'En Sevilla quedan [los mis amores] presos/per cordón de mis cabellos' (Frenk 234), '[My love] is imprisoned in Seville/by a ribbon of my hair.' A whole network of associations between eyes, seeing and looking, present in CA (5, 10–12, 22–4), occurs across the corpus, notably in lines like 'véante mis ojos', 'let my eyes see you' (C 10; Alín 363; Frenk 218, where the next line, 'y muérame luego', connects eyes and death as San Juan does in CB 11). The glance of the Beloved is equally common, as plea, complaint or warning, in both secular and sacred contexts (Frenk 190, 231, 487). Frenk also records a whole series of poems which connect 'ojos' with love, loss, suffering and death (156, 174–9, 181–2, 400).

I do not mean to propose *cancionero* poetry as yet another source which helps to unlock the mystery of San Juan's poetry. I merely note its presence in the 'Cántico', as the visible sign of a much larger oral culture which finds its voice alongside the others in his *liras*. Complaints of love also find expression in the highly charged language, full of questions, exclamations and complaints, of devotional works like the *Soliloquia*.[50] Its Augustinian filiation is not difficult to see: its tone is confessional, it cites Augustine's famous words 'Da quod jubes et jube quod vis' (PL 40, 880; compare *Confessions* x.29; 37), and it includes a passage closely modelled on Augustine's famous questions to the created order in his search for God (*Confessions* vi.10). But it is only partly Augustinian. It does not tell the story of a young man's life and conversion; it is an intimate dialogue between the soul and her Creator, full of passionate longings and prayers (as long sections of the *Confessions* are). Nor does the language of darkness betray any influence of the pseudo-Dionysius: it is never a symbol for divine otherness, nor is it given a positive role to play on the journey; it stands only for human ignorance and death (e.g. 865, 872–4, 878, 892). While San Juan will teach that in the dark night of the spirit God appears to have abandoned the soul, the whole weight of the argument in the *Soliloquia* is that the soul is responsible for any breakdown in their relationship, and it puts greater emphasis on the work of the devil and the terrors of hell than he does. Its language is often biblical, but in comparison with him, textual quotations are fewer and further between.

San Juan refers this work several times in his commentaries. In S 1.5.1 he quotes a series of antitheses contrasting divine goodness with human sinfulness from its second chapter (866). His translation of the Latin is exact, though he shortens it. The so-called 'pregunta a las criaturas' of C 4–5 derives from the version in chapter 31 of the *Soliloquia* (888) of the famous passage in the *Confessions* (vi.10): in C 4.1 and 5.1 San Juan amplifies the sense of the Latin.[51] Several more general aspects of his language and teaching may owe their inspiration to the *Soliloquia*. Its chapters use nuptial imagery, with God as the soul's spouse or Bridegroom (865, 868, 894), and God is often described in terms of hiddenness (865, 873, 889–90, 898) and beauty (865, 888). The *Soliloquia* develops the theme of the creature–Creator relationship in similar fashion to San Juan's relentless exposure of the incompatibility of love for things and love for God (S 1.4–10): if the soul desires anything other than God, it will be 'nec summum bonum, ergo nec Deum, sed potius creaturam. Cum autem creaturam desiderat, continuam famem habet; quia licet quod desiderat de creaturis, adipiscatur, vacua tamen remanet, quia nihil est quod eam impleat nisi tu, ad cujus imaginem est creata' (887), 'neither the highest good, therefore not God, but rather a creature. When she desires a creature, she suffers continual hunger. What she desires and obtains from a creature leaves a vacuum, as there is nothing that can fill this but you, in whose image she is created.' The second chapter speaks of the creature's relapse into death and nothingness without the creative Word, 'per quod omnia conservantur, sine quo omnia annihilantur' (869), 'by whom all things are maintained, without whom all would be brought to nothing', a passage reminiscent of S 2.5.3, where San Juan explain that God indwells every creature, which without this 'substantial' union would simply cease to be.

The presence of the *Soliloquia* is strongest in the first ten stanzas of the poem. We have already noted the unusual correspondence between the opening of the poem and a passage in the treatise.[52] Many of the ideas are commonplace in the spiritual literature San Juan had read, and some have biblical origins: the initial question of the poem also reflects the enemies' taunt, 'Where is thy God?', from Psalm (41.2[42.3]), which begins with the simile of the hart, 'Quemadmodum desiderat cervus ad fontes aquarum', 'As the hart panteth after the water brooks.' But the presence of so many of them in the *Soliloquia* suggests the work had left its mark. The first stanza bears other traces of the *Soliloquia*, with its 'con gemido' and 'salí [. . .] clamando', the sighing and calling out, echoing the Latin's 'gemitus nostros' (885), 'clamo' (866) and 'Clamabo, Domine, antequam transeam' (867), 'our groaning', 'I cry out', 'I shall cry out, Lord, before I pass on.' The question to the creatures and their reply is thoroughly Augustinian, but their role as 'mensajeros', messengers who cannot give the soul what she seeks (C 6) is like that of the external senses in the *Soliloquia*: 'Misi nuntios meos omnes sensus exteriores, ut quarerem; et non inveni, quia male quaerebam' (888), 'I sent all my external senses as messengers, so that I could search; and I did not find, because I searched wrongly.' Medical imagery, particularly in respect of the sight of the Beloved as a cure, is common to both: 'Munda me, mundans virtus, sana oculos meos, ut sanis te contemplar oculis' (894), 'Cleanse me, with virtue's cleansing, heal my eyes, that I may contemplate you with sound eyes', makes the same kind of connections between sight and healing as C 10 and CB 11, while the repeated phrase 'lumen oculorum meorum' (864–5, 870, 880), 'the light of my eyes', is present in C 10's 'y véante mis ojos,/pues eres lumbre dellos'. Such links are not confined to the 'Cántico', either: 'Ego autem stans in hac nocte tenebrosa' (885), 'I, standing in this dark night', makes the dark night into a first-person experience, as in the 'Noche', while the paradox of the gentle fire and its secret light, 'O ignis qui semper ardes, et nunquam extingueris, accende me [. . .] Ignis sancte, quam dulciter ardes, quam secrete luces, quam desideranter aduris!' (893), 'O fire ever burning and never extinguished, set me on fire [. . .] Holy fire, how sweetly you burn, how secretly you shine, how longingly you scorch', shows close parallels with lines in the 'Llama' like '¡O llama de amor viva,/que tiernamente hyeres' and 'donde secretamente solo moras'.

Both works use polyptoton in similar contexts: 'O vita, cui omnia vivunt; vita, quae das mihi vitam; vita, quae es mea vita; vita, per quam vivo, sine qua morior' (865), 'O life, to whom all things live; life that gives life to me; life which is my life; life by which I live, without which I die', becomes in C 8:

Mas, ¿cómo perseveras, ¡o vida!, no viviendo donde vives, y haziendo por que mueras [. . .]	But how do you persevere, oh life, not living where you live, and treating so that you die [. . .]

'Totus totum me tibi offero: totus spiritus, totum cor, tota vita mea vivat tibi, vita mea' (880), 'Wholly I offer my whole self to you: let my whole spirit, my whole heart, my whole life live to you', is emphatic in the same way as CA 19:

Mi alma se a empleado, y todo mi caudal, en su servicio.	My soul has been employed and all my treasure, in his service.

More generally, the anguished questions and exclamations and antitheses of the *Soliloquia* find their densest expression in C 6–10. In his commentaries, too, San Juan uses many of the biblical texts found clustered in the *Soliloquia*, like the important 'Vere tu es Deus absconditus', 'Verily thou art a God that hidest thyself', of Isaiah 45.15, alongside John 1.18, where the Son is proclaimed as the one who makes this hidden God known (CB 1.3). *Cancionero* love poetry also delighted in abstract and paradoxical arguments, but there are strong grounds for believing that the *Soliloquia*, which we know San Juan to have read as bearing all the authority of the greatest Doctor of the Western Church, provided another model in his search for a language to express the inexpressible.

Surely no other Golden Age poet embraces so many different poetic traditions. San Juan's cultural inheritance is rich and complex, and rooted in traditions familiar and unfamiliar to us. His *liras* fuse the distinctive voices of biblical language and imagery, classical and Renaissance poetry, popular love songs and devotional literature, into a poem which contains them all but transcends the sum total of its parts. Consciously or unconsciously, his imagination was receptive to them all and capable of reworking them into his own distinct and original poetic voice. The ease with which he incorporates them implies, as Cristóbal Cuevas has suggested, that his intellectual stature 'no está tan lejos como se pudiera creerse del ideal de teólogo humanista', 'is not as far as one might suppose from the ideal of the humanist theologian'.[53] But while critics have argued about the relative weight to be given to these and other traditions in the poem, beyond the identification of sources lies a harder question about the meaning and purpose of his integration of them into a single work. Can we go as far as to say that this union of separate traditions, Eastern and Western, sacred and secular, popular and *culto*, represents its subject, the union of lover and Beloved?

When San Juan locates classical 'ninfas' in the biblical world 'de Judea' (CA 31) he is providing in miniature an example of something characteristic of his poetic diction throughout the *lira* poems. His paradoxes and oxymora, rooted in Petrarchan and *cancionero* traditions – life which is death, wounds which are sweet – are familiar enough, but nymphs from Judaea are disconcerting. Yet such an expression replicates in respect of source the oxymora of the poetic text, by the sharp juxtaposition of two images which are as incompatible as a classical nude between the pages of a Bible. Such a process is original to San Juan in the poetry of the Golden Age, and affects the

'Cántico' most of all his poems. Since for him no word or image can adequately describe the mystical union of the soul with God, all words and images, no matter what their origin, are equally wanting, and equally appropriate. The language of the Bible, certainly, has a privileged place in this respect, given its revelatory nature. The language of Christian devotion, in the liturgy and in spiritual reading, is likewise privileged, because it is largely nourished by scripture. But it also follows that many kinds of human language have a contribution to make in the attempt to represent through finite language the union of the finite self with the infinite God. Each inevitably fails, but together they can achieve more than separately. All, like the creatures of C 5, bear traces of the Beloved's passage through them, but the divine language of the Bible integrates them and enables them to find coherence in their unlikeness.

The ever-changing flow of images in the 'Cántico' seems to represent in poetic terms an important element in San Juan's teaching, that attachment to any particular image or idea about God is spiritually destructive.[54] No sooner is the Beloved described as one thing than he is already something else. That has an important consequence for understanding the poetic text. The language of his poetry itself becomes a witness to the unitive experience it represents through its transcendence of the divisions literary critics assume must exist between sacred and secular, popular and learned, Eastern and Western. Whereas it comes from different places, it always points to the same end and becomes a sign of the union he struggles to articulate. Whatever divisions may exist between them in the finite world, each is equal in its capacity to become signs of transcendence. Whereas the critic asks how a poem can adopt so many styles yet retain coherence, the poet knows that at one level his words clash with each other and at another speak in complete harmony. In this way, the language of the 'Cántico' both affirms and overcomes difference. Its words can be seen simply for what they are, because they show identifiable things, but they undermine presuppositions about the kind of poem it is, and ask for a more careful and sensitive reading. The poetic world of the 'Cántico' is one, therefore, in which the familiar can be encountered as strange, and the strange become familiar. It offers a new hearing (or reading) of its raw material, words, so that they speak with unaccustomed power and communicate across cultures and centuries. In Christian terms, this rebirth of language has a Pentecostal and a sacramental quality.

In CB 12.7 San Juan provides an explanation for the linguistic innovations of the poem. Through the union of love each attribute is exchangeable for the other:

> Y tal manera de semejanza hace al amor en la transformación de los amantes, que se puede decir que cada uno es el otro y que entrambos son uno [. . .]. En la unión y transformación de amor el uno da posesión de sí al otro, y cada uno se deja y [. . .] trueca por el otro, y así cada uno vive en ol otro, y el uno es el otro y entrambos son uno por transformación de amor.

> And love creates such a manner of likeness in the transformation of the lovers that it can be said that each is the other and that both are one [. . .].

> In the union and transformation of love each gives possession of the self to the other, and each leaves self and [. . .] is exchanged for the other, so that each lives in the other, and the one is the other and both are one by transformation in love.

The language of the poem witnesses to the way in which love (here, divine love embracing humanity) creates 'semejanza', likeness, between otherwise separate entities, so that the one is transformed into the other. The word 'semejanza' is essential to understanding both the language and the teaching of San Juan, and acts as a point of connection between his poety and his prose. It is the best language can do to utter anything meaningful about mystical union as it responds to love, which is the only power capable of bringing likeness out of unlikeness; 'figuras, comparaciones y semejanzas', 'figures, comparisons and likenesses' are integral to the poem's strange diction, as the prologue to the *Cántico* maintains.[55] It represents the exchange of selves that the lovers experience in mystical union by the interchangeability of attributes between them, the attraction of hosts of metaphors to each and to both, the many literary languages it speaks. Their multiplicity makes San Juan's verse quite unlike the Renaissance pastoral of Garcilaso, with its more limited range, links it to a long Christian tradition of applying many biblical images to Christ, and demonstrates what Fray Luis de León meant when he wrote of metaphor as a linguistic phenomenon which reflects creation itself.[56] But it also opens the poem out to many potential readers, and perhaps helps to explain why an age which has largely lost the spiritual understanding of human beings and their world which San Juan's writing so powerfully celebrates can be so moved by his poetry.[57]

NOTES

1 An earlier version of this section appeared in my *El poeta y el místico* (El Escorial: Swan, 1985), pp. 195–214, but has not appeared in English until now.
2 Bernard Sesé, 'Estructura dramática de la *Noche oscura* (tres aspectos del poema)', *Actas*, I, pp. 245–56, calls it 'un pequeño drama', 'a little drama' (p. 246).
3 José C. Nieto, *San Juan de la Cruz: Poeta del amor profano* (San Lorenzo de El Escorial: Swan, 1988); his emphases.
4 See below, pp. 255–6.
5 See my *The Strife of Tongues* (Cambridge: Cambridge University Press, 1988), pp. 27–34, 87–8.
6 R. O. Jones, *The Golden Age: Prose and Poetry* in *A Literary History of Spain* (London: Ernest Benn, 1971), p. 111.
7 Luce López-Baralt, *Asedios a lo indecible: San Juan de la Cruz canta al éxtasis transformante* (Madrid: Trotta, 1998), p. 151.
8 For a similar example of 'desdoblamiento' in the 'Llama', see below, pp. 246–7.
9 For discussion of this, see Luce López-Baralt, *Asedios*, p. 172. Sarmiento's translation follows the strict grammatical sense.
10 'Notada' can carry the meaning of 'censured', as its equivalent once did in English (Sebastián de Covarrubias, *Tesoro de la lengua castellana* (Barcelona: Horta, 1943), p. 831, under 'nota'; used in this sense by Teresa, *Fundaciones*, 15.5), though San Juan interprets it as the soul not being prevented by any of the jailers from escaping out of her captivity (S1.1.15).

11 Jorge Guillén, *Lenguaje y poesía* (Cambridge, Mass.: Harvard University Press, 1961), p. 80, notes how the image of the 'muro', 'wall' in CA 30/CB 21 'se yergue con una prodigiosa densidad de materia penetrada de espíritu', 'rises up with a marvellous density of matter penetrated by spirit'.

12 Compare conventional Petrarchan usage, where lilies represent fair skin, even in its bolder recreations, like Góngora's Galatea in the *Polifemo*, who is made to become 'the scythe of her lilies' as she rises from the grass.

13 Contrast, for example, the association of 'noche oscura' with lack of 'ventura' in the sense of good fortune in the *cancionero* verse 'Parióme mi madre/una noche escura/cubrióme de luto/faltóme ventura' (*Lírica española de tipo popular*, ed. Margit Frenk (Madrid: Cátedra, 1994), p. 160).

14 *The Poet and the Mystic* (Oxford: Oxford University Press, 1977), pp. 110–12; *El poeta y el místico*, pp. 152–3.

15 Dámaso Alonso, *La poesía de San Juan de la Cruz* (Madrid: Aguilar, 1966), pp. 136–8.

16 The call to go forth is characteristic of the Song, e.g. the 'egrediamur' of 7.11.

17 The line 'con ansias en amores inflamada' admits of two grammatical interpretations; the soul departs inflamed by anxiety in love, reading 'ansias en amores' as a single phrase, or she departs anxiously, inflamed by love, 'con ansias, en amores inflamada', two separate phrases. The BAC edition gives the latter; San Juan assumes the former (S 1.14, N 2.11.1–2).

18 For Juan Goytisolo's modern reworking of the image of wounding, see my 'La presencia de San Juan de la Cruz en la literatura del siglo XX. España e Inglaterra', in *El sol a medianoche*, pp. 189–203. Elizabeth Smart's *By Grand Central Station I Sat Down and Wept* (London: HarperCollins, 1991 [1945]) does something similar with Song texts.

19 *Metamorphoses*, IV, 93–6, trans. Frank Justus Miller, Loeb Classical Library, 3rd edn (Cambridge, Mass: Harvard University Press, 1977), pp. 184–5. My attention was first drawn to this passage by Eric Southworth, of St Peter's College, Oxford. Luce López-Baralt, *Asedios*, p. 150, points to the Castilian translation by Jorge de Bustamente as possibly read by San Juan. It is hard to imagine San Juan turning naturally to Ovid in his maturity, but he may have studied this passage in Latin with the Jesuits in Medina.

20 *Garcilaso de la Vega: Obra poética y textos en prosa*, ed. Bienvenido Morros (Barcelona: Crítica, 1995), pp. 167–8.

21 Sebastián de Córdoba, *Las obras de Boscán y Garcilasso trasladadas en materias Christianas y religiosas* (Zaragoza: Juan Soler, 1577), cited here from *Sebastián de Córdoba: Garcilaso a lo divino*, ed. Glen R. Gale (Ann Arbor: University of Michigan, 1971), p. 186.

22 Critics have given the name *contrafacta* to spiritualized versions of secular poems (and vice versa).

23 These seem to me more obvious than the parallels from Sufi literature given by Luce López-Baralt, *Asedios*, pp. 155–9. Nor is San Juan's night a stage on the journey, as with them, but, as he makes clear, both the journey and its goal.

24 *The New Sunday Missal* (London: Geoffrey Chapman, 1982), p. 163. See J. Sullivan, 'Night and Light: the Poet John of the Cross and the *Exsultet* of the Easter Liturgy', *EphCarm*, 30 (1979), pp. 52–68. The Latin text of the *Exsultet* invokes 'haec nox' four times, interspersed with the exclamatory 'O vere beata nox!', a repetition mirrored in San Juan's poem.

25 See above, pp. 86, 91, 104–6; also George Tavard, *Poetry and Contemplation in St John of the Cross* (Athens: Ohio University Press, 1988), p. 49.

26 The poem exists in two principal versions, CA and CB. There are few differences of expression between them, but the order of stanzas is radically altered in CB. A new stanza, CB 11, is introduced between CA 10 and 11; CA 15–24 become CB 24–33; CA 25–6, CB 16–17; CA 27–8, CB 22–3; CA 29–30, CB 20–1; CA 31–2, CB 18–19. These changes, and the extensive reworking of the commentary, have led a minority of critics to dispute the authenticity of the second redaction. For a good summary of the case for and against, see Eulogio Pacho, *Reto a la crítica: Debate histórico sobre el Cántico espiritual de s. Juan de la Cruz* (Burgos: Monte

Carmelo, 1988). I follow CA for the poem, as closer to the experience which inspired it, and CB for the commentary, reflecting San Juan's final version. For a critical approach which regards these issues as irrelevant to the production of meaning, see David Brian Perrin, *Canciones entre el alma y el Esposo of Juan de la Cruz: A Hermeneutical Interpretation* (San Francisco: Catholic Scholars Press, 1996), especially pp. 316–67.

27 The rhetorical trope is prosopopoeia. Rivers sometimes speak, in imitation of classical tradition; see, for example, Fray Luis de León's 'Profecía del Tajo'.

28 The added stanza (CB 11, present in all the seventeenth-century editions, which otherwise follow a modified form of CA known as CA') recapitulates the images and themes of the opening stanzas – desire for his presence, sight, beauty, wounding, death, love, face.

29 For example, Góngora's early sonnet (1582), '¡Oh claro honor del líquido elemento!'. This is one of the places where Luce López-Baralt, *Asedios*, pp. 42–53, sees clearest parallels with Sufi mysticism.

30 Represented dramatically by Frida Kahlo's painting 'The Wounded Deer' (1946).

31 This pattern is interrupted by CB, which removes CA 15 to CB 24. Here the CA version of the poem is better, because the description of the Beloved and the marriage-bed of union share the same syntax; López-Baralt, *Asedios*, pp. 74–5.

32 On this ending, see my '"Aminadab tampoco parecía": presencia y ausencia en el "Cántico" y en el "Cantar"', *Ínsula*, 537 (Septiembre 1991), pp. 10–11.

33 *The Poet and the Mystic*, especially pp. 81–117; *El poeta y el místico*, pp. 117–60.

34 For a sequential account of the poem which sees it as a coherent representation of mystical experience achieved in the past and hoped for in the future, see L. J. Woodward, 'Verb Tense and Sequential Time in the *Cántico espiritual* of San Juan de la Cruz', *FMLS*, 27 (1991), pp. 148–58.

35 *The Poet and the Mystic*, pp. 91–6, 106–12; *El poeta y el místico*, pp. 131–6, 146–53.

36 On the range of San Juan's imagery, see Elizabeth Teresa Howe, *Mystical Imagery: Santa Teresa de Jesús and San Juan de la Cruz* (New York: Peter Lang, 1988).

37 See Thomas Traherne (1637–74), *Centuries of Meditations*, quoted in *The English Spirit*, ed. Paul Handley and others (London: Darton, Longman and Todd, 1988), pp. 120–4. Wordsworth's phrases are from his 'Ode on Intimations of Immortality'.

38 For examples from his prose in the *Llama de amor viva*, see below, pp. 250–1.

39 For example, W. G. Tillmans, *De aanwezigheid van het bijbels in het "Cántico espiritual" van San Juan de la Cruz* (Brussels: Paleis der Academiën, 1967); *The Poet and the Mystic*, pp. 60–9; *El poeta y el místico*, pp. 93–102; Francisco Contreras Molina, 'El Cantar de los Cantares y el Cántico espiritual', *SJC*, 11 (1993), pp. 27–73; Perrin, *Canciones entre el alma y el Esposo*, pp. 154–159.

40 Athalya Brenner, *The Song of Songs* (Sheffield: Sheffield Academic Press, 1989), pp. 31–2.

41 Marcia Falk, *The Song of Songs: A New Translation and Interpretation* (San Francisco: HarperSanFrancisco, 1990), p. 139.

42 *The Poet and the Mystic*, especially pp. 81–117; *El poeta y el místico*, pp. 119–60.

43 Lines 2278–2310; II.17.

44 Luce López-Baralt, *Asedios*, p. 45.

45 See George H. Williams, *Wilderness and Paradise in Christian Thought* (New York: Harper, 1962); Stanley Stewart, *The Enclosed Garden: The Tradition and the Image in Seventeenth-Century Poetry* (Madison: University of Wisconsin, 1966); Christopher Hill, *The English Bible and the Seventeenth Century* (London: Allen Lane, 1993), pp. 126–53.

46 Casiodoro de Reina's translation (1569) follows the Vg: 'Huye, o Amado mío, y sé semejante al gamo, o al cabrito de los ciervos'; see facsimile edition (Sociedades Bíblicas Unidas, 1970), p. 1322.

47 Compare Garcilaso, sonnet 8, 'De aquella vista pura y excelente/salen espírtus vivos y encendidos'. Luce López-Baralt refers to this 'inesperada reescritura espiritualizante de la mirada unitiva de los neoplatónicos' (*Asedios*, p. 65), 'unexpected spiritualizing rewriting of the unitive look of the neo-Platonists'.

48 Luce López-Baralt, *Asedios*, pp. 39, 54; 'estos *loci* giratorios e inestables nos reservan la sorpresa adicional de que deben ser entendidos como *un* solo espacio unificado: el del alma convertida en Dios' (p. 89), 'these moving, unstable *loci* surprise us additionally by needing to be understood as *one* single unified space, the soul converted to God'.

49 I have used the Frenk anthology and *Cancionero tradicional*, ed. José María Alín (Madrid: Castalia, 1991) for my illustrations, cited henceforth by number of entry rather than page. On popular elements in the poem, see Dámaso Alonso, *La poesía de san Juan de la Cruz*, pp. 78–110; Ricardo Senabre, 'Sobre la composición del Cántico espiritual', *Actas*, I, pp. 95–106 (pp. 98–101).

50 See above, p. 5.

51 The original Latin reads: 'Interrogatio creaturarum, profunda consideratio ipsarum: responsio earum, attestatio ipsarum de Deo, quoniam omnia clamant, Deus nos fecit', followed (as in the *Confessions*) by a reference to Romans 1.20, which San Juan also cites.

52 See above, p. 5.

53 Cristóbal Cuevas, 'El bestiario simbólico en el «Cántico» de San Juan de la Cruz', in *Simposio sobre San Juan de la Cruz* (Avila: Miján, 1986), pp. 181–203 (pp. 197–8).

54 Luce López-Baralt, *Asedios*, p. 88.

55 See below, pp. 228–31.

56 See my *The Strife of Tongues*, pp. 8–12, 171–2.

57 'Juan's *Cantico* can [. . .] be read meaningfully (interpreted) in the twentieth century as it was in the sixteenth because of the text's innovative metaphorical references'; Perrin, *Canciones entre el alma y el Esposo*, p. 194.

5

Endings and Beginnings

El está sobre el cielo y habla en camino de eternidad; nosotros, ciegos, sobre la tierra, y no entendemos sino vías de carne y tiempo.

He is above heaven and speaks in the way of eternity; we, blind, upon earth, only understand ways of flesh and time. (S 2.20.5)

San Juan's writing career did not stop when he escaped from prison. During the years that followed, he completed the 'Cántico', wrote the 'Llama' and some shorter verses, but also began work on the prose commentaries to the *lira* poems, which in a sense he never completed. If the first response to his own experience, both of human exclusion and divine union, expressed itself in poetry, he began to see that his own verses provided the opportunity for him to give a more considered account of the journey he believed they depicted, by using the words they offered, and the questions they provoked in their hearers, to offer a different picture of the soul's journey to God. Literary critics have often ignored these commentaries, just as theologians have the poetry. Relatively little attention has therefore been paid to the connections between them.

His poetry can stand on its own. But the prose commentaries cannot be ignored in a full account of his writing. For them, he turned to other generic models, notably the biblical commentary and the devotional treatise, as he sought to explain the meaning of each image and phrase of the poem, and from them construct his teaching about the soul's journey to God. The apparent boldness of a procedure in which a writer who protested his obedience and submission to the Holy Catholic Church treated his own poetic text as if it were equivalent to the inspired text of scripture on which the authority of the Church rested, is mitigated in two ways. Many of the images he uses are themselves borrowed from biblical language and, as the prologue to the *Cántico* announces (.4), he grounds the teaching he intends to derive from them in the authoritative text of the Bible. His writing comes full circle: biblical imagery inspires him in the creation of his own verse, and his own explanations of its meaning send him back to the Bible. In becoming his own interpreter he also becomes an interpreter of scripture, which is why it is difficult to write about San Juan as a critic of his own poetry or as a biblical exegete in separation from each other.

Just as we should never overlook the daily round of *lectio divina* when assessing the place of the Bible in his work, so we should always bear in mind that his spiritual teaching was the fruit not only of his own experience, but also of his interaction with friars, nuns and laypeople over whom he exercised authority or who sought his advice. That wider context will become clearer from an account of the remaining period of his life. His surviving letters, together with two shorter works, the *Dichos de luz y amor* and the *Cautelas*, will illustrate how much his spiritual teaching owed to the knowledge and practical experience he gained from this process, and serve to introduce some of its main themes.

AFTER PRISON

Inevitably, Fray Juan's escape has been given a miraculous tinge by hagiographical tradition. The reality was more prosaic: a new, more sympathetic gaoler, who allowed him out into the adjoining guest room while the community was enjoying its siesta; a balcony window left open near his cell, deliberately or not we cannot tell; a pair of blankets torn into strips and knotted together; a hazardous descent to a wall below, with a sheer drop into the gorge of the Tagus, and to certain death, if he lost his footing. Early in August 1578, at the dead of night, with two visitors fast asleep in the guest room, he let himself down, found himself short of the wall, and jumped the remaining few feet to safety. Following it, he came to a stop by the walls of an adjacent convent, but managed to climb over them into the street. He stopped briefly in the entrance of a house, and made his way to the Discalced convent, where the nuns took him in and sheltered him. Soon afterwards one of the canons of the Cathedral, Pedro de Mendoza, arranged for him to stay in the Hospital de Santa Cruz, to recover from his ordeal. Within two months he was on his travels again, to the Discalced Chapter at Almodóvar del Campo (Ciudad Real), between Toledo and Córdoba, called in response to the crisis provoked by the new nuncio's removal of Gracián as visitor. In a letter of September 1578 Teresa expressed her continuing anxieties about Fray Juan's health.[1] Evidently still weak, and suffering the effects of his imprisonment, he was accompanied to Almodóvar and thence to Beas by two of Mendoza's servants, to attend to his needs.

Despite uncertainties as to its legality, the chapter made three important decisions. It elected Antonio de Jesús as Provincial; it sent delegates to Rome to seek formal separation from the Calced; and it appointed Juan as superior of El Calvario, a remote monastery in northern Andalusia, to which, still accompanied, he set out. In Madrid, Sega, the nuncio, was furious when he learnt of the meeting, declaring it null and void, imprisoning any leaders of the Reform he could lay his hands on, and excommunicating the participants. Juan, fortunately, and perhaps deliberately, was out of his immediate reach as he made his way to his new charge. For some time he stopped at the convent of the Discalced nuns Teresa had founded in Beas de Segura in 1575, to the Prioress of which, Ana de Jesús, he would in due course dedicate the *Cántico* commentary, and who would herself take the Carmelite Reform into France and the Low Countries.[2]

For the next few months, Fray Juan led his community of 30 friars, and each weekend took the strenuous but beautiful walk of six miles or so each way across the hills to confess the Beas nuns. After the horrors of prison these were happy times for him, and productive in another way. For it was at Beas, in response to the sisters' questions about the meaning of his poetry, that it first occurred to him to write down explanations of his verses. Much of the rest of his life was engaged, as time permitted, in preparing and revising his prose commentaries. His long practice in the confessional and in spiritual conversation with his fellow-religious, hearing accounts of their inner life and responding to their questions, as well as correcting their mistakes, meant that by the time he began to write his commentaries he already knew the twists, turns and pitfalls of the journey which they would trace.

He had already, it seems, developed the practice of writing down brief statements of his teaching on scraps of paper, for the nuns to read and consider. The *Dichos de luz y amor* is a collection of spiritual aphorisms dating from this period.[3] Their dense, paradoxical tone gives some of them an epigrammatic quality: '¡Oh dulcísimo amor de Dios mal conocido! El que halló sus venas descansó' (16), 'Oh sweetest love of God, so little known! The one who discovered its veins found rest'; 'Un solo pensamiento del hombre vale más que todo el mundo; por tanto, sólo Dios es digno de él' (34), 'One single human thought is worth more than the whole world; therefore, only God is worthy of it'; 'No sabe el hombre gozarse bien ni dolerse bien, porque no entiende la distancia de el bien y y de el mal' (62), 'Human beings do not know how to rejoice or to grieve properly, because they do not understand the distance between good and evil.'

Others sum up a particular aspect of his teaching. Some speak of the need for complete dependence on God and rejection of all that is less: 'Mas estima Dios en ti el inclinarte a la sequedad y al padecer por su amor, que todas las consolaciones y visiones espirituales y meditaciones que puedas tener' (14), 'God values in you more your inclination to dryness and to suffering for his love, than all the consolations, spiritual visions and meditations you may have'; 'No te hagas presente a las criaturas si quieres guardar el rostro de Dios claro y sencillo en tu alma; mas vacía y enajena mucho tu espíritu de ellas y andarás en divinas luces, porque Dios no es semejante a ellas' (25), 'Do not make yourself present to the creatures if you wish to keep God's face clear and simple in your soul, but empty your spirit and remove it far from them and you will walk in divine light, because God is not like them.' Some use biblical language: the tree must be cultivated to bring forth its fruit in due season (5–6; Psalm 1); others take natural images, like the flight of birds or flies caught in the honey, and build teaching on them (22–4, 31). Flowers wither quickly, so 'escoge para ti un espíritu robusto no asido a nada [. . .] porque la sabrosa y dulce fruta en tierra fría y seca se coge' (41), 'choose for yourself a robust spirit, not attached to anything [. . .] because sweet and tasty fruit is picked from cold, dry earth'. Others are startling in their simplicity: 'Secado se ha mi espíritu porque se olvida de apacentarse en ti' (38), 'My spirit has dried up because it forgets to feed on you'; 'A la tarde te examinarán en el amor' (59), 'In the evening you will be examined in love.' The opening verse of the 'Cántico' is present too, though in a more positive form: 'Señor mío, no eres tú extraño a quien no se extraña contigo. ¿Cómo dicen que te ausentas tú?' (49), 'My Lord, you are no stranger to those who are not strangers to you. How can people say that you are absent?'

In June 1579 Fray Juan moved with three of the friars to Baeza, to found the first Discalced college in Andalusia. The handsome Renaissance buildings of the town, which make it so rewarding to visit today, were new or in the process of construction when Fray Juan arrived. It was a flourishing place of some 20,000–25,000 inhabitants, its prosperity based on agriculture, salt, wool and silk, with its own university, founded in 1538 for the study of arts and theology, and associated particularly with the religious reformer known as the Apostle of Andalusia, San Juan de Ávila. The Discalced friars were anxious to establish a university presence in Andalusia, following the example of Salamanca and Alcalá, partly to strengthen their own intellectual life, partly because universities proved a good recruiting ground for novices. Baeza seems to have been a place of unusual religious fervour, even by the standards of the time, and large numbers of pious women, *beatas* – perhaps as many as a thousand – frequented its churches and sought direction from its priests, monks and friars. Unsurprisingly, it had witnessed its own outbreak of *alumbrismo*.[4] The College was inaugurated on Trinity Sunday 1579, with episcopal and local support, and soon began to attract the interest of clergy and lay people as well as its first novices. Here Fray Juan continued a ministry of teaching and spiritual direction, as well as attending to the administrative duties his Rectorship involved and to the artistic embellishment of the chapel by a local painter, Juan de Vera. Documents have recently come to light which show how the community was donated property nearby, including a farm a few miles away, from which some of its needs could be supported.[5] His visits to the sisters at Beas became less frequent, but the fact that he continued to visit them once or twice a month and to correspond with them demonstrates the special place this community had in his affections. A serious outbreak of influenza swept through Spain in 1580 and among its victims was his mother Catalina in Medina del Campo, who had remained close to the Discalced sisters there. Baeza was badly affected too, and the college became a temporary hospital, with all 18 friars affected. Fray Juan's nursing experience must have been put to good use.

Pope Gregory XIII's Brief *Pia consideratione* (22 June 1580) granted the Discalced permission to elect a Provincial distinct from the Calced. The Provincial Chapter at Alcalá in March 1581, attended by Fray Juan, was the first since separation. There were now 22 houses, some 300 friars and 200 nuns.[6] Gracián, Teresa's protégé, was elected Provincial and Fray Juan the third of four *definidores* or general councillors, whose duties involved carrying forward the policies of General Chapters between meetings (*consejeros* were also appointed, to deal with the provincial level of the Order's life). At the Chapter, constitutions for the friars and nuns were approved, new foundations were received and the first steps were taken towards involving it in missionary activity in Africa. The first expedition would suffer a disastrous accident, when the boat was in collision with another and the friars were all drowned; the second was attacked by English pirates, but in due course the Order succeeded in reaching the Congo. But tensions were also beginning to surface among the Discalced, described by historians of the Order in terms of a conflict between rigorists like

Antonio de Jesús (and later Doria) and those who preferred the gentler and more humane style adopted by Teresa, followed by Gracián and Fray Juan.

One of his shortest works, the *Cautelas*, was written at El Calvario for the Beas nuns as a summary of advice for those who wished to follow the monastic life.[7] It provides three strategies to adopt to counter the three traditional enemies of the soul: the world, the flesh and the devil. The introductory remarks provide a concise commentary on large sections of the *Subida-Noche*:

> El alma que quiere llegar en breve al santo recogimiento, silencio espiritual, desnudez y pobreza de espíritu, donde se goza el pacífico refrigerio del Espíritu Santo y se alcanza unidad con Dios, y librarse de todos los impedimentos de toda criatura deste mundo y librarse de las astucias y engaños del demonio y libertarse de sí mismo, tiene necesidad de ejercitar los documentos siguientes; advirtiendo que todos los daños que el alma recibe nacen de los enemigos ya dichos, que son: mundo, demonio y carne.
>
> El *mundo* es el enemigo menos dificultoso. El *demonio* es más oscuro de entender, pero la *carne* es más tenaz que todos, y duran sus acometimientos mientras dure el hombre viejo.
>
> Para vencer a uno destos enemigos es menester vencerlos a todos tres: y enflaqueciendo uno, se enflaquecen los otros dos; y vencidos todos los tres, no le queda al alma más guerra. (p. 57)

> The soul that desires quickly to reach holy recollection, spiritual silence, and nakedness and poverty of spirit, in which the peaceful refreshment of the Holy Spirit is enjoyed and unity with God is gained, and to free herself from all the burdens of every creature of this world and from the wiles and deceits of the devil and become free of herself, needs to practise the following counsels, noting that any harm that comes to the soul arises from these three enemies: the world, the devil and the flesh.
>
> The *world* is the least difficult enemy. The *devil* is harder to understand, but the *flesh* is the most persistent of all, and its attacks last as long as the old man lasts.
>
> To conquer any one of these enemies it is necessary to conquer all three. Once one is weakened, the other two grow weak; and once all three are conquered, the soul is free of warfare.

The length of sentence is typical of the age. Less so are the *culto* words, stemming from traditions of devotional literature, but Latinate for all that: 'pacífico refrigerio' and 'impedimento', 'astucias', 'documentos'. At first sight the teaching seems conventional enough, but its categorization of the world as the least difficult of the three to resist, the devil as hard to understand and the flesh as the hardest to overcome, is worth comment, if only because the teachings of the *Subida-Noche* will bear it out. Anyone who has embraced the religious life has already abandoned the world, so this is not the struggle it might be for those who have not. The devil often works in subtle, insidious ways, especially through visions and revelations, when the soul may interpret as divine what is demonic. But the flesh is the most stubborn foe because it drives human desires and leads the will into making wrong choices. The fact that all three are connected, as the dark nights of the soul themselves are, should warn against any facile schematization.

In his advice about the world he warns first to avoid loving some people more than others: 'tengas igualdad de amor e igualdad de olvido, ahora sean deudos, ahora no', 'be equal in your love and equal in your forgetting, whether people are relatives or not'.[8] The point is not to encourage inhumanity, but one equal love for everyone under God: 'Tenlos todos por extraños, y desta manera cumples mejor con ellos que poniendo la afición que debes a Dios en ellos' (p. 58), 'Treat them all as strangers, for this way you fulfil your duty towards them better than placing the affection due to God on them.' The same advice attaches to possessions and desires, for food, clothing or anything else, since there is no higher objective than the kingdom of God. Such a way leads to 'silencio y paz en los sentidos', 'silence and peace in the senses'. His most forceful comments, though, are devoted to the damage done to life within the community if members start paying attention to the attractions or shortcomings of other members, or start finding fault with individuals or community life. There will always be something to trip up on in religious communities, he warns, whether you live among angels or demons, therefore the tongue must be kept firmly under control. This is less a cultivated neo-Stoical indifference to material things than a common-sense attitude trained to be aware of how destructive petty jealousies and differences are in the intense life of a small community which holds everything in common. Detachment from such affections or concerns is vital, or they will come to occupy the central place in the mind of the religious which should be reserved for God alone.

In his advice against the devil, he begins with the important point that the devil usually leads religious astray under the appearance of good, not evil. Religious must therefore be on guard against anything that seems good, unless under obedience: the superior should be held in no less regard than God. This apparently astonishing claim is connected with San Juan's view that attitudes towards superiors can also be destructive when they come to dominate the thoughts of a friar or nun. Whether the superior is severe and makes you suffer, or gentle and amenable, the aim is to become indifferent to personal qualities and cultivate the habit of obedience. Humility in word and deed is the best remedy against such temptations. The third enemy, the flesh, is glossed as the need to overcome the self and its sensuality. San Juan teaches that religious enter the community to be worked upon by others, like the image on which sculptor, painter and gilder exercise their arts. Good works must be undertaken whether or not they are personally congenial; spiritual exercises should not be practised for the pleasure they bring or neglected because they are hard. Indeed, to do them precisely because one is resistant to them helps to cure self-love and gain the love of God.

This short work, like the similar 'Cuatro avisos a un religioso para alcanzar la perfección', 'Four counsels for a religious to attain perfection', the context and date of which is unknown, belong very much to a monastic environment. The tone of self-denial and self-abasement which characterizes them is not an end in itself, but a means towards achieving a life in which individual obsessions do not threaten the good of the whole community, and in which feelings and experiences, instead of being accepted uncritically, are subject to relentless analysis, especially where they threaten to become a substitute for God.

Having travelled to Ávila and failed to persuade Teresa to go south for the foundation of a Discalced convent in Granada, Fray Juan left for Beas at the end of 1581, to prepare for this. The nuns were lodged at first in the private house of Doña Ana de Peñalosa, because neither the necessary licence from the Archbishop nor the property they had been negotiating to buy were forthcoming. He now became Prior of the Granada monastery, a position he would occupy three times over the next six years, his longest stay in one place. This seems to have given him the opportunity, despite all the burdens of office, to continue working on his commentaries and to write the last of them, the *Llama*, in the space of a fortnight, if his secretary, Fray Juan Evangelista, is to be believed. Doña Ana was to become one of his most faithful disciples, following him in 1588 to Segovia, and after his death making arrangements for his burial and tomb. It was to her, a laywoman, that he dedicated the *Llama*.

Granada, with a population of around 33,000, was in the process of being rebuilt. Fray Juan's residence there covered the period between the resettlement in other parts of Spain of a large part of the *morisco* population following the Moorish revolt of the Alpujarras in 1568–70, and the eventual forcible expulsion of the remaining *moriscos* between 1609 and 1614. During his time at least eight *autos-da-fe* were held in the Plaza Nueva, at the foot of the steep hill leading down from the monastery into the city, or by the church of Santiago. But his writings are silent about these.[9] As Prior, he was expected to lead his growing community, attend to its spiritual formation and material needs, all of which he did, alongside a ministry of direction to the sisters and to a range of local people, by no means all drawn from the ranks of the noble and rich. Care of the sick and the poor was another aspect of his ministry: hunger and plague broke out in 1584 and 1585, and even poor monasteries found themselves sought out for charity. There was manual work too, following the Order's decision at Alcalá that no superior should be exempt from this. The monastery occupied a hill adjacent to the Alhambra, which had been the site of Moorish dungeons in which Christian prisoners had been kept (hence its name, 'Los Mártires'). Fray Juan oversaw the provision of water via an aqueduct, which solved a serious problem, and there is some evidence that Fray Juan's brother Francisco paid a visit to assist in the operations.[10]

During the years in Granada Fray Juan travelled widely. It has been calculated that he must have covered at least 25,000 kilometres during his lifetime, usually with a companion, much of it on foot or by mule: strict rules governed the way in which Discalced friars were permitted to travel.[11] In May 1583 he attended the Provincial Chapter in Almodóvar, presided over by Gracián, at which he was re-elected Prior of Granada, despite his own opposition to re-elections. A new African mission was approved, as well as the foundation of Discalced houses in Italy, to be undertaken by the rising star of Nicolás Doria, a Genoese banker who had come to Seville in 1570 at the age of 21, but had then passed through a conversion experience, turned his back on the world, become a priest in 1576 and joined the Carmelite Reform while it was still in crisis in 1578.[12]

Two years later Fray Juan travelled to Lisbon for the next Chapter, at which the absent Doria was elected Provincial, setting into motion a power struggle with Gracián which would lead to the latter's expulsion from the Order soon after Fray Juan's death, and be the indirect cause of Fray Juan's own exclusion, shortly before his death, from the affairs of the Order he had co-founded. Here, he was elected second *definidor*, and the first mission, of 12 friars, was sent to Mexico. A story told of him at this time has the ring of truth about it. In Lisbon there was a Dominican nun, Sor María de la Visitación, who was reputed to have the stigmata. Many churchmen, including Fray Luis de Granada, were persuaded by her claims and paid great attention to all she said. Fray Juan was very sceptical about such manifestations. Many years later, Gabriel de Cristo, Discaled Prior in Lisbon at the time of the Chapter, would recall what a fellow-Discalced on his way by the shore to see this prodigy, had told him:

> Arrimado a estas paredes hallé este día al padre fray Juan de la Cruz [. . .] con una Biblia en la mano, ocupado, como solía, en contemplación, al cual dije que, si gustaba, fuésemos los dos a ver la monja de las llagas, y el padre fray Juan de la Cruz me respondió: «¡Vaya de ahí! ¿Para qué quiere ver un embuste? Calle, verá cómo lo descubre Nuestro Señor». Con esto, dejándole yo allí en su ocupación, me fui. Y después, como habéis visto, sucedió todo, en los añós siguientes, como él lo había antes dicho.[13]

> That day I found Father John of the Cross [. . .] leaning up against the wall with a Bible in his hand, engaged, as usual, in contemplation. I said to him that if he liked we could both go to see the nun with the wounds, and he replied: 'Good heavens! What do you want to go and see a fraud for? Calm down, you'll see how our Lord unmasks it.' So leaving him there to his business, I went off. And afterwards, as you know, in the years to come everything turned out as he had earlier said.

The story is undoubtedly told to credit Fray Juan with the gift of discernment of spirits, but its emphasis on suspicion of extraordinary phenomena and on contemplative prayer through scripture is entirely consistent with the tenor of his writings.

The Chapter was effectively adjourned until October, at Pastrana, east of Madrid, so that Doria could be present. His growing hostility towards Gracián became apparent, as well as his desire to reform the governance of the Order, reflected in a new arrangement whereby a simple majority vote from among the *definidores* and the Provincial was deemed sufficient, with the stipulation that it should be called unanimous, so that those who objected to a new policy were required to support it, as an act of cabinet solidarity. Fray Juan's position remained secure, however: he was elected second *definidor*, and under another plan proposed by Doria, in which each of the four *definidores* was made Vicar General of one of the new vicariates, he stepped down as Prior of Granada in order to assume the responsibilities of Vicar General of Andalusia, working closely with Doria and meeting with him and the others at least once a year. At least Fray Juan was able to remain in the monastery with his new responsibilities. Before the Lisbon Chapter he had been present at the foundation of a convent in Málaga (February), where he saw the sea for the first time. He visited it again in May to comfort the sisters, after one of the nuns had committed suicide by throwing herself out of a window.

1586 was an especially busy year. In May he travelled to Córdoba to be present at the foundation of a Discalced monastery there; in October he visited the recently admitted monastery in La Manchuela (Jaén); in December he was with the nuns in Caravaca (Murcia) for the foundation of another new monastery. He paid two further visits to the sisters in Málaga. In the midst of all this, he had to attend the first of the meetings of the Junta (also known as the *Definitorio*) in Madrid in August and September, which introduced further changes. The traditional Carmelite breviary of the Jerusalem rite was replaced with the Roman breviary, breaking perhaps the last link with the origins of the Order. A Discalced Procurator General was to be sought from Rome so that the business of the Discalced could be effectively represented there. It was agreed that the body of Teresa should be returned from Ávila to Alba de Tormes, where she had died, and that her books should be printed (San Juan refers to this in CB 13.7).

A journey to Bujalance early in 1587, in connection with another foundation, was interrupted by a summons from Doria to meet him in Madrid, for reasons which are not clear. On his way back he made a diversion to visit the sisters in Caravaca (Murcia), but by the spring of 1588 was on the road again, this time to Valladolid, as far north as he was to reach. Here the Junta gathered in advance of the forthcoming Provincial Chapter, at which Fray Juan finished his term of office as *definidor* and Vicar General of Andalusia, and was re-elected Prior of Granada. The issuing of the Papal Brief *Cum de statu* by Sixtus V on 10 July 1587 marked a further stage towards the full independence of the Discalced. It gave them the right to appoint their own Vicar General, and to divide what had hitherto been a single Discalced Province into several, which would together form the Congregation of the Discalced. It also ordered Doria to summon the first Chapter General of this new Congregation, which duly took place in Madrid in June 1588. This marked the high point of Fray Juan's involvement in the governing of the Order, for he was appointed first *definidor* under Doria, now Vicar General, and third of the six *consiliarios* who were appointed to govern the Order with him. This new administrative body, the *Consulta*, was to be based in the monastery in Segovia, where Fray Juan was to become Prior, heralding at last his return to Castile.

The establishment of the *Consulta* led to further internal dissension. Gracián opposed it, because it seemed to him to go against the spirit of the Teresan Reform, as did Ana de Jesús, because it threatened to undermine the considerable independence the Teresan constitutions gave to the nuns by placing them under the authority of the friars: they lost their freedom to choose their own confessors and to re-elect their Prioresses and were required instead to deal with the distant, male-only *Consulta*.

Doria, however, regarded Gracián as too lax, made accusations, including sexual impropriety, against him, and deprived him of any voice in the Order's affairs for the next two years. Though Doria has often been presented as the villain of the piece, a lover of the letter rather than the spirit of the Reform, authoritarian and severe, it is probably true that the Order had grown to such an extent that it was no longer possible to govern it as it had been in its early years, largely through its Priors. It also seems to be the case that Gracián, in Lisbon in the early days of the Spanish Crown's rule over Portugal, had some contact through his visitation of a Calced convent there with the movement known as *sebastianismo*, which looked for the miraculous return of the young king Sebastián who had lost his life with so many members of the Portuguese nobility at the battle of Alcazarquivir in Morocco in 1578, precipitating the loss of Portuguese independence through the intervention of Philip II.[14]

Segovia, a city of some 18,000 inhabitants and at this stage still a flourishing centre of the wool and textile industry, was to be Fray Juan's home for all but the last few months of his life. Though he travelled less, he wrote little more, save letters and perhaps some final revisions to the *Llama*. On the other hand, he remained busy in his ministry of spiritual direction, with the internal affairs of the Order, and with extending and rebuilding the Segovia monastery, built on a plot taken over from an abandoned Trinitarian house too close to the river Eresma for comfort. Of all the monasteries with which he was associated, Segovia is the easiest for the modern pilgrim to visit. Set outside the city walls, close to the Templar Church of Vera Cruz, and with splendid views across the river to the Alcázar towering above, one can see exactly where Fray Juan acquired additional land, how he moved the buildings away from the river, and built a garden under the cliffs which marked the new boundary. The route up into the city is the one he took on his visits to confess the Discalced nuns, established there since 1574.

By 1590 tensions within the Order had reached crisis point. Gracián had been effectively dealt with by removing him from the *Consulta* in 1588 and keeping him at a distance in Portugal, but he continued to make his views known and Doria was minded to expel him altogether. Meanwhile, the nuns had attempted to bypass Doria's authority by appealing directly to Rome and gaining a Brief from Sixtus V (5 June 1590), confirming Teresa's constitutions and empowering intervention only by the Vicar General and a special Commissary. Fray Luis de León, the first editor of the works of Santa Teresa, and the Archbishop of Évora, were appointed to execute the Brief, but Doria went straight to the king and successfully obtained a stay.[15] Fray Juan may not have been especially enamoured of Gracián's behaviour, nor did he think the nuns had behaved particularly well, but he was not in favour of so radical a step as his expulsion. He expressed his reservations about the extreme policy Doria was pursuing, as well as the growth in legislation within the Order, which may have led Doria to assume that he was aligning himself with the opposition.[16] For the time being, the peace held. By the General Chapter of June 1591, in Madrid, Gracián seemed ready to return in obedience to Castile and Fray Juan continued to counsel moderation with respect to him as well as the nuns. Doria had gained a Counter-Brief, though this did not arrive until after the Chapter had ended. But after the elections

Fray Juan found himself relieved of all his responsibilities within the Order. Some scholars believe that at this point he was offered, or offered himself, for service overseas, in Mexico. He seems to have been given the opportunity to choose a community, perhaps to prepare himself for the new mission until the fleet was ready to set sail the following summer, and opted for the remoteness of La Peñuela, back in northern Andalusia, desiring, it appears, a life of withdrawal and anonymity, away from the conflicts within the Order, which must have distressed him. He bade farewell to his community in Segovia and travelled southwards, via Toledo. Doria's triumph would be complete when in 1592, after the death of Fray Juan, he expelled Gracián from the Order, punished María de San José and Ana de Jesús, who had led the nuns' opposition, and became the first General of the Discalced. Gracián led an eventful life thereafter: he went to Rome to seek justice, was captured by Turkish pirates and imprisoned in Tunis for two years, was ransomed and, after some years in Spain, went to Belgium, where he returned to the Calced Carmelites, though faithful to the spirit of Teresa, before dying in Brussels in 1614.

LETTERS

Only a few of San Juan's letters have survived, none from before 1581, and most from the last three years of his life. The bulk must have been lost or destroyed: according to his early biographers, shortly before he died he ordered a bundle of his letters and papers to be burnt, probably to spare his closest collaborators any persecution they might suffer on his account from Doria and those who were taking the Order in a different direction.[17] Yet they are an invaluable and little-studied resource for appreciating the context of his prose writings and spiritual teaching. Many of the most characteristic elements of his teaching and style are found in them, not now in the form of impersonal prose treatises, but as direct advice given to particular individuals, and accompanied by a good deal of personal reflection; indeed, they offer the only reliable access we have to the man himself. Some of them show him as a practical man, dealing with the business of foundations; others reveal an unexpected warmth and affection of tone. Almost all of them are addressed to women: only 6 of the 34 extant letters have male addressees (10, 13, 18, 24[?], 25, 33), and these, with one exception (13) deal primarily with the affairs of the Order.[18] Several are clearly replies to earlier letters; often Fray Juan apologizes for having delayed answering. Communication seems to have taken place through a network of official messengers but also informally, as friars and nuns travelled (19). In one of his last letters (29), to Ana de Peñalosa, he has taken advantage of two servants, presumably hers, to take it to her, and he expects it to reach her before a previous letter (lost) he had written to her from Baeza.

One letter (6) stands out as revealing a cannier side to Fray Juan in his work for the Order. Writing to Ana de San Alberto, Prioress of Caravaca, in June 1586 he describes the Córdoba foundation with evident pride – the pomp and ceremony, the crowds as large as for Corpus Christi, all the clergy and the guilds, the bishop's sermon in praise of the Order. He has now come to Seville, 'en la traslación de nuestras monjas, que han comprado unas casas principalísimas, que, aunque costaron casi catorce mil ducados, valen más de veinte mil', 'for our sisters' move: they have bought some very fine houses, which, though they cost only 14,000 ducats, are worth more than 20,000'. After describing his hopes for a possible male foundation in Écija, for which as yet he has no commission, and his forthcoming journeys thence to Málaga and to the Junta in Madrid, he passes to a more practical concern. The Caravaca sisters had come into dispute with the local Jesuits over a property which lay between their two sets of buildings as both communities were extending their premises. The sisters had apparently neglected to come to a formal written agreement with the Jesuits, who were now causing difficulties: 'Pesado me ha de que no se hizo luego la escritura con los Padres de la Compañía, porque no los tengo yo mirado con ojos que son gente que guarda la palabra, y así entiendo que no sólo se desviarán en parte, mas, si si difiere, se volverán de obrar en todo, si les parece les está bien', 'I am sorry the document was not signed at once with the Fathers of the Company [Jesuits], because in my view they are not people who keep their word, and so I feel sure that they will not only change their mind in part but, if there is a delay, will completely turn away from it, if they think it is to their advantage.' So, without telling anyone, she should start negotiations to buy the disputed premises, effectively beating the Jesuits at their own game, 'que ellos, como ven que tienen cogida la cuerda, ensánchanse; y va muy poco que después se sepa que las compramos sólo por eso de redimir nuestra vejación', 'because when they see they have got you by the rope they delay; and it does not matter if it then becomes known that we bought them only to be free of this irritation'. He adds: 'El librico de las *Canciones de la Esposa* querría que me enviase, que ya a buena razón lo tendrá sacado Madre de Dios', 'I would like you to send me the little book of the *Songs of the Bride*, as no doubt [Francisca de la] Madre de Dios will have finished copying them', a unique reference in his own writing to the textual transmission of his works.

Other letters deal with problems within the Order. The tenth, addressed to Fray Ambrosio Mariano, Prior of the Madrid house, from the time when Fray Juan was a member of the *Consulta* and senior *definidor*, reports that the *Consulta* had decided that novices should not be passed from one novice-master to another, which is damaging to their progress, but remain with one. To María de Jesús, Prioress of Córdoba, he answers a series of queries she has raised (letter 14, June 1589) about the use of the discipline, rising excessively early and permission for confessors, doctors, barbers and officials to enter the convent in case of necessity. Later (letter 21, June 1590) he advises her to worry less about the temporal affairs of her house, which God will attend to: 'la casa más la ha de gobernar y proveer con virtudes y deseos vivos del cielo que con cuidados y trazas de lo temporal y de tierra', 'you should rather govern the house and furnish it with virtues and living desire for heaven than with temporal and earthly worries and plans'. To the Vicar General Doria he reports (letter 18, September 1589) that the *Consulta* has considered what to do with the question he has raised of receiving novices in Genoa 'sin saber gramática', 'not knowing grammar'. Its view is that 'poco importa no la saber, como ellos entiendan el latín con la suficiencia que manda el concilio de manera que sepan bien construir', 'it is not important if they do not, as long as they understand as much Latin as the Council [of Trent] requires, so that they can construe it properly', a revealing comment about the educational requirements of the new generation of Discalced in Doria's own city.

The sense of having begun a new work in the Reform shines through another letter to the Prioress of Córdoba (letter 16; 18 July 1589). God has brought the sisters into 'casas tan pobres y con tantos calores', 'houses so poor and in such great heat', to show them the meaning of what they have professed. He tells them, by paradox and antithesis, to take care to conserve the spirit of poverty and contempt for all things which had animated them from the beginning, 'porque el pobre de espíritu en las menguas está más constante y alegre, porque ha puesto su todo en nonada y nada, y así halla en todo anchura de corazón', 'because the poor in spirit are more constant and happy in want, since they have placed their all in nothing, nothing at all, and therefore find in everything freedom of heart'. He reminds them that they have been chosen as the foundation stones on which future vocations will be built, so that they 'se aprovechen de este primero espíritu que da Dios en estos principios para tomar muy de nuevo el camino de perfección', 'should make the most of this first spirit God gives at such beginnings, to set out all over again on the road of perfection'. Similar advice is given in letter 17, to Magdalena del Espíritu Santo in Córdoba three weeks earlier, with an injunction reminiscent of the paradoxical antitheses in S 1.13.1: 'Para tener a Dios en todo conviene no tener en todo nada', 'To possess God in everything, you should possess nothing in everything.'

All through his letters run phrases and expressions found in his prose commentaries and popular poems. He longs to see Ana de San Alberto 'con gran desnudez de espíritu y tan sin arrimo de criaturas que todo el infierno no baste a turbarla' (4), 'in great nakedness of spirit and so free of creaturely dependence that all hell cannot disturb you' – echoing here not only his own *glosa* 'Sin arrimo y con arrimo' but also Teresa of Ávila's 'Nada te turbe', with its verse about standing firm when hell assails the soul.[19] His gift for vivid similes is seen in his letter (8) to the Beas sisters, in which he encourages them to concentrate on their vocation 'y no andar luego a buscar cosas nuevas', 'and not go looking at once for new things', because this engenders a kind of restlessness which leaves 'el espíritu flaco y vacío y sin virtud interior', 'the spirit weak and empty and without inward virtue', just as one should not keep eating when suffering from indigestion. To a girl from Ávila who is wanting to become a nun and has asked him some questions, he replies (letter 12) that to avoid sin she should shun people and conversation as far as she can, keep God's law assiduously, be moderate in ascetic practices and follow her mother's advice. To keep the mind and heart fixed on the glory to come, 'tenga toda la riqueza del mundo y los deleites de ella por lodo y vanidad y cansancio [. . .] y no estime en nada cosa alguna, por grande y preciosa que sea, sino estar bien con Dios, pues que todo lo mejor de acá, comparado con aquellos eternos bienes para que somos criados, es feo y amargo', 'hold all the riches of the world and its delights as mire and vanity and weariness [. . .] and value nothing as anything, however great and precious it is, because the best of this world, compared with those eternal gifts for which we are created, is ugly and bitter' – advice which closely repeats the teaching of S 1.4 and which is followed by greetings to her mother, clearly not something he sees as contradicting what he has just said about detachment.

Some of his briefest statements are among his most powerful and direct utterances: 'Si en algún tiempo, hermano mío, le persuadiere alguno, sea o no prelado, doctrina de anchura y más alivio, no la crea ni abrace, aunque se la confirme con milagros; sino penitencia y más penitencia y desasimiento de todas las cosas; y jamás, si quiere llegar a la posesión de Cristo, le busque sin la cruz' (24; undated fragment): 'If at any time, my brother, anyone – be he a superior or not – should persuade you of an easier and more pleasant teaching, do not believe or embrace it, even it is confirmed by miracles; instead, penitence, more penitence and detachment from all things. And if you wish to come to possess Christ, never seek him without the Cross.' The comment about miracles and the way of the cross is entirely characteristic, as his long discussion of mystical phenomena in the *Subida* amply shows. In another undated fragment (32), he writes, reflecting no doubt on his own exile to La Peñuela: 'Ame mucho a los que la contradicen y no la aman, porque en eso se engendra amor en el pecho donde no le hay', 'Love much those who contradict you and do not love you, because in this way love is born in the breast which has none.' More simply and famously: 'Y adonde no hay amor, ponga amor, y sacará amor' (27, fragment), 'And where there is no love, put love, and you will bring love forth.'

In a number of places in the letters one also notes stylistic features found in his more developed writing. His paradoxical turn of phrase is applied to his own situation as much as others': 'es lima el desamparo, y para gran luz el padecer tinieblas', (letter 1, July 1581), 'vulnerability is a file, and suffering darkness brings great light'. Playing on the paradox, he adds that he has much else to say: 'Mas escribo muy a oscuras [. . .] por eso ceso sin acabar', 'But I am really writing in the dark [. . .] so I finish without ending' (letter 1). The Bible is less central to this more personal discourse, though the allusion to Jonah and the whale in this letter or, in a fragment of the fifth, to Gideon's soldiers as types of those who empty themselves of reliance on creaturely aids, remains present. The seventh letter (November 1586, to the Beas sisters) is an exception, as it contains a short but dense exegesis of two apparently unrelated symbols, the crown and water, through a series of Old Testament texts to encourage the nuns to continue to progress 'en Cristo, cuyos deleites y corona son sus esposas', 'in Christ, whose delights and crown are his brides'. Crowns are seen as pointing the soul upwards to the day of the soul's coronation, when she will receive from above 'aguas de deleites in[te]riores', 'waters of inward delights'.

One of the most consistent features of his letters is his insistence on faith, especially when events seem to be conspiring against his correspondents. On three occasions (4, 20, 29) he deals with scruples, that over-punctilious concern with trivial matters which is common in the religious life. He shows himself to be wise and balanced, notably when addressing an unknown nun in the days leading up to Pentecost (20). His first piece of advice is to concentrate on the feast and its meaning – the coming of the Holy Spirit and his continual presence. In this way he brings her back to the essentials of liturgy and doctrine. He then advises her not to go to confession, presumably because this would only exacerbate her difficulties. But, he adds, if she does she is not to confess involuntary thoughts, which are to be disregarded, but to confine herself to general points about her failings of memory, understanding and will. She should also confess any excess of words or her lack of attention to speaking in truth and purity. In terms of works, she should only be concerned about the 'recto y solitario fin', 'true and solitary end' she seeks, God alone. There is no need to go into detail, even though refraining from doing so is painful to her. She should make her communion at Pentecost and on other days when she normally would. His final advice is intended to help her connect her own troubles with Christ's suffering, rather than become absorbed in them, and is offered in terse and alliterative language: 'Cuando se le ofreciere algún sinsabor y disgusto, acuérdese de Cristo crucificado y calle', 'when upsetting or unpleasant things come along, remember Christ crucified and be silent'. Equally, negative experiences are set in the context of spiritual growth: 'Viva en fe y esperanza, aunque sea a oscuras, que en esas tinieblas ampara Dios al alma', 'Live in faith and hope, even if darkly, for in such darkness God protects the soul.'

The opinion Fray Juan gave about the case of an unnamed Carmelite nun for the Discalced Vicar General, Doria (25), reveals a more critical assessment of spiritual claims very much in line with the teaching of the *Subida-Noche*. He finds four lesser defects in her and one which is fundamental. She seems to have 'mucha golosina de apetito', 'a very greedy appetite', for prayer, whereas truly spiritual people always show 'gran desnudez', 'great nakedness'. She shows too much confidence in herself and is not concerned about 'errar interiormente', 'inward error'. She wants to persuade everyone that what she has experienced is good and abundant, whereas the truly spiritual seek only to be accounted as nothing. Her style and language are inappropriate, a point San Juan elaborates in his chapter on preaching (S 3.45): the wrong kind of spirituality will betray itself in the language in which it expresses itself. The spirit she claims to have 'enseña estilo más sencillo y sin afectaciones ni encarecimientos, como éste lleva', 'teaches a simpler style, without affectation or exaggeration, as here', while 'todo esto que dice: «dijo ella a Dios, y Dios a ella», parece disparate', 'everything she says about "she said to God, and God said to her", seems nonsense'. But above all, she seems entirely lacking in the fundamental virtue of humility. If her experiences were truly of union with God she would be bound to write a good deal about this, because it is their first consequence. People who seek consolations in prayer, whose pride leads them to suppose that God has favoured them and that everyone else must be told, and who write about their experiences in inappropriately self-aggrandizing language, are in his view lacking the most basic element of the spiritual life, humility. Prayer does not exist for their personal indulgence or to enhance their reputation for sanctity, and any genuine encounter with the divine will lead the soul to the keenest possible awareness of her own worthlessness in comparison. So his conclusion is a hard one: she must not write any more about it or talk to her confessor about it, and she must be tested 'en el ejercicio de las virtudes a secas, mayormente en el desprecio, humildad y obediencia', 'in the exercise of virtues as they are, particularly in contempt, humility and obedience'.

The thirteenth and longest letter, written to one of his male charges, has sometimes been appended to the end of the unfinished third book of the *Subida*, since it deals with spiritual joy, one of the four passions San Juan announces he will deal with in the active night of the spirit (S 3.16.2), but never does. It comes in response to an earlier letter soliciting advice on how to mortify and expunge all affections for whatever is not God. The will naturally seeks enjoyment from spiritual things, but God cannot be limited to human desires or pleasures in this way, however lofty they may seem to be. For the will has never enjoyed God as he is, so cannot know what that might be. That is why to be united with God it must purge itself of all other appetites and affections, which will always be self-centred, to concentrate solely on loving God. Desire for God cannot unite the soul with God; only divine love has that unitive power, and the soul's work is to make room for this to operate. As always, he is making an absolute distinction between creature and Creator, and warning his correspondent not to confuse the means with the end: 'Que, pues Dios es incomprehensible e inaccesible, la voluntad no ha de poner su operación de amor para ponerla en Dios, en lo que ella puede tocar y aprehender con el apetito, sino en lo que no puede comprehender ni llegar con él', 'For, since God is incomprehensible and inaccesible, the will must not apply its operation of love to what it can touch and know of God with its appetite, but to what it cannot understand or reach in this way.' Feelings, however spiritually exalted, must therefore be left behind: their absence is not an absence of God, nor their presence a sign of his (compare C 1.4), because spiritual feelings and desires can no more capture God than can human language. What is required is a complete emptiness and nakedness of all appetite for anything before God, 'para que Dios la hinche y llene de su amor y dulzura, y estarse con esa hambre y sed de sólo Dios', 'so that God can expand the soul and fill her with his love and sweetness, and to be hungry and thirsty for God alone'.

Most surprising, perhaps, is the degree of genuine personal feeling some of his letters reveal. In the second (March 1582), soon after his arrival to be Prior in Granada he writes to one of the Beas sisters: '¡Ojalá v[uestra] m[erced] con sus hermanas moraran en ella [Granada], por que las pudiera yo en algo dar contento', 'If only you and your sisters lived here, so that in some way I might please you.' Later, in a letter addressed to them all (letter 8; November 1587) he excuses his slowness in replying not as a lack of will on his part but because writing and speaking are not of the essence: what counts is 'el callar y obrar', 'being silent and doing works'. Having advised Ana de San Alberto how to deal with her scruples (letter 4), he tells her that if she wishes to share her troubles with him, 'váyase a aquel espejo sin mancilla del Eterno Padre que es su Hijo, que allí miro yo su alma cada día', 'go to that spotless mirror of the Eternal Father, which is his Son, for there I see your soul every day'. But he can equally well muse on his own experience: 'Esto por mí lo veo, que cuanto las cosas son más mías más tengo el alma y corazón en ellas y mi cuidado [. . .] Bueno estoy, aunque el alma muy atrás', 'I see this for myself – the more things I have the more my soul and heart focus on them, and my worry [. . .] I am fine, though my soul is very backward' (letter 11; to a laywoman in Granada, from Segovia, January 1589). Many of his letters end with greetings, usually to sisters or laywomen by name, rather like the Pauline Epistles, the apparent misogyny of which needs to be read against these personal touches.

Fray Juan's last days can be traced in the series of letters he wrote from Madrid and La Peñuela in the late summer of 1591, which, despite the poignancy of their tone, reveal that the teaching he had so often given to others he had now to apply to himself. To Ana de Jesús, in Segovia, he writes before setting out from Madrid (letter 26; 6 July 1591), to tell her to give thanks that matters have not turned out as she would have wished. Freed from all burdens in the Order, a life of peace, solitude and forgetting of self and the creatures beckons him, though he is still fearful that he may be required to return to Segovia. His final greeting is tender, as if he knew this were a kind of farewell: 'Pero, ahora sea yendo, ahora quedando, doquiera y comoquiera que sea, no la olvidaré ni quitaré de la cuenta que dice, porque con veras deseo su bien para siempre', 'But whether going or staying, wherever and however it may be, I shall not forget you, nor abandon the debt you mention, because truly I desire your good for ever.' Six weeks later, having recently arrived at La Peñuela, he is writing in the same vein to Ana de Peñalosa, about the freedom and space he finds in his isolation, 'aunque el alma muy pobre anda', 'though the soul is in a very poor state'. The contrast he draws between handling crops and being manipulated by people betrays a deeper feeling about his fate: 'Esta mañana habemos ya venido de coger nuestros garbanzos, y así, las mañanas. Otro día los trillaremos. Es lindo manosear estas criaturas mudas, mejor que no ser manoseadas de las vivas'; 'This morning we have just come from picking our chick-peas – that's how our mornings are spent. Tomorrow we'll clean them. It's lovely to handle these dumb creatures – better than being handled by living ones' (letter 29, 19 August 1591). To a friar who has expressed fears for his future in the Order he writes at about the same time (letter 33; a fragment): 'Hijo, no le dé pena eso, porque el hábito no me lo pueden quitar sino por incorregible e inobediente, y yo estoy muy aparejado para enmendarme de todo lo que hubiere errado y para obedecer en cualquiera penitencia que me dieren', 'My son, do not be concerned about this, because they cannot take my habit from me unless I am incorrigible or disobedient, and I am very ready to make amends for all my errors and to comply with whatever penitence they may give me.'

His final letter (34), addressed to Ana de Peñalosa, is written on 21 September as he is about to leave for Úbeda, 'a curar de unas calenturillas', 'to be treated for a bit of fever', from which he has been suffering for about a week with no improvement. He looks forward to returning soon to La Peñuela, for which he departed a week later. The Úbeda monastery had been founded four years earlier. Its Prior, Francisco Crisóstomo, is thought to have borne a grudge against Fray Juan ever since on a visit to the community in Seville some years earlier, he had been reprimanded, with Fray Diego Evangelista (recently appointed by the *Consulta* as Visitor to Andalucian houses in connection with the investigations against Gracián), for spending too much time outside the monastery.[20] Once there, his condition rapidly deteriorated. The testimony of those who were present indicates that he was harshly treated during his final illness by both men, though a visit at the end of November by the Provincial, Antonio de Jesús, his companion all those years ago in Duruelo, seems to have alleviated the situation, and to have engendered a change of heart on the part of the Prior. The accounts of Fray Juan's last days and his death just after midnight on 14 December 1591, influenced, no doubt, by the desire to present the sufferings of Fray Juan's last weeks in the most Christlike fashion, emphasize his resignation, devotion and faith, despite the pain he must have experienced from the suppurating ulcers which had spread from his legs to other parts of his body. He is supposed to have asked to have passages from the Song of Songs recited to him in place of the traditional commendation of his soul, and, as the bell for matins rang, to have exclaimed that he was going to sing them in heaven. His last words are recorded as those of Christ on the cross: 'Into thy hands, Lord, I commend my spirit.' But the real miracle is surely how more than 400 years after the suffering and death he sought in a distant place, this friar of small stature and unprepossessing appearance came to be known all over the world for the beauty of his poetry and the profundity of his teaching.[21]

NOTES

1 *Obras* (ST), p. 928.
2 See Sister Anne Hardman, *Life of the Venerable Anne of Jesus* (London: Sands, 1932), Ildefonso Moriones, *Ana de Jesús y la herencia teresiana: ¿humanismo cristiano o rigor primitivo?* (Rome: Teresianum, 1968); Concha Torres Sánchez, *Ana de Jesús (1545–1621)* (Madrid: Orto, 1999).
3 *Obras* (SJ), pp. 42–56.
4 See Álvaro Huerga, *Los alumbrados de Baeza* (Jaén: Diputación Provincial, 1978).
5 See Gabriel Beltrán, 'San Juan de la Cruz en Baeza: Textos y notas del Libro de Protocolo del Colegio de San Basilio', *SJC*, 14 (1994), pp. 233–47.
6 Figures from José Mariá Javierre, *Juan de la Cruz: Un caso límite* (Salamanca: Sígueme, 1992), p. 740.
7 *Obras* (SJ), pp. 57–61.
8 On the theme of 'igualdad de amor', see below, pp. 179–82.
9 Teresa mentions such events, *Fundaciones*, 12.3.
10 The monastery was pulled down in the nineteenth century, but the aqueduct and the grounds remain.
11 Federico Ruiz, ed., *Dios habla en la noche* (Madrid: Espiritualidad, 1990), pp. 254, 303; Javierre, *Juan*, p. 920.
12 On Doria, see *Dios habla en la noche*, pp. 315–16.
13 Cited from Crisógono de Jesús, *Vida y obras completas de San Juan de la Cruz* (Madrid: BAC, 1964), p.250.
14 Javierre, *Juan*, p.1018. For a more favourable view of Doria and a more critical account of Gracián, see Joachim Smet, *The Carmelites: A History of the Brothers of Our Lady of Mount Carmel* (Darien, IL: The Carmelite Press, 1988), II, pp. 102–131. Smet sees the conflict between them as stemming from the former's 'rigid asceticism' and the latter's 'activism', representing 'two divergent concepts of the Carmelite vocation'; p. 126.
15 For the role of Luis de León as defender of the privileges of the Discalced nuns, see *Obras*, I, pp. 942–50; C. P. Thompson, *The Strife of Tongues* (Cambridge: Cambridge University Press, 1988), pp. 122–3, 269.
16 Javierre, *Juan*, p. 1051, notes that the 59 paragraphs of the Teresan constitutions had grown to 461 by Doria's death in 1594.
17 See above, p. 47.
18 Some are autographed (2, 7, 10, 12, 14, 16, 19–22, 28, 34); the rest have survived only in manuscript copies or more recent photocopies. Several exist only as fragments.
19 See above, pp. 61, 81.
20 Javierre, *Juan*, pp. 845–6, says that Francisco Crisóstomo was a novice in Granada who did

not fit in, so Fray Juan asked for him to be sent somewhere else; see also p. 928. Cf. p. 1088, where this is said to have happened in Seville for the reasons given above.

21 No physical likeness of San Juan from his lifetime seems to have survived. Fray Eliseo de los Mártires, who professed in Granada and later became the first Discalced Provincial of Mexico, collected together a number of the sayings of Fray Juan known as the *Dictámenes del espíritu*, which begin with the following description: 'Fue hombre de mediano cuerpo, de rostro grave y venerable, algo moreno y de buena fisonomía; su trato y su conversación apacible, muy espiritual y provechoso para los que le oían y comunicaban', 'He was a man rather small in build, with a serious and venerable face, rather dark and of goodly appearance. His dealings with people and his conversation were pleasant, very spiritual and beneficial to all who heard him or talked with him.' A nun, María de San Pedro, remembered him less flatteringly but more realistically: 'un hombre no hermoso y pequeño; traslucía un no sé qué', 'a little man, not good-looking; something shone through him'.

6

Music from the Past

Lead me from the unreal to the real; lead me from darkness to light; lead me from death to immortality.

(The Upanishads)

Thoughts like these, from the Hindu scriptures, have been voiced by mystics of all times and places: human experience of the world is unreal, in comparison with the real world, unseen but ever present, surrounding us; we think we live in the light, whereas we live in darkness and ignorance in comparison with the light of this unseen world; we think we are alive, but we are as dead in comparison with the true, immortal life of the world beyond sense and time. Mystical literature abounds in antithetical formulations of this kind. Plato said the same; San Juan could be said to have written an extended gloss on these words. The teachings of the great mystics often express themselves in similar concepts and images, even when there is no possibility of mutual influence, which suggests that they may be expressing a constant in human experience and its encounter with whatever name it uses for God.[1]

The origins of the Western mystical tradition lie in the remotest past, but certain moments in its development have affected it deeply.[2] Some have much wider cultural significance, like Plato's allegories of the cave in the *Republic* and the charioteer in the *Phaedrus*, and his picture of the soul as imprisoned in the body.[3] In the first, Plato raises fundamental questions about human knowledge and its limitations. It is as if human beings were prisoners chained to their places and able only to see flickering shadows on a screen in front of them thrown by a fire above and behind them, of which they are unaware. Because they have always been there, they believe that the shadows are reality. If one were freed and able to ascend into daylight, he would at first be dazzled; once accustomed to the light, he would realize the error of his former companions. If he returned he would be unable to see the shadows because of the brightness of the world he had left behind. But if he tried to tell his fellows that they were fools and blind, they would laugh at him, say that his visit to the upper world had ruined his sight, and that the ascent was not even worth the attempt.

This allegory of the human condition proposes that the light by which we see and know is but a shadow in comparison with the true light of the realm of Ideas and Forms. That light is accessible only to the soul, but the soul is imprisoned in the body and can hardly even remember that such a realm exists. The philosopher María Zambrano, a great admirer of San Juan, recalls in her *Filosofía y poesía* that Plato's metaphor for the soul's imprisonment in the body was submarine, not terrestrial. The sea both erodes and deforms it, encrusting it with shells, seaweed and rocks, so that it can no longer be seen as it is (the sense of Shakespeare's image of 'sea-change' in *The Tempest*). This prison is therefore like an organism to which fresh layers are constantly being added, with the result that it becomes correspondingly more difficult to imagine what it would be like free of such accretions or how it could act independently of them.[4]

Whether or not San Juan was aware of the exact Platonic image, its sense remains basic to his thought. Already suffering the effects of original sin, the soul is unable to act in conformity with its divine origin, because the deposits of repeated mistaken choices build up like accretions, and the choices themselves become so habitual that they appear neutral or even good. People get used to thinking about themselves and their world in a particular way, which slips into becoming the only way they think. They remember particular pleasures and want to repeat them because they are gratifying. Ingrained habits of thought and desire lead them to make the same choices, over and over again, which accumulate to damage their capacity to respond to God, or lead them to feel that he is irrelevant.[5]

The allegory of the charioteer describes the opposing forces of reason and sensuality in the soul. Souls which do not attain to the contemplation of perfect justice and knowledge find themselves as in a chariot no longer under the control of the charioteer, reason. One kind of soul strains upwards to the vision of reality, but because the horses are unruly has only an impaired vision. Another sort tries to reach the upper world, but the horses jostle and trample each other and drag the soul down to confusion and toil, where it feeds only on 'mere opinion' instead of the vision of reality. San Juan, like many mystics, sees the pull of the senses as working against the desire of the spirit to rise above the earthly and material; indeed, the practice of asceticism, presupposed in his teaching, is intended to subdue the sensual appetites of the body through rigorous disciplines like fasting and other physical deprivations and discomforts, and break the will and its habitual choice of evil. The antithesis of sense and spirit is one of the foundations on which San Juan's work rests, but, as we shall see, his aim is to restore a right relationship between the two, in which the senses act under the direction of the spirit, moving the will to the choice of the good.

Plato's philosophy, adapted and modified over the course of many centuries by classical and Christian thinkers, up to the Renaissance neo-Platonists of the late fifteenth and early sixteenth centuries, profoundly affected the development of Christian theology and spirituality. His underlying contrast between 'that which always is and never becomes' and 'that which is always becoming and never is' found fertile ground as Christianity developed in the Roman Empire, and discovered in Graeco-Roman philosophy a useful ally for distinguishing between the eternal and changeless nature of God and the world of flux and change in which things come to be and cease to be. The Christian Gospel proclaimed that in the Incarnate Son the divine Word was united with human flesh and entered the world of corruption and change to redeem it; 'that which always is' became flesh, so that 'that which is always becoming' might have eternal life. The Incarnation, which united the two realms, made it possible for the eternal being made known in the temporal though creaturely relationship with the Word made flesh. The necessary connection between an incarnational theology and San Juan's mysticism has not always been well understood.[6]

Two particular moments in the development of the Western mystical tradition require attention. The first is the account St Augustine gives in the *Confessions* (ix.10) of what has come to be called the vision of Ostia. Waiting with his mother to board a ship, not long before her death, he converses with her of the life of the saints in heaven. As they talk, their souls are lifted upwards, through the heavens with their celestial bodies, beyond the region of their own souls, to the eternal pastures of truth (significantly, Augustine is echoing Song 1.6). As they speak, so for a fleeting instant they touch and are one with uncreated Wisdom.[7] The vision describes a journey upward, to a place of eternal light and knowledge and a fleeting union with the source, and it shows the strong influence of the mid-Platonism associated with the philosopher and mystic Plotinus (c. 205–70), whose *Enneads* Augustine had studied. But Augustine's account also provides an authoritative account of a mystical experience from the greatest of the Latin Fathers, to add to St Paul's ascent to the third heaven, in 2 Corinthians 12.2, mentioned by San Juan on three occasions.[8]

However, San Juan is more closely associated with the symbol of the dark night and with a way he describes as 'no saber', not knowing, ultimately derived from Dionysius the Areopagite, whose works had appeared in Latin translation in Western Europe by the ninth century. The identification of the author with the person of that name converted by St Paul in Athens (Acts 17.34) endowed his writing with great authority.[9] The pseudo-Dionysius wrote several treatises, but the one which was to mark the Western tradition so indelibly was far and away the shortest, the *Mystical Theology*. It is the foundation of the so-called *via negativa*, the study of God by negation (also known as apophatic theology, and of especial importance in the spiritual literature of the Orthodox East). It begins with an invocation to the Holy Trinity, dwelling in a deep but dazzling darkness. Human language and concepts cannot penetrate this mystery, for God is above and beyond them, unreachable, unknowable. They can only say what God is not, and the closer we approach him the more conscious we shall be of darkness. San Juan had read this treatise, and cites its author.[10]

The pervasive presence of Dionysian negative theology can be seen in the anonymous medieval English *Cloud of Unknowing*, probably from the fourteenth century.[11] The Augustinian world of ascent to the region of light and knowledge has been replaced by a Dionysian one of ascent into cloud, darkness and not knowing. The author addresses the *Cloud* to a disciple, advising him to try to forget all created things. At the start, only darkness will be encountered, as it were a 'cloud of unknowing' between the soul and God and 'a cloud of forgetting' between the soul and the creatures (3–5; compare S 1.3–5). God is incomprehensible to our intellect, but not to our love (4; C prologue). You must strike at this cloud with an arrow of eager love; all thought must be left behind, even holy meditation on the Passion or on the goodness and mercy of God, in order to penetrate this cloud of unknowing

(6–7; S 2.13). All that is required is a naked, loving attention directed towards God, naked because it is not clothed in words, ideas or images (7; San Juan frequently uses expressions like 'advertencia amorosa', 'loving attention', and 'desnudez', 'nakedness'). Never in this life can you have a clear vision of God, but if you allow him to lift you up into this cloud, you will have some awareness of him. You should try to be like Mary (the type of contemplative life) rather than Martha (the active life), a traditional distinction found in almost all Spanish spiritual writing of the sixteenth century.

If you continue striking against this cloud, it is possible that God will send an arrow of spiritual light which will pierce it, and reveal to you some of his secrets, of which it is not possible or lawful to speak, but which will make you burn in love towards him (2 Corinthians 12.2; N 2.12–13). Any 'consolations', like sounds, sweetness, joy, which come suddenly from the outside, may be good but they may equally be evil (S 2.16–30; 3.7–13; Teresa, *Fundaciones*, 8). The hard ascent of the mountain is prefigured in the person of Moses in the cloud of Mount Sinai (S 1.5.6). Just when God appears to have abandoned the soul, he returns suddenly and inflames it with greater passion than before (the trajectory of the *Cántico*, especially CB 1–15).

These are only some of the parallels which can be drawn. They demonstrate how the influence of Dionysian negative theology had developed to become a symbol for the whole spiritual journey, and how that influence had become generalized in mystical writing. Similar expressions, ideas and biblical allusions are found in works which were separated by centuries and existed in isolation from each other. Because San Juan cannot have read the *Cloud*, it provides a good example of the nature of the tradition which nourished him – a living tradition, not only read about in books, but heard in sermons and talked about in spiritual conversation, especially in monastic tradition. One does not need to posit a direct chain of transmission to argue that a work like the *Cloud* belongs to the same world as San Juan's: better, perhaps, to think in terms of a substratum of common experience, expressed in terms drawn from a common tradition.

Not all mystical writing used the language of cloud and darkness. Other medieval English mystics cultivate other parts of the tradition: Richard Rolle's *The Fire of Love* knows little of anguish or suffering, and expresses the mystical journey in terms of fire, light, heat, love, joy and sweetness – images which are frequent enough in San Juan. Julian of Norwich's *Revelations of Divine Love* recount a series of visions which occurred during a severe illness over a period of a month, and wrestle with profound theological problems of goodness and evil, and divine justice and mercy.[12] Santa Teresa has less to say about dark nights, perhaps because her struggles to be taken seriously as a woman of prayer and as a monastic Reformer involved her in years of personal turmoil.

One thing the *Cloud* and the *Fire* and almost all medieval mystical treatises agree about, however, is that the spiritual journey they teach is accessible to everyone, not only or mainly to the learned. To follow it only love is required, and all have the capacity for loving, regardless of the level of their knowledge or intellectual accomplishment. Time and again one comes upon statements to the effect that those excluded from power and education (the poor and simple, women) can travel this road – even, presumably, the illiterate, as long as they are well guided.[13] Theirs is a spirituality for the marginalized, an alternative to the inaccessibility and the sterility of the religion of the established order, the world in which the clerks (men) studied scholastic theology, in Latin, and disputed abstruse theological questions. Mystical literature in this tradition opened up a way of prayer and growth in the Christian faith for those who were not content with a merely superficial practice, yet lacked the qualifications for deeper study. It is therefore no accident that women's voices found expression in mystical texts – Julian of Norwich and Margery Kempe in England, Saints Catherine of Siena and Catherine of Genoa in Italy, and Hildegard of Bingen and Mechtild of Magdeburg in Germany, long before Teresa. For some women, entry into a convent was the only way open to them to a world in which women could live in relative independence of men, for example in escaping from arranged marriages, as Santa Teresa describes in the book which tells of her first foundations of Discalced Carmelite convents.[14]

Augustine's vision of knowledge and light and the Dionysian language of darkness marked the language of Western mysticism. But from the Cistercian spirituality of St Bernard onwards, a strongly affective element entered the tradition, and love wrested the primacy from knowledge as both the means to union and the goal itself. No longer was mystical union thought of as primarily intellective, the human mind illumined by the wisdom of God. Now the mystic seeks to burn for and in the love of God, as lover with Beloved, rather than to be one with the divine Mind.[15] This distinguishing of knowledge and love is most clearly expressed by San Juan in the prologue to the *Cántico*, dedicated to Madre Ana de Jesús: 'aunque a V. R. le falte el ejercicio de teología escolástica con que se entienden las verdades divinas, no le falta el de la mística, que se sabe por amor en que no solamente se saben, mas juntamente se gustan' (.3); 'although Your Reverence lacks the use of scholastic theology, by which divine truths are understood, she is not lacking in mystical theology, which is known through love, and by which divine truths are not only known but enjoyed'. She has not studied theology as priests must, but she has an advantage over them, for she knows God through love, not as an object of intellectual investigation, and in such love she savours his delights. Love, as San Juan will go on to explain, is the principle which makes union with the infinity of God possible. Knowledge alone cannot do that, since human knowledge is finite, must enter the darkness to be reborn as faith; knowledge through love unites both the mind and the will with God.

The distinction is an ancient one, symbolized in Christian tradition by the coming to Christ's birth of both wise men and shepherds. The wise men come prompted by intellectual searching, the study of the stars, while the shepherds are drawn by wonder and love, so memorably expressed by Sidney Godolphin (1610–43) in his poem 'Lord when the wise men came from far'. The magi have studied the heavens and the laws of nature, and seek to ascend from their studies to discover the First Cause of all. The simple shepherds come in response to the angelic voices and seek the Child with humility and love. When they reach the manger, the magi must leave behind all their knowledge, to marvel at the wondrous birth, as the shepherds do intuitively: 'Wisemen, all wayes of knowledge past/To th'shepheards wonder come at last'.[16] The poem ends by showing how, when we raise our eyes to heaven and confess our pitiful state with thanksgiving, 'Then though wee do not know, we love', as Madre Ana does.

The terms 'mystical theology' and 'mysticism' are themselves open to misunderstanding. Dionysian language provides San Juan with the fundamental symbol of the dark night and the paradoxes of light and darkness, knowing and not knowing, though he extended its scope to cover the whole of the human journey towards God. He uses the term 'mystical theology' to refer to the direct experience of God, rather than in its primary, Dionysian meaning of a theology which proceeds by way of negations, though his approach to language provides evidence for this sense too.[17] He makes it a synonymn of infused contemplation (S 2.8.6; N 2.5.1), and translates it as 'sabiduría de Dios secreta o escondida', 'the secret, hidden wisdom of God' (CB 39.12). It is linked with 'amor secreto', 'secret love', which inspires the soul to leave all behind her and ascend to God (N 2.20.6). Dionysius is concerned to establish that human language and concepts can never capture the essence of a God who is beyond any affirmation or negation of his being which we might make. His work is metaphysical and speculative, while San Juan turns negation into the basis of his practical teaching on the spiritual journey, retaining images of darkness to speak of the divine Being, but also of all that impedes the soul from reaching God – sensual and spiritual appetites, or love for the creatures, which is a dark night for the soul (S 1.3–10). Faith too – the road by which we travel – is darkness because it proceeds by a way of 'no saber', 'not knowing' or 'unknowing' (S 2.2–4). The dark night of San Juan is therefore all-embracing: it is the negation of creaturely appetites at the start of the journey (asceticism, mortification), the route taken (faith) and the goal sought (the hiddenness of God). It is the ultimate development of the *via negativa*; beginning from the Dionysian darkness, it radiates inwards to cover areas never before so powerfully explored and mapped. San Juan differs from Dionysian negative theology in another respect. Whereas in the *Mystical Theology* Dionysius denies that neither affirmations nor negations, simple words nor images, can express anything at all about God, San Juan, paradoxically, both denies and affirms. He creates in his poetry whole constellations of images which move the reader by their beauty. Though they are but a 'no sé qué', a stammering of the inexpressible glories of God, they are indeed 'something', not nothing; that 'something' which has overflowed from his experience, and which in his commentaries he will endeavour to expound.

A significant part of the the history of the Western mystical tradition also lies in its engagement with the Bible, and in that history one book more than any other has pride of place – the Song of Solomon, called in the Vulgate 'Canticum Canticorum', the Song of Songs. As Jean Leclercq pointed out to his audience of young Benedictines 40 years ago, this was 'the book which was most read, and most frequently commented in the medieval cloister', for its teaching about 'loving, disinterested contemplation'.[18] Since the eighteenth century, critics have generally viewed the Song as a collection of oriental erotic poems, with no real unity other than that imposed on it by its editor(s). Parallels have been drawn with Syrian and Egyptian love lyrics, in which similar images, so strange to Western eyes, have been found. It is widely celebrated as love poetry of the highest order, delicate, rich and sensuous, while in recent years feminist commentators have found in it an equality and mutuality in the depiction of male–female relationships which redresses the predominantly patriarchal balance of the Bible.[19] Its attribution to Solomon has long been discounted, and few scholars are prepared to argue that its primary, intended meaning is spiritual, though it is a late book and by the time it was written and/or edited nuptial imagery was already well established as a metaphor for the relationship between God and his Bride, Israel.[20]

From the first Christian century till the rise of historical criticism, the Song was universally read by Jews and Christians as a love song between, variously, God and Israel, God and the soul, Christ and the Church. This was the tradition which exercised an unmistakeable influence over the literature of Western mysticism, and which San Juan inherited and used in an entirely natural manner. Malón de Chaide, writing in the same decade as San Juan was preparing his commentaries, put it succinctly: 'Habla el Señor con el alma debajo de metáfora de matrimonio, y llama al alma su esposa, y él se dice nuestro esposo. Y de este lenguaje y estilo de hablar está llena la Escritura Sagrada, particularmente los Cantares y los Profetas', 'The Lord speaks to the soul under the metaphor of marriage, and calls the soul his bride, and himself our husband. Holy Scripture is full of such language and manner of speaking, especially the Song and the Prophets.'[21] It is this tradition which explains why the poetic voice of San Juan's verse is so often the feminine 'esposa' in dialogue with her 'esposo', whatever conclusions one may wish to draw in our own age about a male poet adopting the feminine perspective. It may be, as critical consensus now suggests, that the Song only became accepted into the canon of scripture because Jews and Christians, discomfited by its frankly erotic language, attributed it to Solomon and had given it a spiritual interpretation. Homer's commentators, after all, had tried to resolve the apparent mismatch between the greatness of his poetry and the profundity of his thought on the one hand and his ready acceptance of an anthropomorphic polytheism on the other, by insisting that the latter was not to be taken literally.

The allegorizing tradition associated with Philo of Alexandria (c. 20 BC–c. AD 50), a Jewish scholar deeply influenced by the Hellenic culture of that city, passed into early Christian thinking. Origen (c. 185–c. 254), one of the greatest of the early Christian theologians, turned the Jewish interpretation of the Bridegroom of the Song as God and the Bride his chosen people Israel into the wedding song of Christ the Son of God and the Church, the new Israel. Most influential of all were the 86 sermons St Bernard of Clairvaux (1090–1153) preached on the Song, which only reached the beginning of the third chapter, such were the riches a skilled exegete could glean from it.[22] These introduced a more affective, individualizing exegesis, in which the biblical poem becomes the story of Christ's love for each soul and the soul's response. If at first his explanations seem artificial and arbitrary, a closer reading reveals a great sensitivity to the language of the Song, combined with a solidity of theological and spiritual teaching, imaginatively related back to the text. Dipping into these sermons is a good way of entering the cast of mind with which San Juan read the Bible. He read the Song as divine poetry, let its music be heard through his own poems, and expounded it as such in his commentaries.

I have tried to pinpoint a few of the elements which in different ways reached San Juan, and establish a context in which mystical experience and the forms of expression it used were subjects of authoritative analysis. I have tried, all too briefly, to show how the Western mystical tradition shifts from an Augustinian rising to the light of knowledge to a spirituality which seeks Love through love in the darkness, and how the Song of Songs is consistently read as the love song between Christ the Bridegroom and his bride, the soul. I have not wanted to think in terms of precise sources or of intertextuality, but rather to identify the living tradition in which San Juan worked, so that his own contribution to it, through the dark nights of the soul, may better be appreciated.

THE COMMENTARIES

San Juan wrote three or four treatises, depending on how the relationship between the *Subida del Monte Carmelo* and the *Noche oscura del alma* is viewed. Each is cast in the form of a commentary on one of his poems, though the *Subida* and the *Noche* pay less attention to this than the *Cántico espiritual* and the *Llama de amor viva*. The genre of these works is difficult to fix. They are part poetic gloss, part biblical commentary, part ascetic and moral treatise, part devotional text, with numerous digressions; but the balance between these elements is a shifting one.[23] Historically, the *Cántico* came first; by 1579 San Juan had begun to write commentaries on individual verses of the poem at the request of nuns who found his poems beautiful but beyond their comprehension. The *Subida* and the *Noche* were written at different times during the early 1580s, but develop the same fundamental teaching, based on the symbol of the dark night of the soul. There are a number of cross references between them, while the *Llama* (1.25) refers to *Noche* as part of the *Subida*, suggesting that San Juan thought of them as one work. Critics have argued as to whether they should be considered a single work, two separate works, or a diptych, but the modern consensus prefers to acknowledge a community of subject matter in two distinct works, the *Noche* dealing with the most original part of San Juan's teaching, and representing to a small extent his attempt to return to the principle of expounding the meaning of the poem, more or less abandoned in the later stages of the *Subida*.[24] The *Llama*, and most of all, the *Cántico*, passed through a process of continual revision, which has excited a great deal of critical heat and correspondingly little light (to which I do not propose to add).[25]

The *Cántico* exists in two distinct redactions, CA and CB, as well as a number of intermediate forms. While individual copyists of the poem certainly introduced alterations, by design or in error, nothing suggests that CB was the work of a reviser who was uncomfortable with San Juan's doctrine or style.[26] He was in the habit of rewriting his work: no one has seriously disputed the authenticity of the second redaction of the *Llama*, and it is not surprising that the *Cántico* should have passed through a similar process, especially as the poem itself (which in any case grew from 31 to 40 stanzas) is much longer. In any case, a convincing explanation for the reordering of its verses and the consequent changes made to the commentary can be given. In the 'Argumento' added to the second redaction, San Juan makes it clear that the *Cántico* deals with the whole spiritual journey, from the moment a soul begins to serve God, to the beatific vision beyond the highest state of perfection accessible in this life, the spiritual marriage, and that the last five stanzas refer to the eternal enjoyment of the presence of God in the life of the world to come. That this is entirely consistent with San Juan's original purpose is proved by the reference already present in CA 1.4 to the soul's desire to see God in glory (that is, beyond death). Given that he was not writing for publication and had to prepare his revisions in whatever time he could snatch from more pressing duties, one would hardly expect them to have been thoroughly edited. I shall base this chapter on the second redaction of the commentary, since this represents, as far as we know, San Juan's final, most considered version.

The overall structure of each prose commentary is fairly straightforward. The *Cántico* is patterned according to the three traditional ways of the mystical journey, the purgative way of beginners (C 1–5), the illuminative way of proficients (CB 6–13; CA 6–12) and the unitive way of the perfect (CB 14–40; CA 13–39). The spiritual betrothal (CB 13; CA 12) and the spiritual marriage (CB 22; CA 27) take place within these stages, though this is not explained until the commentary is well advanced (CB 22.3; CA 27.3). The *Llama* is more of a unity, with the important exception of a long digression on spiritual direction. The *Subida-Noche* divides the image of the dark night into four parts, the two active nights of sense (S 1) and spirit (S 2–3), and the two corresponding passive nights (N 1, N 2).

There are four major reasons why modern readers find these works difficult. The first is that they turn beautiful lyrical poems into what seem like arid and didactic exercises. Once we begin to see how San Juan's mind works and the kinds of connections the exposition makes between poem and Bible, the tension between the two extremes becomes less uncomfortable. The *Cántico* and the *Llama* both pay close attention to the imagery of the poems on which they are based in a way the *Subida-Noche* does not. In this, the relation between poem and commentary is largely tangential, and much of the exposition is independent of the verse, which seems more like a pretext on which to hang a more evidently systematic account of the inner life of the soul by concentrating on the first line.[27]

The second difficulty is the problem of finding one's way. As Eulogio Pacho has pointed out, the main lines of the argument, especially in the *Subida*, quickly become muddied 'en una maraña de temas y esquemas cada vez más complicados y minuciosos', 'in a tangle of themes and schemes of increasing complexity and detail'.[28] His commentaries proceed in a disconcerting way, announcing schemes but failing to complete them, and apparently losing sight of their objectives in a mass of subdivisions and digressions. Almost always the structure of his argument as a whole has to be borne in mind in order to assess the place of any individual part of it. It is easy to lose the overall orientation of the work in these excursuses, which may themselves be the result of an often interrupted process of composition or of hurried revisions. For example, S 1 begins with a complex piece of biblical exegesis which divides the night into three parts, in counterpoint to its overall fourfold scheme. It continues by making a fundamental distinction between sense and spirit and analyses two kinds of harm caused by the sensual appetites of the soul, which are described in a series of five verbs, expounded in its central chapters (6–10). S 2–3 explain the active night of the spirit as this affects the three faculties in turn, the intellect (S 2), the memory (S 3.1–15) and the will (S 3.16–45), to which the three theological virtues of faith, hope and love correspond. Thus two further triple perspectives are introduced, which control the exposition. N 1 begins with a series of chapters patterned on the seven deadly spiritual sins (1–7), which San Juan himself admits are really out of place (1.1), while towards the end of N 2 a miniature treatise on the ten steps of the mystical ladder of divine love, prompted by the image of the 'secret ladder' in the second line of the second verse of the poem, interrupts the exposition of the passive night of the spirit.[29] As if that were not enough, San Juan introduces subdivisions into these larger structures, like the different kinds of 'apprehensions' at the beginning of S 3 and the four 'affections' of the will in S 3.16. These structural inconsistencies are partly the result of following the flow of the poem, but they also seem inevitable, given the mode of exposition San Juan has chosen. Each time he describes the dangers and the benefits of particular experiences, he tends to repeat himself, as if he wished to communicate important points about them in general but found himself constrained by the divisions and subdivisions he had already introduced to reiterate them.

In the middle of the second book of the *Subida* he offers an apologia for his method:

> dejado que es materia que pocas veces se trata por este estilo, ahora de palabra como de escritura, por ser en ella extradordinaria y oscura, añádese también mi torpe estilo y poco saber. Y así, estando desconfiado de que lo sabré dar a entender, muchas veces entiendo me alargo demasiado y salgo fuera de límites que bastan al lugar y parte de la doctrina que voy tratando; en lo cual confieso yo hacerlo a veces de advertencia, porque lo que no se da a entender por unas razones, quizá se entenderá por aquéllas y por otras, y también porque entiendo que así se va dando más luz para lo que se ha de decir adelante. (S 2.14.14)

> apart from the fact that the subject-matter is infrequently dealt with, in talking or in writing, because it is obscure and out of the ordinary, there is also my clumsy style and lack of knowledge. So, lacking confidence in what I shall explain, I see that often I go on too much and exceed the limits appropriate for the place and aspect of the doctrine I am dealing with. I confess that I sometimes do so deliberately, because what cannot be explained by some words perhaps will be explained by others, and also because I think that in this way more help is given for what is to be said later.

The unusual nature of the subjects he is treating imposes, it seems, a structure which is less disciplined than it might be, though despite the modesty of his claims this clearly has advantages and is not entirely accidental.

Third, San Juan addressed himself to a very limited readership; not to the general public, but to a small number of friars and nuns of the Discalced Carmelite Order who had advanced far on the road and who needed better guidance than was available from spiritual treatises or their confessors.[30] They lived in a monastic environment in which ascetic and penitential practices were taken for granted, and San Juan might well have believed that outside such a context it was impossible to understand his teaching, or, worse still, that it would prove misleading. Put another way, almost all readers of San Juan find themselves at a much earlier stage of the journey than that presupposed for 'beginners' at the start of the *Subida*. The fourth difficulty is that his terminology is often difficult to grasp, and when he does use apparently familiar words their meaning may have changed over the centuries, or have a precise technical significance for him.

Issues of genre, structure, audience and lexis can, however, be identified and explained. When a writer's ideas and the way in which they are communicated are rooted in structures of belief which are no longer common currency, it becomes essential to grasp the foundations on which his analysis of the human self and its search for a hidden God is constructed, and to translate them into terms which can be understood today. San Juan's belief that each human person is a child of God, created in the divine image and likeness, and made to live in communion with God, underlies all his teaching. His prose writings are directed towards helping his readers discover the infinite God who dwells within them, recognizable in their deepest needs, and for whom there can be no finite substitute. He sees all human desire and potential as finding true fulfilment only in transforming union with God the Holy Trinity. This is a radically different picture of humanity from the one drawn by the twentieth-century trinity of Darwin, Marx and Freud, and it is bound to affect the reading of San Juan profoundly. He may be regarded as a fossil of a species driven to extinction by the Enlightenment and scientific rationalism; as a dreamer after heavenly treasure, excluded by class and poverty from earthly riches; or as a man whose frustrated sexual desires were sublimated into religious devotion. Such views create a distance between author and reader, and (perhaps) the comfort of detachment and the illusion of objectivity in assessing his work as a thinker and a theologian. It is easy to let our own preconceptions go unchallenged while we question his. So the first task is to understand what he was trying to say.

San Juan's teaching rests on a number of fundamental principles which need to be grasped before the particular details of his argument can become clear. They are characteristically woven into the dense texture of his writing, and need to be picked out, so that the complex patterns of discourse he creates do not overwhelm the larger design. Before any assessment of the significance of his teaching can be attempted, these broad principles must be established, since they govern his analysis of the human self and its quest for fulfilment. They are by no means self-evident at first reading.[31]

His subject is the human search for God (the active part of the dark night) and the divine search for humanity (the passive). His most famous creation, the 'dark night of the soul', is endowed in his thought with a precision and a scope evident from the outset, unlike its looser contemporary usage.[32] To achieve his aim, he undertakes an analysis of the human personality, its constitution, its conflicts and its potential which finds its fullest and most systematic expression in the *Subida-Noche*. He divides his famous symbol into the night of the senses and the night of the spirit, each of which presents a double aspect of activity and passivity. The commentary follows this fourfold structure: the active night of the senses (S 1), the active night of the spirit (S 2–3), the passive night of the senses (N 1) and the passive night of the spirit (N 2). The two nights of the senses occupy relatively little space, since they relate to ascetic principles and the practices familiar to his monastic audience (though the passive night of the senses marks the beginning of contemplation). But the active night of the spirit is five times the length of its sensual counterpart, and the passive night of the spirit about twice, and in each case the commentary is unfinished. The reason for this disparity is that, as the prologue to the *Cántico* states, 'para los principiantes hay muchas cosas escritas' (.3), 'there are many things written for beginners'; there is no shortage of material to guide people through the nights of the senses. But the nights of the spirit, little understood, present a much graver problem to spiritual directors, whose charges may well have advanced further on the journey than they have themselves. San Juan's originality as a spiritual theologian rests largely on the fact that he was the first writer ever to undertake so complete an analysis of the higher reaches of prayer. For this reason, his attacks on inexperienced spiritual directors in the prologue to the *Subida*, and the lengthy and passionate digression on the same topic in *Llama* 3.30–62, form an integral part of his argument.

San Juan's prime concern is the inner life of the individual. When he uses the word 'alma', 'soul', he means the whole inner life of a person, not that part which according to many religions survives physical death. It therefore includes conscious and unconscious modes of operation of the self, and a range of feelings and desires, many construed in negative terms, which would not generally now be associated with the concept of 'soul'. This can be seen from the way in which he divides the soul into a 'sensitive' and a 'spiritual' part. He does not regard these as entities or locations, but rather as modalities of the inner life which are easy to distinguish at their extremes and useful for the sake of analysis.[33] N 2.2.1 uses vivid metaphors borrowed from the language of the laundry and the orchard to focus the distinction between sins and underlying sinfulness: the 'manchas', 'stains', of the old man (the flesh, the senses) remain in the soul and require 'el jabón y fuerte lejía' (2.1), 'the soap and strong lye' of the passive night of the spirit; sinful branches may have been lopped from the senses, but not until the roots have been extracted from the spirit is the process complete.

His distinction between sense and spirit is a version of the Pauline antithesis between the flesh and the spirit or the old man and the new (Romans 8, to which San Juan frequently returns: S 3.2.16, C 3.10, L 2.32). This has often been interpreted negatively, as denial of the body and exaltation of abstinence from all kinds of bodily desire. That is not quite what Paul or San Juan had in mind; both are more nuanced than that. The beginning of the *Subida* contains a number of statements which correct such misinterpretations. First, any disorder or imperfection in the senses stems from disordered human reason. Sin is therefore diagnosed as a spiritual sickness, the consequence of wrong choices of the will, which then manifest themselves in the misuse of the senses. For that reason, it is the human spirit that requires purification (S 1.1–2).

The soul, where the image and likeness of God is to be found, is the proper place to search for him. She is created expressly for the purpose of communing with him, but is full of other kinds of knowledge and desire, the power of which should not be underestimated. Following his Aristotelian–Thomist training, San Juan regards knowledge of the outside world as mediated purely through the five senses: 'el alma luego que Dios la infunde en el cuerpo, está como una tabla rasa y lisa en que no está pintado nada, y si no es lo que por los sentidos va conociendo, de otra parte naturalmente no se le comunica nada', 'when God infuses the soul into the body, it is like a smooth, flat tablet on which nothing is written, and apart from what she comes to know through the senses, nothing is communicated to her naturally from any other source' (S 1.3.3). If the discovery of an unknown creature were to be reported to us without any indication as to its appearance, we would be none the wiser, any more than people born blind can have white or yellow described to them (S 2.3.2). In a more Platonic mode, the soul is also described as in a dark prison, unable to see anything except through its windows, which are the senses. The Platonic doctrine of *anamnesis*, of the soul's buried knowledge of her true origins, is Christianized, conventionally enough, as the indwelling of the Holy Trinity hidden deep within her.

What she sees, hears, tastes, touches and smells becomes part of her inner life by a process of internalization and abstraction from the data provided by sense perceptions. The faculty of understanding or intellect ('entendimiento') enables her to have thoughts and ideas about them. These are conserved within the soul or the imagination ('fantasía'), while the faculty of will ('voluntad') governs choices about them. The 'sensitive' part of the soul represents that part of the inner life which is lived under the sway of sensual desires: when, for example, someone is overpowered by anger, lust or envy, or is greedy for worldly recognition or full of ambition. But such feelings may equally motivate those who seek the spiritual life: they may wish others to believe that they are acting for the glory of God, whereas their true motives are self-centred, since they desire to impress others with a show of devotion or the favours God has granted them. The sensitive part of the soul, therefore, can, if unchecked, distort religious practice and turn it into a manifestation of misplaced human desire. A great deal of the power of San Juan's analysis of the active night of the senses lies in his unmasking of religion of this kind, which speaks the language of serving God but which exalts the self above all else.

The 'spiritual' part of the soul represents that deeper, hidden mode of being of which we are not normally aware, but which is closer to its true nature and purpose, its centre. The aim of the ascetic life (works of mortification and self-denial) is to break the senses' stranglehold on motive, thought and action, so that the spiritual nature of the soul, governed by reason and enlightened by faith, can reassert its primacy. The objects of our choice are not bad in themselves; no created thing can be, for all were made good in the mind and purpose of God. While discussing certain mystical states, San Juan mentions an objection to his teaching: 'Dios no destruye la naturaleza, antes la perfecciona' (S 3.2.7), 'God does not destroy nature, but rather perfects it.' Though he argues that much needs to be forgotten in the early stages of the journey, he is not a Manichaean or other kind of dualist, and his teaching should not be regarded as a denial of creation or the body. What he does is to unmask the 'belittling imperialism' of the senses under which unredeemed humanity lives, largely unaware of its power, to reorder the soul's faculties towards God as the object of the mind's contemplation, the will's choices and the memory's contents.[34] So complete a reversal of accustomed priorities cannot be achieved without terrible struggle, but the conflict and pain of the dark nights are worthwhile because they open the way to the new humanity.

The distinction San Juan makes between the active and passive modes of the soul's journey (S 1.13.1) also needs explanation. The active, logically, includes everything human power can achieve to assist progress; in Martin Thornton's happy phrase, it is 'the art of co-operating with grace'.[35] The passive sounds like a state of inertia, which it is not. Put one way, it is the direct action of God on the soul and is a gift, not an achievement or reward for work done. It belongs as such to the wisdom and liberty of God, and is given according to his unfathomable purposes. Put another way, when the soul is passive, she is in a state of receptiveness. Her natural processes are stilled and her faculties are no longer occupied with particular images, concepts, memories or desires. Instead they experience a 'simple' or 'general' desire for God, the reduction of desire to its barest essentials, desire-in-itself for God-in-himself, rather than desire aroused, say, by an act of meditation on a moment from the life of Christ. The soul waits upon God with 'advertencia amorosa', 'loving attention': that is her whole work and activity. If waiting brings only darkness and a keen sense of the absence of God, this must be borne patiently and faithfully, and must not affect the normal commitments of daily living. For through bearing the pain and suffering of these passive nights, the soul is brought to greater knowledge of herself and of God.

Passivity, therefore, is neither a state of idleness nor the complete abandonment to the will of God which has traditionally been associated with the heresy of Quietism.[36] It involves the letting go of everything which hinders the work of God in the soul and is best understood as a different form of activity: the activity of being receptive to something from beyond herself. In S 2.15.2 San Juan likens it to having the eyes open and receiving light, which suggests that it is not a state of complete absence of human activity but of preparation to receive a gift. It is not hard to find other analogies. In order to become wholly engrossed in a play or a piece of music, the mind needs to be cleared of other, extraneous concerns. If it finds itself contemplating shopping lists, unanswered letters or the person in front, even if it is thinking devotional thoughts, it will not be free to concentrate on the spectacle or the sound. When it becomes free, it is not in a state of idleness, in which things float in and out of the mind with no particular purpose, but in a state of receptiveness which allows all its faculties to be wholly engaged in the act of watching or listening. It can be very difficult to move from everyday activity to this receptive mode. San Juan's active nights of sense and spirit, the ways in which the soul may habituate herself to emptying the faculties of all their other concerns, are intended to enable her to become receptive to what God will give her in the passive nights, gifts for which will there will be no room if she is busy with other concerns.

San Juan approached the task of expounding his poem as a man of his age, and must first be judged on that basis. Despite the many difficulties his commentaries present to modern readers, they should not to be discarded as curiosities for that reason alone. They offer fascinating glimpses into the way a sixteenth-century mind worked and their very strangeness can be refreshing. I have chosen the *Cántico* commentary as the best place to study San Juan's work as an interpreter of language. It expounds every image and line of the poem, shows San Juan's sense of how their meanings cohere with the witness of scripture, and thereby associates them with and tests them against the whole history of salvation, not simply an individual's experience. For such reasons, it offers the clearest examples of the exegetical techniques found also in the other commentaries, and shows the process by which San Juan converts poetic image into spiritual truth. I then pass in the following chapter to the *Subida-Noche*, his most systematic treatment of the spiritual life, before finally tackling the *Llama,* where poetry is made to bear a sustained doctrinal weight.

San Juan's explanations in the *Cántico* can appear pedantic, as if imposed on the poem some time after its composition, and robbing it of its much-admired lyrical qualities. In a world in which the same image of flowers represents worldly pleasures in v. 3, the stars of heaven in v. 4 and the soul's virtues in CB 17, what hermeneutic can there be but an arbitrary and inconsistent one? The first line of the seventh verse confirms this view: 'Y todos quantos vagan/de ti me van mil gracias refiriendo' ('And all who contemplate/Go telling me a thousand gracious things about you'). It uses a *culto* verb derived from Latin: those who 'vagan' are not, as might be supposed, those who drift through life, but 'todos cuantos vacan a Dios', 'all those who contemplate God', because the Latin 'vacare in Deo' had acquired the technical meaning of 'to be fully occupied in God', hence, 'to contemplate' (7.6).[37] This surprising observation changes the apparent sense of the verse and enables San Juan to connect the argument with the preceding verses. The 'messengers' of the sixth verse are irrational creatures, that is to say, those parts of the natural creation which had, surprisingly, through the trope of *prosopopoeia*, responded in the words of the fifth to the Bride's request in the fourth for news of her Beloved. Only rational creatures – the human and angelic creations – are able to have knowledge of God and consequently possess the ability to contemplate him.

Critics have felt uncomfortable with such interpretations. Ynduráin, for example, rejects it forcefully, and his opinion may stand for the critical approach to the poem which either discounts the commentary or (as he does) makes only selective use of it.[38] It is undeniably true that this Latinate definition is not implied by the poetic text on its own and that a more natural reading would identify the shepherds moving towards the hill (v. 2) with the messengers of v. 6 and 'todos cuantos vagan' of v. 7, since all seem to be engaged in the same activity, bringing news of the Beloved. The critic must decide what to do with San Juan's own precise markings of meaning, particularly in cases like this. But the fact that San Juan's interpretation is not necessary does not mean that it must be ruled out. No critic proposes that Góngora's Latinate usages are to be ignored when they may have a commoner meaning; quite the contrary, much time is spent pointing them out. Other writers of the age used 'vacar' in a similar way, even if they did not turn it into 'vagar'.[39] Those who disregard San Juan's commentary in their approach to the poem at least act with consistency, though at the risk of ignoring what a poet writes about his own work. Those who admit some of San Juan's interpretations but not others need to establish firm criteria for their judgements. The issue arises with 'vagar' because, like other words and images in the poem, it admits of a secular sense and the commentary, while sometimes nodding in that direction, consistently chooses a religious one.[40] Modern critics may feel it inappropriate to apply the language of human love to the love of a God in whom they may or may not believe, especially when an apparently innocent philological comment about the meaning of *vacare* opens Pandora's box. But their discomfort is itself culturally conditioned: one of the challenges any critic faces is to understand and take account of the limitations imposed by one's own world view.

To alleviate this discomfort, five general points need making. First, it should not be assumed that all San Juan's explanations are subsequent rationalizations. Because he was steeped in a tradition of exegesis of the Song of Songs which understood it as a love song between Christ and the soul, and because he was familiar with the interpretations given to it by monastic writers like Bernard of Clairvaux, his own poetic images which most closely imitate the Song's – like the garden, the wine cellar, the little vixen, the dark but comely Bride – are more likely to have come to him attached to pre-existing meanings than to have had meanings invented for them by him. That is certainly the case with the identity of the protagonists: it is inconceivable that he would have thought of the Bride and the Bridegroom as other than the soul (or the Church) and the Word (or Christ). In that respect the *Cántico* commentary was no different from the poetry: some of its explanations came to him as given, others he had to work out for himself.

Second, San Juan wrote in an age which saw and made connections which ours does not:

> This verse marks that, and both do make a motion
>   Unto a third, that ten leaves off doth lie:
>   Then as dispersèd herbs do watch a potion,
> These three make up some Christian's destiny:
> [. . .] for in ev'rything
> Thy words do find me out, and parallels bring,
>   And in another make me understood.[41]

Herbert's poem articulates a hermeneutical principle widely accepted from the early Christian era until historical scholarship began to question the Bible's status as a single authoritative text, and it encapsulates San Juan's exegetical procedure, which is as much of his age as that of the sermons of John Donne and Lancelot Andrewes. Frequently he argues from a catena of texts drawn from different parts of the Bible but which have something in common, if only a word or an image. The New Testament itself provides the warrant: the argument of the first chapter of Hebrews is notoriously difficult to follow without seeing that the author is demonstrating the nature of Christ's Sonship, proclaimed in the first three verses, through a series of seven texts from the Psalms and two from Isaiah in the rest. Unless the principle is grasped, the argument can appear bewildering. Such familiarity with the Bible is closely connected with the monastic practice of *lectio divina*: as O'Reilly comments: 'In this way a memory of the text was built up, based not only on the sight of the words but on their pronunciation and sound. The reader's mind became a concordance, able to link passages spontaneously according to sound and meaning.'[42] No other literary text was used by San Juan in such a manner.

Third, San Juan's age had a naturally allegorical frame of mind. Interpretations which seem arbitrary to a twentieth-century reader would have seemed much less so to his contemporaries. Secular and sacred examples abound. In Gaspar Gil Polo's pastoral romance *Diana enamorada* (1564), a continuation of Montemayor's *Diana*, a white stag with black spots and golden horns appears during the festivities of the final book, only to be revealed as a 'moral enigma' representing the human heart.[43] Cervantes's last work, *Los trabajos de Persiles y Sigismunda* (1616), based on the *Aethiopica* of Heliodorus, contains several allegorical episodes, including one in which the hero sees a tableau of sensual and chaste love, but does not realize until afterwards that it was a performance rather than a dream or vision.[44]

Fourth, different kinds of meaning were understood to cohere within the same text. The literal sense might establish the precise meaning of the words, but the allegorical, moral and mystical senses would build on this to apply the text to the history of the Church, the life of the Christian on earth and the soul's journey to God. Malón de Chaide's exegesis of Jeremiah 2.25, describing those who believe their lives have been so sinful that they can have no hope of salvation, displays many of the same features as San Juan's:

> Y así dejan de volverse a Dios, como lo dice Jeremías: *Prohibe pedem tuum a nuditate, et guttur tuum a siti. Et dixisti: Desperavi; nequaquam faciam, adamavi quippe alienos, et post eos ambulo.* Mira la locura de mi pueblo, dice el Señor, que diciéndole yo: "Pueblo mío, ¿por qué pudiendo andar calzado en el invierno, queréis andar descalzo? ¿por qué pudiendo tener refresco en el verano y beber frío, queréis perecer de sed?" Más claro: ¿por qué, alma, pudiendo andar vestida de gracia, que es ropa que os tendrá el frío de la desnudez del pecado, queréis andar desnuda y sufrir los hielos de los vicios? ¿Y por qué, pudiendo hallar refresco, contra el calor desordenado de vuestras pasiones, en mí, que soy fuente de vida eterna, queréis más secaros al ardor de vuestros pecados, para haceros madero seco para arder siempre en el infierno? (*La conversión de la Magdalena*, I, 79)

> And thus they fail to turn to God, as Jeremiah says: *Withhold thy foot from being unshod, and thy throat from thirst; but thou saidst, There is no hope: no; for I have loved strangers, and after them will I go*. Behold the folly of my people, says the Lord [the author gives his Spanish version]. More clearly: why, o soul, since you can walk clothed in grace, which will keep away the coldness of the nakedness of sin, do you wish to walk naked and suffer the iciness of vice? And why, since you can find refreshment in me, the fountain of eternal life, against the disordered heat of your passions, do you wish to dry yourself out in the heat of your sins, so that you become dry wood which will burn for ever in hell?

Jeremiah has God addressing his unrepentant and idolatrous people, who have turned away from his laws to follow other ways, the 'strangers' of the text, which seem to have nothing to do with the soul, sin and damnation. But Malón de Chaide, like San Juan, moves quite naturally from the history of Israel to the life of the individual through allegorizing the imagery of the text, and interprets them as vices.

Fifth, the reader must expect a degree of discomfort because that is, for San Juan, the inevitable result of using an imperfect instrument, human language, to represent inexpressible truths. The connections he makes may not entirely convince, but one of the consequences of his understanding of the insufficiency of language is that language does not behave in an ordered or straightforward way. The seams will show, as much in his prose as his poetry. On the basis of his theory, it is no more possible to construct a wholly consistent and persuasive argument than to produce an immediately intelligible poem. Though longer, fuller, and intended to explicate the imagery of the poem, the commentary can never be more than another kind of stammering witness to the experience which the poetry first sang.

NOTES

1 This issue has been much debated, and scholars have reached radically different conclusions: compare W. T. Stace, *Mysticism and Philosophy* (London: Macmillan, 1961); R. C. Zaehner, *Mysticism Sacred and Profane* (Oxford: Clarendon, 1957). For more recent debate on the subject, see *Mysticism and Philosophical Analysis*, ed. Steven T. Katz (London: Sheldon, 1978); *Mysticism and Language*, ed. Steven T. Katz (New York: Oxford University Press, 1992); Steven Payne, 'The Christian Character of Christian Mystical Experience', *Religious Studies*, 20 (1984), pp. 417–27, and *John of the Cross and the Cognitive Value of Mysticism* (Dordrecht: Klouwer, 1990), especially pp. 92–116.

2 On this, see Cuthbert Butler, *Western Mysticism*, 3rd edn (London: Constable, 1967); Marie M. Goudreau, *Mysticism and Image in St John of the Cross* (Frankfurt: Peter Lang, 1976); Rowan Williams, *The Wound of Knowledge* (London: Darton, Longman and Todd, 1979); Andrew Louth, *The Origins of the Christian Mystical Tradition* (Oxford: Oxford University Press, 1981); Bernard McGinn, *The Foundations of Mysticism* (London: SCM Press, 1992).

3 On the cave, see *Plato: The Republic*, Penguin Classics, 2nd edn (Harmondsworth: Penguin, 1974), pp. 317–20; on the soul, p. 444; on the charioteer, *Plato: Phaedrus & Letters VII and VIII* (Harmondsworth: Penguin, 1973), pp. 50–66.

4 María Zambrano, *Filosofía y poesía* (México: Fondo de Cultura Económica, 1987 [1939]), p. 49.

5 Calderón gives powerful dramatic expression to this in some of his *autos sacramentales*; witness the puzzlement of the characters at the presence of a cross among the items they can choose as they acquire their props in *No hay más fortuna que Dios* (Manchester: Manchester University Press, 1949).

6 Iain Matthew, 'The Knowledge and Consciousness of Christ in the Light of the Writings of St John of the Cross' (D.Phil. thesis, University of Oxford, 1991), pp. 182–202, redresses the balance.

7 One unusual aspect of the vision of Ostia is that it is shared. I am grateful to Dr. A. Lappin of Manchester University for drawing to my attention another example, from the *Cantigas de Santa Maria*, 295. At least one of Santa Teresa's visions was witnessed by a number of people (*Vida* 7.8).

8 S 2.24.3; CB 13.6; 19.1.

9 This identification was not challenged in the sixteenth century. He appears to have been a Syrian monk, c. 500, now commonly known as the pseudo-Dionysius (or Denys). See Andrew Louth, *Denys the Areopagite* (London: Geoffrey Chapman, 1989); Denys Turner, *The Darkness of God* (Cambridge: Cambridge University Press, 1995), pp. 19–49.

10 S 2.8.6; N 2.5.3; CB 14–15.16; L 3.49.

11 See *The Cloud of Unknowing*, trans. Clifton Wolters, Penguin Classics (Harmondsworth: Penguin, 1961).

12 See *Rolle: The Fire of Love*, trans. Clifton Wolters, Penguin Classics (Harmondsworth: Penguin, 1972); *Julian of Norwich: Revelations of Divine Love*, trans. Clifton Wolters, Penguin Classics (Harmondsworth: Penguin, 1966).

13 *Rolle: Fire*, p. 46; Bernardino de Laredo, *Subida del monte Sión*, in *Místicos franciscanos españoles* (Madrid: BAC, 1948–49), II, p. 34; see also my *The Poet and the Mystic* (Oxford: Oxford University Press, 1977), p. 4, for other writers who make this point.

14 *Fundaciones* 11, 22, 26.

15 San Juan's older contemporary, Fray Luis de León, retains the more traditional, Augustinian longing for light and wisdom in his religious poems; see my 'La tradición mística occidental: dos corrientes distintas en la poesía de San Juan de la Cruz y fray Luis de León', *Edad de Oro*, 11 (1992), pp. 187–94.

16 *The Oxford Book of Seventeenth-Century Verse* (Oxford: Clarendon, 1934), p. 572.

17 See below, pp. 235–6.

18 Jean Leclercq, *The Love of Learning and the Desire for God* (London: SPCK, 1978 [New York: Fordham University Press, 1961]), pp. 106, 108.

19 See, for example, Marcia Falk, *The Song of Songs: A New Translation and Interpretation* (HarperSanFrancisco, 1990).

20 For a persuasive argument in favour of the spiritual meaning of the Song as primary, see Sister Edmée SLG, 'The Song of Songs and the Cutting of Roots', *Anglican Theological Review*, 80 (1998), pp. 547–61.

21 Malón de Chaide, *La conversión de la Magdalena*, ed. Félix García (Madrid: Espala-Calpe, 1957–9) II, p. 82; he is commenting on Hosea 2.2..

22 *Bernard of Clairvaux: On the Song of Songs*, trans. Kilian Walsh, 4 vols (Kalamazoo, Michigan: Cistercian Publications, 1979–83).

23 For discussion of their genre, see Eulogio Pacho, 'Cántico espiritual', in *Introducción a la lectura de San Juan de la Cruz* (Valladolid: Junta de Castilla y León, 1991), pp. 459–64; Cristóbal Cuevas, 'La literatura como signo de lo inefable: el género literario de los libros de San Juan de la Cruz', in *La literatura como signo*, ed. José Castillo Romera and others (Madrid: Playor, 1981), pp. 98–106, David Brian Perrin, *Canciones entre el alma y el Esposo of Juan de la Cruz: A Hermeneutical Interpretation* (San Francisco: Catholic Scholars Press, 1996), pp. 208–226).

24 See, for example, the summary of the argument in José Damián Gaitán, in *Introducción a la lectura de San Juan de la Cruz*, pp. 373–80.

25 For forms of reference to these works, see Note on References, p. ix; on the major changes to the 'Cántico' and its commentary, above, p. 113.

26 For a fascinating account of some of these altered readings, see María Jesús Mancho and José Antonio Pascual, 'La recepción inicial del «Cántico espiritual» a través de las variantes manuscritas del texto', *Actas*, I, pp. 107–22.

27 The first line of the poem is the ostensible text for S 1.1–13; N 1.1–10; 2. 5–10. S 2–3 are supposed to relate to the second verse of the poem, but apart from its appearance at the start of S 2 it plays no further part in the commentary. The third verse is briefly glossed at the end of N 2, before the work peters out.

28 In his prologue to the *Subida* in his *Obras completas* (Burgos: Monte Carmelo, 1982), p. 129.

29 He attributes the work to St Bernard and St Thomas, but it was probably the work of the Dominican Helvicus Teutonicus (13–14Cs); see *Obras* (SJ), p. 402.

30 The *Llama* is unusual in having been dedicated to a laywoman closely connected with San

Juan and the Discalced. On the author–reader relationship in San Juan, see Perrin, *Canciones entre el alma y el Esposo*, pp. 273–94.

31 S Prol. 3; see also Gaitán, *Introducción a San Juan de la Cruz*, p. 364.

32 A number of critics raise the question of its broader application to twentieth-century theological, philosophical, social and political problems; for example Augusto Guerra, 'Para la integración existencial de la *Noche oscura*', *Experiencia y pensiamento*, pp. 225–50; Camilo Maccise, 'Lectura latinoamericana de San Juan de la Cruz desde una perspectiva liberadora', *Experiencia y pensiamento*,, pp. 271–95; Juan Martín Velasco, 'Experiencia de Dios desde la situación y la conciencia de la ausencia', *Actas*, III, pp. 213–47; Alfonso Álvarez Bolado, 'En medio las afueras de la sociedad secularizada: mística y secularización', *Actas*, III, pp. 249–76; Michael Buckley, 'Atheism and Contemplation', *Theological Studies*, 40 (1979), pp. 680–99.

33 Iain Matthew, 'The Knowledge and Consciousness of Christ in the Light of the Writings of St John of the Cross' (D. Phil. thesis, University of Oxford, 1991), p. 119, remarks that the centre of the soul is not spatial but ontological; the same is true of all the 'parts' of the soul. For the linguistic implications of this, see below, pp. 234–8. I disagree with Alain Cugno, whose definition of San Juan's 'alma' is more concerned with 'the bodily nature of the soul, the process of salvation as it concerns the body'; *Saint John of the Cross*, pp. 112–13.

34 The phrase is Iain Matthew's, p. 141.

35 Martin Thornton, *English Spirituality* (London: SPCK, 1963), p. 25.

36 On Miguel de Molinos and Quietism, see *The Oxford Dictionary of the Christian Church*, 3rd edn, ed. F. L. Cross and E. A. Livingstone, pp. 1100–1, 1357.

37 See Mancho and Pascual, 'La recepcion', *Actas*, I, pp. 117–18.

38 Domingo Ynduráin, ed., *San Juan de la Cruz: Poesía* (Madrid: Cátedra, 1994), pp. 59–61.

39 For example, Fray Luis de Granada, *Introducción del Símbolo de la Fe*, ed. José María Balcells (Madrid: Cátedra, 1989), p. 196: 'vacar en silencio a Dios'. While Sebastián de Covarrubias (*Tesoro de la lengua castellana* (1611), Barcelona: Horta, 1943) only gives the literal meaning of 'vagar', and attacks 'vagabundos' (p. 989), *Diccionario de Autoridades* (III, (p. 410) includes the element of 'sosiego', but regards it as archaic. It defines 'vacar' in the sense of contemplation of divine mysteries (p. 406).

40 San Juan mentions human lovers in order to establish the spiritual sense in CB 9.3, 14–15.28, 32.2, 36.1.

41 *The H. Scriptures.* II, in Louis L. Martz, ed., *George Herbert and Henry Vaughan* (Oxford: Oxford University Press, 1986), p. 50; lines 5–8, 10–12.

42 Terence O'Reilly, 'St John of the Cross and the Traditions of Monastic Exegesis', in *Leeds Papers on Saint John of the Cross*, ed. Margaret A. Rees (Leeds: Trinity and All Saints College, 1991), pp. 105–26 (107); reprinted in *Variorum*, VII.

43 Rafael Ferreres, ed., *Clásicos castellanos* (Madrid: Espasa-Calpe, 1953), pp. 224–5.

44 Juan Bautista Avalle-Arce, ed., *Clásicos Castalia* (Madrid: Castalia, 1969), II. p. 15.

7

The Interpreter

'Entremos más adentro en la espesura.'

'Let us go further into the thicket.'

(CA 35)

To open up the *Cántico* to those who find it impenetrable, I have chosen to explore a number of tracks. I begin with a sample, the exegesis of the first five verses of the poem. I pass to San Juan's careful attention to the words of the poem, especially where he pauses on what might seem insignificant grammatical details or stylistic variants, and derives meaning from them. I then explore his freedom of movement across the corpus of the sacred text, as he brings into relationship texts from widely separated passages to aid the exposition of his own images. I examine the patterns of association he creates through this process, as he moves beyond the simple cashing of his own images for their spiritual sense to produce a rich and complex text, more akin to English metaphysical or Spanish *conceptista* writing than to the models of devotional writing he inherited.[1] I conclude by looking at the significance of the themes of mutuality and participation as they emerge from the *Cántico.*

THE FIRST FIVE VERSES

The commentary opens with a characteristically dense argument about the hiddenness of the divine Beloved, which is provoked by the opening cry of the poem, '¿Adónde te escondiste, Amado?', 'Where did you hide, Beloved?', and which introduces passages of biblical exegesis and statements of general theological principles to explore different notions of hiddenness. It begins with the Son who is hidden 'in the bosom of the Father' (John 1.18), beyond human eyes and understanding, for 'Verily thou art a God that hidest thyself' (Isaiah 45.15; C 1.3).[2] San Juan then distinguishes God's being in itself (his essence) from human awareness of him in religious feelings and experiences, the presence of which is not to be confused with God's, nor the lack of them with his absence (C 1.4). The soul's cry in the poem is one with the Bride's request in Song 1.6[.7] for the Beloved to disclose the place of his midday rest (C 1.5).[3] The essence of the Holy Trinity is imprinted within each soul, present but hidden; therefore, to find God the soul must look not to the world outside but within the self, as the *Soliloquia* teaches (C 1.6). Many biblical injunctions represent this process: Christ's command to pray to the Father in secret (Matthew 6.6) and his parable of the buried treasure of the Kingdom (13.44) suggest the need to withdraw into the self and to search beneath the surface (CB 1.9). In this life the soul cannot reach the full vision of God, but she may, like Moses sheltering in a cleft in the rock, be permitted a vision of the 'back parts' of God (CB 1.10; Exodus 33.23). To achieve this, she must likewise be sheltered, 'hidden', from all else which might engage her attention. San Juan returns to this text in CB 19.4 (CA 32.4), expounding the image of the 'haz', or 'face' of the Beloved, again in the context of hiddenness ('Escóndete, Carillo'), and in 'las subidas cavernas de la piedra', 'the lofty caverns of stone' of CB 37.4 (CA 36.4), which are 'bien escondidas', 'well hidden'. This shows how consistently San Juan associated the same word in his poem with the same biblical text.

In his treatment of the single image of hiddenness San Juan distinguishes two kinds, which correspond to the human and the divine elements in the journey. Divine inaccessibility or absence is defined in terms of God's hiddenness within the soul; the soul's route towards this is by way of purgation of her former habits and desires by faith and love, which requires her to 'hide' from her previous affections. In the poem the question is addressed by the Bride to the absent Beloved; in the exposition the interpretative process is at work, initiating a dialogue between the unidentified authorial voice and the reader/soul, so that the commentary conserves the direct speech of the poem but to articulate what the poem does not reveal: the identity of the protagonists, the twofold meaning of hiddenness and the interior starting point of the journey the rest of the poem will trace (CB 1.7–12).

The Beloved's vanishing leaves the Bride 'con gemido', groaning, which, San Juan explains, is 'anejo a la esperanza' (1.14), 'close to hope'. Her anguished plea is not a sign of desperation because San Juan associates it with Romans 8.23, where Paul speaks of humanity groaning within as it awaits redemption. The image of the Beloved fleeing as the stag, is traced back to the simile in Song 2.9 and is judged appropriate because stags appear and disappear swiftly, just as God sometimes appears suddenly to inflame the soul and at other times, as here, cannot be found. The wounds suffered by the soul are 'heridas de amor' (C 1.17), like fiery arrows plunged into the soul, but because they inflame desire for God they bring delight. The conventional paradox of pleasurable pain is developed in the commentary through a classical allusion and the creation of a further paradox: these flames consume and transform the soul, which, like the phoenix, becomes a sign of new life rising from death (C 1.17), while the wound can, paradoxically, only be healed by the one who caused it.[4] The soul's actions to remedy her loss mirror the Bride of the Song, who twice leaves her home to search the city by night for the one she loves (Song 3.2; 5.7), and on the second occasion is mysteriously wounded by the watchmen. The poem's disparate images – setting forth, absence, wound – thus find their point of cohesion in the biblical text. So in the poem the soul went forth – 'salí' – in forgetfulness of self and leaving all behind, in search of a cure from the one who wounded her, only to find that he has gone. San Juan's use of the Petrarchan paradox of pleasurable pain is not merely decorative. Having explained the Bride's distress as a sign of hope, he ensures that each element of his exposition – the stag, the wound, the phoenix, the healer, the search – is made to participate in its oppositions.

The exposition of the verse reaches its climactic point with the Song texts because there San Juan found in one place the fundamental images of the stanza: an absent Beloved, a going forth, a wounding and a cry of pain, the simile of the stag. Hence the argument of the exposition depends on implicit verbal connections between the poem and the Bible, which the commentary elucidates. But the explanation of the second verse seems more arbitrary: why should shepherds represent either the soul's desires or angels who bear her prayers, or the 'majadas' (sheepfolds) the angelic choirs who take them to the 'otero' (hill), God? The fluidity of interpretation, with two possible meanings attributed to shepherds, one of which also applies to sheepfolds, does little to encourage the view that San Juan was working with a coherent exegetical theory in mind. But his explanation is prompted by the poem's change in verbal address, from a singular 'Amado' in the first verse to the plural 'pastores' in the second. Shepherds feed flocks; these shepherds, whoever they may be, feed the soul with her proper food, desire for the Beloved. They act as intermediaries, as the spiritual equivalents – angels – of those employed by profane lovers to prosecute their suit, and their prayers rise to the divine height (hence the image of the 'otero', 'hill'). There is an intellectual connection to be grasped between the imagery of the poem and the activities of the shepherd go-betweens who are asked to tell the soul if perchance they *see* her Beloved. The verb 'viérdes' triggers further biblical references: God *sees* those who are in distress; he *sees* the affliction of his people Israel and comes to deliver them (Exodus 3.7–8), just as he *hears* the prayer of Zacharias for a child (Luke 1.13; my emphases).

In the poem, the Bride expresses her distress to the shepherds by three verbs, 'adolezco, peno y muero', 'I suffer, grieve and die'. They form a natural enough rhetorical gradation. But San Juan treats each separately, applying them respectively to the three faculties of the soul – intellect, will and memory. One senses that the search for patterns is being imposed on the poem, since there is no apparent reason why one should be any more appropriate than another for the faculty to which it is assigned, let alone to the three corresponding theological virtues of faith, love and hope (C 2.6). The biblical texts adduced only complicate the matter, particularly when San Juan turns to Lamentations 3.19 and announces that its three images of poverty, wormwood and gall correspond to the three verbs in turn, and gall to each of them.[5] He reaches this conclusion by the well-established principle of exegeting one difficult text by another. Poverty refers to the intellect, which is to possess the treasures of Christ's wisdom and knowledge (Colossians 2.3); the bitterness of wormwood, to the will, which is to taste the sweetness of God, symbolized in the scroll sweet to the taste but bitter to the stomach (Revelation 10.9); and gall, to the memory and to the other faculties, because it signifies the lack of God, which is death to the soul (Deuteronomy 32.33, which contains the same image).

San Juan states that the third stanza belongs to the context of the soul exercising herself in the active and contemplative ways and rejecting the three enemies we encountered in the *Cautelas* – the world, the flesh and the devil. The poem seems to give no hint of this, but he takes his cue from its first word, 'buscando', the soul's active 'searching', and connects it with the Gospel saying 'Seek, and ye shall find' (Luke 11.9), and the night-time search of the Bride of the Song through the streets of the city (3.1–4). To search for God by remaining in bed at night is useless without this active going forth, as it requires no work on the soul's part, whereas those who rise early find Wisdom seated at their door (Wisdom 6.13–15). The mountains and the riverbanks along which she searches represent the contemplative and active lives; the former because they are lofty, the seat of the virtues, and the latter because they are low-lying, where mortification must be practised. The flowers which remain unpicked are the pleasures and delights of this life, whether temporal riches, sensual indulgence or spiritual consolations. The wild beasts, fortresses and frontiers of the last two lines (the alliteration in 'f' in the original – 'flores', then 'fieras', 'fuertes', 'fronteras' – is notable) represent the world, the devil and the flesh. Loss of friends and status, lack of worldly pleasures, and mockery from those who stay behind are beasts which cause fear and inhibit progress, though more advanced souls will suffer more inward trials and tribulations. The fortresses are the Devil, cunning and strong, who arms the world and the flesh to make war on the soul (Psalm 53.5 [54.3]; Ephesians 6.11–12). The frontiers mark the boundary between flesh and spirit, of which Paul writes (Galatians 5.17; Romans 8.13).

These first three stanzas describe the way of self-knowledge, which is the beginning of knowledge of God (C 4.1). Now the soul turns outward to the realm of creation to see if she can glean any knowledge of her Beloved there. This transition is marked by the poem's first exclamation after the direct questions and statements of the preceding stanzas, and by an appeal to the elements of nature planted by the Beloved's hand to give witness to his presence.[6] Following Romans 1.20, a text frequently appealed to in the construction of natural theologies because it envisages creation as a book to be read for signs of the Creator, and quoting from the *Soliloquia*, San Juan interprets the woods and thickets as the four elements, because of the density and multiplicity of life each contains, created directly by God.[7] But the 'prado de verduras', the green meadow enamelled with flowers, is given an unexpected meaning, as a metaphor for the eternal pastures of the heavens, spangled with stars. Before one is tempted to dismiss this as too forced, it should be remembered that Golden Age writers often followed their classical predecessors in imagining the heavens in terms of the pastoral landscapes of the heavens, the Elysian fields. Fray Luis de Granada uses precisely the same image of enamelled flowers for the stars; Fray Luis de León Christianizes the tradition in his ode 'Alma región luciente'; a generation later Góngora evokes spring at the beginning of his *Soledades* through a complex allusion to the constellation of Taurus, where the Sun 'en campos de zafiro pace estrellas'; 'in sapphire fields feeds on stars'.[8] San Juan's apparently eccentric interpretation is therefore following a venerable tradition of Christian pastoral, in which the green, flowering pastures of heaven are distinguished from those of earth by their beauties which never fade and by the brightness of their inhabitants.

In the fifth verse Creation replies that it bears witness to the Creator through the beauty with which he endowed it when he created all things through his Word. In the poem San Juan compresses Augustine's questioning of the elements about God and their reply that he made them, but that they were not themselves God (*Confessions*, x.6), into a single line of alliterative poetry: 'pasó por estos sotos con presura', 'he passed through these groves swiftly'. In his commentary, he stresses both the multiplicity and the loveliness of the creatures, though they only hint at the Beloved's presence, works of a moment in comparison with the work to which he hastens, the Incarnation of the Word, in which the being of the creature was united to the being of the Creator and all the creatures were raised to divine beauty. San Juan interprets the goodness of creation (Genesis 1.31; C 5.4) through Christ's words in John 12.32, 'And I, if I be lifted up from the earth, will draw all men (Vg 'omnia', all things) unto me', where the lifting up of the risen Word made flesh beautifies and dignifies all creation. Though briefly sketched in, the theology is profound, in that the purpose of the Incarnation and the power of the Resurrection are understood to reach into the whole creation, and not just its human inhabitants. This is achieved 'con sola su figura', 'by his face alone', a less puzzling image when San Juan cites Hebrews 1.3, in which the Son is described as 'the brightness of his [the Father's] glory, and the express image of his person' (Vg 'figura substantiae eius').

A CAREFUL READER

One could proceed through the whole exposition in this manner, providing what in effect would be a commentary on a commentary on the poem. But the exegesis of the first five verses should be sufficient to familiarize the reader with the mind-set of San Juan. So I turn instead to other features of the commentary, in order to explore its strange territory more selectively.

Occasionally San Juan surprises us by attention to small changes in the grammar of the poem which might well pass the reader by, but which become the foundation for complex arguments in the commentary. We have already noted this in the change of the Bride's address from a singular 'Amado' to the plural 'pastores' of the second verse.[9] Further examples of careful reading of his own verses are not hard to find. When the Bride reaches a moment of crisis and is vulnerable to the devil, who wants to disrupt her progress, the verse (CB 16; CA 25 has 'Cogednos') reads 'Cazad*nos*', 'hunt us', not 'Cazad*me*', 'hunt me', because it is the mutual delight of Bride and Groom which is now at risk to the 'raposas', the 'vixen' of the sensual appetites, which feign sleep then pounce on their prey to make war on the soul's tranquility. A more complex point is made about the first person plural of 'hazemos una piña', 'we make a cone', four lines on. The argument is almost as tightly constructed as the image, and turns on multiplicity and unity. The cone or bouquet of roses forms a single object composed of many others in close relationship with each other; hence, in the spiritual sense, it represents the many perfections and virtues of the soul, now manifest and fully activated, and constituting 'una sólida perfección', 'one solid perfection' (16.9), which in this state are offered all together to the Beloved. But the first person plural also leads San Juan into one of the great controversies of his age, the relationship between faith and works in human salvation, as well as between the active and passive modes of his own doctrine of the dark night. The soul cannot make this self-offering without the assistance of the Beloved; their joint enterprise is indicated by the verb, 'hazemos', for human effort alone is insufficient and is always in need of grace. The roses, interpreted positively, not in their traditional Golden Age role as reminders of the ephemeral beauties of human love or as snares to trap the unwary into desires which cannot be fulfilled, affirm the beauties of creation as they participate in the mutual exchange of gifts between Lover and Beloved.[10]

Equally, adverbs, prepositions and pronouns receive comment. The line 'acaba de entregarte ya de vero', 'Yield yourself at last, and truly' (C 6) is a case in point. San Juan takes 'de vero' as a marker in the poetic text for a distinction he makes elsewhere between secondary knowledge of God through the creatures (reading the book of creation, as in C 4–5) and primary knowledge of God in his essential being (L 4.5). His argument is far more complex than the two words would appear to indicate. The more the soul learns of her Beloved the greater her hunger and pain. But the creatures, as messengers who bring her news of him, are mere crumbs which cannot satisfy or heal, because they are 'remotos' and 'ajenos', distant from and other than the goal she seeks, and unable therefore to lead her to it. The commentary contrasts the Bride's desire for the full self-bestowal of the Beloved, which the poem indicates by 'de vero', with the partial bestowal she has hitherto known through these messengers. Almost half the admittedly brief commentary on the verse concentrates on this single adverbial phrase.

In CB 17 (CA 26) two prepositions catch the expositor's interest to mark another distinction. The Spirit-wind acting within the 'huerto' of the soul reawakens the love that seemed to have become dormant. The Bride says 'aspira *por*', 'blow *through*' and not '*en* mi huerto', '*in* my garden', to mark the difference between potentiality and actuality. Though divine grace has infused virtues *in* her, she does not always sense their activity. Once the wind is blowing *through* the garden the flowers are no longer tightly closed buds but yield up their fragrance (17.5–6). The Bridegroom now comes to feed '*entre*', '*among*' the flowers of his garden (17.10; Song 6.1–2; [AV .2–3], not simply '*en*', '*on*' them, because the soul is 'ya guisada, salada y sazonada con las dichas flores de virtudes y dones y perfecciones, que son la salsa con que y entre que la pace', 'now cooked, salted and seasoned with the said flowers of virtues, gifts and perfections, which are the sauce with which and among which he feeds her' (my emphases). 'Entre' establishes the image of the flowers among which the Beloved feeds in the poem as flowers of the soul's virtues in the commentary. Once the poem's flowers are allegorized into virtues in which the Beloved delights, the otherwise surreal image of a male lover feeding among flowers becomes a dense theological statement of the new relationship which exists between the poem's protagonists.

The image of the bouquet returns in a different form, the garlands of flowers and emeralds woven into a strand of the Bride's hair (CB 30, CA 21), where another first person plural, 'haremos las guirnaldas', 'we shall make garlands', provokes an exegesis which helps to clarify the relationship between the active and passive nights in the *Subida-Noche*.[11] The Bride has come to be like the queen at the king's side in Psalm 44.10 [45.9], because she has been beautified by her Lord: all gifts come from on high (James 1.17). Therefore, the garlands (her virtues) are jointly worked: 'las virtudes no las puede obrar el alma ni alcanzarlas a solas sin ayuda de Dios, ni tampoco las obra Dios a solas en el alma sin ella' (30.6); 'the soul cannot work virtues or acquire them alone, without God's help, but neither can God work them alone in the soul, without her'. Biblical confirmation for this teaching is found in another first person plural future, the 'correremos' of Song 1.3. Here, the grammar of the poem acquires theological significance through the grammar of a biblical text, to demonstrate that human virtues, which are God's gift, once active need to be perfected by divine love in order to flower (30.8) – 'en tu amor floridas', 'flowering in your love'.

In view of the remarks made about the interpretation of 'vagar' in the poem, it is interesting to note that San Juan comments elsewhere on the precise meaning of unusual verbs.[12] In the line 'las jóvenes discurren al camino', 'the maidens run to the road' (CB 25), he takes the maidens to be souls renewed by their encounter with God and defines the verb as 'corren por muchas partes y de muchas maneras' (CB 25.4), 'they run in many directions and in many ways', that is, they run about on the way to eternal life through the many kinds of spiritual works in which Christ's followers are engaged.[13] He supports his exegesis from the biblical use of 'currere' (Song 1.3; Psalm 118 [119.]32), correctly perceiving in the second case that to run in the way of the Lord's commandments means to perform his will. Similarly, in the line 'por eso me adamabas' (CB 32), 'for that reason you loved me greatly', the verb is defined as 'amar mucho [. . .] como amar duplicadamente, esto es, por dos títulos o causas' (CB 32.5), 'to love a great deal [. . .] as if to love in double measure, that is, for two reasons or causes'.[14] This he links through its shared rhetoric of emphasis with the 'grace upon grace' which the incarnate Word has brought (John 1.16), because it is the Beloved's grace present within the Bride which causes him to fall in love with her so powerfully.

On the other hand, the poem is sometimes interpreted in a way which strongly suggests that the poet himself has come to see new meanings in the words he had originally used. This is hardly surprising, given his remarks in the Prologue about the correspondence between word and meaning in the poem being only approximate. The clearest example comes in the exposition of the image of the 'llama que consume y no da pena' in CA 38, which follows immediately on 'la noche serena', anticipating the central images of San Juan's other two *lira* poems. One might have thought that the verb 'consume' would have taken him to Moses and the burning bush which was not 'consumed' (Exodus 3.2), but the Vulgate uses the verb 'combureretur', whereas Deuteronomy 4.24, which San Juan does cite, has 'Deus tuus ignis consumens est', 'thy God is a consuming fire'. In the commentary San Juan takes his argument a stage further through a word-play which is not evident in the poem, from the biblical 'fuego consumidor' to 'consumador', one which brings consummation in love, to connect the flame which in this life consumes with some pain, in order to prepare the soul for the joyful consummation of her journey in the life to come.[15]

CONNECTIONS BETWEEN THE VERSES

In cases like these, verbal morphology, prepositions, adverbial phrases and individual words are given a prominence in the exposition which they do not seem to have in the poem. But the commentary is also sensitive to the more literary features of the poem, like the patterns of imagery which extend over several verses. Images of wounding and dying occur across the first 12, framed by the image of the stag. In C 7.2–3, San Juan recalls that he had used 'herida' for wound in the first verse, but is now using the verb 'llagar'. Remembering the threefold 'adolezco, peno y muero', 'I suffer, grieve and die', of the second, he explains that the Lover suffers in three different ways, depending on the source of her information about the Beloved. The 'herida' is caused by the creatures, the lowliest works of God; the 'llaga', by knowledge of the Incarnation of the Word and the other mysteries of faith. Both these wounds are associated with texts from the Song. The 'daughters of Jerusalem' (Song 5.8) represent the wound of the creatures because, like the Bride's question to the creatures in stanza 4, the biblical verse is cast in the form of an appeal for them to tell her Beloved of her pain, 'Quia amore langueo', 'for I am sick of love'. The 'llaga', deeper and more enduring than 'herida', is caused by knowledge of the higher works of God, as shown in Song 4.9, which he translates 'Llagaste mi corazón en el uno de tus ojos y en un cabello de tu cuello' (cf. AV, 'Thou hast ravished my heart'), where the eye stands for faith in the Incarnation and the hair for the love of it.[16] The third and worst kind of suffering, like death (the poem's 'muriendo'), is caused by a 'toque' or 'touch' of the highest knowledge of God, so lofty that it can be expressed only as 'un no sé qué' which the stammering of contemplatives provokes, and which belongs to the category of mystical experience proper. San Juan does not explain what it is or how it relates to this stage in the Beloved's progress, but he chooses two biblical examples of what he calls this 'amor impaciente', 'impatient love', Rachel's desire for a child (Genesis 30.1) and Job's desire for an end to his agony (6.9), appropriate, because both, like the poem, express a wish to die if the request is not granted.

This discussion leads naturally into the next verse (C 8), which develops the theme of living death. San Juan notes that the paradox of not living where one lives is due to the soul's true life being located in the object of her love (God) rather than in her body, a characteristic leap from the popular paradox in the verse (living but not living), through a philosophical principle (one lives where one's love is), to the spiritual lesson of the commentary. Taking two of the best-known biblical texts which state that all life is lived in God (Acts 17.28 and John 1.3–4), San Juan recognizes the hyperbolic nature of the poetic language ('encarecimiento'), and introduces another principle, that of the contraries, to explain the soul's suffering in terms of the conflict between her natural life in the body and her desire for life in God. That the arrows which bring this living death should be called 'toques de amor', 'touches of love', is not surprising, given the conventional armoury of Cupid; a little more so, perhaps, is San Juan's statement that they 'fecundan', 'fertilize' the soul and heart with understanding and love for God. But the sexual imagery the commentary develops is suggested by the verse's reference to conception – a conceiving of the Beloved within the soul; in this case, of God's greatness, beauty, wisdom, grace and virtues.

The commentary on v. 9 opens with the simile of the stag (CB 9.1), representing the wounded soul as she seeks a remedy for her pain, obtainable only from the one who caused it and the death she seeks through the power of his love; we are still in the realms of 'impatient love', of longings not yet satisfied. Though the wounded stag does not appear in the poem at this point, the commentary remembers the image from the first verse and anticipates its reappearance in the twelfth. When the Bridegroom speaks for the first time in the poem (CA 12), his reply to the Bride's plea for him to reveal himself transmutes them both into images from the natural creation: he calls the soul 'paloma' and himself 'el ciervo vulnerado'. The 'herida', which the Beloved's flight 'como el ciervo' causes in the Bride at the start of the poem, has led to his appearance now as 'el ciervo vulnerado', 'the wounded stag'. Doves and wounded stags have a long history in Christian art and their presence here is not in itself remarkable. What is more significant is the coherence of image and sense across these stanzas, in poem and commentary alike. Deliberately harking back to the imagery of groaning and wounding in the first verse of the poem, San Juan writes of the Bridegroom that 'él también al *gemido* della viene *herido* del amor della' (CB 13.9, CA 12.9), 'he also comes in answer to her *groaning wounded* by love for her' (my emphases). The wounded stag now takes refreshment on the hill from the breeze of the dove's flight. At this point the poem juxtaposes two different images of air, 'vuelo' (flight) and 'aire' (breeze), and through making a careful distinction between them San Juan establishes a precise theological point. The flight of the lover's ecstasy, which occurs in the second line of the stanza, is caused by a wind of love. San Juan correctly notes that the Bible often uses wind as an image of the Holy Spirit, the third Person of the Trinity; the wounded stag is a metaphor for the Son, the second Person of the Trinity, who is drawn to the soul not by her ecstasy, but its cause, divine love already at work within her. San Juan wants to make it clear that her ecstasy is the result of divine initiative, not human effort, and to drive the lesson home, he appeals to St Paul's great hymn to love in 1 Corinthians 13, which shows that ecstatic religious experiences are of no value without love, the bond of perfection (Colossians 3.14).

The next verse (CA 13, CB 14) also contains a double image of air, in the Bride's description of the Bridegroom as 'el silbo de los aires amorosos', 'the whistling of the loving breezes'. San Juan develops the point he has just made about 'al aire de tu vuelo', to explain why the singular 'aire' of the previous verse has now become the plural 'aires': they are the virtues and graces of the Beloved which at this moment of betrothal flow into the soul. Their whistling is described as a very lofty and delightful knowledge of God brought about in the intellect when God's virtues touch the substance of the soul, the highest point reached so far in the journey. The fact that the poem mentions 'aires' and 'silbo' in the same line encourages San Juan to interpret the former as a 'toque' from God in the substance of the soul, on the grounds that breezes are felt, whereas the latter is a sound heard by the 'ear' of the soul, which is the intellect. To distinguish the touch of the wind from its sound may seem to be a rationalization, and to do so in Thomist terms, with reference to the passive or possible intellect (that is, received with no activity on the soul's part) an unlikely one. But he is drawing attention to continuities of imagery between two verses which constitute a break in the poem's narrative, as the Bride turns from complaint and longing to her hymn in praise of the Beloved, who has suddenly revealed himself. Each uses the same images of the other: while at the start he fled like a stag leaving her wounded, he now appears as himself the wounded stag; he appears in the breeze caused by her flight of rapture, she describes him as the whistling of the breezes. This mutual exchange of attributes between Lover and Beloved in the poem becomes the exchange of gifts and virtues between Bride and Bridegroom in the commentary. It is of a different order from the exchange of attributes critics have noted in Góngora's reworkings of classical allusions.[17] His are intended to breathe new life into poetic conventions; San Juan's, to represent in the poem's imagery the mutuality of loving between its protagonists, and to explore in the commentary the origin and nature of that love.

Rhetorical features of the poem also attract attention. On two occasions the verb 'mirar' is repeated within a verse, in CB 19 (CA 32), 'y mira con tu haz', 'mas mira las compañas'; 'look with your face', 'look at the companies', and, more obliquely, in CB 33 (CA 24), 'ya bien puedes mirarme/después que me miraste', 'well may you look at me/after you looked at me'. In both cases the repetition signals a similar point about the relationship between divine initiative and human response. In the first, the soul is asking the Beloved to fall in love with the virtues and graces with which he has himself endowed her. San Juan's answer to the puzzle 'How can the beloved be asked to fall in love with himself within the Bride?' is given as he analyses the movement of the text from 'mira' to 'mas mira'. The 'haz' (an archaic Spanish word for 'face') is God's, a connection supported indirectly by scripture, in the sense that the text cited (Exodus 33.23) tells of how Moses was *not* permitted to see God face to face, as the soul now desires. The second 'mira' is interpreted as a request for God to 'amar y hacer mercedes', 'love and perform mercies' as he looks on the 'compañas', the gifts, graces and virtues he has already bestowed upon the soul as his betrothal gift and her dowry. As he has already implanted in her the gifts for which she now asks him so that he will love her, he can indeed love himself through them within her: though his by origin, once bestowed they become her 'compañas'. The second case is just as complex. The verse twice refers to the Bridegroom's looking upon her, first to tell him he may, then to recall when he did. The commentary clarifies the mystery: his first look gave her grace and beauty, so that when he looks again he will see them in her and increase them. By her own nature, sinful, imperfect and lowly – the 'color moreno', 'dark colour' of CA 24 (CB 33) – the soul cannot deserve his glance (33.4–5), but through his beauteous gaze the dark stain of sin has been replaced by the grace and beauty he has poured out upon her.[18] The commentary implies that the verse's polyptoton is deliberate, and must be given due weight.

In both cases, San Juan builds a coherent theological structure on a word repeated in the poem, reading it through biblical passages about the consequence of seeing God, which is to die. For the Bridegroom to look upon the soul in her sinfulness would mean her certain death; but from the betrothal onwards a change has taken place in their relationship: his virtue and grace are to be found within her, obliterating her sin and raising her creatureliness by divine gifts, so that when he looks on her, she lives. One may not agree with the exegesis; one may assume it to be *a posteriori*, as San Juan ponders why the same word is repeated across these verses; but the one thing one cannot do is to complain that he has neglected the rhetoric of the verse or constructed an argument which does not match it. But he does not always do this: in CB 31 (CA 22), the verse where 'mirar' first begins to play an important part, the repetition of 'en mi cuello', 'on my neck', is noted but passes without comment.

A further example of a distinction San Juan makes in what might otherwise be taken as simple rhetorical variation occurs with 'al monte y al collado', 'to the mountain and the hill', where the lovers will go to see the divine beauty, CB 36 (CA 35). The association of 'monte' with the mountain and house of the Lord in Isaiah 2.2–3 leads him to interpret it as '*la noticia matutina* y esencial de Dios, que es conocimiento en el Verbo divino' (36.6), 'the *morning knowledge* of the essence of God, which is knowledge in the divine Word', while the 'collado' is the lowlier knowledge of God through the creatures, 'la *noticia vespertina* de Dios, que es sabiduría de Dios en sus criaturas y obras y ordenaciones admirables' (36.6), 'the *evening knowledge* of God, which is knowledge of God in his creatures, works and admirable counsels'.[19] This latter knowledge belongs to a much earlier stage of the journey, the *interrogatio creaturum* of stanza 4, but it is not to be rejected here – rather, wholeheartedly embraced, since union with God leads to a radically new vision of the whole creation and is part of the 'hermosura del Hijo de Dios en que desea el alma ser ilustrada' (36.7), 'beauty of the Son of God in which the soul desires to be illumined'. The identification of 'collado' with this lower knowledge is also argued from Song 4.6, with its 'mons' of myrrh and 'collis' of incense. Myrrh from the mountain is a higher kind of spice than incense from the hill, hence it represents the clear vision of God rather than knowledge of God derived from the creatures. The distinction is not arbitrary, since Spanish 'monte' is generally higher than 'collado'.[20]

Further indications of the way San Juan respects both the poetic and theological integrities of the work comes when the commentary is prompted by a recurrent image in the poem to reflect on its shifting senses. We have already looked at the way hiddenness, wounding and the stag are related to one another in the opening stanzas. Much later, the line 'Escóndete, Carillo', 'Hide yourself, Dearest', which introduces CA 32 (CB 19), acts as a cue to return to the theme of hiddenness, and to mark a progression which has taken place in the soul. The poem began with a cry to the absent, hidden Beloved. Now, by calling on him to hide, the very thing which provoked her initial cry of pain, she seems to contradict herself. But the 'Escóndete' of this later verse marks the distance the soul has travelled. She has now found the secret dwelling place of her Beloved within her, and longs for an even closer relationship with him, uninterrupted by distractions, 'muy adentro en lo escondido de su alma', 'deep within the hiddenness of her soul' (CB 19.2). She desires her faculties to be filled with divine glory beyond the power of words to express, as she asks the Beloved to fall in love with the virtues and graces with which he has himself endowed her. She describes herself periphrastically as 'la que va por ínsulas extrañas' (CA 32), 'she who goes by strange islands', an image she had earlier used of him (CA 13), a further poetic representation of the exchange of attributes which has taken place between the lovers since she learnt to find the Beloved by hiding within herself. This second occurrence of the image receives little commentary, other than that the soul is now discovering in them the spiritual knowledge beyond all senses which belongs to him and which he has shared with her (CB 19.7).

The commentary on verses 34–5 develops the relationship between the image of the dove and the call for solitude in the poem. In CA 24 (CB 33) the Bride had attributed to herself 'color moreno', 'dark colour'; now the Bridegroom calls her 'la blanca palomica', 'the white dove', a progression between the verses which is easy to miss but which the commentary clarifies (one of the few places where the CB order of the verses gives greater coherence to the imagery). San Juan goes first to the dove of the Song (1.14[.15], 2.10 [AV, 'my fair one']), denoting the soul's gentleness and loving eyes (34.3), but also to Genesis 8.8–12, because of her likeness to the dove of the Flood narrative. The paragraph which explains why this is so is one of San Juan's densest, but it establishes all the connections he wishes to make between verse and meaning. Like the dove Noah sent forth from the ark, unable to find a place to set her foot until she returns with an olive branch, the soul has left the ark of divine omnipotence at her creation and has wandered across the floods of sins and imperfections, unable to find anything to satisfy her appetite. She comes and goes, seeking God (though San Juan is clear that God has never left her) in 'ansias de amor', 'anxiety of love', until the waters of imperfection subside and she is able to pluck the olive leaf of victory over herself and of peace gained, and return to the ark of God 'blanca y limpia como salió della cuando la crió' (34.4), 'clean and white as she left it when she was created'.[21]

Though the verse (CA 33) does not mention solitude, the commentary introduces it as part of the dove's quest for 'la soledad de todas las cosas', 'solitude from all things' (CB 34.6). This leads naturally into CA 34, with its fourfold anaphora ('en soledad', with the variant fourth line 'a solas'). Solitude, as sought by the dove, now becomes the dominant image for the whole of the journey to union – not simply the solitude practised in monastic life but the absence of all the normal props of daily living, the things and the desires which have had to be left behind in order to discover 'la posesión de la paz de la soledad en su Amado' (CB 35.2), 'the possession of the peace of solitude in her Beloved'.

The 'nido', 'nest', of the verse's second line is the 'perfecta soledad', 'perfect solitude', in which she enjoys union with the Word, and thereby rest and refreshment (35.5), because it is the place where the sparrow finds a home and the swallow a nest (Vg Psalm 83.4 has 'passer' and 'turtur'; San Juan's 'pájaro' and 'tórtola'). Because her natural faculties are empty, she is free to concentrate all her energies on the God who is guiding and raising her to divine knowledge and love. In the third line, 'en soledad la guía', 'he guides her in solitude', following Romans 8.1 (all who are moved by the Spirit of God are children of God), because she has attained perfection. And just as in 31.8 and 32.1 he has spoken of God being in love with the soul, so in 35.7 he comments on the last line of CA 34, 'también en soledad de amor herido', 'also in solitude wounded by love', in similar terms: the soul's search for the Beloved in spiritual solitude, wounded with love for him, has caused him so to fall in love with her that 'él solo la guía a sí mismo, atrayéndola y absorbiéndola en sí' (35.7), 'he alone guides her to himself, attracting her and absorbing him in himself'. Human lovers, San Juan observes, delight to be alone with each other and find other company a hindrance to their full pleasure, because 'el amor, como es unidad de dos solos, a solas se quieren comunicar ellos' (36.1), 'since love is the unity of two single objects, they wish to communicate in solitude' – a neo-Aristotelian dictum which reflects the language of the preceding stanzas as well as being true to the mutual delight of lovers alone with each other. In his commentary, therefore, we see how San Juan reflects on the sequence of images in the poem, gives them a coherence which is not always apparent from the verse alone, and uses them to develop ideas which have already been foreshadowed. Equally, in tracing his images back into scripture and allowing them to bear significant theological weight, he does not forget the fundamental metaphor of human love on which the whole is constructed.

But this solitude has a further level of meaning. The Bridegroom is now her guide (CA 34, line 3), but 'a solas', interpreted as 'sin otros medios, ni de ángeles ni de hombres, ni de formas ni figuras, por cuanto ella por medio de esta soledad tiene ya verdadera libertad de espíritu, que no se ata a algunos de estos medios', 'with no other intermediaries, neither angels nor men, forms or figures, because through this solitude she already possesses true liberty of spirit, which is not dependent on any of these intermediaries'. Like his teaching on faith, San Juan's statement that in union human beings have direct and unmediated access to the Father through the Son is not incompatible with the theology of the Protestant Reformers, though it is reached by an entirely different route, the dark nights of detachment.[22] He returns to this in 35.6, where the unmediated action of God on the soul is characteristic of the spiritual marriage, the end of her quest in this life.

SAN JUAN AS A BIBLICAL EXEGETE

As the passages we have studied already show, the centrality of the Bible to San Juan is beyond question. But little attention has been paid to his exegetical techniques, or to the literary qualities of his interpretations. His most sustained passage of biblical exegesis is found in the *Subida* (S 2.16–22).[23] He regards these chapters as something of a digression, but they are not. Although his exegesis is more extensive and less allegorical than customary, he always comes back to the same point, that private revelations are ambiguous, easy to misunderstand, and potentially dangerous. His mastery of scriptural sources is impressive, as he demonstrates the inadequacy of a literal reading, moving from prophecies which come true but in unexpected ways, through those which are changed because of human response, to those which find their true fulfilment in Christ. Above all, his insistence on the way of the cross and on measuring everything by the final revelation of Christ and the community of believers who interpret and live the Gospel, answers powerfully all those critics who have supposed Christian mystics to be engaged on some kind of private fantasy which has nothing to do with the beliefs of the Church.[24]

These chapters from the *Subida* are important because they show how confidently and persuasively San Juan could handle the Bible as a whole, develop a sustained argument, and apply it to a particular problem. The examples I now look at from the *Cántico* do not demonstrate the same rigour because they are much briefer, but they do help us to understand his exegetical technique, and show how sensitive he is to the language of scripture as it enters into dialogue with his poem. We have encountered the lines 'y véante mis ojos,/pues eres lumbre dellos' (C 10), 'and may my eyes see you,/since you are their light', before.[25] They have many echoes in Spanish literature, both in popular love poetry and more *culto* contexts: one thinks of the imprisoned Segismundo's reaction in Calderón's masterpiece *La vida es sueño* on seeing Rosaura for the first time: 'Pero véate yo y muera' (line 233), 'may I see you and die'.[26] Suddenly death is redefined for him. No longer is it the living death of his solitary confinement, chained up like a wild beast since birth; it is the death which the sight of something beautiful brings. This secular analogue of San Juan's line shows how easily the same clusters of words and images could suggest different meanings in different contexts.[27] Their simplicity might lead one to suppose that San Juan would find little to say about them. He glosses his line as 'let me see you face to face with the eyes of my soul' (10.7), adding that lovers often call the ones they love 'light of my eyes' as a sign of how much they love them. Yet at once, with that leap which is so disconcerting, he is burrowing away in scripture to find three texts connected with sight which fit the soul's desire to see her Beloved. Psalm 37.11 [38.10] is straightforward enough: 'the light of mine eyes [. . .] is gone from me'. The second seems more arbitrary: Tobit 5.12 alludes to the blindness of the old man, who cannot see the light of heaven. Revelation 21.23, with its picture of the heavenly Jerusalem whose light is the Son of God, completes the sequence. These texts have not been chosen at random; they form a meaningful sequence characteristic of the imaginative and cumulative reading of the corpus of scripture practised by older traditions of exegesis. The linguistic features the texts share are used in an incremental way to illustrate the journey from the Beloved's absence to the consummation of love which both poem and commentary represent. The first relates directly to the lover's lack of sight of the Beloved in the poem, the second associates it with the light of heaven, while the third looks to the eschatological fulfilment of the desire expressed in the new Jerusalem. It is true that this application allegorizes the particular context of the second: Tobit's blindness is an element in a Jewish folk tale of great charm, and the 'light of heaven' he desires to see is simply a Hebrew metaphor for daylight. But biblical texts have often been applied to situations far removed from their original contexts, especially when the exegete turns preacher.

A particularly good example of San Juan's imaginative connection beween poetic image and scripture occurs where the tension between the lyrical outpouring of the poem and the commentary's insistence on its spiritual meaning is most keenly felt – the Bride's hymn of praise to the Beloved in CB 14–15 (CA 13–14).[28] According to San Juan, these marvellous verses signify a series of gifts: the richness, refreshment and rest the soul discovers in her betrothal; secret things of God; a divine power which exceeds all other strength; a gentle, enlightening, lofty experience of divine wisdom; and above all, an overwhelming love. The exuberant beauty of the verse leads him first to an affirmation of the beauty of creation, of 'la armonía de las criaturas y hechos de

Dios', 'the harmony of the creatures and acts of God', in which all the divine attributes represented by the imagery 'relucen', 'shine'. He quotes St Francis's exclamation: '¡Dios mío y todas las cosas!', 'My God and all things!' (CB 14–15.5), the conjunction implying that there is no longer a choice to be made between spirit and sense, but that their new relationship means that both can be affirmed, because the soul in union with God values and enjoys his works in creation no longer as objects of her own desiring but as witnesses to his glory.

The first biblical text he introduces is to the many rooms and different foods provided for all kinds of creatures in Noah's ark (Genesis 6.18–22). This becomes a type of the many mansions in the Father's house of which Christ speaks (John 14.2), through the common features of multiplicity of rooms and inhabitants, and because the soul feeds on the divine grandeurs represented by these images from the poem. Remembering his observations about mystical language in the Prologue, he interprets these lines as an 'exceso' expressed by 'la semejanza de la bondad de las cosas' (14–15.5), 'the likeness of the goodness of things'. The goodness and beauty of creation brought into being by God in the external, physical world is analogous to the overflow of language in the poetic world inspired by divine activity within the soul. Passing now to John 1.3–4, 'All things were made by him and without him was not anything made that was made. In him was life', it becomes clear that the theology has advanced from C 4–5, where Creation spoke of the Beloved's swift passage through it but left the soul deprived of him, to one in which she can claim that she possesses all things in him. She has not, however, yet reached the point at which creation is seen as it exists in the mind of God (L 4): 'no se ha de entender que lo que aquí se dice que siente el alma es como ver las cosas en la luz o las criaturas en Dios, sino que en aquella posesión siente serle todas las cosas Dios' (14–15.5), 'it is not to be thought that what the soul is here said to feel is like seeing things in the light or the creatures in God, but that in this possession she feels that all things are God to her'. What seems like pantheism on a superficial reading represents the intermediate stage in the journey, in which the soul, united with God in the mode of betrothal, discovers that her vision of creation has changed from seeing it an external protagonist to her inward possession of what Gerard Manley Hopkins was to call a world 'charged with the grandeur of God'.

The first two images, the mountains and the solitary wooded valleys, require little commentary. But the 'strange islands' do. San Juan begins with the literal sense, of islands far from human commerce, full of plants and animals never before seen, which are the cause of wonder to those who find them – a reflection, surely, of the impact of the Spanish discoveries in the New World. Their metaphorical application to the soul depends on the two meanings he, like Covarrubias (pp. 568–9), ascribes to 'extraño': isolated from people, and excellent above other things. But the word which governs his exegesis is not in the poem: 'novedades', 'new things', and the wonder they provoke. It is God who is 'strange', strange as these islands in his counsels and works, new and wonderful to men, strange even to angels, who contemplate ever new manifestations of divine judgements and works with ever increasing wonder.[29] Given that 'novedad' was often used pejoratively, in the sense of innovations which ran counter to orthodox norms, it is interesting to find San Juan using the expression so confidently of God, perhaps because in the *Confessions* (x.27) and the *Soliloquia* Augustine prays to that Beauty which is ever ancient and ever new.[30] That God is ever new and constantly experienced in surprising and changing ways is true only from the perspective of the creatures, since God is neither new nor strange to himself: San Juan is always careful to maintain the fundamental ontological distinction between God and the creatures (angels included). It is the strangeness of the new knowledge of God the soul acquires in this state of betrothal, and her wonder at its greatness, which creates the links between image and interpretation. She is seeing, as it were, the unvisited shores of the divine self-giving, as new and strange to her as they are essential and eternal to the being of God.

The interpretation of the 'ríos sonorosos' also begins by enumerating their natural characteristics – the force by which they cover everything in their path, filling any hollows or dips, and the sound they make, which drowns out all other noise. One suspects that he has selected these features with an exegesis in mind; but that does not preclude admiring the rich and imaginative use of the Bible which they prompt, especially in the antithesis of power and gentleness. The torrential force of the Spirit sweeps away the rivers of worldly actions and emotions, but gently, for his are rivers of peace ('fluvium pacis', Isaiah 66.12), filling the soul with peace and glory. This divine water likewise fills the lowly places of the soul's humility (Luke 1.52, the Magnificat) and the empty places where formerly her appetites held sway. But its sound occupies San Juan the most, as he builds an exegesis around several scriptural texts, and brings it to an unexpected climax.

The mighty roar of these rivers communicates great delight and strength, for it is an inward, spiritual sound, and, unlike noise, not troublesome to the external senses. Its many biblical witnesses include the mighty rushing wind of the day of Pentecost (Acts 2.2–6); the voice like thunder, heard as Jesus prayed before his Passion (John 12.28–29); the divine voice of power (Psalm 67.34 [68.33b]); the thundering of many waters, sweet as the sound of many harpers harping (Revelation 14.2); the thunder of the four living creatures in Ezekiel's vision (1.24, the source of the text in the Apocalypse); and finally the sweet voice of the Bride, which the Bridegroom asks to hear in Song 2.14. All these mighty sounds combine sweetness and gentleness with spiritual power. All come from God, except the last, which invites a human response. San Juan has not merely piled up as many references as he can find to the noise of water as thunder. Poem and commentary, as San Juan has already explained, mark at this point a significant advance in the soul's journey, the exchange of gifts and pledges in betrothal. As the soul draws closer to God and is more and more filled with his gifts, she becomes more and more like him. When he asks to hear her sweet voice, after a series of texts in which he has spoken to her in power but gently, it is because his work is to bring her to union with himself, and to continue his wooing of her until that union is consummated in marriage. From the single image of 'ríos sonorosos' San Juan brings into relationship a series of biblical sounds which represent powerful theophanies but which give way to a more intimate request, in which God asks to hear a human voice. That voice is precisely the one which speaks in these stanzas.

This tendency to cite a number of biblical authorities and round them off with a text from the Song is found at least ten times in the commentary, and there is good reason for it. In one sense San Juan's poem exegetes the Song by rewriting it, rather than paraphrasing it, as its images combine with others from the Song and other books of the Bible, from secular traditions or his own creation. For San Juan and the tradition in which he was writing, the Song was the love song *par excellence* between God and the soul: nowhere else in the biblical corpus was this the subject of a whole book or dealt with so comprehensively and beautifully. Though expressed in terms of a dialogue between two individual lovers, this tradition saw the nuptial imagery of the Song as representing the whole history of salvation, from Creation to the End, within which the particular journey of the individual soul takes place. The Song's imagery, so central to the poem, is the prime example of the 'misterios en extrañas figuras y semejanzas', 'mysteries in strange figures and comparisons' announced in the Prologue, which even the Holy Spirit must use to express such abundance of meaning.

A good example of the way the Song helps to unravel a difficult image in the poem occurs with the 'semblantes plateados', the 'silvery features' of the 'cristalina fuente' (CB 12; CA 11), in which San Juan finds more than the commonplaces of the Renaissance fountain. They represent the articles of faith, a silver surface for the truths of gold they cover, an idea which supports what he has to say elsewhere about the relationship between words or concepts, at best partial and at worst idolatrous, and the God who is beyond them.[31] He derives his interpretation from a complex piece of exegesis of the picture of a dove covered in silver with wings of gold in Psalm 67.14 [68.13], read through Song 1.10[.11]), which also mentions both precious metals, 'borders of gold with studs of silver' (12.4). The propositions of faith are the silver plating which will be removed when the soul enjoys the pure gold of the vision of God, symbolized in the poem by the 'ojos deseados', the 'longed-for eyes' of the Beloved (12.5). On closer examination, the strangeness of the exegesis is tempered not only by the constants (silver and gold) but also by a second, parallel image. Through faith the soul already has within herself ('en mis entrañas') knowledge of this vision, but as yet imperfect, sketched (the poem's 'dibujados'), inferior to the final painting. Silver and sketch both represent partiality of vision; gold and the final painting its completeness. San Juan proves his point with a text which makes the contrast explicit, Paul's distinction between 'through a glass darkly' and 'face to face' (12.6; 1 Corinthians 13.10).

At other times San Juan brings together a group of ideas derived from images in the poem and concludes his exposition with the Song text to which they are most closely related. In this next example he actively seeks out points of contact between different parts of his own poem and of biblical poetry (31.8–10). His theme is 'y en él [aquel *cabello*] *presso* quedaste', 'and on [that strand of *hair*] you were *caught*' – the Bridegroom's falling in love with the Bride as he becomes caught in a strand of her hair at which he had been looking ('Quando tú me *miravas*'; my emphases). He begins with a definition, 'el *mirar* de Dios es *amar*' (.8), 'When God *looks* he *loves*', and a direct statement from the Bible: we *love* because God *loved* us first (1 John 4.10). In the poem, the Beloved saw her hair *flying* on her neck ('que en mi cuello *volar* consideraste'), which reminds San Juan how, when the soul had earlier flown in rapture at the sight of the Beloved's eyes, he had called his 'paloma' back ('que voy de *buelo*', 'al ayre de tu *buelo*'; 'for I am *flying*', 'in the breeze of your *flight*' (CA 12). The commentary proceeds: 'si Él por su gran misericordia no nos *mirara* y *amara* primero [. . .] y se abajara, ninguna *presa* hiciera [en él] el *vuelo* del *cabellos* de nuestro bajo *amor*, porque no tenía él tan alto *vuelo* que llegase a prender a esta divina *ave* de las alturas', 'if in his great mercy he had not *looked* on us and *loved* us first [. . .] and humbled himself, the *flying* of the hair of our lowly *loving* could not have *caught* him, because its *flight* was not so lofty that it could manage to capture this divine *bird* of the heights'. Moreover, the one eye of the Bride which wounds the Bridegroom in the poem ('en uno de mis *ojos* te *llagaste*') is her single-minded faith: 'en el *ojo* de su fe aprieta con tan estrecho nudo la *prisión*, que le hace *llaga* de *amor*' (.9), 'she tightens the *prison* with so tight a knot in the *eye* of her faith, that it makes a *wound* of *love* in him'. Only then does San Juan cite the Song text (4.9) which inspired the imagery of the verse in the first place. His translation runs: '*Llagaste* mi corazón en uno de tus *ojos* y en un *cabello* de tu cuello' (.10), 'you *wounded* my heart in one of your *eyes* and in a strand of *hair* of your neck'. What seem to be ideas extraneously imposed on the poem are part of a closely argued passage which moves freely between poetic and biblical texts. There are many passages in all his commentaries of equal or greater complexity. The reason they are difficult is not because they lack coherence, but because of the web of connections he weaves. Sometimes the web catches up otherwise unrelated objects, like pomegranates and caverns, through texts from the Song. In the poem, the juice of the pomegranate (CA 36), a fruit traditionally a symbol for the infinite mysteries of God, is to be tasted in the 'subidas cavernas de la piedra', 'lofty caverns of stone'. This image derives from Song 2.14's 'in foraminibus petrae, in caverna maceriae' (AV 'clefts in the rock'), while the stone has been explained as the wisdom of God in Christ (37.3). As caves have many chambers ('senos'), so the pomegranate fruit has 'muchos granicos, nacidos y sustentados en aquel seno circular', 'many pips, which originate and are nourished in its circular heart' – the many attributes, mysteries, judgements and virtues of God 'contenidos y sustentados en el seno esférico de virtud y misterio' (37.7), 'contained and nourished in the spherical heart of virtue and mystery'. Each pip represents one divine attribute or virtue and each is God himself, his eternity signified by the circular shape of the fruit, without beginning or end. San Juan then finds the same truth expressed in a radically different image, the Beloved's belly of ivory, overlaid with sapphire, in Song 5.14. The distance between caves, pomegranates, and now bellies of ivory and sapphire, seems vast, but, just as the metaphysical poet discovers likeness in unlikeness, so he finds correspondences between the circular shape of the fruit and of the belly, and between the inner spaces of the belly and the cave. Hidden within that space, like the pips in the pomegranate, is divine Wisdom, which brings forth the treasures of heaven, represented by the sapphire (a stone both precious and blue), from its mysterious depths.

In the poem, the soul and her Beloved are to enjoy the sweet juice of the pomegranate together. Just as a single juice is expressed from the many pips, so '[de] todas estas maravillas y grandezas de Dios en el alma infundidas redunda en ella una fruición y deleite de amor, que es bebida del Espíritu Santo' (37.8), '[from] all these marvels and wonders of God infused into the soul there redounds within her the fruition and delight of love, which is the drink of the Holy Spirit'. This juice is identified with the 'adobado vino' (CA 16), 'spiced wine' of Song 8.2, while the verbal form 'gustaremos', 'we shall enjoy', shows it once more to be a shared activity, the fruit of mutual love. San Juan does not make all these connections explicit, but he expects his readers to follow them. Passages like these are difficult to unravel because they assume the reader's familiarity with a range of biblical imagery, especially that of the Song, and with the imagery of the poem at other points than the one under immediate discussion.

Whereas most of the images of the poem are traceable to similar images in biblical texts, when it comes to expounding the line 'entremos más adentro en la espesura' (CB 36, CA 35), 'let us enter further into the thicket', San Juan uses a whole range of biblical texts to define an image which is his own creation. The thicket represents the marvellous works and deep judgements of God, because they are so many, so deep and unsearchable (36.10; Romans 11.33). It is their abundance which makes them 'thick' and justifies the image; equally, they could be called 'cuajada', a curious choice of word, meaning 'set', as milk coagulates to become cheese. The sense only becomes apparent when another biblical reference is given, because 'cuajada' translates Vg 'coagulatus' in the text 'Mons Dei, mons pinguis, mons coagulatus' of Psalm 67.[68.]16 (lost in English versions but of interest to contemporary exegetes since it was expounded by Malón de Chaide and by Fray Luis de León).[32] Its intrusion into the otherwise unrelated image of the thicket is due to the fact that just before, in 36.6, San Juan has been distinguishing 'monte' from 'collado', two lines earlier in the poem. 'Monte' in Spanish of this time normally meant high ground covered in trees or vegetation, so its association with thickets is natural rather than forced.

San Juan gives the poem's 'adentro' its full weight, in the sense that it indicates a fuller and deeper appreciation of the sweetness and desirability of the judgements of the Lord (Psalm 18.10–12 [19.9–11]); but he links both it and the image of the thicket to a wider frame of reference, through a series of connections which draw together ideas which concern him. To know God more profoundly is to be able to bear more joyfully the sorrows and travails of the world (36.11). Therefore the thicket also represents the many sufferings the soul must endure on this road, 'porque el padecer le es medio para entrar más adentro en *la espesura* de la deleitable sabiduría de Dios, porque el más puro padecer trae más íntimo y puro entender' (36.12), 'because suffering is the means for her to enter further into *the thicket* of the delightful wisdom of God, because the purest suffering brings with it the most intimate and pure understanding'. Indeed, it takes the soul to the very threshold of death in her desire to see God, as Job's cry in 6.8–10 shows. Suffering itself is linked with the way of the cross, which is also called 'espesura', hence it enables the soul to participate in Christ's own saving journey, which is the work of divine Wisdom. San Juan makes Paul's prayer in Ephesians 3.13–19 the biblical authority for his argument, since it too links suffering and knowledge, and the love of God through Christ. But his closing sentence also alludes to Matthew 7.13–14: 'Porque para entrar en estas riquezas de su sabiduría la puerta es la cruz, que es angosta, y desea entrar por ella es de pocos, mas desear los deleites a que se viene por ella es de muchos' (36.13), 'for to enter into these riches of his wisdom the gate is the cross, which is narrow, and few there be who desire to enter it, but many there are who desire the joys that are reached thereby'. The emphasis on the way of the cross derived from the image of the thicket through the common property of wood which both possess turns the exegesis into a kind of conceit, and confirms what the *Subida-Noche* will teach about the pain of the dark nights. These are not some private agony endured for some private gain; they participate in the central and defining mysteries of the Christian faith, like the cross.

BIBLICAL ARCHETYPES

If the Song offers the fullest biblical picture of the journey of any soul to union, the use San Juan makes of biblical archetypes indicates that the individual's experience is also to be checked against episodes from the lives of the great figures of both Testaments. Given the close relationship between seeing and dying in the poem, it is natural that San Juan several times recalls the story of Moses sheltering in a cleft of rock on Mount Sinai and permitted to see only of the 'back parts' of God (Exodus 33.20), because no one can see God and live (v. 20; CB 11.5).[33] When the Bride has progressed sufficiently, indirect vision is no longer adequate, so she asks to see the 'haz', or face, of the Beloved (19.4). Moses is, of course, the divinely appointed liberator of Israel from bondage in Egypt. San Juan refers to the Exodus narrative many times (e.g. L 3.38), always to show how God delivers the soul from bondage to her past. This individualizing exegesis must be understood correctly, as only one exegetical strand in the tradition (anagogical or mystical exegesis). Had he been writing a treatise on political oppression he would no doubt have used the same texts differently, as he does, briefly, in S 2.30.3. But Moses is also traditionally a type of the contemplative, because of his intimate relationship with God, initiated at the burning bush and confirmed on Sinai in cloud and darkness.[34]

Other figures from the Hebrew scriptures who are important to San Juan are Noah and Elijah. Noah appears in connection with the image of the dove in the poem (CA 13 and 33), while we have seen how the Ark is the type of the many mansions of the Father (CB 14.15.3). Elijah, the supposed founder of the Carmelite Order, has his own vision of God in the 'still small voice' of 1 Kings 19.12, mentioned in explanation of the line 'el silvo de los ayres amorosos' (CB 14–15.14). The Bride of the Song is not San Juan's only female archetype. The soul's distress in C 7 is attributed to the 'amor impaciente' (7.4), 'impatient love' of Rachel when she found herself childless and her sister not (Genesis 30.1), while Esther plays a significant part in the *Llama* (1.8, 2.31, 4.11–12).

Job and the Psalms provide further archetypal confirmations of his teaching; indeed, there are more references to the Psalms in his commentaries than to any other biblical book (the much shorter Song comes a close second).[35] The texts and images which introduce CB 13 to indicate the passage through the dark nights are all used in association with the passive night of the spirit in the *Noche oscura*: Psalms 96 [97].2–3 (N 2.5.3), 17 [18].13 (N 2.5.3; 16.11) and 138 [139].12 (N 2.7.3), as well as Job 23.3

(N 2.5.6 uses 23.6). A little later San Juan digresses to expound a longer text, Job 4.12–16 (CB 14–15.17), in which Job speaks of hearing a hidden word in the horror of visions of the night, seeing a spirit before his very eyes, and in terror hearing a voice as thin as air. This passage, San Juan asserts, contains almost everything which has been expounded from the moment the soul flew into rapture with the words '¡Apártalos, Amado!'. As nightmares come between sleep and waking, so this experience of ecstasy comes between the sleep of natural human ignorance and the awakening to supernatural knowledge. The text is relevant because it traces the journey through pain and suffering to sudden revelation through the hidden word which led to the soul's rapturous flight – a hidden word, as we have seen, in the poetic sense too, since the cause of her rapture is not textually present in the verse.[36] Job, like the Psalmist, is an Everyman of the spiritual journey each soul is called to undertake.

The five paragraphs he devotes to this text, with its reference to the fears of the night, prepare the way for the next image in the poem, the 'noche sosegada', the calm night. The soul has now entered a spiritual sleep, resting on her Beloved's breast and receiving a profound and dark knowledge of God. It is not simply a dark night, but a peaceful night, because of the calm and quiet the soul enjoys in her resting; and it is a night about to give way to the dawn (the third phase of the natural night in S 1.1.2), because the soul is being lifted out of the darkness of natural modes of knowing towards the supernatural knowledge of divine light. Since this line contains one of the few examples of San Juan's most famous symbol outside the 'Noche oscura' and 'Fonte' poems, it is important to note how consistent his exegesis is with that of his more systematic treatment of the image in the *Subida-Noche*. The dark night is relative, in the sense that it obscures only in order to enlighten. This 'noche sosegada/en par de los levantes de la aurora', 'calm night before the rising of the dawn', is an omen of transition, now described as 'entre dos luces' (CB 14–15.23), 'between two lights', neither wholly night nor wholly day. The soul does not see God with full clarity but she does participate to some extent ('algo') in divine light. Continuing his exploration of the imagery of sleeping, dreaming and waking, San Juan then tells us that when the soul has reached the restful state of the coming dawn the understanding rises far above all natural knowledge into the divine light, like someone waking into unexpected light from a long dream (14–15.24). It is this state which David describes in Psalm 101.8 (102.7), under the image of the *passer solitarius*, the solitary bird on the rooftop, a symbol for contemplation through its position above the lower realm and through the five properties it possesses.[37] It is now that the soul hears the famous 'música callada', the silent music of the poem.

San Juan uses a wide range of Pauline teaching, because Paul has much to say about the vision of God and union with Christ. The soul only wishes for death in CB 11 because death is a precondition for the vision of God (2 Corinthians 5.4; Philippians 1.23); only then will she no longer see 'through a glass, darkly' (1 Corinthians 13.12). The transformation of lovers each into the other (CB 12.7) represents Paul's 'I live: yet not I, but Christ liveth in me' (Galatians 2.20). The rapturous flight of the soul in CB 13 is like Paul's famous out-of-the-body experience in 2 Corinthians 12.2–4, while the revelation of knowledge through the Spirit in 'el silvo de los ayres amorosos', is beyond the power of words to capture, as Paul there explains (CB 14–15.15, 18). San Juan believes that Paul's experience, despite his protestations of uncertainty, cannot have taken place in the body, because flesh cannot participate in so lofty a vision (CB 19.1). The frequency with which he returns to these Pauline texts suggests that he had a high regard for Paul as a spiritual guide, surely because Paul's theology embraces both the cosmic mystery of Christ crucified and risen for the reconciliation of the universe to God, and an intensity of personal spiritual life transformed by the indwelling Christ.

More traditional biblical typologies are also present in his exposition. CA 28 is the most directly allegorical of all the stanzas. As we have seen, in Christian tradition, where Eve, the mother of all, fell by eating the forbidden fruit of the tree in Eden, Mary brought restoration to all by her obedience to God's will at the Annunciation. The typological relationship between the two events (Genesis 3. 6–19; Luke 1.26–38) is a commonplace of paintings of the Annunciation: one thinks of Fra Angelico's version in the Prado, with Mary receiving the angel's message in humble obedience in the foreground, while in the background Adam and Eve, clothed and eating an apple, with guilty expressions on their faces, are about to be expelled from the Garden.[38] The subject of this verse, San Juan tells the reader, is primarily the mystery of the Incarnation: humanity's Fall at the tree of knowledge and its redemption by the Bridegroom on the tree of the cross. The betrothal of the soul is therefore set in the context of Christ's betrothal to the human race on Calvary, and is part of a universal call to participate in the life of God which is centred on the way of the cross. The fact that this is symbolized by the 'manzano' again reflects traditional exegesis, which connected the tree of Eden and the tree of the cross as they spanned the history of salvation from Fall to Redemption through Song 8.5b, 'Sub arbore malo suscitavi te; ibi corrupta est mater tua, ibi violata est genitrix tua', 'I raised thee up under the apple tree: there thy mother brought thee forth: there she brought thee forth that bare thee.' But once San Juan has established the doctrinal framework of the verse, he announces disconcertingly (CB 23.6) that this betrothal of God with humanity is not its subject, and that the verse refers to the betrothal of God with his people in Ezekiel 16.5–14. As he does not expound this passage here or anywhere else, we are left to guess how its rich imagery might have related to the poem.[39]

For a final example, we may take the exposition of the garlands of flowers and emeralds in CB 30, where the verse is interpreted ecclesiologically, in terms of the Church, rather than of the individual soul, addressing Christ. The garlands are composed of the white flowers of virgins, the bright flowers of the Doctors and the red flowers of martyrs. The picture San Juan draws is iconographical: he sees Christ in heaven adorned with the garlands they bring, in a celestial representation of Song 3.11 (30.7). These garlands are 'en un cabello mío entretejidas', 'woven into a strand of my hair': just as garlands are held together with a thread, so love binds together the virtues (Colossians 3.14). Without it, 'se desatarían todas las virtudes y faltarían del alma [. . .] De manera que no basta que Dios nos tenga amor para darnos virtudes, sino que también nosotros se le tengamos a El para recibirlas y conservarlas' (30.9), 'all the virtues would be undone and would be absent from the soul [. . .] So it is not enough for God to love us to give us virtues, but we too must love him to receive them and keep them.' Curiously, San Juan first explains the strength of this love by a comparison of unlikeness, a text which refers to the scaly armour of the Devil (Job 41.6–7 [15–16]): if he is capable of such fearsome protection, how much more awesome and beautiful is the love which binds soul and Christ together (Song 7.1, 6.3[.4]). In her weakness the soul had desired this love when she asked to be strengthened by flowers and apples (Song 2.4[.5]), the former representing the Bridegroom, who in Song 2.1 calls himself the flower of the field and the lily of the valley. Though this joining cannot be described (31.2) it is hinted at in the knitting, 'conglutinar', of Jonathan's soul to David's in 1 Samuel 18.1, a human image of God's far greater love 'siendo Dios el principal amante, que con la omnipotencia de su abisal amor absorbe al alma en sí con más eficacia y fuerza que un torrente de fuego a una gota de rocío de la mañana' (31.2), 'since God is the principal lover, who by the omnipotence of his inexhaustible love absorbs the soul into himself with greater force and power than a torrent of fire absorbs a drop of morning dew'.[40]

So it is that Moses seeing the back of God in the cleft of the rock, Elijah hearing the still, small voice, Noah and the dove, Rachel longing for a child, David in joy and despair, Job in his suffering, Paul in his rapture and in his theology of transformation in Christ, together with other passages interpreted typologically or ecclesiologically, become the soul's companions along the way, from her first cries of help to her longing for completeness and permanence in union with God beyond death. Though only particular moments of their stories concern San Juan in his elucidation of the meaning of his poem, by associating them with it he provides a larger frame of reference and a compelling model for any soul who sets out on the road to union. The journey he traces is one he sees woven into the fabric of scripture. Without these companions, there would always be the risk of departing from the Church's teaching. Like the *romances*, they provide the wider narrative framework for the enterprise, the same journey, seen from a different but authoritative perspective.

THE ART OF EXEGESIS

Because San Juan tells us in passages like those we have discussed what his poetry means, the critical question of authorial intention is sharply posed, the more so because the meaning he attaches to it is so out of keeping with the spirit of our age. It is one thing to understand how San Juan proceeds in his interpretations, quite another to ask to what extent his procedure is justified. One answer is an historical one: whereas other exegetes might have disagreed with him over the details, they would not have quarrelled with the techniques in themselves, universally agreed and practised. But can his method have any value today, when historical criticism and textual analysis have for so long dominated biblical study? I believe that it may. The Bible was written over many centuries and came to be what it is through complex processes of editing and translation. That is one way of looking at it. But its place in the Church and the way it has inspired art and literature derive from a sense of its oneness and uniqueness, its mystery and its revelation. San Juan treats scripture as a whole and ranges freely through it, finding points for meaningful comment where words and images recur or complement one another, rather than pointing out where an historical detail is wrong or a manuscript reading problematical. That is how he knew and cherished it. In preaching and in devotional literature the great figures of the Bible, and many of the great stories associated with them, still acquire a universal significance applicable to any particular situation. So, for example, the slavery of the children of Israel in Egypt and their epic journey across the Red Sea and the wilderness to the promised land become in different ages and contexts archetypal narratives of other experiences of oppression and liberation, as the presence of figures like Moses and Joshua in the spirituals of the black slaves in America so powerfully shows.

But in the end it must be the artistic quality of San Juan's exegesis that persuades, as he brings texts from different parts of the Bible into close relationship with each other and allows each to shed new light on the other. When, for example, he takes the text 'quia amore langueo' from Song 5.8 to illustrate the paradoxical concept of a sickness which is beneficial, he goes straight to Christ's words in John 11.4, 'this sickness is not unto death' (N 2.19.1), lifts them out of their particular context (the illness and subsequent death of Lazarus) and applies them to the soul's sufferings in the dark night, which will be her road to union, because 'this sickness is not unto death, but for the glory of God'. He does not violate the sense of the original, but allows both texts to make the significant point that not all unpleasant experiences are negative: some are necessarily painful in order to prepare the way for a greater joy. The Bride of the Song will be united with her Beloved after suffering in his absence and being wounded in her search. Lazarus will be raised from the place of death. So the soul needs to understand and participate in this pattern revealed in scripture, passing through pain and darkness not as ends in themselves, but as a means to a better end.

San Juan's method demands of the reader a degree of intellectual agility more commonly reserved for the *conceptista* writing of the following century. Rosamund Tuve notes 'how like "Metaphysical wit" is to medieval habits of mind', in the ability of both to make dense and often paradoxical associations between different images and ideas. She adds: 'Once establish the habit of freely reading New Testament meanings back into Old Testament images – and multiple significance, deep reach into primitive levels of meaning, follow quite naturally. Liturgy, iconography, and homily had firmly established this as habitual even in ordinary lay thinking.'[41] Much the same could be said of San Juan's commentaries as of Herbert's poetry. The procedure can seem loose and disjointed to readers unfamiliar with it, yet within a single paragraph he will expound an image from the poem, relate it to one or more biblical texts, derive a piece of teaching from it, and in the process create new expressions of his own, often condensing these various elements into paragraphs of striking prose.

Mutuality

If there is one theme more than any other which distinguishes the *Cántico* from the systematic presentation of the journey to union in the *Subida-Noche*, it is mutuality. Given that the fundamental metaphor of poem and commentary alike is marriage, this is not surprising. This teaching on 'igualdad de amor', the equality of loving between the soul and God given in union, is grounded in Romans 5.5, where the indwelling Holy Spirit becomes the point of access between the soul's longing for God and God's coming to the soul, made possible only because God has already given himself to her. We have seen it in the attention San Juan draws to grammatical details of the poem, like the first person plural verbs, which indicate the full participation of both protagonists in the story, and in his insistence that the divine virtues of the Beloved, once communicated to the Bride and freely accepted by her, become the means whereby he falls in love with her. The mutual gaze of the lovers, which begins in CA 11–12, redeems the myth of Narcissus: the Bride may fall in love with herself because she is falling in love with herself recreated through him. In CB 19 God is understood as asking, paradoxically, to fall in love with himself within the Bride. The priority of saving action is God's; the soul's work is one of preparation and disposition to receive such gifts, not one of earning them by her own merits. This teaching is developed in CB 28 and given its fullest form in CB 38–39. Philosophical commonplaces about the nature of love are woven tightly together with biblical passages to develop the theme of mutuality.

The point of all the soul's strivings – the active nights, in the scheme of the *Subida-Noche* – is to make room for God. His desire is not to belittle but 'de engrandecer el alma', 'to magnify the soul'. Insofar as human effort is directed towards this end, it works in harmony with God's own gifts to the soul. The greatest of these is to make her like himself – 'igualándose consigo', 'making her his equal' – through love, the property of which is to 'igualar el que ama con la cosa amada', 'to make equal the one who loves with the thing which is loved'. Because the soul is now perfected in love she is, in San Juan's bold language, equal with him (not, of course, in terms of her being, but because her own loving is one with his): 'en la cual igualdad de amistad todas las cosas de los dos son comunes a entrambos', 'in this state of equality in friendship all things each possesses are common to both' (28.1), as Jesus shows when he calls his disciples his friends and shows them all that the Father has revealed to him. In it, the faculties of the soul are wholly occupied in the service of the Beloved; so too the passions which formerly controlled the soul's behaviour. It is as though acting in complete accordance with God's will has become natural and habitual for her (28.5).

One thing is needful for this, 'la asistencia y continuo ejercicio de amor en Dios' (29.1), 'the presence and continual exercise of love in God'. The text San Juan chooses to introduce the exposition of the next verse, Luke 10.42, had been used for centuries to argue that Jesus privileged Mary, the type of the contemplative who has the one needful thing, over Martha, the type of the active. He parallels this text with Song 3.5, where the daughters of Jerusalem, interpreted as the creatures, are urged not to disturb the Bride's sleep (Mary's contemplation). In an age obsessed with activity, San Juan's conclusions can seem both self-indulgent and escapist. For he goes on to say that, while until this point it has been appropriate for the soul to exercise herself in the active as well as the contemplative life, she should now abandon the former to concentrate exclusively on the latter, just as the Magdalene spent 30 years in the wilderness, 'porque es más precioso delante de Dios y del alma un poquito de este puro amor y más provecho hace a la Iglesia, aunque parece que no hace nada, que todas estas obras juntas' (29.2), 'because a tiny bit of this pure love is more precious in the sight of God and benefits the Church more, even if it seems she is doing nothing, than all such works together'.

The rhetoric needs some qualification, especially as San Juan, like Santa Teresa, found himself all too often in the midst of ecclesiastical and monastic politics and encumbered with responsibilities which he must have felt were taking him away from his true vocation. For the next paragraph reads more like a plea than an attack:

> De donde cuando alguna alma tuviese algo de este grado de solitario amor grande agravio se le hacía a ella y a la Iglesia, si, aunque fuese por poco espacio, la quisiesen ocupar en cosas exteriores o activas, aunque fuesen de mucho caudal [. . .] Al fin, para este fin de amor fuimos criados. Adviertan, pues, aquí los que son muy activos, que piensan ceñir al mundo con sus predicaciones y obras exteriores, que mucho más provecho harían a la Iglesia y mucho más agradarían a Dios [. . .] si gastasen siquiera la mitad de este tiempo en estarse con Dios en oración, aunque no hubiesen llegado a tan alta como ésta. (29.3)

> Hence when a soul possesses something of this degree of solitary love great harm would be done to herself and to the Church if even for a short time she was expected to be occupied in exterior or active matters, even if they were of great import [. . .] In the end, we were all created for this end of love. So let those who are very active and think to gird the world with their preaching and exterior works note that they would benefit the Church and please God a great deal more [. . .] if they spent only half the time being with God in prayer, even if they had not reached so lofty a state as this.

San Juan's point is not that the soul should disengage from the real world, but that by learning greater attentiveness to the will of God through prayer, her capacity to do truly good works (as opposed to those done grudgingly or to impress others) for his sake alone, will increase. Then, souls 'harían más y con menos trabajo con una obra que con mil, mereciéndolo su oración, y habiendo [c]obrado fuerzas espirituales en ella; porque de otra manera todo es martillar y hacer poco más que nada, y a veces nada, y aun a veces daño', 'would do more and with less effort through one work than through a thousand, their prayer meriting it, and having gained spiritual strength through it; otherwise, it is all hammering away and doing little more than nothing – sometimes nothing, and sometimes even, harm'. Those who insist on the outward show of good works need to grasp 'la vena y raíz oculta de donde nace el agua y se hace todo fruto' (29.4), 'the vein and the hidden root from which the water comes and everything is fruitful'. CB 29 thus becomes the soul's bold answer to those who accuse her of shunning the important affairs of the world, heard more strongly in the twentieth century than the sixteenth: what is the point of these contemplatives? why don't they do something useful instead of shutting themselves away and praying? San Juan's answer is that effective action in the world depends on attentiveness to God in prayer. Without this, a great deal of time and effort will be expended to little advantage, and may even be harmful, because the soul will not be experienced enough to know what truly constitutes a good work before God.

In CB 38, what the soul 'pretendía', 'was claiming' is 'la igualdad de amor con Dios', 'equality of love with God', perfected only beyond death (1 Corinthians 13.12), when her loving will be wholly divine (38.3). San Juan is careful to stress that the soul's faculties retain their independence, but are so fully engaged in God that they are as one: 'ama el alma a Dios con voluntad y fuerza del mismo Dios, unida con la misma fuerza de amor con que es amada de Dios. La cual fuerza es en el Espíritu Santo [. . .]' (38.3; Romans 5.5), 'the soul loves God with the very will and power of God himself, united with the very power of love by which she is loved of him. This power is in the Holy Spirit.' This is San Juan's most sustained exposition of the theme, and one of the few places where his pneumatology is to the fore.[42] In the following stanza, the image of the blowing breeze, 'el aspirar del aire', is given full Trinitarian weight: the soul's transformation would be incomplete 'si no se transformase el alma en las tres Personas de la Santísima Trinidad en revelado y manifiesto grado', 'if the soul was not transformed in the three Persons of the most Holy Trinity in a revealed and manifest degree', which is 'a ella de tan subido y delicado y profundo deleite, que no hay decirlo por lengua mortal, ni el entendimiento humano en cuanto tal puede alcanzar algo de ello', 'of such lofty, delicate and profound delight to her that it cannot be spoken of by mortal tongue nor can human understanding as such attain to anything of it'. The halting language of the previous stanza with its threefold 'aquello', 'that thing', and the five images which now appear to define it (breeze, nightingale singing, thicket, calm night, painless burning flame), bear testimony in their strangeness to the inexpressibility of an experience which is altogether divine.

Though the language of the poem and the commentary has been firmly centred on the mutual relationship of Bride and Bridegroom, their union brings about the soul's total transformation in the Trinity, experienced often in this life, but not with the clarity of the life to come (39.4; Galatians 4.6). It completes the work begun at creation, when humanity was made in the image and likeness of God (Genesis 1.26). This, for San Juan, is what John the Evangelist means by becoming the children of God (1.12) and by the union of believers with the Father through the Son (39.5; 17.20–24); and what St Peter means by our becoming 'compañeros' ('partakers') of the divine nature. Here, at the summit of the human journey, the soul 'se hace deiforme y Dios por participación', 'becomes deiform, God by participation'. The word 'participation' must be given its full weight, since it is San Juan's chief safeguard against any heterodox account of union – that the soul's individuality is submerged in the divine being so that they are no longer distinguishable, for example, or that the soul actually becomes God by nature. God by divine grace, perhaps; but divine only in the sense that, free now of all obstacles which prevent her from realizing her true goal, she participates in the Holy Trinity so completely that she has no understanding, willing or loving which is not at one with God's. She remains, and always will, a creature; but her creatureliness no longer stands in the way of her self-identification with God. She possesses by participation what God possesses by nature (39.6), so that souls become 'dioses por participación, iguales y compañeros suyos de Dios', 'gods by participation, equals and companions of God'. That is the work of love, its highest work: to bring into a relationship of intimate and mutual delight Creator and creature. It is, one might say, the moment when the listener is so fully engaged in the beauty and power of the music so as to be no longer aware of any distance between it and the self. The listener becomes one with the music by participating in it, not through becoming the music itself. In the life of eternity this union becomes the soul's constant possession, not simply a foretaste experienced for fleeting moments. This vision of the destiny of humanity is perhaps not without its importance in a world in which human beings seem so often to be machines or consumers, or reduced to biological essentials.[43]

I hope this selective reading of the exposition of the 'Cántico' poem will have helped to ease the discomfort readers face when they try to follow San Juan's arguments, and to introduce the critical problems raised by the relationship between the poem and the commentary on the one hand and the content of the commentary on the other. San Juan seems to move in a disconcerting way from one point to the next, to make many assumptions when expounding his images and biblical texts, and to impose on a beautiful and mysterious love poem an interpretation which deprives the great majority of readers from participating in its beauty and mystery by insisting that its meaning is inward and spiritual. Readers who respond to the poetry are therefore apt to be confused and deterred by the commentary, and ask themselves whether it can possibly express what San Juan had in mind when he composed these ardent verses in his dark prison. Since it is subsequent to them, it is tempting to conclude that inspiration and lyrical eroticism have been betrayed by prosaic hindsight. But a more considered reading reveals a mind at work with a remarkable sensitivity to language and a gift for making surprising and original connections between the human language which can scarcely articulate itself when it encounters God, and the divinely inspired language in which God addresses humanity. In the *Cántico* San Juan searches creatively for points of contact between it and the spiritual and biblical tradition which nourished and inspired him, and the careful and subtle way he relates what he says in the commentary back to his poem and to scripture through attention to language and imagery can enhance the reading of all three.

NOTES

1 See my *The Poet and the Mystic* (Oxford: Oxford University Press, 1977), ch. 6 (*El poeta y el místico* [El Escorial: Swan, 1985], ch. 6), for a different but (I hope) complementary account of the relationship between the poem and the commentary. For a pioneering interpretation based on the critical theory of Paul Ricoeur, see David Brian Perrin, *Canciones entre el alma y el Esposo of Juan de la Cruz: A Hermeneutical Interpretation* (San Francisco: Catholic Scholars Press, 1996).

2 Isaiah 45.15 is used with John 1.18 in *Soliloquia*, 889; *Soliloquia* also adds Exodus 33.20, which San Juan uses with John 1.18 in S 2.8.4, 3.12.1.

3 A text frequently used in religious poetry; see, for example, the last verse of Luis de León's ode

'Alma, región luciente'.

4 San Juan returns to the traditional paradox of Christ the wounded healer when Christ reappears as the wounded stag in CB 13 (CA 12). For a twentieth-century reworking, see T. S. Eliot, *Four Quartets*, 'East Coker', IV: 'The wounded surgeon plies the steel/That questions the distempered part'.

5 Edward Perronet (1726–92), in his much-adapted hymn 'All hail the power of Jesu's name', uses the same text: 'Sinners, whose love can ne'er forget/The wormwood and the gall'. Entitled in one version 'The Spiritual Coronation, Cant. iii.11', it is associated with the crowning of Solomon in the Song (hence its refrain 'And crown him Lord of all'); see John Julian, *A Dictionary of Hymnology* (London: John Murray, 1892), pp. 41–2. This is a good example of the continuity of exegetical tradition across temporal and confessional boundaries.

6 Ricardo Senabre, 'Sobre la composición del Cántico espiritual', *Actas*, I, p. 105, notes that the 'garden planted by my hand' is a literary topos of Ciceronian origin, used famously by Fray Luis de León in his 'Oda a la vida retirada', and here adapted to express the traditional Christian doctrine of the creation through the second Person of the Trinity.

7 On the four elements in the poem, see Manuel Alvar, 'La palabra y las palabras de San Juan de la Cruz', in *Presencia de San Juan de la Cruz*, ed. Juan Paredes Núñez (Granada: Universidad de Granada, 1993), pp 183–215; especially pp. 189–93.

8 Fray Luis de Granada, *Introducción del Simbolo de la Fe*, ed. José María Balcells (Madrid: Cátedra, 1989), p. 186. On Fray Luis de León, see my *The Strife of Tongues* (Cambridge: Cambridge University Press), pp. 242–5; Góngora, *Soledad primera*, line 6. Fray Luis de Granada also uses the image in reverse, that is, 'los prados verdes, pintados de diversas flores [. . .] como otro cielo estrellado', 'the green meadows, painted with various flowers [. . .] like a second starry heaven' (p. 240).

9 See above, p. 157.

10 Compare a similarly positive use in Lope's sonnet 'Con qué artificio tan divino sales' (*Rimas sacras*) and George Herbert's 'Life' and 'The Rose'. Such a use, surprisingly, seems commoner in religious than secular poetry (cf. Góngora's sonnet 70, 'La dulce boca').

11 See below, p. 177.

12 See above, pp. 149–50.

13 Covarrubias does not give such a definition for 'discurrir'; *Diccionario de Autoridades*, however, does: 'Andar, caminar, correr por diversas partes o parajes' (I, p. 299), 'walk, go, run in various directions or to various places'.

14 Covarrubias describes 'adamar' as archaic: 'es término de que usan los romances viejos', 'a term used in the old ballads' (Sebastián de Covarrubias, *Tesoro de la lengua castellana* [1611] (Barcelona: Horta, 1943), p. 110). *Autoridades* is more explicit about its source and meaning: 'amar con pasión, y vehemencia. Es voz de poco o ningún uso, y puramente latino' (I, p. 77), 'love passionately and ardently. A word rarely if ever used, purely Latin.'

15 The CB commentary at this point is fuller than its CA predecessor (38.14), which lacks any biblical references.

16 San Juan's distinction is confirmed by Covarrubias, who defines 'llaga' as meaning 'lo mesmo que herida' (*Tesoro*, p. 774), and as having a specific religious sense, the wounds of Christ.

17 For example, 'pavón de Venus es, cisne de Juno', 'she is Venus's peacock and Juno's swan', *Polifemo* 14. On the transference of attributes, see A. A. Parker, *Luis de Góngora: Polyphemus and Galatea* (Edinburgh: Edinburgh University Press, 1977), pp. 24–5.

18 For a similar exegesis, see *Bernard of Clairvaux, On the Song of Songs*, trans. Kilian Walsh (Kalamazoo, Mich.: Cistercian Publications, 1979–83), Sermon 25; II, pp. 50–7.

19 See below, pp. 268–9.

20 Covarrubias defines 'collado' as 'tierra levantada, pero la que no llega a serlo tanto que la llamamos monte', 'high ground, but not so high that we call it mountain' (p. 337); *Autoridades* agrees (I, p.416).

21 The second line of the 'Noche oscura' poem uses a similar expression, 'ansias en amores'.

22 One imagines his criticism of the Protestant teaching would have been that such access cannot be immediately available to the believer, because it is the result of a long and arduous journey of spiritual growth.

23 On these chapters, see José C. Nieto, 'Mystical theology and "salvation-history" in John of the Cross: two conflicting methods of Biblical interpretation', *BHR*, 36 (1974), pp. 17–32. For San Juan's use of the Bible, see Jean Vilnet, *Bible et mystique chez saint Jean de la Croix* (Desclée de Brouwer: Paris, 1949); Francisco Brändle, *Biblia en san Juan de la Cruz* (Madrid: Espiritualidad, 1990).

24 For example Karl Barth, *Church Dogmatics*, 13 vols (Edinburgh: T. & T. Clark, 1936–77), II. 1, 11; 2. 319–20; III. 4, 59; IV. 4, 11; see my *The Poet and the Mystic*, pp. 147–50; also Steven Payne, 'The Relationship between Public Revelation and Private Revelation in the Theology of Saint John of the Cross', *Teresianum*, 43 (1992), pp. 175–215.

25 Above, p. 108.

26 Pedro Calderón de la Barca, *La vida es sueño*, ed. Ciriaco Morón Arroyo, 18th edn (Madrid: Cátedra, 1991).

27 The fact that in certain contexts death can be a metaphor for orgasm does not mean that it always must be, any more than it does in English literature of the period.

28 Alvar calls these lines 'los más bellos e intensos versos de la lírica española', 'the most beautiful and intense lines in Spanish lyric poetry'; Manuel Alvar, 'La palabra y las palabras de San Juan de la Cruz', *Presencia*, p. 192.

29 Compare Charles Wesley's lines from 'And can it be': ''Tis mystery all: the Immortal dies!/Who can explore his strange design?/In vain the first-born seraph tries/To sound the depths of love divine.'

30 Cf. Covarrubias on 'novedad': 'suele ser peligrosa por traer consigo mudança de uso antiguo' (p. 831), 'is usually dangerous because it implies a change in ancient custom'. For a telling example, see *The Strife of Tongues*, p. 36. But *Autoridades* is closer to San Juan: 'Figuradamente se toma por la extrañeza o admiración que causan las cosas, hasta entonces no vistas ni oídas' (II, p.683), 'Figuratively, it is used for the strangeness or wonder caused by things not previously seen or heard.'

31 See below, pp. 234–8; also George Tavard, *Poetry and Contemplation in St John of the Cross* (Athens: Ohio University Press, 1988), pp. 101–2.

32 AV has 'the hill of God is as the hill of Bashan; an high hill as the hill of Bashan'. See Malón de Chaide, *La conversión de la Magdalena*, ed. Félix García (Madrid: Espasa-Calpa, 1957–59), I, p. 143; Frey Luis de León, 'Monte' in *De los nombres de Cristo*, *Obras* (FL), I, pp. 483–500; *The Strife of Tongues*, pp. 187–9.

33 Cited four times in the *Cántico* (CB 1.10 and 37.4, as well as these) and the *Subida*; twice in the *Llama*.

34 See *Gregory of Nyssa: The Life of Moses*, trans. Abraham J. Malherbe and Everett Ferguson (New York: Paulist Press, 1978).

35 For San Juan's use of St Gregory's *Moralia*, see Lawrence Sullivan, 'The *Moralia* of Pope St Gregory the Great and its Influence on St John of the Cross (A General Approach)', *EphCarm*, 27 (1976), pp. 453–88; 28 (1977) pp. 59–103.

36 Thompson, *The Poet and the Mystic*, pp. 84–5.

37 These properties have given rise to much debate, since no source for them has yet been located in the expected places (biblical commentaries, medieval or ancient bestiaries). San Juan also explains them in the *Dichos de luz y amor*, 120 (BAC p. 52), where they appear in a slightly different form; he also refers to it briefly in S 2.14.11. Luce López-Baralt, in *Huellas del Islam en la literatura española: De Juan Ruiz a Juan Goytisolo* (Madrid: Hiperión, 1985), pp. 59–72, and *San Juan de la Cruz y el Islam* (Mexico: El Colegio de Mexico, 1985), pp. 269–71, finds close parallels with bird symbolism in Sufi mysticism, taken up in Goytisolo's *Las virtudes del pájaro solitario*. Jacobo Sanz Hermida, 'El *passer solitarius* sanjuanista, algunos aspectos', *Actas* I, pp. 309–23, has argued for identification with a real bird, *Monticola solitarius*, the blue rock thrush, a striking bird of steep and rocky country which San Juan would have seen often

enough in his long walks between El Calvario and Beas (and which may still be seen in such country in many parts of Spain): 'Pico sorprendentemente largo [. . .] Se posa con facilidad en zonas abiertas en una roca' (*Guía de campo de aves de España y de Europa*, ed. Bertel Bruun, Håkan Delin, Lars Svensson, revised edn (Barcelona: Omega, 1990), pp. 254–5); 'Surprisingly long beak [. . .] Likes to perch on a rock in open country.' He also traces the European literary antecedents of three of the characteristics, leaving only the upturned beak and the indeterminate colour to be accounted for (the male is blue, but the female generally dark brown). The identification of this bird with the 'sparrow alone upon the housetop' of the AV was repeated, curiously, by Geoffrey Lee Martin in a report about its first-ever appearance in Australia (*Daily Telegraph*, 14 November 1997, p. 24). Domingo Ynduráin, 'El pájaro solitario', *Actas* I, 143–61, stresses how San Juan, typically, turns a biblical context of abandonment and distress into an affirmation of joy and suggests that Islamic writers may well have used common Greek or neo-Platonic sources. He suggests that the bird belongs symbolically to the tradition of the phoenix, with elements of the dove and the sparrow (144–6). One should not perhaps discount the possibility that San Juan was being inventive, bringing together a number of already-existing ideas. *Autoridades*, interestingly, has a special entry under 'pájaro solitario', which confirms the identification with the blue rock thrush (female): 'Ave algo mayor que el gorrión. Su color es negro con unas pintas blancas muy menudas, sembradas por todas las espaldas. Llámase así, porque por la mayor parte vuela solo. Es de la especie y linaje de los tordos, y por eso le dicen algunos tordo loco. Habita ordinariamente en los tejados de las casas viejas, y desiertas de moradores. Su canto es muy suave [. . .] Lat. *Solitarius avis* [. . .] El verdadero espiritual solitario ha de tener las mismas condiciones y costumbres que el pájaro solitario' (III, p. 172); 'Bird somewhat larger than the sparrow. Dark, with very small white streaks all along its back. So called because it generally flies alone. Of the same family as thrushes; sometimes called the mad thrush. Usually lives in the roofs of old, abandoned houses. Has a very gentle song [. . .] The truly solitary spiritual person must have the same state and habits as the solitary bird.' Unless this reflects knowledge of San Juan, one must presume a common tradition. The biblical *passer solitarius* is used by Quevedo in his love sonnet 'Más solitario pájaro ¿en cuál techo?' (*Francisco de Quevedo: Poemas escogidos*, ed. by J. M. Blecua (Madrid: Castalia, 1972), pp. 157–68), itself derived from Petrarch's sonnet 'Passer mai solitario in alcun letto' (see Ynduráin, *Actas*, I, 158). For its presence in English literature, see the opening lines of Robert Southwell's 'David's *Peccavi*' ('In eaves sole sparrow sits not more alone') and John Clare's delightfully domesticated 'sparrows on the cottage top' in 'Lord, hear my prayer' (in *Chapters into Verse*, I, 202; 314). The image could also be used more polemically: the Elizabethan separatist Henry Barrow, replying from his prison to Lancelot Andrewes, who had told him that he should rejoice in his solitary, contemplative life, said: 'You speak philosophically but not christianly. So sweete is the harmonie of God's grace unto me in the congregation, and the conversation of the saints at all tymes, as I think myself as a sparrow on the howse toppe when I am exiled from them'; quoted in Patrick Collinson, 'Separation In and Out of the Church: The Consistency of Barrow and Greenwood', *The Journal of the United Reformed Church History Society*, 5 (1994), 239–58 (p. 253).

38 The reversing of the name 'Eva' in the Angel Gabriel's greeting to Mary, 'Ave Maria', became a typological topos, as demonstrated by the hymn 'Ave maris stella'.

39 This paragraph is a CB addition, and reflects the discomfort provoked by the rearrangement of the stanzas, which here seems to have created rather than solved a problem for San Juan. 24.1–3, which follow, betray signs of haste and repetition.

40 The use of *culto* words like 'conglutinar' (in this case directly from the Vulgate) is not infrequent in San Juan; compare 'regraciar', 'adamar' in CB 31.10, 32.2; CB 32.5. It represents one of the linguistic strategies he adopts, though for reasons different from Góngora's: he is not interested in ennobling the vernacular but with trying to express the inexpressible.

41 Rosamund Tuve, *A Reading of George Herbert* (London: Faber & Faber, 1952), pp. 55, 79.

42 See Tavard, *Poetry and Contemplation*, pp. 194–200.

43 There is a striking correspondence between San Juan's teaching on the sharing of divine

virtues and participation in God in a quite unrelated but contemporary work, Jerónimo Merola's *República original sacada del cuerpo humano* (Barcelona: Pedro Malo, 1587): 'Porque lo que pretende el hombre es hazer vna circulación y boluerse a Dios de quien tiene su origen, y esto mediante la virtud, con la qual viene a hazerse tan virtuoso, tan perfecto, y semejante a Dios, que por la similitud es atrahído por el summo bien (porque Dios enamórasse del ánima, viendo en ella muchas cosas suyas, que puede dezirse que se enamora de sí mesmo en el ánima) para que allí le goze de manera que se haga otro como Dios por participación y fruyción'; 'the aim of man is a movement of return to God by means of virtue, through which he comes to be as virtuous and perfect as God, and like him. By likeness he is attracted to the highest good (for God falls in love with the soul, seeing so much of himself in her, that it can be said that he falls in love with himself within the soul), so that he can enjoy him in that state in such a way that he becomes as it were another God by participation and fruition'; cited by Ronald Truman, 'Analogy and Argument in Jerónimo Merola's *República original*', in *The Discerning Eye: Studies Presented to Robert Pring-Mill on his Seventieth Birthday* (Llandysul: Dolphin, 1994), note 7, pp. 49–50. From this it would appear that such ideas enjoyed greater currency than has hitherto been supposed.

8

The Pattern of the Night

We carry with us the wonders we seek without us: there is all Africa and her prodigies in us.

(Sir Thomas Browne, *Religio medici)*

The context of the *Subida* is firmly practical. The most striking feature of the Prologue is the force with which San Juan writes against those who have the care of souls but insufficient understanding to nurture them. His emphasis on the suffering and the damage that inexperienced confessors and spiritual directors can inflict on souls ready to enter the dark night of contemplation calls forth some of his most passionate prose writing: he describes confessors who make souls go backwards by imposing on them many general confessions instead of encouraging them when they are ready to progress as 'crucificarles de nuevo' (5), 'crucifying them anew'. Bad directors keep souls in infantile dependence, mistaking symptoms of lack of progress for depression or malice, so that when they are ready to walk they have had no guidance. He feels constrained to write in order to put an end to such errors, so that souls may be free to progress safely on 'un altísimo camino de oscura contemplación y sequedad' (4), 'a very high road of dark contemplation and dryness'. He is clear where the boundaries lie between such souls and those suffering from depression or falling into evil ways, and this will form an important part of his subsequent analysis. His 'doctrina sustancial y sólida' (8), 'substantial and solid doctrine', is therefore provided for souls in crisis, so that they and their confessors may be able to distinguish when they are being called to the dark night of the soul's purgation from states which are caused by psychological problems or sinful desires. These moments of crisis will therefore demand his particular attention, to show how they may be points of transition to the next stage of the journey instead of insurmountable obstacles to its continuation.

Like the *Cántico*, the beginning of the exposition proper provides a good illustration of the difficulties that modern readers face. Having established the sense–spirit polarity, San Juan explains why this moment of transition is called night (S 1.2) through a series of arguments complex in structure, briefly elaborated. He gives three reasons, each threefold in form. First, it is called night because of its point of origin: the soul must abandon her pleasure in worldly things, and this negation is night to the senses. It is also night because of the road which must be followed, faith, which is dark as night to the intellect. It is night too by virtue of its goal, God himself, who is a dark night to the soul in this life. The symbol therefore covers the whole journey, its human and divine aspects, from start to finish; it is all-embracing, comprehensive, multivalent, dynamic, and will mean different things at different points along the way.

Second, he confirms his interpretations from the Bible, as promised in the Prologue, to demonstrate that his doctrine of the dark night is not his own invention but found in the authoritative word of scripture. In the Book of Tobit, young Tobias is commanded by the angel who accompanies him on his journey to spend three nights alone before he may marry his bride, whose first six husbands have all unfortunately been killed by the Devil on the night of their honeymoon.[1] In the first night he is told that he should 'quemase el corazón del pez' (S 1.2.2), 'burn the fish's heart', which prompts the exegetical connection: the human heart is to burn all her other affections in the fire of divine love. In the second night Tobias is to be admitted 'en la compañía de los santos patriarcas' (.3), 'into the company of the holy patriarchs', which is faith, since they are the fathers of faith. In the third, he will receive 'la bendición', 'the blessing' (.4), which is the union of Bride and Beloved. He will be joined to his wife 'con temor del Señor', 'with fear of the Lord', since such fear, when perfect, transforms the soul in love (an unstated but implicit reference to 1 John 4.18, 'perfect love casteth out fear'). For twenty-first-century readers, this is a very obscure passage on which to hang the whole doctrine of the dark night. But San Juan is scrupulous in establishing direct verbal connections between his teaching and scripture. By making the association with Tobit, he introduces into the commentary biblical images which are central to his poetic endeavour: the journey beset by tribulations, the night, and the celebration of marriage.

Third, having established the symbol as scriptural, San Juan illustrates it from nature: 'estas tres partes de noche todas son una noche' (.5), 'these three parts of the night together form one night'. The divisions are to be understood as parts of a greater whole. As darkness falls, things recede; at midnight faith walks in deepest darkness; as daybreak approaches, God's presence is about to dawn. The pattern he establishes is repeated in the many analogies he will draw from nature and art in support of his argument. The experience needs to be placed in the context of biblical faith before it can be correctly interpreted, but nature has its part to play in the creation and exploration of this ascent of the mountain which is also a journey through the night.

SUBIDA – BOOK I: DESIRE AND DETACHMENT

The third chapter introduces the concept of 'privación', by which San Juan means the deliberate depriving of the senses of all the objects the soul normally desires and takes pleasure in. At first sight this seems a daunting and inhuman task, but privation has a positive and liberating role to play in his teaching. The active night of the senses means more than a matter of not possessing things: just because one does not have something does not mean one does not want it (1.4). His teaching is therefore directed towards understanding the mechanisms which govern desire and its pleasure, in order to subordinate them to the will of God, in which the soul's true fulfilment is to be found. He argues from three principles. The first is the commonplace Aristotelian one, that two 'contraries' cannot co-exist within the same subject (4.2); that is, one cannot in any final sense love the creatures and love God, because one cannot be both an idolater and worship him.[2] The second is a metaphorical antithesis which represents the ontological gulf between God and everything created, and which is prolonged through the many antithetical forms of expression the treatise contains: pleasures derived from created objects are 'puras tinieblas', 'pure darkness' before his pure light. There is an absolute and unbridgeable distinction between Creator and every created thing in terms of being; between infinite, self-sufficient Being itself and all finite and dependent forms of being. The creatures depend entirely on God for their existence, 'de manera que todo el ser de las criaturas, comparado con el infinito [ser] de Dios, nada es' (4.4), 'so that all creaturely being, in comparison with the infinite being of God, is nothing'. To seek union with created things is to be united, in this strict ontological sense, with 'nothing'. This would seem to rule out any possibility of a human relationship with the divine. Hence the third principle is crucial: 'el amor hace semejanza entre lo que ama y es amado', 'love creates likeness between lover and what is loved' (4.3). The argument may be summed up as follows: the creaturely and the divine are incompatible as objects of the soul's ultimate desire, yet it is the work of love to unite the lover with whatever is loved. To love the creatures is to become one with them, to be in union with nothing; to love God is to become one with him who is all in all.

We need to be careful before jumping to the conclusion that San Juan has a negative view of creation in itself. This early stage in the treatise represents the beginning of a process which is intended to lead to union with God and the deification or 'transformación en Dios' (4.3), 'transformation in God', of the soul. The creatures will, in due course, assume their proper place as free and independent objects and will at the end of the journey be affirmed in all their variety and beauty (*Llama* 4.4–5). But before that can happen a great deal needs to be done. For now, his focus is on the way human desire becomes attached to created objects as substitutes for God, exploits them for its own satisfaction, and comes to regard them as ends in themselves, thereby disabling the soul from progressing towards her true fulfilment in God. It is the nature of human desire and attachment which is at issue, not the nature of the objects they seek to possess. The creatures are not in themselves valueless or worthless, because they are all God's good creation. But if the soul mistakes any of them for its ultimate good, which they cannot be because they are finite and subject to change, decay and death, she will never find the fulfilment she seeks. They are the soul's brothers and sisters, offspring of a common divine source. Her journey is to be one with that source, not with the siblings.

If the exactness of San Juan's analysis is not grasped, the series of antitheses which follows can easily mislead. All the beauty, goodness, wisdom, power, pleasures and riches of the created order, compared with the absolute reality of these attributes in God, are ugliness, malice, ignorance, servitude, torments and poverty. The work of the active night of the senses is to enable the soul to enter into this new knowledge and love of God. Its privations are not ends in themselves, but undertaken for this greater good. San Juan is at his most Dionysian here, denying any kind of progression by analogy from human notions of goodness and the like to the nature of God. One example provides a telling illustration, since it looks far beyond Carmel. Worldly power, in comparison with the liberty and lordship of God, is 'suma servidumbre y angustia y cautiverio' (4.6), 'the greatest slavery and anguish and captivity'. Therefore those who hanker after high political office and great estates become slaves to them, and the freedom they think to possess is an illusion, because it is not based on the evangelical doctrine that the first shall be last and the last first. Similarly with riches: expounding Proverbs (8.4–6, 18–21), he insists that they are not to be found in piling up treasures on earth. It is not hard in our own time to think of examples of the corrupting and enslaving nature of political power, or the burden and misery which excessive material wealth can bring. Later (S 2.7.12), San Juan suggests that the mighty will be judged accordingly. In neither example does the thing sought possess in itself the power to satisfy the desires which those who seek it are deluded into believing it can. From these rare glimpses into the world of *Realpolitik* one senses how sharp San Juan's social criticism could be. His teaching about the human self and its capacity for self-delusion and error is equally radical and just as uncomfortable.

He now describes how human appetites inflict both negative and positive harm on the soul. Negatively, they deprive her of the spirit of God; positively, they weaken her: 'la cansan, atormentan, oscurecen, ensucian y enflaquecen' (6.1), 'weary, torment, darken, soil and weaken' her. When the soul feeds on created things, she becomes ever hungry for more, and is excluded from staying her hunger in God. Chapters 7–10 examine the positive evil she suffers as a result, through careful attention to the verbs he has just used, and through a series of analogies. Tormented by desiring more and more, the soul can no longer see her way clearly, just as the moth is drawn to destruction in the lamp which attracts it, or the fish is lured to the bait by the fishermen's lights (8.3). The term 'apetitos' is another of those which can mislead. In a significant clarification (1.11) San Juan makes it clear that he does not mean natural or involuntary human appetites for food, drink, sleep and so on, but those which involve a deliberate choice of the will. These, even if they are apparently trivial, must be rooted out, so that the will becomes free to desire God alone. By way of illustration he lists a series of 'imperfecciones habituales', 'habitual imperfections' – excessive talking, preferences for particular people, clothes, books, food, even monastic cells. Once more, the problem is not that they are bad in themselves, but that when the soul becomes attached to them it fails to realize how dependent it has become on them, because they seem insignificant. But birds, he explains, are trapped more easily by fine wire than thick rope, while the 'remora', a very small fish, can becalm a ship by attaching itself to it.[3] So the 'thread' of such attachments must be broken and the obstacles they create removed if the precious cargo of spiritual riches is to come safely to port.

How, then, is the soul to enter this night of the senses? San Juan provides a number of 'avisos', 'counsels' (S 1.13), which he says are short and few, yet helpful and comprehensive. The soul should cultivate 'un ordinario apetito', a habitual desire, to imitate Christ in everything, and to renounce all sensual pleasures which are not for the glory of God. Mortification of the four passions of joy, hope, fear and sorrow, which motivate human desire, is to be achieved by actively cultivating an attitude summarized first in a series of antitheses: seeking not the easy, but the difficult; not the restful, but the laborious; not the most, but the least; and so on, desiring always to 'entrar en toda desnudez y vacío y pobreza por Cristo de todo cuanto hay en el mundo' (13.6), 'to enter in complete nakedness and emptiness and poverty of all that there is in the world for the sake of Christ'. These antitheses (1.13.11), inspired by a set of maxims in Bernardino de Laredo's *Subida del monte Sión*, and also found on a drawing San Juan made of the ascent of Mount Carmel, depend on a series of paradoxical negations beginning: 'para venir a gustarlo todo,/no quieras tener gusto en nada', 'in order to come to enjoy everything,/desire no pleasure in anything'.[4] Three exercises are recommended with the aim of despising the self and desiring others to despise one in equal measure (13.9). This language of self-abasement is troublesome to modern tastes and appears masochistic, but San Juan is describing the beginning of a process designed to lead to the highest possible affirmation of humanity. What sounds like an unhealthy tendency to self-loathing must be seen as the first part of a process intended to cure the self of false diagnoses of its spiritual health, which then distort its relationship with others. This work of detachment can best be understood if the perspective of the whole journey is kept in mind. To develop San Juan's own metaphor of ascending a mountain, it corresponds to the part of the climb when the body is most acutely aware of aching muscles and developing blisters, resulting from the unaccustomed exercise. The pain is not sought for its own sake, but it is a necessary stage for the summit to be gained.

SUBIDA – BOOK 2: THE DARK WAY OF FAITH

The defining concept of the second book, which begins the active night of the spirit, is faith, the journey itself, and the second part of the symbol of night. Having introduced it in the first two chapters, San Juan proceeds to explore the meaning of faith according to its theological definition as 'un hábito del alma cierto y oscuro' (3.1), 'a sure and dark habit of the soul'. The phrase means that faith becomes, through constant practice, a habitual state, like the 'ordinary appetite' to follow Christ mentioned above, rather than a conscious act at any given moment; it becomes part of the soul's natural behaviour, just as skills are acquired which by practice become second nature, as long as they are kept in good repair. Musicians, for example, do not have to think consciously about the notes printed on the score; once the art of reading musical notation has been mastered, they can concentrate on interpretation and performance. But faith is also 'dark'. Its darkness, however, is neither an innate quality, nor one the soul can acquire by her own efforts. It is a gift, the presence of the dazzling light of divinely revealed truths, which blinds the intellect, just as the rising sun eclipses the moon and stars. Faith therefore is received as darkness, because its source is an overwhelming light which throws all human light into shadow. The analogy is important, because San Juan is not rejecting reason by exalting faith, as if reason were fatally corrupted by the Fall, any more than in his discussion of detachment he rejects the creatures by his language of nothingness. Faith is light and the creatures are good, but the limited nature of human knowledge and wilful human misuse of the creatures turn their light and goodness into a form of enslavement. What the soul experiences as the darkness of deprivation is the breaking free of these limitations and abuses. San Juan proposes the purification of reason, so that it can regain its rightful place in the soul. But he does make a sharper distinction between reason and revelation than is sometimes found in Catholic theology, and his insistence that faith 'es consentimiento del alma de lo que entra por el oído' (3.3) 'is the soul's consent to what enters her through hearing' strikes a note familiar in Reformed theology, which emphasized the receiving in faith of the preaching of the word.[5]

The double paradox of faith is that 'con su tiniebla alumbra y da luz a la tiniebla del alma' (3.5), 'by its darkness it illumines and gives light to the darkness of the soul'. Its work, to bring the soul to union with God, is described in two comparisons, the first traditional in devotional literature. When the sun shines through glass, it reveals all the specks and imperfections of the glass. If this were perfectly clean, the sun would shine right through it, and the glass and the rays would become indistinguishable from one another. The distinct nature of the glass would remain, but it would be wholly transparent to the light. The second comparison is more original. A picture may be painted in many delicate shades and tints. Someone with poor eyesight will only see a little of its beauty, but the better the eyesight is, the more of the picture's subtleties will be appreciated. Between the two comparisons, and providing their theological rationale, comes a bold statement about union, which still lies in the future: 'el alma más parece Dios que alma, y aun es Dios por participación' (5.7), 'the soul seems more God than soul, and is even God by participation'. Once no created object comes between the soul and God, she sees the divine beauty as never before, even though her creaturely status remains unchanged.

After this initial discussion of faith, the commentary, still attached to the first line of the poem, settles into the structure outlined in the sixth chapter: the purgation of the three faculties of intellect, memory and will by the corresponding theological virtues of faith, hope and love. Here and in the following chapters several of the terms San Juan uses most frequently – faith, detachment, creatures – are defined, explained and related to each other, since each forms part of the dark night of mystical theology. The theological virtues are so named because they are gifts of God, and thus are not limited by the finitude of creatures. The content of the faculties in their natural state is to be purged away, so that they are entirely open to the proper object of their contemplation. San Juan does not pretend that this is easy. He identifies the road up this mount of perfection with the 'straight gate' and 'narrow way' of Matthew 7.14, and with the way of the cross (Mark 8.34–5). He has harsh words for those who prefer to look for spiritual consolations (7.5), for a pleasant and undemanding religion, which makes them 'enemigos de la cruz', 'enemies of the cross'. Faith, therefore, is inseparable from the way of the cross. The soul is called to be despised and rejected as Christ was, and to die to her own self the death he died in his human nature, abandoned by God in order to redeem humanity. Some critics have treated San Juan as a mystic of a universal kind who happened to be a Christian, but might just as well have been a Buddhist. There are indeed many connections between different mystical traditions, but this strongly evangelical statement of the *via crucis* places San Juan firmly within the core of Christian belief, and makes an important connection between the individual road to God and the salvation brought to the whole created order through the death and resurrection of Christ. Chapters 8–9 further define the nature and role of faith through a new philosophical tenet: that all means must be in proportion to their end. To reach a city I must use the means – the road – which leads me to it. To burn a log in the fire the means must be appropriate – heat, not air, water or earth. San Juan's examples introduce a theological point implied in the earlier discussion of detachment from creaturely appetites but which will control the analysis of the purification of intellect by faith through the rest of the second book, that no creature can be a means of proximate union with God. Though everything which exists bears a trace of its divine origin and is related to God as creature to Creator, none, however noble, is like him in essence, and an infinite gulf separates them from him in being (S 2.8.3). 'Creature', a term of much wider reach than we might suppose, is not restricted to physical objects, but also includes mental images and concepts, an idea which will become important later in the treatise. Even great fathers of faith, Moses, Isaiah and 'Elijah our father' (8.4) are shown in scripture as unable in the flesh to see God as he is. Hence faith is 'sola el próximo y proporcionado medio para que el alma se una con Dios' (9.1), 'alone the proximate and proportionate means for the soul to be united with God'. It is not something the soul strives to discover, for it is revealed as gift as she perseveres in the purgative way. The work of faith is to propose to us the very nature of God. It teaches that he is infinite, Three and One. Therefore faith and only faith possesses that essential likeness which can make it the immediate means to the end. At this point San Juan returns to the image of faith as darkness: the highest contemplation, which brings the loftiest knowledge of God, is the 'rayo de tinieblas' (8.6), the 'ray of darkness' of Dionysian mystical theology, in which the clearer divine truths are in themselves, the darker and more unknown they are to us. He demonstrates that faith is rightly so considered by a series of biblical texts which tell of God's self-manifestation in the darkness (9.1–4).

The argument of the commentary becomes notably more complex in Chapter 10, a close analysis of the purification of the intellect in relation to knowledge directly given to the soul through the theological virtue of faith. Natural knowledge originates with sense perceptions, but supernatural knowledge comes in four forms. It can be perceived physically, by the external senses; or by the imagination; or spiritually, in distinct forms (visions, revelations, locutions, spiritual sentiments), or indistinctly: this he calls 'confusa, oscura y general' (10.4), 'confused, dark and general'. This last kind San Juan defines further as 'la contemplación que se da en fe', 'contemplation given in faith', which will mark the beginning of his most original contribution to mystical theology. But before he passes to this he writes two dense and important chapters on the damage that supernatural knowledge experienced through the exterior senses or in the imagination can do, and he has a shock in store for those who believe that such experiences are of the essence of mysticism.

He first summarizes the kinds of representations of supernatural objects which come into the minds of those at prayer via the external bodily senses:

> Acerca de la vista se les suele[n] representar figuras y personajes de la otra vida, de algunos santos, y figuras de ángeles buenos y malos, y algunas luces y resplandores extraordinarios. Y con los oídos oír algunas palabras extraordinarias, ahora dichas por esas figuras que ven, ahora sin ver quién las dice. En el olfato sienten a veces olores suavísimos sensiblemente, sin saber de dónde proceden. También en el gusto acaece sentir muy suave sabor, y en el tacto grande deleite, y a veces tanto, que parece que todas las médulas y huesos gozan y florecen y se bañan en deleite, cual suele ser la que llaman unción del espíritu, que procede dél a los miembros de las limpias almas. (11.1)
>
> Concerning sight: figures and people from the next life are often shown to them – saints, good and evil angels, lights and extraordinary radiances. With their ears they hear extraordinary words, sometimes spoken by the figures they see, at others without seeing who is speaking. Their sense of smell sometimes detects very sweet fragrances, sensually, without knowing where they come from. Their sense of taste often experiences a very sweet savour, and of touch, great pleasure, sometimes to such an extent that it seems as if their very bone and marrow is rejoicing and flowering and being bathed in delight. This is generally called the anointing of the spirit, which proceeds from him to the limbs of pure souls.

Here for the first time in the treatise experiences are described which seem plainly mystical. San Juan's advice could not be more uncompromising: 'totalmente han de huir de ellas [. . .] siempre se han de tener las tales cosas por más cierto ser del demonio que de Dios' (11.2–3), 'they are to be completely shunned . . . such things are always to be held to be more certainly of the devil than God'. His rejection, consistent with his principles, is based on the kinds of dangers he perceives in accepting them. First, souls who have these experiences will be tempted into vanity and thence into error, believing themselves more highly favoured than others by God because he has granted them such blessings. Second, they will become dependent on their consoling power, as felt by the senses, instead of on the dark way of faith and nakedness of spirit, which is the only means to union. Third, their source is ambiguous: the devil is entirely capable of sending them into the soul, and even if they come from God, to shun them causes him no offence, since they will in any case produce the effect he intends. They cannot actively be sought by the will, since they are received passively and are therefore involuntary. When they do occur, the soul must exclude them. The more often they are allowed entry, the greater the danger of demonic intervention. They must therefore all be rejected, 'negarlas todas' (11.8). This advice is repeated in his subsequent discussions of other psychosomatic phenomena: in 17.7–9, for example, San Juan stresses their creatureliness, and repeats that no such forms or images can in themselves bring about union with God.

There is a stern warning running all through San Juan's teaching which makes its first appearance here. The spiritual journey has many hidden dangers and obstacles.

Like a game of snakes and ladders, the nearer one is to the end, the further there is to fall, and, more troublesome still, the temptations are harder to spot because so much progress has been made and they have become so inward and subtle. That is why the only sure route to union is the way of faith, which, expecting nothing, remains open to God, to press on to its goal.

San Juan now sets out the contrast between meditative and contemplative prayer which is central to his teaching. The average reader may sense little distinction between them. But San Juan teaches that in the dark night God calls souls to leave behind the former and to embrace the latter, since failure to be sensitive to this moment of transition risks damaging spiritual progress severely. Meditation and contemplation must be distinguished in consequence of the antithesis already established between creature and Creator. Meditation takes place in the imagination, and 'es acto discursivo por medio de imágenes, formas y figuras, fabricadas e imaginadas por los dichos sentidos' (12.3), 'is a discursive act by means of images, forms and figures, created and imagined by the said senses'.[6] It lay at the heart of a great deal of Catholic devotional practice, and many spiritual directors taught that it was dangerous to abandon it for forms of prayer which were not dependent either on words spoken aloud (vocal prayer), or on mental pictures, such as imagining Christ crucified or tied to the column, or God in great majesty on his throne, or divine glory as a most beautiful light (the examples San Juan gives of topics of mental prayer).[7] This suspicion of any less focused forms of prayer is directly challenged by San Juan, and lies at the heart of his attacks on spiritual directors who do not recognize that some of their charges are being called beyond meditation by God, for the reasons he gives here.

The simile he chooses, the stairway, from the second verse of the poem, was commonly used in devotional writing to describe the ascent to God (he himself does so in N 2.19–20). The creatures – in this case, discursive meditations – are the steps on the stairway, and each step must be left behind to reach the level ground at the top of the stairs. Many spiritual people err because they believe that they must hold on to meditative prayer, even though they find no profit in it and become increasingly troubled and wearied by their apparent failure. They need guides who have negotiated the stairway, not inexperienced directors who try to hold them back. San Juan will return to this theme in connection with his analysis of memory.[8]

Not everyone who can no longer meditate is ready to be lifted into contemplation, which is why in S 2.13.2–4 he proposes three signs which must be present concurrently for the correct diagnosis to be made: the soul cannot meditate profitably and finds only dryness where before she found refreshment; she has no desire to fix the imagination or senses on any particular object (which would mean she was still attached to it); and, surest of all, she 'gusta de estar a solas con atención amorosa a Dios sin particular consideración' (13.4), 'likes to be alone in loving attention to God without any particular thoughts'.[9] Then the work of meditation is ended: it has served its purpose. This new knowledge brings with it a kind of prayer no longer attached to specific images of God, which is brief but penetrates the heavens. In it the soul becomes like the 'pájaro solitario' (14.11), the solitary bird on the roof (Psalm 101.8 [102.7]), and like the Bride of Song 6.11 [12], who can only say 'Nescivi', 'I knew not'.[10] Here San Juan makes a clear connection between passivity – openness to receiving the gifts of God – and ineffability.

Words are an impediment to her now, so it is not surprising that she cannot describe what she is experiencing. But San Juan nevertheless illustrates his point with several metaphors. The child is ready to be weaned, and should not be made to suckle again; the shell has been removed from the kernel and cannot again be removed (14.3); water is being drunk from the source and there is no need to transport it via 'los arcaduces de las pesadas consideraciones y formas y figuras' (.2), 'the aqueducts of weighty thoughts, forms and figures'; food is already cooked and digested (.7). Similar metaphors were used by Santa Teresa (e.g. *Vida* 11.7), and their presence here perhaps reflects the conversations they shared. The nature of this 'noticia general', 'general knowledge' unattached to any specific object or concept, inspires, paradoxically, a fresh version of the comparison with the sun's ray (14.9; see also N 2.8.3), which is only visible because of all the motes and dust particles floating in the air. Without these particles, which diminish its clarity and purity, it could enter one window and leave by another without our seeing it. Once the intellect has been purged of particular knowledge for which it uses words and pictures, it can receive the light of divine knowledge without hindrance.[11]

At this point San Juan turns away from his theme to answer the question he had no doubt been asked by some of his charges: why, if they are so dangerous, does God grant such visions (S 2.16.13)? In his long analysis of biblical examples, which we mentioned earlier, he stresses the dangers of defective interpretations of prophecies and revelations.[12] The same problem affects locutions and revelations: people who make that mistake will miss the spiritual sense God has enclosed in them, 'el cual es dificultoso de entender, y [. . .] muy más abundante que la letra y muy extraordinario y fuera de los límites de ella' (S 2.19.5), 'which is difficult to understand, and [. . .] much fuller than the literal sense and very extraordinary and beyond its limits'. The examples he gives show how the sense of a particular revelation may be modified by the response it engenders, so that souls should not assume they have understood its meaning.

Having concluded his biblical excursus San Juan passes in S 2.23 to visions which are received supernaturally, passively, but distinctly in the soul. He understands the spiritual senses to function by analogy with the bodily ones: the mind can 'see' or 'hear' things without these taking any apparent physical shape or form. Experiences of this kind he calls visions if seen in the mind's eye, revelations if they bring new understandings to the mind, locutions if they are heard within the soul, and 'sentimientos espirituales' (23.3), 'spiritual sentiments', if perceived there as spiritual fragrances or other delights. These are all of a higher order than the visions previously described, because they are spiritual. Though his teaching about shunning them remains generally consistent, he identifies some important exceptions.

The first category, visions of 'corpóreas sustancias' (24.5), physical objects, may be of any material thing in earth or heaven, but come directly and supernaturally to the intellect, like St John's vision of the heavenly Jerusalem in Revelation 21. They happen 'como si se [. . .] abriese una clarísima puerta, y por ella viese [una luz] a manera de un relámpago, cuando en una noche oscura súbitamente esclarece las cosas y las hace ver clara y distintamente y luego las deja a oscuras', 'as if a very bright door were being opened, and through it [a light] could be seen, as when a flash of lightning on a dark night suddenly illumines things and enables them to be seen clearly and distinctly and then leaves them in the dark', with only an impression left in the imagination. Their effects are good, though the devil can use them, as perhaps when Christ was shown all the kingdoms of the world in his temptations (Matthew 4.8). Then they bring dryness of spirit (not of course to Christ, though San Juan does not make the point). Visions of immaterial substances, like souls or angels, are much rarer: Paul, Moses and Elijah are mentioned (24.3). Even unseen, their effects may be felt, as 'suavísimos toques y juntas' (.4), 'gentlest touches and unitings', which leave the soul strengthened in virtue. But the soul must not seek her treasure in such visions: however lofty they may be, they remain creatures, and the Creator is reached only by 'la pura fe y desnudez a oscuras de todo eso' (24.8), 'pure faith and nakedness in darkness of all such things'.

The second category, revelations, consist of 'entender y ver verdades de Dios o de las cosas que son, fueron y serán' (26.2), 'understanding and seeing truths about God or about things which are, were, and shall be', that is, about either the Creator or the creatures. The former are incomparably more nourishing, and may consist of a very high knowledge of divine attributes like omnipotence or goodness. It is not surprising that he regards these experiences as unitive, safe from demonic interference, since they come directly from God, unmediated by any creature. He calls them 'divinos toques' (26.8), 'divine touches' which bring 'ciertos recuerdos de Dios', 'certain remembrances of God', and he regards them as very powerful and creative.[13] They are the first experiences he records which are not to be rejected. But revelations of created things fall under the old suspicion. They may take the form of insights into the hearts and actions of other people, and San Juan is quick to point out that the devil can be very active here, bringing to mind 'pecados ajenos, y conciencias malas, y malas almas, falsamente y con mucha luz, todo por infamar' (26.17), 'the sins of others, and bad consciences, and bad souls, falsely and with great clarity, all for the sake of slandering'.

He divides the revelation of secrets and hidden mysteries similarly, into those which concern God in himself, and those which concern the nature of God as seen through his works. Of the first kind, which includes the mystery of the Trinity, he says little. The second may be 'acerca del universo en general' (27.1), 'about the universe in general' as well as 'de reinos, provincias y estados y familias y personas particulares', 'about kingdoms, provinces, estates, families, and individual people'. But they can also include doctrinal statements (other than those about God in his being). Here he is adamant that there can be no such thing as a new revelation of the faith, since it has been revealed once and for all. He prefers to call these the 'manifestación o declaración de lo ya revelado' (27.2), 'manifestation or explanation of what has already been revealed'. The devil can be very active here, too, so that 'en cuanto [a] lo que toca nuestra fe se nos revelase algo de nuevo o cosa diferente, en ninguna manera habemos de dar el consentimiento' (27.3), 'if in anything concerning our faith something new or different should be revealed to us, in no wise are we to give it our consent'. The devil, he says, deceives first by proposing truths, then probabilities, so that he introduces his lies gradually, like the 'cerda', the needle used for sewing leather, which has to be very thick to pierce the hide, but which introduces in its wake the much thinner thread.

Locutions, the third category, are divided into three kinds, 'palabras sucesivas, formales y sustanciales' (28.2), 'successive, formal and substantial words'. The terminology is strange, but San Juan's brief definition of each helps. 'Successive words' are ones formed by the recollected soul about the matter it is considering and sound like words and expressions which occur to someone so engrossed in an activity that they flow with unexpected ease. Unusually, he provides a direct, first person example, more in the spirit of Teresa:

> Yo conocí una persona que, teniendo estas locuciones sucesivas, entre algunas harto verdaderas y sustanciales que formaba del Santísimo Sacramento de la Eucaristía, había algunas que eran harto herejía. Y espántome yo mucho de lo que pasa en estos tiempos, y es que cualquiera alma de por ahí con cuatro maravedís de consideración, si siente algunas locuciones de éstas en algún recogimiento, luego lo bautizan todo por de Dios y suponen que es así, diciendo: «Díjome Dios», «Respondióme Dios»; y no será así, sino que [. . .] ellos las más veces se lo dicen. (29.4)

> I knew a person who had these successive locutions, and among some which were very true and meaningful about the Most Holy Sacrament of the Eucharist, there were some which were clearly heretical. And I am greatly fearful of what is happening nowadays, when any soul at all, who after a moment's contemplation experiences such locutions in recollection, baptizes everything as God's and imagines it so, saying: 'God told me', 'God replied'; and it is not so; rather [. . .] most of the time they are talking to themselves.

Worse still, such people become so full of themselves and talk such palpable nonsense that only the severest treatment will rid them of it. This is not a problem which has disappeared, as any priest or minister will testify. San Juan's good sense wins through, and together with his spiritual perceptiveness, forms a powerful alliance against self-deception. It almost goes without saying that these experiences too are to be rejected, for though the Spirit always speaks the truth the soul in question may not be advanced enough in faith and love to preserve the message ungarbled.

A further danger is demonic interference. When Satan sees that people are attached to such locutions, he starts suggesting ideas and words to them, all 'verosímiles' (29.10), plausible. Those who make pacts with him often communicate in this way, as do heretics and heresiarchs. San Juan knew neither Luther nor Calvin, and probably had little grasp of Reformed theology, but he did at least on one occasion exorcise over a period of months a nun whom he discovered had made a pact with the devil, an experience which may have been in his mind as he wrote these words.[14] He proposes a test whereby their source may be determined: if they are accompanied by reverence and love for God, it is a sign that the Spirit is at work; if self-generated, their effect is neutral; if demonic, they will incline the soul to vanity, which may manifest itself as false humility and love, difficult from the outside to distinguish from the genuine thing. The lesson is clear: seek to strengthen the will to serve God, be content with the Church's teaching, obey divine law, and the soul will not go astray.

Another kind of locution, 'palabras formales' (28.2), 'formal words', is given to the spirit distinctly, passively, as from a third person. Though they may occur at any time, even outside recollection, their effect is negligible. They should be discussed with the confessor, but can be disregarded, since they may be demonic and are not an immediate means of union. But 'palabras sustanciales', 'substantial words', which are also passively received, have a performative effect: 'en la sustancia del alma hacen y causan aquella sustancia y virtud que ellas significan' (28.2), 'they cause in the substance of the soul that substance and virtue which they signify'.[15] For example, the soul receives the locution 'no temas' (31.1), 'fear not', and is at once strengthened and calmed. Santa Teresa records exactly such an experience, when the books through which she had been helped were prohibited and the Lord said to her: 'No tengas pena, que yo te daré libro vivo', 'Do not be distressed, for I will give you a living book.'[16] They are 'de tanto momento y precio, que le son al alma vida y virtud y bien incomparable, porque la hace más bien una palabra de éstas que cuanto el alma ha hecho toda su vida', 'of such moment and value that to the soul they are life and virtue and incomparable benefit, because one such word does more good than all she has done throughout her life'. These are also to be accepted – a second exception to the general rule – because they imprint on the soul the reality signified by the word. Only if the soul had entered a voluntary pact with the devil could there be any danger of such words being imprinted with malice aforethought. The final category, 'spiritual sentiments', belongs primarily to the treatment of the will (Book 3), though they often affect the intellect. For them San Juan prefers the term 'toques', 'touches'. They may be brief or more lasting, but leave 'un subidísimo sentir de Dios y sabrosísimo en el entendimiento' (32.3), 'a very lofty and nourishing sense of God in the understanding', and should be passively accepted, in a spirit of humility, so that God may work through them whatever he intends (.4) – a third exception to the rule.

In his discussion of these experiences, San Juan deals for the first time with phenomena normally considered mystical, only to inject a healthy dose of scepticism into his analysis. In the case of revelations from God, substantial words and spiritual sentiments, San Juan identifies passive and unitive elements within the active night, suggesting that though the nights are presented consecutively, as their systematic treatment demands, they are experienced simultaneously, as God's work in the soul parallels the soul's own work of detachment. These chapters are also important for providing a counterbalance to what might be thought of as the individualizing approach of the treatise. San Juan is doubtless using his experience as a confessor, reflecting on the many nuns and friars who have been struggling with the phenomena he analyses. His warnings against new interpretations of scripture or against too much doctrinal speculation are, with one exception, as close as he comes to tackling one of the issues raised by the Protestant Reformers.[17] His rooting of mystical experience in the way of the cross, his use of scripture to demonstrate how revelations can deceive, and his warnings against using them to depart from Catholic truth, set his teaching on faith in an ecclesial dimension far removed from a purely private or subjective religion.

SUBIDA – BOOK 3: RELIGIOUS EXPERIENCE AND PRACTICE

In many ways the treatment of the purgation of memory by hope (S 3.1–15) parallels that of the purgation of the intellect by faith. San Juan makes the same division between natural and supernatural knowledge which had governed his earlier analysis (3.1.2), while the effect of divine 'toques' on the memory is as powerful as they had been on the mind, to the extent that the soul seems to swoon and to become oblivious of everything (S 3.2.5–6). In such a state her memory becomes so absorbed in God that it can forget its normal activities, like eating and drinking. Then, the soul does only those things which God moves it to do, since he has become the sole content of her memory. But this is part of the process of perfecting, so that once union becomes habitual and memory is divinized such lapses no longer occur. Mary, he says, is an example, since from the beginning she was raised to this high state and 'nunca tuvo en su alma impresa forma de alguna criatura, ni por ella se movió, sino siempre su moción fue por el Espíritu Santo' (3.10), 'never had imprinted on her soul the form of any creature, nor was moved by such, but always by the Holy Spirit'. The Virgin Mary thus becomes the perfect type of the contemplative.

His treatment of memory is especially interesting for its links with twenty-first-century views of psychological health. Memory can exert a terrible power, repressing fearful or threatening incidents, or allowing them to haunt and to disable individals. The psychologist Bruno Bettelheim's experiences in a concentration camp enabled him to understand the extreme oddities and disorders of children no one else could deal with, because he remembered how he and others had reacted to constant, life-threatening situations. San Juan's insights may not be as striking, but they are no different in kind. In setting out a process by which the memory is purged of the burdens and pleasures of the past, which can inhibit a creative response to the present and future, he shows how from a Christian perspective the weight of the past can be lifted and replaced by a renewed confidence and purpose in the self and its potential, and makes a valuable, if unexpected, contribution to the study of the human psyche (in the original sense of soul).[18]

Memory for San Juan is not simply about the past: it also governs the way the present and the future are imagined – 'memory is the capacity to be present to, mentally to "possess", whether the object be past, present or future'.[19] God is the goal of all human hoping (as of thinking and loving), and pictures of an imagined future can be just as much an obstacle to reaching him as memories of a particular past, since both depend on creaturely constructs. San Juan does not describe the techniques by which the memory is to be emptied, but he emphasizes why this is necessary, what the dangers of failing to do it are, and the benefits it brings. If the memory is not purged, the soul remains in damaging subjection to the effects of its imperfections, appetites and false views and opinions (3.3.2); to demonic interference (3.4), which can only enter through the working of the faculties; or to the passions associated with remembering (3.5). To these dangers correspond, by virtue of the doctrine of contraries, the benefits of purgation: peace in the soul, resistance to demonic suggestions, and receptivity to the movements of the Spirit (3.6).

Admitting that it seems impossible for anyone to have a memory so purged, San Juan insists that though God does more to achieve this than the soul does, nevertheless the soul must do all she can to enter into 'esta negación y vacío de formas' (2.13), 'this negation and emptiness of forms', by not allowing anything derived from knowledge gained through the five senses to be retained in the memory's archive. Such emptying does not prevent the soul from performing her necessary actions: God will ensure that these happen insofar as they need to. San Juan saves the objection that 'doing nothing' (2.15) seems a waste of time for the passive night.[20]

Following the pattern established in S 1.6, failure to empty the memory of its natural content is seen as causing positive and negative harm. Positively, it leads to the retention of all kinds of false impressions, imperfections and sensual attachments, not all of which are necessarily pleasurable – fear, pain and hatred are there alongside vain pleasures and aspirations; negatively, to the retention of all kinds of emotions from the past or concerning the future which trap the soul in their ever-changing moods, and prevent her from moving from the limited realm of human understanding to the One who is beyond it (5.2–3). The purpose of this radical treatment of memory is to close off all distractions and interruptions from below and to create a space of receptivity in which the memory will be open only to communication from God through the theological virtue of hope. When, for example, he passes to consider visions, revelations, locutions and spiritual sentiments within the memory which are supernatural in origin, he is examining the same phenomena as in the equivalent chapters of the previous book, but from a different perspective – not as knowledge revealed to the mind, but as the 'imagen, forma y figura, o noticia impresa' (7.1), 'image, form and figure, or impressed knowledge' deposited there, 'a veces muy viva y eficazmente', 'sometimes very vividly and effectively'.

What San Juan appears to mean is this: many people carry in their minds good and bad memories which determine their hopes and fears. Never to move beyond their reach is to remain locked into them. He does not counsel repression, because he knows they must be brought into the open, but, as with the other faculties, he is anxious that once recognized they should be allowed to depart, so that the soul can progress to 'unión de Dios en esperanza pura y entera', 'union with God in pure and full hope'. Hence:

> cuanto más la memoria se desposee tanto más tiene de esperanza, y cuanto más de esperanza tiene tanto más tiene de unión de Dios, porque, acerca de Dios, cuanto más espera el alma tanto más alcanza, y entonces espera más cuando se desposee más, y cuando se hubiere desposeído perfectamente, quedará con la posesión de Dios en unión divina. (7.2)

> the more the memory dispossesses itself, the more hope it has, and the more hope it has, the greater its union with God, since, in divine matters, the more the soul hopes for the more she obtains, and as she hopes for more the more she is dispossessed, [so that] when she is perfectly dispossessed she will have possession of God in divine union.

It is hard not to hear in these words lines from San Juan's poem 'Tras de un amoroso lance': 'porque esperanza de cielo/tanto alcanza cuanto espera', 'for hope of heaven/obtains all that it hopes for'.[21]

The dangers of clinging to natural memories correspond to those of not disengaging the intellect from its habitual modes of thought. The soul cannot judge what their origin is: 'muchas veces pensará que son las cosas de Dios y no será sino en su fantasía, y muchas que lo que es de Dios pensará que es del demonio, y lo que es del demonio que es de Dios' (8.3), 'many times she will think they are things of God, but will be nothing but her fantasy; many times what is of God she will think is of the devil, and what is of the devil, of God'. She may be tempted to vanity, proud of having been granted such wonderful experiences, an attitude San Juan describes as 'pestífero', abominable in God's sight (9.3), since true virtue lies in humility, not self-congratulation. The devil, who likes souls to enjoy the 'sabor y deleite' (10.2), 'savour and delight' of these communications rather than love of God, will gradually deceive her into accepting his lies. Great error can therefore result from failure at the outset to renounce apparently trivial things. As long as the memory houses something other than God, it cannot be open to direct communication with him, will imagine that God is actually like these creaturely memories, and therefore remains trapped within their hold. The purgation of the memory ends with a clarification which looks back to the discussion of images retained by the faculties and forward to the closing chapters of the *Subida* and their analysis of religious practices. San Juan wishes to make it plain that in teaching the rejection of these interior images he is not in agreement with those Protestant Reformers who, inspired by Satan, have torn down images of God and the saints (15.2). His interior iconoclasm is not matched by an exterior one. His concern has been to point out the difference between a creaturely image of God and God in himself, so that people do not mistake the means for the end. Images in churches are a means towards an end, and as long as they do not become ends in themselves are a good and sure guide to move souls from 'lo pintado a Dios vivo, en olvido de toda criatura y cosa de criatura', 'what is painted to the living God, in forgetfulness of every creature and creaturely thing'.

If the chapters on memory have been shorter and less coherent than those on the intellect, when San Juan passes to the active night of the spirit as it affects the third faculty, the will, he pulls no punches. Though he states that he will conduct his argument in terms of the four passions ('afecciones') which move it (16.2) – joy, hope, pain and fear – he only manages to complete some of the first, though he does point out how closely they are connected (16.5), and proves it with an extraordinary piece of exegesis of Ezekiel's vision (1.4–21).[22] He identifies six sources of joy: from possessions (riches, estates, positions, children, relatives, marriages and so on; 18–20); natural gifts (physical beauty, intelligence; 21–3); the five senses (24–6); moral gifts (virtues, good works; 27–9); supernatural gifts (healings, miracles, prophecies, discernment of spirits, speaking in tongues; 30–2); and spiritual gifts (images, churches, holy places, ceremonies, sermons; 33–45). A wide range of human experience, sacred and secular, is therefore held open to scrutiny.

The required attitude towards material possessions is expounded in a straightforward way. San Juan does not view pleasure taken in them as a positive form of harm, since they are not intrinsically evil, but as privative, depriving the soul of something better, and causing her to regress on the spiritual road and to forfeit a right judgement about them (19.3). If not cured, the will expands to desire more and more of them, with the result that souls are in a state of 'gran tibieza en las cosas espirituales [. . .] ejercitándolas más por cumplimiento o por fuerza o por el uso que tienen en ella que por razón de amor' (19.6), 'great lukewarmness in spiritual things [. . .] practising them more because they ought to be or through necessity or habitual use than for the sake of love'. Eventually, God is altogether abandoned in favour of greed and avarice, the things of salvation are treated as irrelevant, and every talent is applied to worldly affairs. The final result is pure idolatry: the worship of money instead of God. This San Juan finds all too prevalent in his own age. Such pleasures, however small, must be rooted out from the very beginning: 'una centella basta para quemar un monte y todo el mundo' (20.1), 'one spark is enough to burn a mountainside and the whole world'. Detachment produces the virtue of generosity, together with freedom and peace in mind and soul. For the wrong kind of joys leads inevitably to a possessiveness which enslaves the soul. That is not to say that the soul can take no delight in any created thing: 'adquiere más gozo y recreación en las criaturas con el desaproprio dellas [. . .] y más clara noticia dellas' (20.2), 'she acquires more joy and recreation in the creatures from not appropriating them [. . .] and a clearer knowledge of them', another paradoxical statement which shows how San Juan's negations always point to a greater good. A modern analogy might be the difference between the experience of pleasure in seeing a wild flower and leaving it where it is for it to complete its cycle and for others to enjoy it, and in picking it (or worse still, uprooting it) to bring it home, which is selfish, possessive and destructive. Detachment from all things means that all can be enjoyed as if possessed (.3).

The snares of human beauty and sexual desire are a constant theme of love poets as well as ascetic writers. They play a relatively small part in San Juan's teaching, but he is quite realistic about them. It is, he says, very difficult for a spiritual person to avoid becoming entangled in this way (21.1), and constant reminders are needed that all physical beauty is as nothing and will return to dust and earth. He singles out fornication as particularly harmful, and briefly (and exceptionally) waxes eloquent on the destructive power of sex:

> cada día por esta causa se ven tantas muertes de hombres, tantas honras perdidas, tantos insultos hechos, tantas haciendas disipadas, tantas emulaciones y contiendas, tantos adulterios, estupros y fornicios cometidos y tantos santos caídos en el suelo [. . .] ¿Hasta dónde no llega la ponzoña

> deste daño? ¿Y quién no bebe poco o mucho deste cáliz dorado de la mujer babilónica del Apocalipsis? (Revelation 17.4; S 3.22.3–4)

> every day as a result of this we see so many deaths of men, so much honour lost, so many insults given, so many estates frittered away, so much rivalry and conflict, so many acts of adultery, assaults and fornication committed and so many saints brought down to the ground [. . .] Where does this harmful poison not reach? And who does not drink little or much from this gilded chalice of the Babylonian woman?

One may partly agree with the first part of the outburst, since sexual passion can wreak terrible damage, while the second reminds us that not even Discalced Carmelite friars are immune from such temptation.[23] But San Juan understands the real harm to be spiritual: lust which is allowed free rein causes a kind of self-esteem which devalues others; it arouses deceitful and vain praise for the object of desire, and leads to the blinding of reason and spirit. So to renounce it increases humility, love of others and tranquillity of soul (3.23). The temptation to indulge in sexual pleasure calls forth strong words no doubt because it is so common; but they are neither disproportionate nor obsessive. His sense of the difference between desiring to possess another person for one's own gratification, rather than appreciating that person for his or her own qualities, may strike an unexpected chord in modern readers, but it is entirely consistent with all he teaches about the close relationship between detachment and freedom.

A case in point comes in 3.24, when San Juan discusses sensual pleasures. Why should it be spiritually detrimental to listen to a piece of good music or contemplate a wonderful view? There is a right use of such pleasures, he explains, which is to lift them up to God; otherwise they can easily become a form of recreation rather than prayer, which will not kindle the will to love God more:

> todas las veces que oyendo músicas [. . .] y viendo cosas agradables, y oliendo suaves olores [. . .] se pone la noticia y afección de la voluntad en Dios dándole más gusto aquella noticia que el motivo sensual que se la causa [. . .] es señal que saca provecho de lo dicho y que le ayuda lo tal sensitivo al espíritu. (24.5)

> each time music is heard [. . .] or pleasant things are seen, or sweet scents smelled [. . .] the will's knowledge and affection is placed in God, which gives it greater pleasure than its sensual causes [. . .], then this is a sign that a benefit is being gained and that something so based in the senses is helping the spirit.

Some of the wrong uses of such pleasures have social implications. Pleasure taken in sweet odours can give rise to disgust for the poor, presumably because they smell (25.4); and the pleasures of the table, as well as leading to gluttony and drunkenness, can also issue in lack of charity towards them and one's neighbours. Only the snares of touch are treated more expansively, and include 'molicie' (defined in *Autoridades* II, 591, as 'pecado torpe contra natura', 'a lewd sin against nature').[24] The corresponding benefits of denial are greater recollection in God, the conversion of the sensual into the spiritual, and a hundredfold increase in the temporal and spiritual joys of the will (San Juan is alluding to the parable of the sower in Matthew 19). In this last case, he stresses that the increase in joy as a result of detachment applies as much to profane as to divine joys, since they are part of the soul's knowledge and contemplation of God. Adam and Eve in Paradise ate and drank and saw its beauty without sin before the Fall, since reason ruled their senses; but until these are subjugated to the spirit, dangers remain.

The discussion of moral gifts raises the disputed question of the place of good works in Christian teaching. When rightly possessed, they are superior to most of the kinds previously described, because they bring actions into conformity with the right use of reason: 'no puede el hombre humanamente en esta vida poseer cosa mejor' (27.2), 'in this life man can possess nothing better in human terms'. They produce good works; but these are acceptable only insofar as their motivation is the love of God. Hence Christians should note that 'el valor de [. . .] buenas obras, ayunos, limosnas, penitencias, [oraciones], etc., [. . .] no se funda tanto en la cuantidad y cualidad de ellas, sino en el amor de Dios que él lleva en ellas' (27.5), 'the value of [. . .] good works, fasting, alms, acts of penitence and prayers [. . .] is not so much founded on their quantity and quality, as on the love of God which [the Christian] brings to them'. The wrong kind of motivation creates a judgemental attitude towards others which is hypocritical, and a desire for good works to impress others. San Juan certainly does not believe that good works in themselves lead to salvation, since unless they are done for the love of God, not self, they bring no benefit – a view which might not unreasonably be termed 'justification by love', and which nicely balances and reconciles one of the great disputes of the Reformation era.

San Juan attacks those who wish to perpetuate their name by displaying their shields in churches, for them to idolatrize and for others to admire. Good works should be hidden, the left hand not knowing what the right hand is doing (Matthew 6.3). People who are motivated by show will not make any progress towards perfection, because as soon as the going gets hard they will give up. They have a higher opinion of their deeds than is warranted, and become incapable of receiving any advice on how to leave their vanities behind. The result is that love of God and neighbour become attenuated. San Juan's psychological perception is surely sound: we can all recognize ourselves in such people, and San Juan is honest enough to say that 'apenas hallarán uno que puramente se mueva a obrar por Dios sin arrimo de algún interés de consuelo o gusto' (28.8), 'hardly anyone can be found who is moved to good works purely for God's sake without the prop of some consolation or pleasure'. In place of false gods like self-interest and the desire to impress others by one's virtue, he points to the benefits of actions not tainted with them: increased resistance to the devil, more perfect works, poverty of spirit, gentleness, humility and prudence, all of which make the soul more pleasing to God (3.29).

The category of miracles and other supernatural phenomena has come to prominence in recent years through the claims of some evangelistic campaigns and charismatic movements which place a high value on healings, prophecies and glossolalia (speaking in tongues). It is therefore salutary to listen to what a voice from an age generally thought of as more susceptible and superstitious than ours has to say. San Juan does not deny that miracles may happen, but he questions their role as a means of union with God. They may bring material benefits to their recipients, but they can be performed without grace or love, even for one's own pleasure and profit, as scripture shows in the case of Balaam, Solomon and Simon Magus. Christ's teaching (Matthew 7.22–3) does not accept them as guarantees of salvation. Miracles, prophecies and the like can be deceptive or even demonic, when based on a pact with Satan – hence the existence of witches and magicians.[25] Reliance on miracles as proof of God's favour undermines faith, since belief becomes dependent on them instead of on God. In a telling passage of exegesis San Juan shows how the disciples first heard about the Resurrection before they saw it, and therefore had (or did not have) faith in it before Christ appeared to them. The status of miracles is far too ambiguous: faith does not need them. When the soul deprives herself of delight in them, God is exalted, rather than the miracles themselves or those who perform them, and faith, hope and love command the will, rather than proofs and pride. San Juan would have been no friend to healing crusades which boast of evangelists' powers to cure or to forms of worship which equate the presence of the Holy Spirit with speaking in tongues, any more than he was to miraculous claims in his own time. His reasons would have been based on the theological distinction between the creatures and the Creator, the finite and the infinite, and on the impossibility of the former as a means to union with the latter.

The kinds of visions and raptures San Juan later describes as imperfections (N 2.2), were common enough in sixteenth-century Spain, and there are plenty of cases in which they were found to be the result of delusion, madness or even demonic pacts: 'hace el demonio a muchos creer visiones vanas y profecías falsas; [. . .] les procura hacer presumir que habla Dios y los santos con ellos, y creen muchas veces a su fantasía' (N 2.2.3), 'the devil makes many believe in vain visions and false prophecies [. . .] and tries to make them suppose that God and the saints are speaking to them, and they frequently believe what they imagine'. The result is that such people are seized by vanity and arrogance, and like to make outward show of their raptures so that others will think they are saints. This is a dangerous state, especially as it appears to belong to a more advanced stage on the journey than the miracles mentioned in S 3. Attachment to such experiences mistakes a particular moment along the way for the desired goal, and strengthens the hold of the deadliest and subtlest of all sins, spiritual pride.

San Juan defines the last of his category of joys, spiritual gifts, as 'todos aquellos que mueven y ayudan para las cosas divinas y el trato del alma con Dios, y las comunicaciones de Dios con el alma' (S 3.33.2), 'all those which move and assist in divine matters and the soul's dealings with God, and God's communications with the soul'. The subject matter is familiar and relates to another of the great controversies of the century, the place of art and ritual in Christianity. Chapters 35–45 have been studied from many perspectives: by Protestants anxious to claim San Juan as a crypto-Protestant, and by Roman Catholics protesting that his are mainstream Catholic views.[26] Such polemical approaches are unproductive; of greater interest are the unexpected points of contact between the two positions which can be appreciated at the distance of four centuries. As a faithful Catholic, San Juan begins his discussion with an implicit reference to the Tridentine decree on the purpose and use of images (35.3): they exist to encourage reverence toward the saints, to move the will and to arouse devotion, and as long as they serve these ends they are necessary. The Council of Trent's attitude to religious art was, contrary to popular belief and later practice, in some ways quite puritanical, and this is reflected in San Juan's words about images needing to be proportionate to their ends, rather than drawing attention to their cost or artistry. Therefore, in accordance with his underlying theology of faith, not creatures, as unitive, he develops an approach to religious art and practice which has much in common with Erasmus at the beginning of the century, and provides a point of convergence between Protestant and Catholic tradition.

Having established the proper use of images, he moves to condemn the 'uso abominable' (35.4), 'abominable use' some people make of them by dressing them up in fine clothes, for their own amusement and vanity, like dolls, so that some of them, in his vivid phrase, do nothing but 'canonizar sus vanidades', 'canonize their vanities'. By contrast:

> la persona devota de veras en lo invisible principalmente pone su devoción y pocas imágenes ha menester y de pocas usa y de aquellas que más se conforman con lo divino que con lo humano, conformándolas a ellas y a sí en ellas con el traje de otro siglo y su condición [. . .] Ni [en] esas de que usa tiene asido el corazón, porque, si se las quitan, se pena muy poco, porque la viva imagen busca dentro de sí, que es Cristo crucificado. (35.5)
>
> the truly devout person centres devotion principally on what is invisible, and needs few images and uses few, and then only those which conform more to the divine than the human, because both they and he in them are conformed to the dress and condition of another age, not this one [. . .] Nor is his heart fixed on those he does use, because if they are removed he is very little troubled, because he seeks the living image within himself, which is Christ crucified [. . .].

The spirit is to fly to God, but the more the soul becomes attached to a particular image, the less it can, because it is trapped in the means, not on the way to the end. Almost everyone has a favourite rosary, but God hears prayers regardless of material and colour (.7); such attachments are like the woodworm, which gnaws away at the good wood (.8). The efficacy of images lies in the faith and purity of heart of the person who prays before them, not in their instrinsic value; for this reason God often works miracles through plain ones (36.1–2). Pilgrimages are best undertaken alone, because many people treat them as recreation rather than devotion (36.3). There are images which have a profound and lasting effect on a soul (4); Santa Teresa certainly records such experiences (*Vida* 27.2; 32.1; 38.17–18). But it is easy to mistake artistic appreciation of an image for true devotion. Speaking or moving images may be the work of the devil, not God (5); San Juan would not have been impressed by weeping and bleeding Madonnas in our own time. Since images exist to awaken the soul to things invisible, devotion should attach to the substance of the latter and disregard the 'accidents', their artistic qualities or supposed miraculous powers (3.37).

If over-decoration of oratories (3.38) runs the risk of drawing attention away from the living truth towards the artistry itself, it is equally important that artistic work should be reverently and worthily done, not badly or crudely. San Juan's preference is for simplicity, which, as he points out, is not at all the same as poorly executed art which detracts from devotion (38.2). Nor should feasts be interspersed with 'cosas ridículas e indevotas para incitar a risa a la gente', 'ridiculous things lacking in devotion, to make people laugh'. While a certain amount of sensual pleasure in all these things may be appropriate to arouse the devotion of beginners, it must quickly be left behind. Churches are not to be enjoyed for themselves: they are images of the living temple within (40). There are places in which God has given particular mercies to individuals, who may return there in order to recall them, as long as they do not become attached to the time and place (42); though the soul is better than any physical location for God to be found (42.4). Holy places chosen by God as places for his worship, like Mount Sinai or Mount Horeb, are mysteries pertaining to his will alone.[27] Failure to adhere to these principles leads to a kind of devotional tourism, flitting from one place or lifestyle to another, because of an inability to persevere in one place or state (41) – a phenomenon not unknown in our own age. Prayer should be practised in places most conducive to spiritual adoration. Though San Juan prayed in the countryside and encouraged his friars to do so, here he specifically rejects the ideal of the *locus amoenus*, since it provides too much sensual pleasure; better a solitary and rough place, as the Saviour chose (39.2). He does not discount the value of beautiful places to arouse devotion naturally (41.1), but points out that anchorites and hermits chose to live in vast deserts or shut themselves up in narrow cells in caves, as St Benedict did for three years (.2).

Commenting on rituals ('ceremonias'), San Juan identifies a type of obsessive personality which insists that they must be carried out in precise detail or else the liturgy will prove invalid (43.2). Christ taught only one prayer, the *Pater noster*, which requires but the privacy of one's own room (Matthew 6.6) or a desert place (Luke 6.12). There is nothing wrong with particular devotions, like novenas or fasting, as long as their performance does not become an end in itself. Last of all, he looks at preaching, where, as we have seen, the outward, sensual part lies in rhetorical adornments, the verbal equivalents of over-dressed images, whereas the power of the word is spiritual, not vocal.[28] Though he is careful not to condemn good style and rhetoric in itself (5), his judgement on preaching ought to be taken to heart by all who engage in that art:

> Que comúnmente vemos que [. . .] cuanto el predicador es de mejor vida mayor es el fruto que hace, por bajo que sea su estilo y poca su retórica y su

> doctrina común, porque del espíritu vivo se pega el calor; pero el otro muy poco provecho hará, aunque más subido sea su estilo y doctrina, porque, aunque es verdad que el buen estilo y acciones y subida doctrina y buen lenguaje mueven y hacen [más] efecto acompañado del buen espíritu; pero sin él, aunque da sabor y gusto el sermón al sentido y al entendimiento, muy poco o nada de jugo pega a la voluntad, porque comúnmente se queda tan floja y remisa como antes para obrar, aunque haya dicho maravillosas cosas maravillosamente dichas, que sólo sirven para deleitar el oído como una música concertada o sonido de campanas; mas el espíritu, como digo, no sale de sus quicios más que antes, no teniendo la voz virtud para resucitar al muerto de su sepultura (45.4).[29]
>
> We often see [. . .] that the better the life of the preacher is the greater the fruits of his labours, however low his style and poor his rhetoric and commonplace his teaching; for heat is kindled by the living spirit. The other kind of preacher will have very little effect, though his style and doctrine be higher; though it is true that good style and actions and high doctrine and good language are of greater effect when accompanied by goodness of spirit. But without this, even though the sermon gives pleasure to the senses and the understanding, very little or nothing substantial stays with the will, which generally remains as weak and reluctant to do works as it was before, even if he has said marvellous things marvellously spoken, which simply serve to delight the ear like harmonious music or the ringing of bells; but the spirit, as I say, does not leave its bounds more than before, since his voice has not the power to raise the dead from the grave.

That a post-Tridentine mystic should have written so critically of many of the religious practices of his day may come as a surprise. But once the basis of his teaching on faith has been grasped, his warnings against a religion based on externals follow the same logic as those against reliance on visions and other strange phenomena. All religious practices and habits in the active night of the spirit are subject to the same criterion: the darkness of faith and poverty of spirit over against attachments to particular experiences or places. San Juan's teaching has an impressive purity and integrity about it. It goes to the root of the matter. He certainly does not believe that the practice of religion is good in itself. He subjects it to exactly the same kind of penetrating analysis as he does the life of the senses, and for the same reasons. As with all the other 'creatures', things which are good in themselves can be perverted by human misuse into a form of idolatry. Too much of what passes for religious devotion is unmasked as a form of self-interest and self-regard, a mistaking of the means for the end. Sermons and images, from that perspective, are identical. Protestants need his insights, for the word can be idolized, as well as works of art. But they are an important corrective to religiosity of any kind, in any age.

THE *NOCHE OSCURA* – BOOK 1: SINS OF THE SPIRIT

Much of the first book of the *Noche* is really a prolongation of the active night of the spirit, or even a return to the stage of beginners, as N 1.3.3. makes clear: 'convendrá tocar aquí algunas propiedades de los principiantes', 'it will be appropriate to deal here with some of the properties of beginners'. Once again the structural boundaries of the work are unclear: though N 1 is concerned with the passive night of the senses, San Juan does not reach this till Chapter 8. He begins with the traditional schema of the seven deadly sins, but as they affect the inner life. Thus, unrecognized spiritual pride leads to self-satisfaction and a desire to teach rather than to learn spiritual things. It leads people to seek out confessors congenial to their own view of their experiences, and to enjoy putting these on public display. They paint their sins in the best possible light, or become impatient because they feel they should already be saints. Excessive zeal also leads to spiritual anger among those who 'querrían ser santos en un día' (5.3), 'would like to be saints in a day'. Spiritual greed is found among those who cannot get enough of 'religion' and spend all their time listening to religious teaching, reading religious books, collecting images and rosaries and the like, which can never be substitutes for the interior poverty of spirit they should be seeking. Even simple objects can be a snare: from his own experience as a confessor he recounts two cases, of someone who possessed a crude cross made from a holy branch and a needle for ten years till he removed it, and someone else who, unconcerned with the beauty of the object, was nonetheless attached to a rosary made out of fish bones.

Spiritual lust brings San Juan back to the relationship between the sensual and spiritual parts of the soul, and to the common phenomenon of prayer and worship being interrupted by lustful thoughts and images. This happens because the pleasure gained from such spiritual exercises passes to the senses, which allow such distractions to enter the sensual part of the soul. The devil, too, can be active, trying to disturb the soul and put it off prayer, by placing 'cosas muy feas y torpes' (4.3), 'very ugly, filthy things' in the imagination, especially among those with a tendency to depression. The very fear of such interruptions is enough to cause them, he remarks; one tries to avoid something so much that for that very reason it comes into one's mind. Other souls, of a different personality type, are so suggestible that once these distractions occur they are overwhelmed by them. All such experiences are subject to the same, sure test: if they increase one's love of God, they are purely spiritual, but if they lead to a cooling of spiritual ardour, they are the result of vice: 'eso tiene el espíritu de Dios, que lo bueno aumenta con lo bueno, por cuanto hay semejanza y conformidad' (4.7), 'for the spirit of God has this property, that it increases the good with the good, because of the likeness and conformity between them'. There is a degree of psychological perception about his analysis here which must reflect his awareness that different people react in different ways to the same stimuli.

Spiritual anger may be directed at the sins of others, but often occurs when the soul, like a child removed from the mother's breast, is irritated that the delights of deep recollection are over. This is less a fault than an 'imperfección que se ha de purgar por la sequeded y aprieto de la noche oscura' (5.1), 'imperfection which must be purged by the dryness and stress of the dark night'. Spiritual gluttony manifests itself in those who are gluttons for punishment – people who become so caught up in ascetic practices that 'algunos se matan a penitencias y otros se debilitan con ayunos más de lo que su flaqueza sufre' (6.1), 'some kill themselves in penitences and others weaken themselves in fasting, beyond what their frailty allows', often in direct disobedience to their spiritual superior. San Juan is scathing about such 'penitencia de bestias (6.2)', 'penitence of beasts', partly because it is of no value, partly because God prefers spiritual sacrifices (1 Samuel 15.22) and partly (no doubt) as a result of his own attempts to ensure that ascetic practices were moderate and appropriate in the Carmelite reform, and the resistance this met.[30] He also criticizes those who try to wheedle their confessors into letting them receive communion frequently.[31] Such people are more concerned to receive pleasurable sensations than to praise God in humility, and display an 'impureza en la fe' (6.5), 'impurity of faith', since it is the invisible grace received through faith which is to be sought. Others go 'andando a caza', (6.6), 'hunting around' for all kinds of favours from God through reading books and meditations, feeling disconsolate if they do not seem to benefit from them. Unless they enter the dark night to be purged of these 'niñerías', 'childish things', they will fall into 'males sin cuento', 'ills without number'. They will certainly not want to enter 'el camino áspero de la cruz' (6.7), 'the harsh way of the cross', the 'tentaciones, sequedades y otros trabajos' (6.8), 'temptations, periods of dryness and other labours' which are part of the dark night and the means by which the Lord cures them.

By the time he reaches spiritual envy and sloth, one senses that San Juan is running out of steam, since so many of the things he has wanted to say about each sin apply to all. To envy the spiritual progress of others and hence to question their virtue reveals a lack of charity. Sloth can lead to the abandonment of prayer when this fails to bring the expected satisfaction. Many who suffer from this 'querrían que quisiese Dios lo que ellos quieren, y se entristecen de querer lo que quiere Dios, con repugnancia de acomodar su voluntad a la de Dios' (7.3), 'would like God to desire what they desire, and grow miserable desiring what God desires, experiencing repugnance in accommodating their will to God's', which is 'midiendo a Dios consigo, y no a sí mismos con Dios', 'to measure God according to themselves, and not themselves according to God'. Everything about the cross offends them, since they only seek to please their own desires.

Finally, in Chapter 8, San Juan reaches the two passive nights. The first, which he says has been written about, is common and happens to many, and is 'amarga y terrible para el sentido' (8.2), 'bitter and terrible for the senses'. Anyone who has given up alcohol or chocolate in Lent will know just a fraction of what San Juan means. The second night is entered only by the few, and 'no tiene comparación, porque es horrenda y espantable para el espíritu', 'is without comparison, because it is dreadful and terrifying to the spirit', and requires a fuller treatment, 'por haber della muy poco lenguaje, así de plática como de escritura, y aun de experiencia muy poco', 'since there is very little said about it, either in speech or writing, and very little experience of it, too'. At the very moment when the inner life of souls seems to be at its most exuberant, full of the light of divine favours, 'oscuréceles Dios toda esta luz y ciérrales la puerta y manantial de la dulce agua espiritual que andaban gustando en Dios todas las veces [. . .] que ellos querían' (8.3), 'God darkens all this light and shuts the door and the spring of that sweet spiritual water by which they enjoyed God as often [. . .] as they desired'. Inner dryness is not necessarily the result of this divine weaning away from maternal dependence; as before, it may be caused by a lack of perseverance in prayer, hence the signs given to distinguish the one from the other.[32] But if it is the symptom of this crisis, every natural sense must be starved so that the spirit alone can be fed. Yet at the same time the soul can sense the effects of God's passive action on her, strengthening her with this inner food, and causing her to desire his presence in quiet and solitude. This is the so-called ligature: God 'ata' (9.7), 'binds up' the inner faculties so that he can work on the soul directly.[33] The purgation and consequent suffering takes place at the sensual level; the spirit, though unable to grasp any particular image or idea, grows stronger all the time.

Those who pass through this night suffer less from the dryness than from the fear that they have gone astray and been abandoned by God. They lose their former tranquillity of spirit and become agitated and distressed. Experienced directors, instead of vainly trying to counsel the resumption of discursive meditation, must leave the soul alone, 'aunque les parezca claro que no hacen nada y que pierden tiempo [. . .] contentándose sólo con una advertencia amorosa y sosegada en Dios' (10.4), 'even if it seems clear that they are doing nothing and wasting time [. . .] contenting themselves alone with a loving and calm attention in God'. Otherwise the soul will regress. It is a good sign if the faculties appear to have ceased all operations, because they will not disturb God's gift of contemplation, which is an 'infusión secreta, pacífica y amorosa de Dios' (10.6), 'secret, peaceful and loving infusion of God', which inflames the soul with love.

Chapters 12 to 13 describe the benefits of this night. The soul is no longer dressed for a 'fiesta', and must put on the garment of dryness and abandonment, which teaches her self-knowledge and awareness of her own misery and God's greatness and excellence. Her attitude changes, as did Job's, when he could no longer find God in his former pleasures and when, in the midst of his sorrows, God spoke to him face to face from the whirlwind, revealing the depths and heights of his great Wisdom – 'cual nunca antes había hecho en el tiempo de la prosperidad' (12.3), 'which he had never done before in the time of his [Job's] prosperity'. The biblical reference is well chosen, since Job's sufferings do lead him to this memorable and quite new encounter with the Creator. Other benefits – spiritual humility, love of the neighbour, obedience, a true measure of the self – are antidotes to the deadly sins themselves.[34] In the midst of this creative dryness, 'cuando menos piensa, comunica Dios al alma suavidad espiritual y amor muy puro y noticias espirituales a veces muy delicadas' (13.10), 'when she is least thinking of it, God sends the soul spiritual gentleness and very pure love and spiritual knowledge, sometimes of a very delicate kind'. The soul 'consigue libertad de espíritu' (13.11), 'achieves freedom of spirit', in which all 12 fruits of the Spirit (Galatians 5.22–3) may flourish. Hence the soul, following the imagery of the poem, can 'leave' the bondage of subjection to the appetites 'without being seen' by her former enemies.

For her 'house' is now at rest: senses, faculties and discursive operations are all stilled.

In this night great temptations and labours nonetheless accompany the soul: the spirit of fornication, tempting her with foul imaginings; the spirit of blasphemy, which almost forces her to utter them; and the spirit of giddiness (Isaiah 19.14), which fills her with scruples and difficult questions for which she cannot find an answer (14.2–3).[35] But without such severe temptations, the soul would not be tested to stimulate its desire for divine Wisdom (14.4). It is impossible to predict how long this night of the senses will last, for that depends on how much imperfection has to be purged and the degree of union to which God wills to raise the soul: the higher this is, the longer and the intenser the temptations will be. Progress in the spiritual life is not a gentle, easy road, but one of confronting obstacles which have actively to be cleared away, or of experiencing burdens which have to be borne passively, without knowing for how long.

NOCHE OSCURA – BOOK 2: THE TERRORS OF THE NIGHT

The first book of the *Noche* has revealed that there can be no short cuts to holiness. Now the passive night of the spirit is approaching, the most original and profound part of San Juan's teaching, though he devotes only three chapters to describing it. Once he has done that, he has nothing more to say, which perhaps explains the unfinished nature of the commentary.[36] It does not immediately follow the night of the senses. It may come many years later, when the soul 'ha salido de una estrecha cárcel' (N 2.1.1), 'has come out of a narrow prison' and finds herself at peace and liberty, delighting in the loving contemplation of God. Even so, there are still times of darkness and dryness, sometimes of great intensity, because the spiritual part of the soul is not yet completely purged, and these act 'como presagios y mensajeros de la noche venidera del espíritu', 'as foreshadowings and messengers of the coming night of the spirit'. This remnant of sensuality is seen in the bodily effects which accompany prayer – raptures, ecstasies and tremblings, which occur when God's Spirit touches the not yet wholly purged soul. These heightened states and extraordinary bodily reactions are discounted by San Juan, and attributed to the weakness of the flesh and a process of purgation as yet incomplete, in which the root of imperfection must be extracted from the spiritual part of the soul, rather than the branches lopped from the sensual. If the night of the senses is rightly called 'cierta reformación y enfrenamiento del apetito' (3.1), 'a kind of reformation and reining in of the appetite', that of the spirit deals with the root cause of sin. Because sin is a spiritual disorder, it manifests itself in certain actions and attitudes, but unless its root causes are uncovered and removed, it cannot be cured. This is a long way from the modern preoccupation with sins of the flesh, and the more significant for it.

What happens to souls in this last night is that God:

> desnúdales las potencias y afecciones y sentidos, así espirituales como sensitivos, así exteriores como interiores, dejando a oscuras el entendimiento, y [la] voluntad a secas, y vacía la memoria, y las afecciones del alma en

> suma aflicción, [amargura y aprieto, privándola] del sentido y gusto que antes sentía de los bienes espirituales, para que esta privación sea uno de los principios que se requiere en el espíritu para que se introduzca y una en él la forma espiritual del espíritu, que es la unión de amor. Todo lo cual obra el Señor en ella por medio de una pura y oscura contemplación. (3.3)
>
> unclothes its faculties and affections and senses, spiritual and sensual, exterior and interior, leaving the understanding in the darkness, the will dessicated, the memory emptied, and the soul's affections in utter affliction, [bitterness and stress, depriving her] of the feeling and pleasure she formerly had in spiritual goods, so that this privation becomes one of the requirements for the spirit, so that the spiritual form of the spirit, which is union in love, can be introduced into and united with it. The Lord works all this by means of pure, dark contemplation.

It is further defined as:

> una influencia de Dios en el alma que la purga de sus ignorancias e imperfecciones habituales, naturales y espirituales, que llaman los contemplativos contemplación infusa, o MÍSTICA TEOLOGÍA, en que de secreto enseña Dios [a] el alma y la instruye en perfección de amor, sin ella hacer nada ni entender cómo. (5.1)
>
> an influence of God in the soul which purges her of her habitual ignorance and imperfections, natural and spiritual, which contemplatives call infused contemplation, or 'mystical theology', in which God teaches the soul in secret and instructs her in the perfection of love, without her doing anything or understanding how.

The next three chapters probe the sufferings of the soul. It is as if she were being swallowed up by the depths, like Jonah into the whale's belly, a 'sepulcro de oscura muerte' (6.1), 'tomb of dark death', which she must enter before her resurrection.[37] Worse still, she feels God despises her and has punished her by abandoning her to the darkness: 'cuando esta contemplación purgativa aprieta, sombra de muerte y gemidos de muerte y dolores de infierno siente el alma muy a lo vivo' (6.2), 'when this purgative contemplation presses, the soul experiences the shadow of death and the groanings of death and the pains of hell in a particularly vivid way'. She feels equally abandoned by friends and every creature, and the three great images of the night – drought, emptiness and darkness – possess her in every part (6.3–4). But it is also a fire to purify her of dross, a forge where she is refined like gold in the crucible, a veritable purgatory in this life, in which hell and perdition open up before her (6.5–6). She finds no consolation, only grief, in any doctrine or spiritual teacher (7.3); she is, in another nightmarish image, like someone 'aprisionado en una oscura mazmorra atado de pies y manos', 'imprisoned in a gloomy dungeon with hands and feet tied up'. There are times of relief, of peace and loving friendship with God, and of an ease of communication with him, which are signs of the healing process which God is bringing about in her (7.4). But after these she is plunged into a still deeper darkness, which even remembrance of these joys is powerless to assuage (.6). Whichever state she is in, deepest darkness or liberty and delight, the soul feels that it will never change. Sometimes the relief is so great that the remaining 'root' of creaturely affections is buried, and she feels a 'no sé qué', an indefinable something yet to be done which prevents her from enjoying the experience as she should. San Juan understands this to be the experience of purgatory itself, transferred into this life, and explains that those who find themselves in it feel that they will never leave it, because the fires of purgatory can only be felt where imperfections remain to be burnt out (7.7). Once this is completed, torments end and only joy is left (10.5). The last of the ten steps on the ladder of divine love (20.5) brings the very few who reach it freedom from purgatory in the life to come, since all necessary purgation by love has been achieved in this life – a bold claim, since it implies that they go straight to heaven.[38]

In this night, prayer becomes impossible, and so does normal human business. The soul becomes so abstracted that she often suffers profound lapses of memory (8.1). But God's purpose is to raise her yet further (9.1), to endow her with 'cierta magnificencia gloriosa en la comunicación de Dios' (9.4), 'a certain glory and magnificence in her communication with God'. There are hints of this as she begins to lose her ordinary sense of things and approach God's: 'anda maravillada de las cosas que ve y oye, pareciéndole muy peregrinas y extrañas, siendo las mismas que solía tratar comúnmente' (9.5), 'she goes about wondering at the things she sees and hears, which appear so strange and unusual to her, though they are the very things she used to deal with all the time'. She is also being prepared for the fulness of peace, which San Juan explains in a complex sentence which repeats the word 'paz' eight times. But first there is war to be waged:

> Esta es una penosa turbación de muchos recelos, imaginaciones y combates que tiene el alma dentro de sí, en que, con la aprehensión y sentimiento de las miserias en que se ve, sospecha que está perdida y acabados sus bienes para siempre. De aquí es que trae en el espíritu un dolor y gemido tan profundo, que le causa fuertes rugidos y bramidos espirituales, pronunciándolos a veces por la boca, y resolviéndose en lágrimas cuando hay fuerza y virtud para poderlo hacer, aunque las menos veces hay este alivio. (9.7)

> This is a painful disturbance full of suspicions, imaginings and conflicts which the soul has within herself, and together with the knowledge and sense of her own miseries, she suspects that she is lost and that good things are finished for ever. Hence this causes in the spirit so deep a pain and groaning, that it brings loud roars and spiritual ragings, sometimes pronounced by the mouth, and resolving themselves into tears when there is sufficient strength and power for it, although such relief is infrequent.

Conscious, perhaps, that in spite of the vivid language he has used, this whole process is difficult to grasp, San Juan elaborates his own version of the traditional comparison of how fire burns wood and transforms it into fire, and applies it stage by stage to the soul:[39]

> el fuego material, en aplicándose al madero, lo primero que hace es comenzarle a secar, echándole la humedad fuera y haciéndole llorar en agua que en sí tiene; luego le va poniendo negro, oscuro y feo y aun de mal olor y, yéndole sacando poco a poco, le va sacando a luz y echando fuera todos los accidentes feos y oscuros que tiene contrarios al fuego, y finalmente, comenzándole a inflamar por de fuera y calentarle, viene a transformarle en sí y ponerle hermoso como el mismo fuego; [en] el cual término, ya de parte del madero ninguna pasión hay ni acción propia, salva [*sic*] la gravedad y cantidad más espesa que la del fuego [. . .] porque está seco, y seco está; caliente, y [caliente] está; claro, y esclarece; está ligero mucho más que antes; obrando el fuego en él estas propiedades y efectos. (10.1)

> for material fire, when it is applied to the wood, first begins to dry it out, forcing its moisture out so that the water it contains weeps; then it turns it black, dark and ugly, even ill-smelling, and, as bit by bit it dries it out, it begins to come alight, as all the ugly and dark accidents which are contrary to fire are removed. Finally, as it begins to heat it and set it alight from without, it ends by transforming it into itself and making it as lovely as the fire is. To reach this end, the wood itself feels nothing and plays no part save being heavier and thicker than fire. Because fire is dry, it too is dry; because fire is hot, hot; because fire is bright, it illumines; it is much lighter than it was. Fire is what causes the wood to have these properties and effects.

The application of the simile is straightforward: the fire represents the purgation of imperfections to the very root, until the soul herself is 'inflamada', as the poem states, aflame with love for God.

Yet even as this is happening, San Juan speaks of a flaring up of love into union, a 'toque en la Divinidad' (12.6), 'touch of the Divinity', which is the beginning of the way of the perfect. It is different from such 'toques' in the night of the senses because it is now experienced in the spiritual part of the soul (13.4). From the outset, he tells us, the soul has travelled with 'ansias de amor', in the fear that God has abandoned her during her trials. But this inflammation of love provokes an 'embriaguez' (13.5), a 'drunkenness' of love and desire, to the extent that 'haría cosas extrañas e inusitadas por cualquier modo y manera, [por] poder encontrar con el que ama su alma', 'she would do strange and extraordinary things in any way she could to be able to find him whom her soul loves'.

Still maintaining a relatively close attention to the poem, San Juan proceeds to explain the words 'secreta', 'escala' and 'disfrazada' from the second line of the second verse of the poem.[40] Dark contemplation is secret because it is difficult to explain to a spiritual director, and because it isolates the soul:

> algunas veces de tal manera absorbe al alma y sume en su abismo secreto, que el alma echa de ver claro que está puesta alejadísima y remotísima de toda criatura, de suerte que le parece que la colocan en una profundísima y anchísima soledad donde no puede llegar alguna humana criatura, como un inmenso desierto que por ninguna parte tiene fin, tanto más deleitoso, sabroso y amoroso, cuanto más profundo, ancho y solo. (17.6)

> sometimes it so absorbs the soul and plunges it into its secret abyss in such a way that the soul sees clearly that it is very distant and remote from any creature, so that it seems that she has been placed in the deepest and widest solitude where no other human creature can reach, like a vast desert which stretches endlessly in all directions, the more delightful, enjoyable and loving the deeper, wider and lonelier it is.

The ladder of the poem is an ancient symbol for ascent to the divine, which San Juan likens to the way ladders are used for taking treasures up into fortresses. He takes the image seriously – the word *Subida* in the title of the treatise means 'ascent'. Ladders enable upward as well as downward movement, so that as the soul ascends, so she is humbled: '[en] este camino el abajar es subir, y el subir abajar' (18.2), 'on this road, to go down is to rise, and to rise, to go down', both happening simultaneously until the ladder is scaled and union with God reached. Not surprisingly, Jacob's ladder is his biblical warrant (18.4; Genesis 28.12): an ascent from self-knowledge on the lowest rung to union at the top. This pattern of exaltation and humility itself corresponds exactly to the pattern of the Incarnation: the descent from glory to humility of the Son of God, and his ascent from shame and suffering to glory.[41] It is part of the way of the cross, and though San Juan does not make this explicit, is another element in his christocentric vision.

The contents of the ten steps of the mystical ladder need not detain us. The devil is unable to enter the purged spirit, which is 'encelada', hidden and safe from his attacks, though he knows that there the soul is communicating with God and does his best to arouse the dormant senses to rebellion. Even this has hardly any effect, and may stimulate the soul to retreat further within her inner refuge, and experience increased joy and peace (23.4). If the senses do become engaged, as when visions are corporeal, then great torments may ensue. Following the theology of Job, in which God permits Satan to trouble his servant as if there were 'cierta paridad entre los dos guerreros' (23.6), 'a degree of parity between the two warriors', San Juan establishes that the soul can become a kind of battleground between good angels and bad, in which the latter cause false visions and the former good, all passively. The distress caused when the devil prevails is a terrible torment, because it comes directly from his naked spirit to hers. Such attacks are permitted by the good angel to prepare and purify the soul to receive even greater mercies and delights from God (23.9–10). There are also experiences which are totally divine, when the soul is truly both in the dark and secure from the enemy. San Juan calls them 'toques sustanciales de divina unión entre el alma y Dios [. . .] el más alto grado de oración que hay' (23.11), 'substantial touches of divine union between the soul and God [. . .] the highest degree of prayer there is'. Finally, when both 'houses' of sense and spirit are quietened, 'esta divina Sabiduría se uñe [*sic*] en el alma con un nuevo ñudo de posesión de amor' (24.3), 'this divine Wisdom becomes united with the soul by a new knot of love's possession'.

The *Noche* treatise tells the other side of the story from the *Subida*: the work of God within the soul, preparing it for union with him. The spiritual life is mercifully not all a matter of human effort. That can proceed only so far, and cannot reach the destination unaided. The passive nights underline that San Juan has no doctrine of justification by works, as though human efforts alone could win salvation, and as if all that God had done in Christ counted for nothing. They show that the divine initiative is at work in both parts of the soul, and that though what God does causes great pain and anguish, it is his activity which brings the soul to her desired end. There are glimpses of this in the *Subida*, but it is much more pronounced in the *Noche*. San Juan's insistence on faith as the only way to union – a theology of *sola fide* indeed – and on the divine prerogative takes him beyond the traditional Catholic–Protestant divide. He is simply too great a theologian to be confined within sixteenth-century polemics. So the *Noche* concludes as love guides the spirit through the dark without disturbance (25.1–4), before it peters out, a poignant confession, perhaps, of the limits both of language and system. San Juan has said all he can say and has wanted to say. He has reached the state of union, and another poem and another commentary must sing its joys.

CONCLUSION

I have tried as far as possible to let San Juan speak for himself, or to clarify as best I can what I think he means in terms accessible to those who do not share his own formation. Occasionally he deals with issues which are not the concern of his intended readership, such as the obligations of family life or the acquisition of wealth and honour, or others which are relevant to people in general, such as sexual or religious practice. Whatever he may say in the Prologue to the *Subida* (.9) about addressing only a few of his fellow-religious, the inclusion of these wider aspects of human experience means that despite having to struggle through many chapters dealing with puzzling inner experiences which they will not have shared, modern readers sometimes emerge onto familiar ground.

Nevertheless, San Juan is easy to misrepresent. Two or three quotations taken out of context can create the impression of a man so obsessed by the dangers of any kind of physical beauty that it had to be spurned. A reading of his three great *lira* poems should be enough to correct this, but their sensual images are rarely integrated into his theology.[42] Careful reading reveals that all San Juan's negations are made for the sake of a greater affirmation. The negative side of his teaching is therefore never an end in itself, but a means towards a more positive end. This can be traced back into the symbolism of the dark night itself. Divine light is experienced as darkness because of its blinding intensity, not because it is by nature dark. In N 2.5 San Juan tackles the paradox of how divine light can be called darkness. His answer goes back to an Aristotelian principle: the brighter and clearer divine things are in themselves, the darker and more hidden they are to the soul. Thus, the brighter the light, the more the owl is blinded; and the more directly one looks at the sun, the more the eye is also (5.3). That is why Dionysius and other mystical theologians call infused contemplation a 'rayo de tiniebla', 'ray of darkness'. It is painful for the soul to receive, because of her remaining imperfections, and she feels that God is against her and she against him (.5). The weight of it is such that sometimes she feels as if her whole being 'debajo de una inmensa y oscura carga está penando y agonizando tanto, que tomaría por alivio y partido el morir' (.6), 'a huge, dark burden, is suffering and in such agony that she would think death a relief and a boon'. Later, San Juan explains that the experience of darkness is soul-engendered, not inherent in the light: 'las tinieblas [. . .] no son tinieblas o males de la luz, sino de la misma alma, y la luz le alumbra para que las vea' (2.13.10), 'the darkness [. . .] is not darkness or evil produced by the light, but by the soul herself, and the light illumines her so that she can see it'. The dark night sometimes seems to be as much about the soul's creatureliness as her sinfulness.[43] Its sufferings are themselves part of the cure of sin, but more importantly, the preparation for a union of love which transcends separation of being.

The time, perhaps, has now come to look back over some of the larger questions raised by the *Subida-Noche*. First, we should remember what the work is and what it is not. San Juan believed he was writing a guide to union with God based on his own experience, and intended for a highly specialized readership. The poem gave him some structure, but the work is inspired much more by his own reading, his inner life and his care of other souls. He had no thought of a wider audience, let alone publication. The treatise should not therefore be judged by the measure of a finished work, with all the loose ends tied up. His desire to incorporate as much experience as possible and in an ordered fashion is constantly in tension with the looseness and repetitiveness of his expository style. That very tension is the source of some of his richest insights.

San Juan's commentaries can give the impression that the spiritual life is characterized by a series of recognizable steps along which the soul must pass. Once the map is unfolded, all the features to be encountered on the way can be identified. Though there is some truth in this, it gives the impression of a system far more finished and fixed than is the case. The commentaries attempt to make sense out of particular elements of mystical experience by locating these within a comprehensive system of theological thought. They break into component parts the undifferentiated nature of that experience, so that these can be examined and related to the principles which undergird the analysis. What appears at a given moment within the system to be a well-defined phenomenon, related to what has gone before and to what will follow, is never experienced with such clarity. But there is a flexibility and a vitality about his teaching which is inherent in the very way he writes, and which makes it a living organism rather than set in tablets of stone. This can be seen in a number of ways: the unfinished nature of the treatises, the repetitions and digressions they contain, and the images of movement and growth which characterize them.

While a system is valuable in creating a logical and ordered sequence of analysis, it can appear to reduce what in life is experienced in complex and non-linear ways to cut-and-dried simplicities. It then becomes hard for the reader to identify with it, because question like 'Which point have I reached?' or 'Have I completed the previous stage yet?' keep interfering with the reading. The system then becomes the meaning of the exercise, not a tool intended to clarify it. San Juan knew perfectly well that the inner life was not reducible to a bare system of universal application, certainly not one produced retrospectively, from the safety of the desired destination, union with God.[44] He himself tells us on several occasions that God leads different souls by different paths, suggesting that there are likely to be as many different trajectories on the journey as there are souls who undertake it.[45] It is therefore a misreading of San Juan to suppose that everyone must travel from a to b in a straight line, and the fact that between a and b he himself follows all kinds of twists and turns strongly suggests that he wanted to avoid creating such an impression. The many different divisions he uses – the three ways, the three theological virtues, the four passions, the four aspects of the dark night, the seven deadly sins, the ten degrees of love – imply that he did not believe there was one rigid pattern to be followed, and that the same journey could be looked at from various points of view. Discrepancies are common enough in his writings and do not require over-ingenious solutions. And if he failed to finish either the *Subida* or the *Noche* in the sense that neither the structure he announces at the outset nor the commentary on the poem is completed, their unfinished state may also act as a textual marker that the journey he traces has no ending in this life, and that there is always more to be said than his words, however wise, can hold.[46]

The dynamism of the metaphor of the journey is important. Only one of his treatise titles embodies it: an ascent, obviously, is one kind of journey, because from the summit both the effort of the climb and the perspective of the route are transformed. But each of the others implies it. The 'Noche oscura' poem recounts a night-time journey to union with the Beloved, and the night of the commentary is a comprehensive symbol for the whole journey, from twilight through midnight towards dawn, as the opening of the *Subida* already announces. The 'Cántico' poem moves too, from a cry of pain caused by the Beloved's absence through searching to union, while the commentary structures this movement according to the traditional threefold way of purgation, illumination and union. The flame of the *Llama* commentary is also dynamic, leaping upwards, an elemental and transforming force. San Juan does not describe a state but a process, a passing through and leaving behind of many states until the soul, in union with God, is free at last to realize her divine and human destiny through a 'reworking from within'.[47] One of San Juan's most important contributions to the history of Christian spirituality is to give a necessary and positive value to experiences of inner frustration and paralysis. Like the dark nights themselves, they have to be faced, but rightly understood and used they become a means of growth.

The analogy San Juan most frequently uses to explain moments of crisis or transition in the journey is that of the the child and parent, expressed in a number of different ways throughout the *Subida-Noche*. It begins in the Prologue itself (.3), where souls are hampered from making progress through inexperience or weakness, and stamp and cry like children who want to walk on their own feet before they have the strength, and resist their mothers' attempts to pick them up. The transition from meditation to contemplation is likened to weaning (S 2.14.3); so too is his teaching on disregarding most kinds of physical visions, which he connects with Paul's contrast in 1 Corinthians 13 between childish and adult experience (2.17.6). The most extended use of the mother–child metaphor occurs at the beginning of the *Noche*, and it acquires an increasing importance through the treatise:

> El alma, después que determinadamente se convierte a servir a Dios, [. . .] la va Dios criando en espíritu y regalando, al modo que la amorosa madre hace al niño tierno, al cual al calor de sus pechos le calienta, y con leche sabrosa y manjar blando y dulce le cría, y en sus brazos le trae y le regala; pero, a la medida que va creciendo, le va la madre quitando el regalo y, escondiendo el tierno amor, póne[le] el amargo acíbar en el dulce pecho y, abajándole de los brazos, le hace andar por su pie, por que, perdiendo las propiedades del niño, se dé a cosas más grandes y sustanciales. (1.2)
>
> Once the soul has determined to be converted to the service of God, God [. . .] nurtures her in spirit and caresses her, like the loving mother with her tender babe, warming it at her breasts, feeding it with nourishing milk and soft, sweet food, and carrying it in her arms and cherishing it. But as the child grows, its mother begins to withhold her caresses and to hide her tender love. She rubs bitter aloes on her sweet breast, puts the child down from her arms, and lets it walk on its own feet, so that as it puts aside the behaviour proper to a babe, it can grow accustomed to greater and more substantial things.

This touching picture suggests that before maturity can be gained, a certain degree of independence is required, and that the process of gaining it sometimes leaves a bitter taste. It is that experience of pain to which the nights of the spirit correspond. Such is the work of 'la amorosa madre de la gracia de Dios', 'the grace of God, that loving mother'. It certainly does not support the notion of religion as a form of infantile dependence. The use of feminine imagery shows that a sixteenth-century friar is perfectly capable of moving outside a patriarchal framework as far as the conception of God is concerned, and that such language is firmly rooted in Christian tradition, and needs to be recovered, not invented.[48] The critique of visions and revelations in S 2, of religious practices in S 3, and the analysis of the seven spiritual sins in N 1, are aimed at showing how all forms of 'childish' religion must be left behind. The one essential virtue which counters their temptations is inward humility.

The terrors of the dark night are a necessary part of growth towards union because they lead beginners from self-indulgent kinds of religion into the demanding way of the cross. This does not happen without protest, just as the child complains when the mother's breast is taken away (N 1.5.1); but, 'destetándolos Dios de los pechos destos gustos y sabores en puras sequedades y tinieblas interiores' (1.7.5), 'God, by removing them from suckling at the breasts of these pleasures and delights in pure interior dryness and darkness', cures them of their dependence and prepares them for the next stage. The greatest of spiritual sufferings come in the passive night of the spirit, but here supremely is the moment at which those on the way begin to emerge at last from babyhood: 'sintiéndolos ya Dios aquí algo crecidillos, para que se fortalezcan y salgan de mantillas, los desarrima del dulce pecho y, abajándolos de sus brazos, los veza a andar por sus pies, en lo cual sienten ellos gran novedad porque se les ha vuelto todo al revés' (8.3), 'God senses that they are now beginning to grow up a little, and so that they can grow stronger and come out of their baby clothes, he puts them down from his arms and gets them used to walking on their own feet, which feels very strange to them, because everything has been reversed'. When this image returns (12.1) it plays on the distinction between drinking milk at the breast and eating bread with the crust on, the milk and solid food of Hebrews 5.12–14, the latter being the fare of the mature. It is clear, then, that the passive night, for all its language of negation, is a means to growth out of infantile dependence on the toys and trinkets of spirituality, towards a maturity which is capable of embracing the way of the cross. San Juan uses other images to describe the journey from the old and familiar to the new and strange, but perhaps remembering his own mother's nurturing of abandoned babies in Medina, finds in the processes of breast-feeding, weaning and learning to walk unaided the loveliest picture of all.

It should now be clear why it is so important to keep hold of the organizing principle and general direction of the commentary. In a curious way, the fragmentation of the structure from the very beginning of the *Subida* has its poetic analogue in the temporal and spatial disruptions of the poetic narrative. Reading San Juan's prose is not like reading a narrative which proceeds in a smooth, linear way. Recurrent motifs characterize the treatise, but the argument follows so many twists and turns that it is difficult to find one's orientation. Its very confusions at the level of internal structure reflect back to the reader a sense of the limits of systematic discourse, and of language itself.

Mystics characteristically deal with feelings and thoughts which lie buried within the soul and which are only accessible by introspection. Reductionist analyses would claim that mystical experience, especially when it expresses itself in erotic language, is a form of sublimated sexuality. I doubt that San Juan's perceptiveness about the self can so readily be dismissed. It stems from too honest and painful an analysis of the self and the hidden forces which shape its behaviour. He teaches detachment, not repression; that is, understanding why certain states and attitudes are obstacles to spiritual growth, rather than burying them in the unconscious; and his aim, as his frequent use of mother–child analogies shows, is the right kind of development towards wholeness and maturity in the soul, whose relationship with the exterior world of creatures is then reordered in mutual freedom when she reaches union with God.

San Juan has also been attacked for being too individualistic, both in his teaching and in his grasp of the Christian faith. But several times in the *Subida-Noche* he touches wider, social questions, by exposing the vanity of the rich and the powerful, or simply by insisting on the need for love of one's neighbour. The context of the work is the life of an individual in a community, the values of which embrace a severe critique of society. He also sets the journey of the individual soul within the whole Christian journey, by his use of scripture, his stress on the way of the cross and his stern warnings against private revelations. But, as the *romances* on the Trinity show, the union of the individual soul with God is only possible because of God's wedding with human flesh and with the whole of the created order. And it is this which, above all else, enables San Juan to affirm at the end of his journey the beauty, worth and dignity of every created thing, great and small.

NOTES

1 Tobit, with other deutero-canonical books, was finally recognized as canonical by the Council of Trent in 1546. Lutheran, Reformed and Anglican confessions regard them as apocryphal, attributing varying degrees of edification to them (see, for example, Article 6 of the Articles of Religion of the Church of England).

2 On the contraries, see George Tavard, *Poetry and Contemplation in St John of the Cross* (Athens: Ohio University Press, 1988), pp. 79–81.

3 San Juan is remembering popular bestiaries and their use in sermon *exempla*; see, for example, T. H. White, *The Book of Beasts* (Gloucester: Alan Sutton, 1984 [Jonathan Cape, 1954]), p. 208.

4 For Laredo's text, see *Místicos franciscanos*, 3 vols (Madrid: BAC, 1948), pp. 409–10. For San Juan's sketch, see *Obras* (SJ), p. 72 (on its origins, see pp. 66–9).

5 *Calvin: Institutes of the Christian Religion*, ed. John T. McNeill, 2 vols (Philadelphia: Westminster, 1960), 4.1.5; 4.8.9.

6 The senses in question are the imagination and the fantasy, both described as 'sentidos corporales [interiores]', 'internal bodily senses', but distinguished from each other in S 2.12.3. Even so, San Juan accepts that for his purposes they are as one.

7 St Teresa seems to differ sharply in this respect, teaching that meditation on the humanity of Christ should never be abandoned, even in unitive prayer; however, E. W. Trueman Dicken who argues convincingly that what San Juan rejects here is the practice of discursive meditation, not the abandonment of any kind of devotion to the human Jesus; *The Crucible of Love* (London: Darton, Longman and Todd, 1963), pp. 279–95.

8 S 3.12; see above, pp. 200–2.

9 These signs do not exactly correspond with a parallel set in N 1.9, where San Juan distinguishes negative dryness in prayer, caused by human failure (e.g. the snares of the seven deadly spiritual sins), from positive dryness, the result of the passive purgation of the senses. But both sets differentiate the positive action of God in the soul from the negative results of human laziness, when the symptoms are similar.

10 On the 'pájaro solitario', see above, pp. 175, 185. 'Nescivi' is used in the commentary on C 7's 'no sé qué' (CB 7.9–8.1) without reference to Song 6.11.

11 'The reason why Meditation is impossible is that, when one takes to prayer, the intellect is engaged in doing something else; viz. contemplating. But this Contemplation is so obscure that it is unperceived. It is subconscious, like the circulation of the blood, but just as real'; *The Spiritual Letters of Dom John Chapman*, ed. Dom Roger Hudleston, 2nd edn (London: Sheed and Ward, 1941), p. 25.

12 See above, pp. 167–8.

13 See CB 25.5–6, on the 'toque de centella', 'touch of spark', in the poem; also the 'toque delicado' of 'Llama', v. 2; L 2.16–10; also S 2.32, below, p. 199. The image of the 'toque' is important to San Juan, and is usually a linguistic marker of an experience to be accepted rather than disregarded.
14 See José Vicente Rodríguez, 'Demonios y exorcismos, duendes y otras presencias diabólicas en la vida de San Juan de la Cruz', *Actas* II, pp. 295–346; especially pp. 308–9, the case of María de Olivares, of the Convento de Gracia, Ávila, 1574.
15 San Juan sometimes uses expressions like the 'substance', 'centre' or 'fund' ('fondo', 'bottom') of the soul to indicate a part which is safe from all demonic attacks; but it is never formally analysed by him, as the sensitive and spiritual parts are.
16 *Vida* 26.6; *Obras* (ST), p. 117.
17 The exception is in S 3.35.4; see below, pp. 206–7.
18 See Ana María Rizzuto, 'Reflexiones psicoanalíticas acerca de la experiencia mística', *El sol a medianoche*, pp. 61–75; C. P. Thompson, 'San Juan de la Cruz, Freud and the human soul', in *Conflicts of Discourse*, ed. Peter W. Evans (Manchester: Manchester University Press, 1990), pp. 166–83.
19 Iain Matthew, 'The Knowledge and Consciousness of Christ in the Writings of St John of the Cross', unpublished thesis (University of Oxford, 1991), p. 79.
20 See above, p. 212.
21 See above, pp. 63–4.
22 The word 'afección' has a particular meaning in San Juan's terminology as the impression one thing causes on another; see *Obras* (SJ), p. 1013.
23 Those who wish to read improving stories about how San Juan dealt with young women who approached him are advised to consult Crisógono de Jesús, *Vida y obras completas de San Juan de la Cruz* (Madrid: BAC, 1964), p. 238; José María Javierre, *Juan de la Cruz: Un caso límite* (Salamanca: Sígueme, 1992), pp. 13–14, 815.
24 Probably masturbation, but possibly homosexual acts.
25 S 3.31.4–5 might well be read alongside Calderón's *El mágico prodigioso* and the episode of the pardoner in *Lazarillo de Tormes*.
26 A good survey of Spanish Protestant attitudes to San Juan is given in Patrocinio Ríos Sánchez, 'Un protestante ante dos místicos: San Juan de la Cruz y fray Luis de León', *Revista agustiniana*, 32 (1991), pp. 1067–93.
27 San Juan does not take these, as modern scholarship does, to be the same place.
28 See above, pp. 4–5.
29 The final phrase echoes John 11.43, where Jesus calls out to the dead Lazarus to come forth from the tomb. San Juan seems to go further than St Augustine, the fourth book of whose *De doctrina christiana* deals with the art of preaching, in terms of the preacher's exemplarity having greater significance than his words: see *Obras de San Agustín*, ed. Balbino Martín, 2nd edn, 22 vols (Madrid: BAC, 1969), XV, especially iv.12–13, 27–8.
30 These strictures on excessive rigour may reflect his experience of the community at Pastrana, which was a source of great worry to Santa Teresa and of continuing tensions within the Discalced Reform.
31 Encouraged in *The Imitation of Christ*, iv.3. Teresa herself recounts how, because she liked to receive large Hosts, San Juan once taught her a lesson by giving her only half; *Cuentas de conciencia*, 25. She also describes problems associated with frequent communion, *Fundaciones*, 6.9–23.
32 See above, pp. 195, 223.
33 On the ligature, see Hudleston, ed., *The Spiritual Letters of Dom John Chapman*, pp. 316–17; Norbert Cummins, *Freedom to Rejoice: Understanding St John of the Cross* (London: HarperCollins, 1991), p. 136.
34 J. V. Rodríguez, 'Noche oscura', *Introducción*, p. 420.
35 This last is the subject of some of his letters; see above, pp. 129–30.
36 Iain Matthew's suggestion, 'Knowledge and Consciousness', pp. 253–4.

37 On this image in his letters, see above, pp. 48, 129.
38 See Matthew, 'Knowledge and Consciousness', pp. 110–11, for San Juan's 'powerful realized eschatology'.
39 For another example of the simile, see Fray Luis de León, 'Esposo', *De los nombres de Cristo*; *Obras completas castellanas*, ed. Félix García (Madrid: BAC, 1957), I, pp. 669–70.
40 For the implications of N 2.17 on San Juan's theory of language, see above, pp. 234–5.
41 See my 'The Many Paradoxes of the Mystics' in *Homenaje a Eugenio Asensio*, ed. Luisa López Grigera y Augustin Redondo (Madrid: Gredos, 1988), especially pp. 484–5.
42 An honourable exception is Hans Urs von Balthasar, *The Glory of the Lord: A Theological Aesthetics*, 7 vols (Edinburgh: T. & T. Clark, 1982–), III, pp. 105–71.
43 Matthew, 'Knowledge and Consciousness', pp. 246, 250.
44 See José Vicente Rodríguez, *Introducción*, p. 407.
45 E.g. S 2.5.10; 2.17.4; L 3.25; and especially N 1.9.9, 1.14.5.
46 In N 2.22.2 he admits that his task is virtually done: 'esta noche [. . .] está ya medianamente declarado y dado a entender', 'this night [. . .] has already been explained to some extent', though he adds 'harto menos de lo que [el]lo es', 'much less than its nature requires'.
47 Matthew, 'Knowledge and Consciousness', p. 143.
48 See, for example, St Anselm, 'Prayer to St Paul' and 'Prayer to Christ', in *Prayers and Meditations of St Anselm* (Harmondsworth: Penguin, 1973), pp. 153–6; Julian of Norwich, *Revelations of Divine Love* (Harmondsworth: Penguin, 1966), pp. 164–71.

9

Silent Music

El está sobre el cielo y habla en camino de eternidad; nosotros, ciegos, sobre la tierra, y no entendemos sino vías de carne y tiempo.

He is above heaven and speaks in the way of eternity; we, blind, upon earth, only understand ways of flesh and time.

(S 2.20.5)

We have already encountered a number of times the central paradox which informs all mystical literature: mystics habitually state that language cannot communicate the intensity of the experiences they are attempting to describe, but language is all they have to achieve this impossible goal. For this reason, William James made ineffability the first of the four marks by which he believed it was possible to recognize an experience as mystical, and his view has been widely accepted.[1] Yet inexpressibility as a defining characteristic of mystical experience needs some qualification. It is often associated with *admiratio*, a sense of wonder which words cannot capture. Nor is it an uncommon reaction to intense human experiences of many kinds – intense love, loss through bereavement, the beauty of nature: 'Sin embargo, algo canta entre estas palabras fugaces./Algo canta, algo sube hasta mi ávida boca', 'Even so, something sings in these fugitive words./Something sings, something climbs to my ravenous mouth', wrote Neruda in his *Veinte poemas*.[2] At such moments, what appear to be tired cliches become filled with meaning for the person who has passed through the experience: 'Words cannot say what I feel.'

But poets have other linguistic resources than everyday speech on which to call, and may capture through image and allusion some fragment of significance. As San Juan shows, both as a poet and as a commentator on his poems, language and literary techniques exist which can be pressed into service to attempt to resolve the dilemma. Indeed, each of the forms of linguistic expression he used – rhetorical techniques, different poetic traditions, the analytical tools of scholastic theology – provided some assistance. In his writings, nevertheless, there is a real tension between the demands of the way of faith – the emptying of the faculties, the dispossession of all mental constructs of God – and the compulsion to express the joy of union. Despite what he says about the need to abandon even meditation focused on pictures from the Bible, scripture contained a treasure-house of images inspired by the Holy Spirit. The writings of the Fathers, Doctors and spiritual teachers of the Church who had wrestled with scripture and sought to expound its significance for Christian lives provided another authoritative source of reflection on its text. San Juan was familiar with them, and had also read at least some of the medieval mystics as well as spiritual writers from the first half of his own century. Nor should one underestimate the importance of oral tradition: conversations, especially those with nuns and friars who had advanced far on the mystical road, both offered him and stimulated him into creating new ways of overcoming the limits of human expression. In all these respects, it is a qualified ineffability to which he is referring when he writes of the impossibility of finding an adequate language for the experience he wished to communicate. It is therefore more accurate to think of language in the first instance as a kind of stammer, which suggests meaning but cannot communicate more than a fractured version of it.

In Christian tradition, there are two main strands of thought about the relationship between language and God. One is positive (the technical term is 'cataphatic'), and sees likenesses between objects and concepts which belong to the world of human experience and the nature of God. Its language is affirmative, and its characteristic modes of expression are simile and metaphor, though it recognizes their limits. God may be described as a rock, but it is his strength and stability which the image suggests, not the nature of his being. It is associated with a theology of immanence of God, which stresses the image and likeness of the Creator in his human creation (Genesis 1.26–7), and leads to a spirituality which rises in steps from the known to the unknown, from contemplation of the book of nature to its Author.[3] The other strand is negative, or apophatic, and denies that human language can convey anything at all about God. It is encountered more in the Christian East than the Christian West, and the name of Dionysius the Areopagite is indelibly associated with it. It springs from the theology of transcendence, which insists on the complete ontological separation between the Creator and creation, on the otherness and unknowability of God and on the impossibility of any language capable of bridging the abyss between the human and the divine. Its spirituality is one of purgation of the soul from its natural concerns and desires, so that it may commune with God in darkness and nothingness. Its language is one of paradox, antithesis and oxymoron, of maintaining two or more contradictory assertions, neither of which is true by itself yet both of which are true when held together, as a sign of some deeper, hidden meaning which, once grasped, can resolve the tension between them.[4]

San Juan is the inheritor of both these traditions. The language he uses reflects both immanence and transcendence. In broad terms, his poetry belongs to the affirmative way, though it contains lines which witness to the insufficiency of language – the 'no sé qué' (C 7) stammered by the creatures, 'y no quieras decillo' (CA 32), 'and do not say it', the repeated 'aquello' (CA 37), 'that thing'. His spiritual teaching, enshrined in his prose commentaries on the poems, focuses largely but by no means exclusively on the negative way. We have noted, nonetheless, that his negations always have a positive intent: he negates the lesser in order to affirm something greater. Human language is bound by its creatureliness. Like any other creature in San Juan's system, it cannot be the direct means of union with God. It falls silent before the ineffable mystery of the Godhead.

San Juan has a lot to say about his own writing in particular and language in general. Here, more than in the little we know about his education and in the virtual absence of any first person references to his experiences and how these inspired him to write, are found at least the outlines of his poetic theory, which proves to be highly unusual, even for an age of faith, as the Golden Age is commonly perceived to be. His words are often enough quoted, but their full significance has perhaps not been sufficiently realized.

The briefest statement of San Juan's mystical poetics – for that is what they are – comes from Magdalena del Espíritu Santo, a nun who had known him early in her religious life and who submitted information to one of his first biographers some 50 years later. Despite the hagiographical overtones of much of this material, there is no compelling reason why she should have invented these words for San Juan. One day, she says, she asked him about his poems, and whether or not God had given him those words so full of meaning and so beautifully expressed. 'Hija, algunas veces me las daba Dios, y otras las buscaba yo'; 'Daughter', he replied, 'sometimes God gave them to me and sometimes I found them for myself.'[5] The meaning is clear enough to dispel any lingering notion of his poetry as an entirely spontaneous creation, a divine infusion if not fury, a view espoused by critics like Menéndez y Pelayo, and implying that San Juan was somehow spared the normal constraints and frustrations of other poets.[6] There is inspiration, there are words and phrases which arrive ready minted in the imagination, as if from nowhere; those San Juan understands to have been given him by God. But there are others for which he has to work, for which acts of conscious creation are required. What is more remarkable is that this twofold source of his poetry matches exactly the fundamental division of his mystical teaching into active and passive spheres. His searching for words parallels the part the soul plays in preparing itself through the mortifications and purifications of the active nights of sense and spirit; his receiving of words, the moments when God takes the initiative and gives the soul growth which it could never earn by its own labours.

More substantial, and in greater need of elucidation, are the prologues he wrote for his three prose treatises, which I shall look at in their probable order of composition.[7] These prologues do not set out to produce a poetic theory: San Juan intends them to assist his readers to follow his expositions. But since the commentaries function in varying degrees as explanations of poetic texts, his remarks have relevance in literary terms too.

The topos of ineffability is the starting point of San Juan's theory. The writer cannot put into words all that he would like to say, and the reader will not find the meaning of his words he does use to be clear or defined, because the subject matter does not permit it. Writer and reader must therefore acknowledge limitations of expression and comprehension. The *Cántico* prologue is as close as San Juan comes to elaborating a poetic theory which relates mystical experience to the begetting of art. In it, he tells us that his verses were composed 'with a certain burning love of God', '*parecen* ser escritas con *algún* fervor de amor de Dios' (.1). The double modifier (literally, they '*seem*' to be written with '*some* fervour'; my emphases) acts to remind the reader that no human expression can be other than an incomplete response to the immense wisdom and love of God. Nor does he believe he can expound the full meaning of his own words, since they cannot convey the breadth and riches of the experiences they symbolize.

But the experiences recorded in the verses are of such power that 'con comparaciones y semejanzas antes rebosan algo de lo que sienten y de la abundancia del espíritu vierten secretos y misterios que con razones lo declaran', they 'overflow in figures and similes' (literally, 'comparisons'), and they are born out of such spiritual abundance that they 'pour out secrets and mysteries rather than rational explanations'.[8] This poetry is an overflow from experience, in one sense prolonging it by representing it in words, in another incapable of containing it within the selected signifier. The notion of language as an overflow of experience is explained more fully in S 2.26.2, when San Juan is writing about a certain type of revelation which 'consiste en entender y ver verdades de Dios o de las cosas que son, fueron y serán', 'consist of understanding and seeing truths about God or about things which are, were, and shall be' – truths, that is, about the Creator or the creatures. The former are incomparably more nourishing, and may consist of a very high knowledge of divine attributes like omnipotence or goodness, which are ineffable. Yet one of the biblical texts he cites to confirm this teaching, Exodus 34.6–7, in which Moses speaks eloquently of God's mercy, goodness and truth, shows how after his vision of the 'back parts' of God in 33.18–23 Moses '*rebosó* por todas aquellas palabras' (.4), '*overflowed* through all those words' to express something he could not otherwise have said (my emphases). San Juan uses the same verb of Moses' words as he does of his own poetry. But this is not a rational, ordered or intelligible overflow, as the secular pastoral eclogues of Garcilaso or the love sonnets of Herrera might be. Unless these images are read in the same spirit of love and understanding which brought them into being, 'antes parecen dislates que dichos puestos en razón', 'they will seem more like nonsense than rationally ordered discourse'.

The irrationality of some forms of erotic love is a commonplace element in pastoral prose and poetry of the age. In Garcilaso's second Eclogue Albanio is driven mad by his unrequited passion for Camila. Pastoral romances are full of lovers who have lost their reason through their lover's absence, faithlessness or death, while jealousy often provokes irrational behaviour. The tension between reason and passion as they struggle for dominance in a lover's heart is a constant theme of Renaissance neo-Platonic love poetry. However, San Juan's description of his poetry as beyond rational discourse and as apparent nonsense should not be pressed too literally, because its explanation lies elsewhere. Human reason itself is an inadequate instrument for conveying the glories of divine union. Its attempts to do so appear irrational because of the inadequacy of a created organ to express truths concerning the uncreated Creator. San Juan may use the same language as his secular counterparts, but to a quite different end. Like many other mystics, he will use images of madness and inebriation (e.g. CB 2.7–11), but to point to a higher order of reason, just as he will use images of darkness to represent the experience of dazzling light.

San Juan's verses, therefore, represent and are witnesses to the mystical experience, but cannot enclose or define it. Poetic space cannot contain the experience it marks, and one of the signs of this is that the poetic language itself is as different from that of other poetry as the experiences represented transcend those of ordinary human experience; unless correctly read, its 'semejanzas' will seem to be 'dislates' rather than 'dichos puestos en razón'. Such strange language is not, however, restricted to human poets, for he goes on to say that the same process is found in scripture, notably in the Song of Solomon. The Holy Spirit cannot use ordinary language ('términos vulgares y usados') to express the fulness of his intended meaning, and therefore 'habla misterios en extrañas figuras y semejanzas', 'utters mysteries through strange figures and likenesses'. Moreover, no interpreter, not even the saints and doctors of the Church, can exhaust the meaning of these: 'lo que dello se declara ordinariamente es lo menos que contiene en sí', 'the explanation of these expressions usually contains less than [literally 'the least of'] what they themselves embody'.[9] Thus the scriptures provide him with the authoritative model not only for his teaching but also for his poetics, consistent with the long tradition which saw the Bible as the divinely inspired model of sacred rhetoric, a literary analogue to its nature as the repository of divine revelation.

The obscurity of biblical language had been dealt with most formatively for Western tradition by St Augustine, who argued in *De doctrina christiana* (II.6) that its presence signalled to the expositor, among other things, a depth of meaning in the text which required great spiritual perception to uncover. San Juan was more likely to have acquired his views from such a source, directly or indirectly, than from contemporary poets. But poetic obscurity was also an idea beloved of the Renaissance neo-Platonists: Ficino had written of how the 'prisci theologi', the ancient theologians (that is, the corpus of wisdom from a variety of pre-Christian sources and associated with the supposed original knowledge of Adam, secret revelations to Moses and other hermetic traditions) had protected sacred truths against profanation from the vulgar with 'hedges of metaphor'.[10] Its application to poetry developed through the sixteenth century in Spain, as poets sought to enrich Castilian by introducing new words drawn from Latin and Greek and borrowing classical syntactical features. The process reached its culmination in the difficult and often obscure poetry of Góngora in the seventeenth century, which he himself justified on the grounds that he wished to protect its core of essential truth from the vulgar horde, even if one suspects that much of his writing was an elaborate and witty game.

But the obscurities and absurdities of his own poetry, the strange and mysterious language which his art, in common with the Bible, has produced, is not for San Juan a form of protection by the elite, a marking off of space which the ignorant have no means of entering. It would be a mistake to imagine that he anticipates Góngora's conscious cult of obscurity any more than his reference to irrationality leads him in the same direction as neo-Platonic love poets. San Juan's role as artist is more limited, since by his own confession in the prologue he is only partly the creator and cannot be the entire interpreter of his verse. Its difficulty does not close it off from those without the educational skills to solve its paradoxes and puzzles; anyone may read it with a level of understanding, provided they are learned in the love of God. And he proves the point that appreciation of verse and commentary alike is unconnected with intellectual accomplishments of themselves by dedicating the *Cántico* to a woman who, as he points out, lacks formation in scholastic theology 'con que se entienden las verdades divinas', 'by which divine truths are understood' but who is skilled in mystical theology, 'que se sabe por amor, en que no solamente se saben, mas juntamente su gustan', 'which is known through love and not only known but at the same time enjoyed' (.3).

Finally, he underlines that his role as expositor is strictly limited. He can only shed 'alguna luz general' (.2), 'some general light' on the verses, because the subject matter, divine love, precludes any fuller account. In any case, he does not want to restrict the sense, since, as he observes, not every palate has the same tastes. Nor is it necessary to tie oneself down to his exposition: 'no hay para qué atarse a la declaración'. He certainly does not mean that any interpretation which occurs to the reader will do, because he follows this statement by explaining that mystical wisdom is not dependent on a precise understanding (presumably of each expression) for its effects of love to be felt in the soul. What he seems to be saying is that the reader should not be worried if it is hard to follow the given explanation; 'something' will be understood, for in the end 'something' (as George Herbert wrote in 'Prayer (1)'), San Juan's 'un no sé qué', 'I know not what', is all that can be understood.

The four paragraphs of this prologue, which constitutes the heart of San Juan's poetic theory, or rather, theology of poetry, contain surprising ideas, often at variance with the theories of his own age, occasionally strikingly modern. He does not read his text as a closed one, and he freely acknowledges that it contains far more than either he or any one reader can wrest from it. But he warns that whoever approaches it with different motives from those which led to its composition will only find nonsense there. Twentieth-century versions of these 'dislates' might be critics who can only find in his poetry the outpourings of a repressed or a sublimated sexuality, or of an unbalanced mind. In any case, his reference to 'dislates' is subtler than it appears. He probably has in mind Paul's words in 1 Corinthians 1.18–31, which contrast the wisdom of the world with the saving foolishness of God, displayed on the cross. His own poetry will be a stammering witness to that divine folly. San Juan thus signals a radical departure from the poetics of the greatest love poets of his century, which gives pause for thought. If his theory is so distinctive, is it surprising that his poetry is so unlike theirs?

The prologue to the *Subida-Noche*, as we have noted, is primarily concerned with the errors of inexperienced confessors who harm souls in their charge, but it too insists on the ineffability of the subject and the consequent obscurity of the explanations, especially at the start. The dark night as doctrine is matched by a linguistic and conceptual dark night: 'por cuanto esta doctrina es de la noche oscura por donde el alma ha de ir a Dios, no se maraville el lector si le pareciere algo oscura', 'inasmuch as the teaching concerns the dark night by which the soul is to go to God, let the reader not be surprised if it seems somewhat dark to him' (.8). He believes the darkness will lighten as the reader proceeds, and that by the end of a second reading a degree of clarity will have been reached, so he does not expect his commentary to be read rapidly or only once. He makes a conventional apology for his lack of knowledge and low style ('mi poco saber y bajo estilo') and warns that the work is not for all spiritual people, and certainly not those who want something sweet and enjoyable. In fact, his intention is only to address 'algunas personas de nuestra sagrada Religión de los primitivos del Monte Carmelo, así frailes como monjas' (.9), 'some members of our holy Order of the primitive [hermits] of Mount Carmel, friars as well as nuns', that is, those Discalced Carmelites who have asked him to explain the mystical journey – not even all members of the Carmelite Reform, and certainly not, it appears, modern readers for whom 'nakedness of spirit' ('desnudez de espíritu'), the last phrase of the prologue, is an almost incomprehensible notion, rather than a studied way of life.

Whether San Juan would have written his commentaries at all if he had not been pressed to do so must remain an open question. But the fact that his intended readership was so limited inevitably imposes constraints on his writing and helps to explain some of the discomfort readers of more recent times experience in approaching him. There are many things he takes for granted which many of his contemporaries in the world beyond the cloister, let alone four centuries later, would have found obscure. Unlike almost all the great figures of Spanish Golden Age literature, San Juan did not write for publication or to be read and admired by the literate classes. Even Santa Teresa reached a wider audience when her works began to be published soon after her death. San Juan's work is more like the record of a private conversation between friends than a form of explanation of his ideas in the public arena, and that must be borne in mind when assessing it.

What is certain is that the stimulus for writing poetry was, in a sense, self-generated, the result of a desire to say something, however inadequate, about experiences so wonderful that they compelled response. In neither case, though, are his stated motives as a writer anything like those of his contemporaries. He does not, as Cristóbal Cuevas notes, seek glory, popularity or fame, nor is he flattering noble dedicatees in order to encourage them to be his patrons.[11] In this respect, San Juan's prologues are very different from those of other Golden Age writers. Theirs are often difficult to interpret, but for other reasons – they are playful (Cervantes), they keep a perhaps ironic eye on the censors, or indulge in the topos of 'I tossed this off in an idle moment in my youth' (Fray Luis de León) – whereas San Juan is telling us that the subject matter itself is the cause of any difficulty the reader may experience, together with his own inadequacies as an expositor.

The prologue to the *Llama*, the shortest of the three, is addressed to Ana de Peñalosa, the devout widow who had followed him from Granada to Segovia. But it does provide two further insights into San Juan's sense of himself as a writer. He explains that he has felt obliged to allow some time to elapse between the writing of the poem and the explanation she has requested, 'hasta ahora que el Señor parece que ha abierto un poco la noticia y dado algún calor' (.1), 'until it seems the Lord has opened up my knowledge a little and given [me] some enthusiasm [for it]'. The treatise evidently had more to do with San Juan finding the words than the Lord giving him them; writing it required both ability and motivation, which were not immediately available. For this hard task he shows a certain (though possibly rhetorical) reluctance. He also clarifies the relationship between his biblically inspired writing and scripture itself. If it is surprising that he expounds his own words in the poetry in the same way as he expounds the biblical quotations which are intended to confirm his teaching, here he depicts the relationship between what he can write and what scripture contains in terms of the distance between what is painted and what is alive ('tanto menor [. . .] como es lo pintado que lo vivo').[12] Nevertheless, 'me atreveré a decir lo que supiere', 'I shall make bold to say whatever I may know.' The distance between the image and reality is a frequent theme of Golden Age literature: one thinks of Calderón's *El pintor de su deshonra*, in which Don Juan Roca is unable to capture the beauty of his young wife on canvas, though he will successfully paint her in blood when, commissioned to paint the portrait of an unknown beauty whom he recognizes to be his abducted wife, he shoots both her and the man he mistakenly believes to be her lover at the end of the play. Likewise, Cervantes makes great play of the distance between the picture and the truth in the *Persiles*.[13]

But the *Llama* prolongs the discussion of language into the beginning of the exposition proper, where San Juan becomes his own literary critic. He notes that the deep feelings expressed in the poem are represented by the frequent exclamations '¡Oh!' and '¡cuán!', which 'dan a entender del interior más de lo que se dice por la lengua; y sirve el '¡Oh!' para mucho desear y para mucho rogar persuadiendo' (L 1.2), 'provide greater understanding from within than can be expressed by the tongue; and the oh! serves to express great desiring and much beseeching by means of persuasion'. Hence the apparently insignificant exclamations around which the whole poem is constructed convey by their very inarticulacy a depth of meaning beyond the reach of more discursive language. The soul's words belong to a language appropriate for communication with God, and are expressive of a greater interior content than words on the tongue can utter: 'Y éste es el lenguaje y palabras que trata Dios en las almas purgadas y limpias, que son palabras todas encendidas', 'And this is the language, these are the words which God speaks in purged and cleansed souls; they are all inflamed words' (L 1.5). This inflammation of language is 'viva', 'living', because it speaks words of eternal life (John 4.28, 6.68) and brings with it a lively enjoyment of God (Psalm 83. [84.]3), 'lo cual es gustar a Dios vivo, esto es, vida de Dios y vida eterna' (L 1.6), 'which is to taste the living God, that is, the life of God and eternal life'. The three words '¡Oh!', 'llama' and 'viva', from the first line of the poem, thus become substantive in defining the nature of the language the poem represents.

San Juan makes many points in a short space. The poem means more than the sum total of its verbal signs; the signified is greater than the signifiers. It therefore uses language in a different way from normal human discourse, for this is language inflamed. It only speaks to those who are pure enough to receive it, otherwise, we may assume (following the remarks in the prologue to the *Cántico*) it will appear baffling. If inflamed language is also living language, witnessing to the eternal enjoyment of God in a union of love, then such language is the closest it is possible to come to a verbal representation of the ineffable.

Language as overflow and language as inflammation are both images of excess. But there is a difference between them. The poetry of the 'Cántico' is, as it were, what has spilled over from the experience and solidified into words which point back to it. The poetry of the 'Llama' is the experience itself, always struggling to find articulation, leaping upwards to become what it is. In analysing the 'Noche' and the 'Cántico',

I argued that the literary texture of the poems seems to bear out his claims. For that reason, there is something as distinctive about his poetic language as there is about his poetic theory, in comparison with his contemporaries who sang of the joys and sorrows of a purely human love.

The nature of this distinctiveness is the theme of N 2.17, an important chapter for understanding that the topos of inexpressibility is not a pretext for avoiding critical analysis but something closely connected with an essential part of San Juan's teaching, in which the three faculties of intellect, memory and will must be emptied of all forms of natural activity. The starting point for this discussion is the 'secreta escala' of the 'Noche oscura' poem (v. 2, l.2), down (or up) which the subject of the poem goes to enter the darkness and to begin the journey to her lover. This 'contemplación oscura', 'dark contemplation' of 'la teología mística' (17.2), 'mystical theology' is called secret because it is infused by divine love and is beyond the capacity of mind, memory or will to grasp.

This emptying of the three faculties must also include all their images and concepts of God. They have to be emptied of such finite things because only when they are so purified can they be free to concentrate on their true object of knowledge and love, the infinite one for which they were created, God himself. That is why San Juan describes knowledge in this state as general or confused ('noticia general', 'confusa'), for it is not like ordinary human ways of knowing, attached to words, concepts or pictures. These have now been purged from the mind, just as all false desires and hopes have been purged from the will and the memory, which instead fix themselves with a 'loving attention' ('advertencia amorosa') on God. Once this process is complete, the soul knows something and knows that this something is knowledge of God. But there are no words or images associated with this knowledge. What the soul does and what she receives in this purified state is no longer bound to the categories of created knowledge which language can name, so that she cannot find 'modo ni manera ni símil que le cuadre para poder significar inteligencia tan subida y sentimiento espiritual tan delicado' (17.3), 'any means or manner or simile which is fitting to be able to signify so lofty an intelligence and so delicate a spiritual feeling'. However much she would like to express it, and however many meanings it might contain, she is unable to do so:

> porque como aquella sabiduría interior es tan sencilla y tan general y espiritual, que no entró al entendimiento envuelta ni paliada [con] alguna especie o imagen sujeta al sentido, de aquí es que el sentido e imaginativa, como no entró por ellas ni sintieron su traje y color, no saben dar razón ni imaginarla para decir algo della.

> because since that inner wisdom is so simple and general and spiritual, and entered the understanding without any species or image subject to the senses, neither sense nor imagination can give account of it or imagine it in order to to say anything about it, since it did not enter them, nor did they perceive its dress or colour.

At the same time, the soul clearly understands this strange knowledge, but, like someone seeing something which has never been seen before, can find no words for it. Divine language functions exactly like this: 'Porque esto tiene el lenguaje de Dios, que, por muy íntimo al alma y espiritual, en que excede todo sentido, luego hace cesar y enmudecer toda la armonía y habilidad de los sentidos exteriores y interiores' (.3), 'the language of God is such that, since it is very intimate to the soul, and spiritual, exceeding every sense, it at once makes all the harmony and skill of the exterior and interior senses cease and fall silent'. San Juan cites the two clearest biblical examples of the inability to communicate, both of which tell of a call by God to speak on his behalf. Jeremiah is called to be a prophet when still a child, and his response in the Vulgate is a tongue-tied stammer, 'A, A, A' (Jeremiah 1.6). Moses at the burning bush argues that he is the wrong person to deliver God's demands to Pharaoh because he is not a gifted speaker (Exodus 4.10). Thus, when God speaks to the soul spirit to spirit, as in these archetypal cases and in unitive prayer, 'todo lo que es menos que espíritu, como son los sentidos, no lo perciben, y así les es secreto y no lo sabe ni lo pueden decir, ni tienen gana, porque no ven cómo' (.4), 'everything which is less than spirit, like the senses, cannot perceive it, and so it is a secret to them and they neither can nor know how to express it, nor do they wish to, because they cannot see how to'. The result of lofty experiences of contemplation is to make the soul aware of the limitations of ordinary language, rather than its impossibility:

> le hace [. . .] ver cuán bajos y cortos y en alguna manera impropios son todos los términos y vocablos con que en esta vida se trata de las cosas divinas, y cómo es imposible por vía y modo natural, aunque más alta y sabiamente se hable en ellas, poder conocer ni sentir de ellas como ellas son, sin la iluminación de esta *mística teología*. Y así, viendo el alma en la iluminación de ella esta verdad de que no se puede alcanzar ni menos declarar con términos vulgares y humanos, con razón la llama *secreta*. (.6)

> it makes her realize how lowly, deficient and to some extent inadequate all the expressions and words which deal with divine things in this life are, and how impossible it is, through any natural means and forms, however loftily and wisely they may be articulated, to know or feel them as they are, without the illumination of this *mystical theology*. Hence, seeing by its illumination the truth that this cannot be grasped or explained in ordinary human terms, the soul rightly calls it *secret*.

It is impossible to give an accurate account of such experiences through a normal use of language, but it is possible to hint at their presence and, by implication, to express something of their power when the writer uses language in unconventional or unexpected ways, so that its very strangeness becomes a textual indication of a meaning it cannot otherwise express. The inappropriateness of finite words to describe infinite realities is made explicit in L 1.10, where, expounding the image of the 'centro' of the soul, San Juan is at pains to state that all such language is metaphorical:

> el alma en cuanto espíritu no tiene alto ni bajo, más profundo y menos profundo, en su ser, como tienen los cuerpos cuantitativos, que, pues en ella no hay partes, no tiene más diferencia dentro que fuera, que toda ella es de una manera y no tiene centro de hondo y menos hondo cuantitativo, porque no puede estar en una parte más ilustrada que en otra, como los cuerpos físicos, sino todo en una manera en más o en menos, como el aire, que todo está de una manera ilustrado y no ilustrado en más o en menos.

> the soul, as spirit, has no height or depth, no greater or lesser depth in its being, as measurable bodies do, for since it contains no parts there is no difference between its inside and outside; it is all of the same kind and has no measurable centre which is more or less deep, because it cannot receive greater illumination in one part than in another, like physical bodies, but is all illuminated to a greater or lesser extent, like the air, which is all illumined or not illumined to the same degree.

It follows that all the spatial or physical language San Juan has to use about the soul and, by extension, about any spiritual entity, cannot be treated literally.

This is equally true of language about God. Here San Juan touches a contemporary theological nerve. He gathers some of his favourite texts in S 2.8.4 to show how even the greatest biblical figures – Moses, Elijah, Isaiah, Paul and John – were unable in their mortal state to see God as he is. Every picture the imagination can create, every supernatural revelation received in the flesh, will be 'muy disímil y desproporcionado [. . .] a Dios' (S 2.8.5), 'very unlike God and disproportionate to him'. Introducing the need for souls to make the difficult transition from meditation to contemplation (S 2.12), he asserts again that all words and images are inadequate for a God who always transcends them. It is the same pseudo-Dionysian view of religious language to which he alludes in the *Cántico* prologue, but its implications are more far-reaching and were to be debated long after his death, because they affect all theological discourse. 'Los que imaginan a Dios debajo de algunas figuras déstas, o como un gran fuego o resplandor, o tras cualesquier formas, y piensan que algo de aquello será semejante a El, harto lejos van dél' (12.5), 'those who imagine God under any of these figures, like a great fire or brightness, or any other form, and think that something of it will be like him, are very far from him'. Beginners may need such meditations to nourish their souls in love, but at some stage they will need to pass beyond them. Since such pictures of God are not God, they can only be creatures, and since finite creatures are an indirect, not a direct means of reaching the infinity of God, they cannot bring the soul to union with him, and must be put aside.

A more scholastic explanation for this is provided in S 3.12:

> las criaturas, ahora terrenas, ahora celestiales, y todas las noticias e imágenes distintas, naturales y sobrenaturales, que pueden caer en las potencias del alma, por altas que sean ellas en esta vida, ninguna comparación ni proporción tienen con el ser de Dios, por cuanto Dios no cae

> debajo de género y especie, y ellas sí, [. . .] y el alma en esta vida no es capaz de recibir clara y distintamente sino lo que cae debajo de género y especie. (12.1)

> all the creatures, earthly or heavenly, and all distinct forms of knowledge and images, natural and supernatural, which can enter the soul's faculties, however lofty they be in this life, bear no comparison or proportion with the being of God, since God falls under neither genus nor species and they do [. . .] and the soul in this life is only capable of receiving what comes into the category of genus and species.

In a 'baja comparación' (12.2), a 'lowly comparison', San Juan endeavours to explain that to confuse the two would be like paying greater attention to the servants (the creatures) than to the king (God). God is not like the images and pictures which the mind stores of him, and Dionysian theological negativities once again become the foundation for the corresponding spiritual discipline: God 'no tiene imagen, ni forma, ni figura' (13.1), 'has no image, form or figure', and the closer one draws to him 'tanto cuanto más se enajenare de todas formas y imágenes y figuras imaginarias', 'the more he is removed from all imaginary forms, images and figures'. As soon as any faculty tries to take an active part in the process it interferes with God's work of passive infusion by introducing a lower, creaturely form of activity, since the faculties can only work with forms, figures and images, which are 'la corteza y accidente de la sustancia y espíritu que hay debajo de la tal corteza y accidente' (13.4), 'the bark [or rind, skin] and accident of the substance and spirit beneath this bark and accident'.

The only language which is of any use is the language of analogy – exactly the point San Juan makes in the prologue to the *Cántico*. Being in love, contemplating a beautiful view or losing someone close can never fully be described; the experience itself can never accurately be represented by the analogies or stammerings which we struggle to articulate in order to communicate it to others. If that is true in purely human terms, it is also true of any experience of God unmediated by what San Juan calls 'created species', that is, beyond the range of words, concepts and images. His contemporary Malón de Chaide connects this with the neo-Aristotelian epistemology of scholasticism. In a surprising attack for an Augustinian on Plato's doctrine of the soul he defends the Aristotelian doctrine of the *tabula rasa*, in which the soul can only come to know through the 'windows' of the five senses. It follows from this that the soul wishing to imagine God and his glory 'no puede pensar sino un Dios con cuerpo, con rostro, con pies y cabeza; y que hay oro, piedras preciosas, plata, ciudades, ríos, fuentes, jardines y cosas de este talle, que ni las hay allá ni aun valieran mucho para allá', 'cannot but think of God with a body, face, feet and head; and that there is gold, precious stones, silver, cities, rivers, fountains and gardens and things of that kind there, which there certainly are not nor would they be much use'.[14] The soul has no other choice than corporeal metaphor derived from her sense-based knowledge – 'las especies o semejanzas de las cosas que tiene en la memoria', 'the species or likenesses of the things she has in her memory' – so that when she wishes to think of heaven, she 'finge solamente las cosas que tiene noticia, que son las que ha visto acá en la tierra', 'imitates only those things of which she has knowledge, which are those she has seen here on earth'. He does not pursue the logic of this view, as San Juan does, to address the whole nature of religious language, but he provides an important witness to the link between Aristotle and Aquinas on the one hand and negative theology on the other.

Ideas of this kind are obviously of interest to contemporary literary theory. Those who have written of the arbitrariness of language, of the way there is nothing fixed about it, of its inability to communicate meaning, should not be surprised that a mystic who has inherited a pseudo-Dionysian attitude to language warns us how slippery language can be, especially when readers assume that his words convey settled meanings. Postmodernist thinkers are not the first to have meditated on the inadequacy of language to perform what it claims to be doing, any more than nineteenth- and twentieth-century theologians are to have questioned the 'literal' meaning of the Bible or the Creeds. But San Juan is emphatically not a deconstructionalist theologian *avant la lettre*. He is simply expressing in his own way a constant trend in Christian thought. Words do not and cannot correspond to the realities they appear to represent when those realities are divine. To treat them as if they did is to make idols of them. In San Juan's terminology, they too are 'creatures', even those words of scripture through which the Creator has spoken, since they are accommodated to human limitations. As such, they can only point to a God who has already passed beyond their range.

In fact, San Juan begins from the same starting point as postmodernism – the unreliability of words – to argue a conclusion in radical opposition to theirs. He agrees that words in themselves can possess no ultimate value or truthfulness, not because none exists, but because they are by their very status as creatures unable to contain such absolutes. He seeks to preserve meaning and value by rescuing language from human attempts to confine God within its constructs. The inadequacies of human language do not therefore point to the failure of all meaning, value and truth but to their affirmation in God, who has made himself known and knowable in the Word made flesh. There is a particular kind of language which, taking its cue from the language of the Bible, can point towards or bear signs of divine truth. Such a language will always be closer to that of poetry than to prose.

This is very evident in the lyrical outpouring of CA 13–14, where San Juan explains that the images in these verses communicate the 'exceso' the soul feels but cannot express when God is everything to her except through 'la semejanza de la bondad de las cosas', 'through the likeness of the goodness of things'. This is cataphatic language indeed, dependent on a theological view which sees creation itself in terms of an overflow of divine energy and love. All the images in these verses, he says, represent what God is 'eminentemente en infinita manera' (14–15.5), 'pre-eminently and infinitely'; each one of them is God, together they are all God, and the soul united to God feels all things to be God. Like language, creation too provides its own inadequate witness to the presence of God. Since both words and created things belong to the same category of finitude and creaturelinesss, they can never be a proximate means to union. But the excess and the likeness present in these images, connecting back to what was said in the prologue about overflow and the language of metaphor, show that the creaturely can become part of the limited resources on which the poet can call to overcome total inarticulacy.

In such ways, embedded in the poem's language lies the same confession of qualified ineffability as the prose commentaries make in more explicit terms. The language of the Bible shares in this ability both to speak about God and to find speech impossible. Though words cannot express the way in which the soul in CB 12.9 thirsts for the presence of God, scriptural words supply the need: Psalm 41.2–3 (the hart thirsting for the waterbrooks), Job 3.24 (the soul suffering for food and roaring as the waters), Song 8.6 (love strong as death and hell), and 1 Chronicles 11.18, when thirsty David's mighty men break through the Philistine ranks to draw him water from the well of Bethlehem. San Juan contents himself by adding simply that the well of Bethlehem was Christ, an exegesis which depends on at least two unstated connections: Bethlehem the birthplace of Christ, and Christ the living water (John 4.14). The exposition of CB 38 is largely concerned with the meaning of the mysterious and twice-repeated 'aquello' and 'otro día' of the verse. This 'other day' is the eternity from which God predestined the soul even before its creation; 'that thing' is part of the topos of ineffability and finds scriptural warrant in 1 Corinthians 2.9 and its source, Isaiah 64.4, as well as in the letters to the seven churches in Revelation 2–3 and other biblical texts, because there is no single name or word which is adequate to convey the joy of eternal life to which the soul has been predestined, 'porque las cosas inmensas esto tienen, que todos los términos excelentes y de calidad y grandeza y bien le cuadran, mas ninguno de ellos le declaran, ni todos juntos' (38.8), 'because it is characteristic of immense things that all excellent, fine, great and good terms fit them, but none can explain them by itself, nor all together'.

Nonetheless, the following verse seeks to represent something of that ineffable thing: in other words, its five images – the breeze, the nightingale's song, the thicket, the calm night, the flame which consumes but does not hurt – are all understood by San Juan as a continuation of the inevitably inadequate exegesis of 'aquello', and stand in apposition to it. The soul cannot express herself as she wishes – 'Yet who can keep from speaking?' (39.1; Job 4.2). In 39.2 the 'aspirar del aire', 'blowing of the breeze', is given full Trinitarian weight: the Spirit lifts the soul in such a way that she 'aspire en Dios la misma aspiración de amor que el Padre aspira en el Hijo y el Hijo en el Padre, que es el mesmo Espíritu Santo que a ella la aspira en el Padre y el Hijo y la dicha transformación para unirla consigo' (39.3), 'breathes in God the same breath of love as the Father breathes in the Son and the Son in the Father, the very Holy Spirit, who breathes this into her in the Father and the Son, together with the said transformation, to unite her to himself'. Here, polyptoton ('aspire', 'aspiración', 'aspira') functions as an indicator of likeness between subject and object, the soul and God, since the same activity is predicated of both.

Such a transformation would be incomplete 'si no se transformase el alma en las tres Personas de la Santísima Trinidad en revelado y manifiesto grado', 'if the soul were not transformed in the three Persons of the most Holy Trinity to a clear and revealed degree'. It brings her 'tan subido y delicado y profundo deleite, que no hay decirlo por lengua mortal, ni el entendimiento human en cuanto tal puede alcanzar algo de ello', 'such lofty, delicate and deep delight that it cannot be spoken of by mortal tongue, nor can the human understanding as such grasp anything of it'. We seem to have come full circle: in one way, something can be uttered; in another, it surpasses language. The contradiction can only be resolved when we realize that both cataphatic and apophatic strategies of language are pointing in the same direction, the first by piling up images to show that even many cannot capture God, the second by embracing silence and refusal to name, to reach the same conclusion by the opposite route. Plenitude and negation are both signs of inexpressibility, and use different linguistic strategies to point to a meaning they cannot contain.

That is perhaps why lovers human and divine are so given to paradox, for it is another form of confession of the insufficiency of language. Each term of the paradox represents an image of the truth, yet each is incomplete without its contradiction, which represents another. Thus, in Petrarchan tradition, when I burn and I freeze at the same time, both terms are equally true and do not cancel each other out. I experience both my fiery passion and her cold disdain, which is to say that I am caught in an impossible situation. But in the hands of San Juan, paradox has a harder task to perform: it marks, verbally and conceptually, the point of breakdown of communication in language by suggesting that somewhere beneath the surface terms of the paradox, but inaccessible to more precise verbal formulation, lies a truth which transcends the limitations of speech. This we have already glimpsed in his popular poems; there are passages in the *Llama*, as we shall see in the last chapter, which use it to extraordinary effect.

Though he does not say so specifically, San Juan does not see his prose writings as moving his readers towards a greater love of God, since they begin from the assumption that they are already engaged in such an exercise. His apologies for his 'bajo estilo' are, perhaps, conventional, but he does connect style with content, pointing out that the teaching itself is demanding and contrasting it with the kind of spirituality which prefers a more pleasurable road:

> Pero paréceme que, aunque se escribiera más acabada y perfectamente de lo que aquí va, no se aprovecharan de ello sino los menos, porque aquí no se escribirán cosas muy morales y sabrosas para todos los espíritus que gustan de ir por cosas dulces y sabrosas a Dios, sino doctrina sustancial y sólida, así para los unos como para los otros, si quisieren pasar a la desnudez de espíritu que aquí se escribe. (S, Prol.8)

> But it seems to me that even if it were written in a more finished and perfect style than it is, only a few would benefit from it, because this book does not contain satisfying moral material for those spiritual people who like to approach God by a sweet and satisfying way, but solid and substantial doctrine for all kinds of people, should they wish to progress to the nakedness of spirit it describes.

He seems to be implying that an over-decorated, over-rhetorical style may be a hindrance rather than a help, since it would suggest that the road to God was paved with pleasure rather than its being the way of the cross.

Elsewhere, San Juan has other things to say about style and content. The third book of the *Subida* ends with a discussion of preaching to which attention has already been drawn.[15] There, he does not make the traditional contrast between style and content, the techniques used and the message they are intended to convey, between the pleasure derived from crafted speech and the truth to be inwardly apprehended. However fine the style and content may be, there is another element essential for the preacher in a way that these are not – the example of a holy life, more persuasive than any human artifice.

Nevertheless, having cited as his scriptural authority St Paul's description of his own preaching (1 Corinthians 2.1–4), he adds, almost as if worried that what he has said is too extreme, that he has no intention of condemning good style and rhetoric, since such language 'aun las cosas caídas y estragadas levanta y reedifica', 'raises and restores damaged and fallen things', just as the wrong kind of language damages and destroys good things. Yet even this nod in the direction of 'deleitar' emphasizes the moral power of language, and the phrase I have just cited suggests that San Juan's own poetry could be read as an attempt to restore the damage done to natural beauty or even human love by language insensitively used. But the success of a sermon is measured by the effect it has on the listener, whether or not it sets the will on fire to do good works, rather than on appreciation of its art. For that, the life of the preacher, a living example of holiness, is the true test. Simply to take pleasure in the words heard and to analyse them from a literary point of view may please the intellect but does not change the person. 'Enseñar', the other side of the equation, resides not only in sound teaching but in the holy life of the preacher, which his words, however poor, will somehow communicate.

We have seen how in several important respects his views about language and writing depart radically from those of his contemporaries. He is different from the love poets of his time in connecting the apparent irrationality of his poetic language with the nature of God and the limitations of finite speech, and different from postmodernist critics in understanding the breakdown of expressible certainties to be a sign of transcendence rather than failure and a call to faith rather than proof of the relativity of all claimed truths. He is different from his contemporaries in the ways he deals with conventional paradoxes, revitalizing them in unexpected ways. He asserts his own obscurity for reasons different from others who adopted a more consciously difficult Spanish style, believing it to be the inevitable consequence of any attempt to write about the deeper things of the spirit rather than of desire for embellishment or praise. The reasons for which he writes and the readers to whom he addresses himself are different from those who sought patronage or fame, and by introducing two other requisities, the spiritual development of the recipient and the quality of life of the originator, to the balance between *prodesse* and *delectare* in works of art, gives a new twist to the old debate. Not to grasp how different a writer San Juan is from almost all his contemporaries (and ours) is likely to lead to inappropriate conclusions about his work.

The problems posed by language for San Juan have now been sufficiently outlined. Language about God is not impossible, but it is only an imperfect response to something greater than it can conceive. Language will always be forced to acknowledge its failure to describe, let alone to capture, the truth it seeks to represent. But to articulate that failure the stammer of language does have certain traditions from which it can draw and a number of techniques it can utilize. The Incarnation is the greatest of the impossible joinings to which the paradoxes of San Juan bear witness and from which they derive their sense. Because it is the unique meeting-point of the divine and the human, it makes physical religious language possible, even necessary.[16] Language itself is redeemed from the curse of conventionality and the burden of the trivial. It becomes sacramental, as it traces and represents the journey of the soul from thoughtless living and pointless goals towards her fulfilment in union with God. Poetry is one way in which this movement can be imagined. It can be charted in prose. But nowhere in San Juan's writing is the union of the two more powerfully demonstrated than in the 'Llama' poem and its commentary.

NOTES

1 William James, *The Varieties of Religious Experience* (London: Collins, 1960 [1902]), p. 367.

2 Pablo Neruda, *Veinte poemas de amor y una canción desesperada* (Buenos Aires: Losada, 1944 [1924]), p. 64; trans. W. S. Merwin, from *Selected Poems. Pablo Neruda*, ed. Nathaniel Tarn (London: Jonathan Cape, 1970), p. 23.

3 See Gabriel Josipovici, *The World and the Book*, 2nd edn. (London: Macmillan, 1979), especially chapter 2, 'The World as a Book' (pp. 25–51). The best-known Spanish example is in Fray Luis de Granada, *Introducción del Símbolo de la Fe*, ed. José María Balcells (Madrid: Cátedra, 1989), pp. 125–231. According to Aquinas, all knowledge of the spiritual must be expressed in analogical terms; see his discussion in 1a.13, 'De nominibus Dei'.

4 For an illuminating study of this tradition, see Denys Turner, *The Darkness of God* (Cambridge: Cambridge University Press, 1995).

5 Eulogio Pacho feels this has been used too uncritically; see *Introducción a la lectura de San Juan de la Cruz*, ed. Salvador Ros and others (Junta de Castilla y León: Valladolid, 1991), p. 448.

6 See above, p. 15.

7 Though the *Cántico* was almost certainly begun first, modern editions print them in what Gaitán has called 'un orden más lógico que cronológico', 'an order more logical than chronological', that is, *Subida-Noche, Cántico, Llama*; José Damián Gaitán, 'Subido del monte Carmelo', *Introducción a San Juan de la Cruz*, p. 368.

8 This emphasis on overflow fits Ricoeur's view of text as containing 'a *surplus of meaning* beyond the intention of the author'; David Brian Perrin, *Canciones entre el alma y el Esposo of Juan de la Cruz: A Hermeneutical Interpretation* (San Francisco: Catholic Scholars Press, 1996), p. 13.

9 Compare Perrin, *Canciones entre el alma y el Esposo*: 'The author is no longer in control of the meaning of the text. Its meaning is now extended to the full range of possibilities opened by the structure of emplotment and the polysemy of words' (p. 174).

10 See Edgar Wind, *Pagan Mysteries in the Renaissance*, revised edn (Oxford: Oxford University Press), p. 169.

11 Cristóbal Cuevas, 'Estudio literario', *Introducción a San Juan de la Cruz*, pp. 129–30.

12 On the relationship between San Juan's exposition of his verses and exegesis of scripture see Cuevas, *Introducción a San Juan de la Cruz*, pp. 157–64.

13 Especially in III.1, 9–10.

14 Malón de Chaide, *La conversión de la Magdalena* (Madrid: Espasa-Calpe, 1957–9), II, p. 148.

15 See above, pp. 208–9.

16 In other words, human love is an analogy of divine love, rather than *vice versa*, 'a remote and weaker image of God's love', as Cugno suggests; Alain Cugno, *Saint John of the Cross: The Life and Thought of a Christian Mystic* (London: Burns & Oates, 1982), p. 111.

10

Language Inflamed

C'est elle [la vérité de l'Évangile] qui accorde les contrariétés par un art tout divin.

(Pascal)

The 'Llama' poem has a different feel from the other *liras*, for several reasons. First, it is written in verses of six lines, not the five normally associated with the *lira*. Second, it seems to describe a state rather than a journey. Third, it consists almost exclusively of exclamations, eight in all, of varying length: in the first two lines of verse two they follow in quick succession, while two (vv. 3, 4) occupy a whole stanza. Fourth, its imagery, while paradoxical, does not seem to be as strange as that of its predecessors, and occasionally betrays a more overt religious meaning.

But the differences should not be exaggerated. First, there were a number of variants of the *lira*, even when allowance is made for the fact that, as San Juan himself points out just before expounding the poem, his model is taken from a verse in one of Sebastián de Córdoba's divinized versions of Garcilaso, an unusual procedure for which he has sometimes been criticized.[1] Second, the image of the flame is dynamic, not static, and the first verse of the poem itself speaks of a process as yet incomplete. Third, exclamations are entirely characteristic of San Juan, even if he is normally more sparing in his use of them. The 'Noche' has three: the repeated '¡oh dichosa ventura!' in the first two verses, and the threefold apostrophe to the night of union (v. 5). The 'Cántico' has several: the appeal to the natural creation (C 4), the complaint of the lover (C 6, 8), the calling out to the fountain and then to the Beloved, whose gaze is too intense to bear (CA 11–12), and the command to the 'ninfas de Judea' not to disturb the lovers. But it is the final point which deserves further comment.

In fact, the language of the poem shows a surprising degree of congruence with the other *liras*. As several critics have noted, the penultimate verse of the 'Cántico' points towards the 'Noche' and the 'Llama':

en la noche serena,	on the calm night,
con llama que consume y no da pena.	with a flame which consumes painlessly.

This same consuming fire is found in the *glosa* 'Sin arrimo y con arrimo', as an image of the transforming love of God:

y assí en su llama sabrosa	and so, in its delightful flame
la qual en mí estoy sintiendo	which I am feeling within myself,
apriessa sin quedar cosa,	quickly, with nothing left,
todo me voy consumiendo.	I am being wholly consumed.

The adjective 'sabrosa', associated in the 'Cántico' with knowledge given by the Beloved in the 'interior bodega' ('allí me dio ciencia muy sabrosa', 'there he gave me most delightful knowledge'; CA 18), recurs in the last verse of the 'Llama', this time in connection with another image found elsewhere (CA 38), breathing, 'aspirar sabroso'.

Many other elements in the poem pick up words and images from others. The plea 'acava ya, si quieres', 'finish, if you will', reworks C 6's 'Acaba de entregarte ya de vero;/no quieras embiarme [. . .]', 'Finish giving yourself truly;/do not send me [. . .]'. The imagery of touching in the second line of the second verse follows the 'Noche' (v. 7), which has a 'mano serena', 'calm hand', wounding the neck rather than a 'mano blanda', 'soft hand' and a 'toque delicado', 'delicate touch'. The paradoxes of life and death in 'matando, muerte en vida la as trocado', 'dying you have turned death into life' offer a highly concentrated version of C 7–8 and the *coplas* 'Vivo sin vivir en mí', with distinct echoes of Pauline theology (spelled out in the commentary). The third stanza, perhaps the most difficult of the four, has fewer such links, but one notes that CA 36's 'subidas cabernas', 'lofty caverns', are now 'las profundas cabernas del sentido', 'the deep caverns of sense', while the combination of 'obscuro y ciego' reminds one of the 'ciego y oscuro salto', 'blind and dark leap' of 'Tras de un amoroso lance', and the 'estraños primores [. . .] junto a su querido', 'strange excellence [. . .] next to her beloved', perhaps, of the 'ínsulas estrañas', 'strange islands' which are among the many images of 'mi Amado', 'my Beloved', in CA 13–14. The last verse contains two further examples. Compare

¡Quán manso y amoroso	How softly and lovingly
recuerdas en mi seno [. . .]	you recall in my breast [. . .]
y en tu aspirar sabroso [. . .]	and in your delightful breathing [. . .]
quán delicadamente me enamoras!	how delicately you fall in love with me!

with CA 17's 'ven, austro, que recuerdas los amores,/aspira por mi huerto', 'come, south wind, recalling love/breathe through my garden', where awakening, love and breathing are brought into a close relationship; and with the sleep of the Beloved on the 'pecho', 'breast' of the lover in the sixth stanza of the 'Noche', while the breeze from the cedars 'aire daba', 'brought a breeze'. The emphasis on secrecy, 'secretamente', also harks back to the 'Noche', through which 'en secreto' the lover journeyed.

Yet despite the ways in which the 'Llama' poem participates in its predecessors, it is different. The exclamations are more concentrated, the imagery seems more abstract, and a number of expressions point to a specifically religious sense in terms which one would expect to find in the commentary rather than the verse – such as 'que a vida eterna save', 'which savours of eternal life', and 'las profundas cabernas del sentido', 'the deep caverns of sense', in both of which cases something is made explicit ('eterna', 'del sentido') which in the other *liras* would have been left open. Equally, the image of the wound 'de mi alma en el más profundo centro', 'in the deepest centre of my soul', uses an expression characteristic of the commentaries.[2] The 'Llama' lacks the lyrical and sensuous images of the others, though it is no less inspired by the intimate metaphors of the language of erotic love. In the first stanza only the wounding flame and the 'tela', 'veil', stand out against intangible words like 'amor', 'alma', 'centro', 'encuentro' ('encounter'); in the second, only the healing wound, the hand and the touch, against 'vida eterna', 'deuda' ('debt'), 'muerte' ('death'). In the third, despite the vivid image of lamps of fire burning in dark caverns, 'sentido' ('sense'), 'primores' ('excellent qualities') and the relatively abstract 'calor', 'heat', and 'luz', 'light', seem to diminish the concreteness of the verse, while in the final verse only the physicality of 'seno', 'breast', survives in a world marked by more abstract adjectives, adverbs and nouns ('manso', 'gentle'; 'amoroso'; 'secretamente'; 'sabroso'; 'bien'; 'gloria'; 'lleno', 'full'; 'delicadamente'). Even the verbs, 'recuerdas' (recalling in the sense of awakening), 'moras', 'you dwell', and 'enamoras', 'you fall in love', do little to counter this.

Yet the language of the 'Llama' poem points systematically to a meaning which lies beyond the conventional paradoxes of *cancionero* or Petrarchan love poetry, while its subtle artistry should not be underestimated. In place of the wound of love which brings both pain and pleasure, or the icy fire of passion and rejection, San Juan establishes a more complex series of relationships between the poem's constitutive images. The link between flame (v. 1) and wound (v. 2) is reinforced by the homophony of 'llama' and 'llaga', the latter defined as 'regalada', 'delightful', with its three successive 'a' sounds. The image which follows, the 'mano blanda', seems to introduce a new idea, though the two stressed and one unstressed 'a's connect it phonically with the flame and the wound. The flame wounds and heals, and the wound becomes a caress; the touch of the hand, with its hints of eternal life, pays all debts. The flame passes through a series of metamorphoses which are grammatically, logically and phonically connected: because it both wounds and heals it is a 'cauterio suave', 'gentle cautery', which in turn becomes the 'regalada llaga'. Three times, therefore, in three different stylistic forms and with close attention to sound, San Juan apostrophizes the wound:

que tiernamente hyeres (adverb, verb)	how tenderly you wound
¡O cauterio suave! (noun, adjective)	Oh gentle cautery!
¡O regalada llaga! (epithet, noun).	Oh delightful flame!

The transition to the '¡O mano blanda!' and '¡O toque delicado!' in the third line of the second verse repeats the pattern established by '¡O cauterio suave!' (exclamation, noun, adjective), and recalls the association made in the 'Noche' between the hand and the action of wounding: 'con su mano serena/en mi cuello hería' (v. 6), 'with his [its] gentle hand/ he [it] wounded my neck'.

The meaning of the last line of the second verse, 'matando, muerte en vida la as trocado', literally 'dying death into life you have changed', is puzzling. Is the subject the 'llama' of the opening exclamation or the 'toque delicado' which immediately precedes it? In a sense it does not matter (nor does the commentary offer much help), since the flame, as we have seen, is interchangeable with wound and hand and touch. While the theme of death turning to life is conventional enough, the presence of 'matando' is not, because it introduces a violent action into the poem. While the Petrarchan lady may kill her frustrated suitor with a look, she certainly does not bring life out of his death. In other words, San Juan has reversed the usual terms of the paradox, reinvigorated it, and suggested to the alert reader that its meaning is other than the one expected. Whatever kind of love this poem celebrates, it passes through death to life. The imagery of transaction – 'y toda deuda paga' – adds another element to the work of the flame, one which in the context of a religious poem cannot but point to the redemptive work of Christ, whose death pays the penalty for human sin and whose resurrection brings life to the redeemed.

The third verse returns to the imagery of fire. The 'llama de amor' has been transmuted into 'lámparas de fuego', 'lamps of fire'. In place of the five separate phrases or sentences of the previous stanza is a single sentence which brings together imagery of darkness, heat and light. The 'resplandores' of the lamps imply both 'calor' and 'luz' in Spanish, so that the two fundamental properties of the flame are held together. But this is the first appearance of light as such in the poem. The 'profundas cabernas' may distantly echo Plato's myth, particularly in their association with blindness, but they are clearly metaphorical, since they are qualified as 'del sentido'. It is this 'sense' which was 'oscuro y ciego', the verb 'estava', 'was', being, as Luce López-Baralt has pointed out, the only past tense in the poem; the others, in vivid contrast with the shifting tenses of the 'Cántico' and 'Noche', are all present, apart from the perfect 'as trocado', making it quite clear that there has been a movement from darkness and blindness to light and heat 'junto a su querido'.[3] This is the only appearance of the imagery of night in the poem, significantly in association with the only verb in a past tense. As we shall see, this matches the commentary's own return from time to time to look back over the journey through the dark night which has led to the living flame.

There is, however, one feature in the third verse which on closer attention seems strange, and makes one wonder about its meaning. The shifting but related images addressed to a second person singular 'tú' by the first person of the poet have implied some kind of dialogue. In the third verse, not only has the singular address become plural – 'lámparas' – but the first person voice appears to become detached and to view itself objectively through an image for itself which is also plural – the 'profundas cabernas del sentido'. The direct address to the subject is then replaced by a reference to 'su', 'their' (or 'her'), not 'mi', 'my' 'querido'. In other words, while the rest of the poem follows the opening – 'you, the living flame of love, have wounded me to the core of my being', the third stanza changes direction – 'you, lamps of fire, make the deep caverns of sense (which was dark and blind) give light and heat next to their beloved'. The identity of the protagonists becomes uncertain: one has to assume that the deep caverns of sense belong to the first person voice, and that 'their' beloved is identical with the living flame, the soft hand, the fiery lamps and so on.[4]

Why should San Juan have departed from his otherwise straightforward syntactical structure? This sense of standing back from the immediacy of the poem's voice as if to observe it is reminiscent of the technique he adopts in the fifth verse of the 'Noche', when the first person's narrative of the journey through the dark night to an encounter with a third person suddenly becomes a direct address in the second person to the night itself, which itself includes as an already accomplished fact the union of the first and third persons, 'amada en el amado transformada', 'lover transformed in the beloved'.[5] The female protagonist of the first four verses is replaced by the night, through which both she and her lover are seen in joyful union. The 'Noche' then resumes the alternation of first and third persons, exchanging caresses and resting in the night-time breezes. Such disruptions, as we have noted, are one of the ways in which San Juan indicates that the subject of his poems is perhaps not as obvious as it might at first sight seem. In the 'Llama', a similar disruption provokes a similar questioning of the meaning of the poem, perhaps because it looks back to a time when darkness and blindness characterized the senses. Now the lamps are blazing, the caverns are filled with their 'resplandores', the 'estraños primores' of the heat and light they emit. We witness an exchange of attributes – heat and light for darkness and blindness – but also the cancelling of distance between what had been radically antithetical entities, 'lámparas' and 'cabernas'. The caverns are filled with strange light and heat, 'junto a su querido', a phrase with strong overtones of union, like its analogue, the 'noche que juntaste/Amado con amada', in the 'Noche'. In other words, the mysterious displacement of persons comes at the very point when both poems make textually present the union of the two lovers they seek to express. Once again, San Juan's strange linguistic techniques become the clue which opens up the meaning of the text.

The last verse, also a complete sentence, marks the poem's closure in several ways. Its most striking feature is the use San Juan makes of two long adverbs, the five syllables of 'secretamente' and the six of 'delicadamente' in the same position in the third and sixth lines, anticipated by the four syllables of 'tiernamente', 'tenderly', in the second line of the poem. Such a procedure is unique in San Juan's art; as a technique it is more closely associated with the *liras* of Fray Luis de León, who sometimes splits the adverb across two lines.[6] The ascending number of syllables of the three examples in the 'Llama' is indicative of the care San Juan takes in constructing his poems, but there is more to it than that. For the last of them, 'delicadamente', itself prolongs the 'toque delicado' of the second verse, while the sense of closure is heightened by the symmetry of the sentence: '¡Quán manso y amoroso' at the start, '[¡]quán delicadamente me enamoras!' at the end.

The fact that the 'Llama' poem picks up so many images from the other *liras* and moves in the direction of explaining itself as a religious poem, together with the charged rhetorical style of the commentary itself, underlines the point that poem and commentary together are both climax and summary of the whole journey. The presence in the poem of a number of expressions which seem to belong more to the language of the commentary prompts the further thought that the boundary between them is less precise than in the other *liras*. It is not simply, as we shall see, that the prose of the *Llama* is highly rhetorical and poetic; the poem itself obscures the distinction by using terms which belong more naturally to the world of San Juan's prose expositions – the 'centro' of the soul, the 'cabernas' which are no longer physical images as in CA 36 ('de la piedra', 'of stone'), but turned into an allegory of 'sentido', a word which represents half the doctrine of the dark night of the soul. In the *Llama*, San Juan comes as close as ever he does to resolving the tensions created in the earlier treatises by the demands of expounding a poetic text in terms of a doctrinal scheme. The gap between poetry and prose, between lyrical and sensuous imagery and didactic, analytical discourse, is effaced. And perhaps in that effacing is found another literary analogue of the subject matter of all his writing, oneness, union.

THE *LLAMA DE AMOR VIVA*

The 'Llama' poem is the least studied of the three great poems, and its accompanying commentary the least studied of the four prose treatises, as critics have observed.[7] As with the earlier commentaries, everything it contains is observed from the summit which has been gained at the end of the journey. Nevertheless, though San Juan tells us that its subject is the unitive life, he looks back at the earlier stages and forward to what is yet to come. Much of it is couched in a language familiar to readers of San Juan's other prose works, and yet it innovates. It is the most finished of them, in the sense that it is more unified in content and style, and that it manages both to expound the images in the poem and the unitive way they are said to describe.[8] It is also theologically the most searching, especially in its exploration of Trinitarian doctrine. Finally, and importantly, it sets the whole journey traced by San Juan in its most complete context, in such a way that without its particular contribution the full force of San Juan's teaching will not be grasped. For it provides the positive and affirmative conclusion in the light of which all the darkness and negations of his earlier treatises must be interpreted.

From its opening words, the *Llama* occupies the heights of mystical experience. The soul, inflamed with the fire of divine love and experiencing 'ríos de gloria' (1.1), 'rivers of glory', is so close to God that only a 'leve tela', 'thin curtain' of mortality divides her from the blessedness of eternal enjoyment of him. Everything she experiences is flame, and that flame of love is the spirit of her Bridegroom (1.3), transforming her as wood becomes fire by burning (a simile explored at greater length in terms of the whole mystical journey in N 2.10). In this state her actions are 'la llama que nace del fuego del amor' (1.4), 'the flame issuing from the fire of love'. Her words too are 'palabras todas encendidas' (1.5), 'all inflamed words', because they are the language of God, which is why the whole poem is constructed from exclamations, which express a greater interior content than words on the tongue can utter. The exclamatory language of the poem continues into the commentary (e.g. 1.36, 2.5, 2.8, 2.16–20).[9]

The structure of the commentary is not as complex as that of the *Subida-Noche*, and, like the *Cántico*, is governed by the need to proceed image by image, phrase by phrase. However, there are four digressions, one of which is substantial. Despite the fact that the verses are said to refer to the 'más perfecto grado de perfección a que en esta vida se puede llegar' (Prol. 3), 'the highest degree of perfection which can be attained in this life', each of the digressions looks back in some way or another to experiences or difficulties encountered on the road towards union, and so introduce depth and perspective into the commentary.

The first occurs in 1.19–26, prompted by the adjective 'esquiva', 'harsh', which the flame now no longer is. San Juan explains how it once appeared to be so by looking back into the dark nights, when it was experienced as a distressingly painful purgation, though its purpose, like that of the refining fire, was good: to purify the dross from the gold. These paragraphs form an interesting commentary on the two books of the *Noche*, to which he refers the reader (1.25), because they are largely concerned with the experience of passive purgation, complete by the unitive way, but under the controlling image of the inconstant flame rather than the dark night. San Juan cites one of the biblical texts previously used in his description of the horrors of the night (Lamentations 3.1–9; N 2.7.2), to explain how both the intellect and the will become a battleground of contrary forces. His writing becomes both dense and rhetorical as it develops the 'contraries' into military images:

> Porque, ¡oh cosa admirable!, levántanse en el alma a esta sazón contrarios contra contrarios; los de el alma contra los de Dios, que embisten el alma y (como dicen los filósofos) unos relucen cerca de los otros y hacen la guerra en el sujeto de el alma, procurando los unos expeler a los otros por reinar ellos en ella, conviene saber: las virtudes y propiedades de Dios en extremo perfectas contra los hábitos y propiedades del sujeto del alma en extremo imperfectos, padeciendo ella dos contrarios en sí. (1.22)

> For (oh wondrous thing!) at this season there arise in the soul contraries against contraries; those of the soul against those of God, which attack the soul, and (as the philosopers say), the presence of one contrary reveals the other more clearly, and each makes war on the soul's person, attempting to expel each other so that they can reign in her; that is, the virtues and properties of God which are perfect in the extreme against the habits and properties of the soul's person, which are in the extreme imperfect, so that she suffers two contraries within herself.

The battle is depicted in terms of the flame of dazzling light shining in the extreme darkness of the soul and forcing out every dark thing which opposes it; of the flame of gentle love meeting the dry and hard resistance of the will; of its breadth and immensity attacking the narrowness of the will, and its sweetness and savour, the bitter and disordered appetites it finds lodged there: a whole series of antitheses which apply the imagery of fire to the faculties and affections of the soul on the battleground of purgation.

The second digression occurs in 2.9–14, where the image of the 'cauterio suave', the gentle cauterization of the wound caused by the flame of love, prompts San Juan to recall an experience of great power and ecstatic delight which, from the way he pictures it in 2.9 (a seraph plunging an arrow deep into the soul and provoking a sudden inflammation) is almost certainly what Teresa describes in her famous Transverberation (*Vida* 29.13–14). He connects it with the stigmata received by St Francis (2.13), as he reflects on the way the herb-tipped arrow penetrates the substance of the spirit but may also leave effects in the flesh. This double reaction is interesting because it helps to define the paradox of the burning at once fierce and gentle in quite different terms from its Petrarchan analogue: 'lo que a su [del alma] corruptible carne es causa de dolor y tormento, en el espíritu fuerte y sano le es dulce y sabroso' (2.13), 'what in her corruptible flesh causes pain and torment, in a strong and healthy spirit is sweet and enjoyable for her. Most remarkable of all is the paragraph which begins by asking how one can rightly speak of this wound caused by the tip, 'que parece quedar en la mitad del corazón del espíritu', 'which appears to lodge in the middle of the heart of the spirit', a phrase which itself combines both physical and immaterial terms (heart, spirit):

> Porque siente el alma allí como un grano de mostaza muy mínimo, vivísimo y encendidísimo, el cual de sí envía en la circunferencia [un] vivo y encendido fuego de amor; el cual fuego, naciendo de la sustancia y virtud de aquel punto vivo donde está la sustancia y virtud de la yerba, se siente difundir sutilmente por todas las espirituales y sustanciales venas del alma según su potencia y fuerza; en lo cual siente ella convalecer y crecer tanto el ardor, y en ese ardor afinarse tanto el amor, que parecen en ella mares de fuego amoroso que llega a lo alto y bajo de las máquinas, llenándolo todo el amor; en lo cual parece al alma que todo el universo es un mar de amor en que ella está engolfada, no echando de ver término ni fin donde se acabe ese amor, sintiendo en sí [. . .] el vivo punto y centro de amor. (2.10)
>
> For here the soul feels something like a very tiny grain of mustard-seed, very bright and ardent, which sends out from itself to the circumference a bright and burning fire of love. This fire, arising from the substance and power of that bright point where the substance and power of the plant lies, is felt subtly diffused through all the spiritual and substantial veins of the soul according to her strength and power. In this she feels the burning so to recover and grow, and love to become so perfected in the burning, that there seem to be in her seas of loving fire which reaches the heavenly and earthly spheres, filling everything with love. It seems to the soul that the whole universe is a sea of love in which she is engulfed, and she can see neither limit nor end where this love might cease, feeling within herself [. . .] the living point and centre of love.[10]

In this passage many of San Juan's techniques as a prose writer in the *Llama* reveal themselves. The use of paradox centres on the antithetical elements of fire and water, in which the brightness and intense burning of fire is related to the love which provokes the experience, and the vast expanse of the oceans to its pervasive effects. Typically, the effect is achieved by concentration on a relatively small number of repeated words and phrases, sometimes with slight syntactical variation, and with frequent alliteration: *vivísimo, vivo, vivo, vivo*; *encendidísimo, encendido*; *fuego, fuego de amor, fuego amoroso*; *ardor, ardor*; *fuego de amor, amor, fuego amorosos, amor, mar de amor, amor, amor*. Together with these go other alliterative series: en*vía*, *vir*tud, *vir*tud, which draw attention to the concentration of *í* sounds at the start; *mostaza, mínimo*; *se siente, sutilmente, todas las espirituales y sustanciales venas, según*; *tanto, ardor, ardor, afinarse tanto, amor, aparecen, mares, amoroso, alto, máquinas, llenándolo, amor*; *sintiendo, sí, vivo*; all exist in close proximity to each other and increase the sense of a series of variations upon a central theme. Typical too is the conjoining of the language of scholastic theology with highly symbolic imagery, and of abstract nouns with others denoting physical space, especially when used of the soul: *circunferencia, máquinas, venas del alma*, for example, alongside the physical but symbolic fire and the abstract love. But most noticeable of all, perhaps, is the way in which from a single point (the tip of the arrow dipped in medicinal herbs) San Juan depicts the sensation rippling through the soul so that it perceives the whole universe as a sea of love. That is why he begins with an image of smallness – the implicitly biblical grain of mustard seed (Mark 4.30–2) – which grows to greatness.

The third digression (2.24–30) looks back over the 'tribulaciones y trabajos', 'trials and tribulations', which have been necessary to reach state of the spiritual betrothal, at the beginning of the unitive way. As he looks back again at the processes of purgation he wonders why so few people ever reach the lofty state of 'perfección de unión de Dios' (2.27), 'perfection of union in God'. He introduces his explanation by observing that though the heights of contemplation are theoretically open to every human being, only the few scale them. Sometimes it is difficult to know what readership San Juan is addressing, because of the tension between statements like this and others to the effect that his commentaries are intended for the tiny minority of those who have set out on this road. Here lies the clue to the resolution of that tension, and an answer to the problem of the intended readership.[11] Human observation demonstrates that the contemplative heights are gained only by what he here calls, borrowing a Pauline phrase (e.g. Romans 9. 21–3), the 'pocos vasos que sufran tan alta y subida obra', 'few vessels who can bear so high and lofty a work'. But God wills all his human children to enjoy perfection. There must therefore be a reason for this disjunction, and it lies in the inability of the majority to tolerate even the slightest discomfort. Many give up at the first difficulties, shunning the straight and narrow way to life and preferring the wide road to perdition, a choice of text which puts one in mind of Bunyan's *Pilgrim's Progress* and the early casualties on the way. In order to reach the high state of the perfect there is only one way, and it passes through suffering, the dark nights of privation which are part of the way of the cross. If souls knew how necessary such suffering was to reach what they desire:

> en ninguna manera buscaríades consuelo ni de Dios ni de las criaturas, mas antes llevar[í]ades la cruz, y puestos en alla, querríades beber allí la hiel y vinagre puro; y lo habríades a grande dicha, viendo cómo, muriendo así al mundo y a vosotros mismos, viviríades a Dios en deleites de espíritu [. . .]. (2.28)
>
> in no way would you seek consolation from God or the creatures, but rather you would carry the cross, and once nailed to it would there drink the gall and pure vinegar; and would count it as bliss, seeing how dying thus to the world and to yourselves, you would live to God in delights of the spirit.

This powerful appeal, in which the reader is asked to imagine him- or herself acting the part of Christ along the *via dolorosa* to Calvary and in the anguish of the crucifixion itself, does not on the face of it belong in a treatise which claims to be about unitive prayer, since it addresses readers reluctant to set out on the road of purgation at all. But it is set in the context of a comment about the disparity between divine calling and human response, and opens the text out to embrace a universal readership. For San Juan, the discomforture of the senses is nothing in comparison with the searching out of the spirit, and he draws a telling contrast between them in terms of the human desire not to be troubled:

> Y si tú no has querido dejar de conservar la paz y gusto de tu tierra, que es tu sensualidad, no queriendo armar guerra ni contradecirla en alguna cosa, no sé yo cómo querrás entrar en las impetuosas aguas de tribulaciones y trabajos del espíritu, que son de más adentro. (2.27)
>
> And if you have not wished to leave behind the peace and comfort of your country, which is your sensual life, not desiring to declare war on it or counter it in any respect, I do not know how you will find the will to enter into the rushing waters of the trials and tribulations of the spirit, which belong more to the inner self.

The 'tú' being addressed here is certainly not the Discalced friar or nun of the prologue to the *Subida-Noche* (.9); it is the voice of the preacher addressing the congregation in vivid metaphor and stern challenge.

The fourth digression (3.27–67) is far and away the longest, and for San Juan's purposes probably the most important. About half the exposition of the third verse is taken up with advice and warnings for spiritual directors dealing with souls at this stage (27–62) and about the stratagems of the devil and self-inflicted harm (63–7). It is San Juan's most sustained treatment of an issue which preoccupied him greatly and which in many ways provided the spur for his prose commentaries. The excursus summarizes the teaching developed more fully (and with many more digressions) in the *Subida-Noche*, but seen here not from the soul's perspective, but from that of the human guides on this divine journey. If we wonder why he chose to insert it at this point in the *Llama*, when he has been describing the anointings in the Spirit which characterize the betrothal, it is because of the ever-present fear of souls slipping backwards, and the need for spiritual directors who are experienced enough to ensure that progress is maintained towards the longed-for union of marriage (3.27). The advice to take care in entrusting the soul to a skilled director is relevant not only to souls at this stage, but for 'todas las demás que buscan a su Amado', 'all the rest who seek their Beloved'. The blind cannot lead the blind (3.29; Matthew 15.14), and the blind in question here are spiritual directors, the devil and the soul herself, each of which can lead the soul astray. But of the three it is the first which concerns San Juan at greatest length.

His starting point is a familiar one: the earlier crisis when meditation must be abandoned for contemplation (S 2.13), and why. The tone of his writing is more direct and forceful than before. He often addresses his audience in the second person singular, as if in conversation with one of its members, or imagining a confessor talking to a soul:

> Y vendrá un maestro espiritual que no sabe sino martillar y macear con las potencias como herrero y, porque él no enseña más que aquello y no sabe más que meditar, dirá: —Anda, dejaos de esos reposos, que es ociosidad y perder tiempo; sino tomá y meditá, y haced actos interiores, porque es menester que hagáis de vuestra parte lo que en vos es, que esotro son alumbramientos y cosas de bausanes. (3.43)

> And a spiritual director comes along who can only hammer and bludgeon away with the faculties like a blacksmith, and because he only teaches that and only knows about meditation, he will say: Come on, stop these periods of quiet, which are idleness and a waste of time. Take up meditation instead, make inward acts, because you must do for yourself what you can; the rest is nothing but illuminations, stuff for simpletons.

The last phrase is quite pointed, in view of the widespread suspicion of the practice of mental prayer and the number of cases of so-called 'alumbrados' the Inquisition uncovered.[12] Even so, a director who persuades a soul that is ready to progress to return to former practices is doing immense damage. Such a man does not understand the absolute need for the emptiness of the faculties, or the barrier which any kind of finite content in them places to God's will. He confuses the soul's work of making herself receptive with idleness, and he does not see that it is the Holy Spirit and not himself who is her true guide (3.46). Such directors 'hacen a Dios grande injuria y desacato metiendo su tosca mano donde Dios obra' (3.54), 'do God great injury and disrespect by clumsily interfering where he is at work'. They have failed to grasp that in this state 'el no volver atrás abrazando algo sensible es ir adelante a lo inaccesible que es Dios' (3.51), 'not to go backwards by embracing something of the senses is to go forwards to the inaccessible, which is God'. Using the making of religious images as a simile, San Juan writes: 'No cualquiera que sabe desbastar el madero sabe entallar la imagen, ni cualquiera que sabe entallar sabe perfilarla y pulirla; y no cualquiera que sabe pulirla sabrá pintarla, ni cualquiera que sabe pintarla sabrá poner la última mano y perfección' (3.57); 'not everyone who can rough-hew the wood can carve the image, and not everyone who can carve can shape and polish it; not everyone who can polish it can paint it, and not everyone who can paint it can put the finishing touches to it and bring it to perfection'. Spiritual directors, in other words, should have a keen sense of what their abilities are, and co-operate with God instead of hindering him. For God leads each soul by different roads: 'apenas se hallará un espíritu que en la mitad del modo que lleva convenga con el modo de otro' (3.59), 'you can hardly find one spirit which follows half the same way as another'. To impose the same spiritual practices on all their charges is to remove from them 'la libertad [. . .] de la doctrina evangélica', 'the freedom of Gospel teaching', while to prevent them from seeking guidance elsewhere reveals the kind of jealousy married people have to face. Some go as far as attempting to stop people from entering the religious life, and he warns that they will not go unpunished for this (.62). San Juan is vehement in his attack on inexperienced, or, worse still, over-confident confessors. His anger is transparent, and the patient tone he usually adopts towards the soul is replaced by a calling to account of those who are supposed to assist her. The difference in tone reflects his belief that those who are called to exercise responsibility in these matters must take great care to do so appropriately. One cannot help but suspect that a great deal of personal experience lies behind these words.

These digressions apart, the image of the flame dominates the commentary to an even greater extent than it does the poem, and the different ways in which it is used, the different ideas to which it is attached and the other images with which it enters into dialogue provide a fruitful way of approaching the exposition. From the outset, the flame is associated with the idea of wounding, through the commonplace paradox of Petrarchan and *cancionero* poetry of the wound which brings pleasure. The flame wounds the deepest part of the soul 'tiernamente', 'tenderly'. The work of love is 'herir para enamorar y deleitar' (1.8), 'to wound in order to cause love and bring delight', and it is ever active, 'arrojando sus heridas como llamaradas ternísimas de delicado amor, ejercitando jocunda y festivalmente las artes y juegos del amor', 'throwing out its wounds like tenderest flamings of gentle love, and exercising the arts and games of love in joyful festivity'. The wounds to which the poem refers are 'llamaradas de tiernos toques', 'flamings of tender touches': the reality in which the images of fire, wounding and touch cohere is love.

This wounding takes place 'de mi alma en el más profundo centro', 'in my soul's deepest centre'. All things tend to their natural centre, and the centre of the soul is God (1.12), which she reaches when she loves God with all her powers. But this centre is more like the mansions of the castle in Teresa's *Moradas* – concentric rooms through which she passes till the innermost one is reached. The soul, San Juan says, has as many centres in God as it has degrees of loving him, and each centre is deeper than the preceding one, until the deepest of all is reached. The highest degree of union in this life, which occurs in this 'deepest centre', is an anticipation of the beatific vision. But he is very conscious that this is controversial and difficult teaching: 'las cosas raras y de que hay poca experiencia son más maravillosas y menos creíbles' (1.15), 'strange things and things of which there is little experience are the most amazing and the least credible'. Hence he cites no fewer than six scriptural texts, and compares the union of love and the union of inflammation in love to the difference between coals which are merely burning and those from which flames are shooting out – which brings the doctrinal exposition back to the fundamental image.

The final line of the first verse, 'rompe la tela deste dulce encuentro', has received a good deal of attention from critics, some of whom have seen in it the erotic metaphor of the breaking of the hymen in the sexual encounter.[13] There is certainly no such reading in San Juan's commentary, nor would we expect one. But the line raises in a particularly acute form the whole issue of erotic language as a symbol for spiritual discourse. The expression 'romper la tela' can have such a meaning in secular love poetry, yet poets used the same stock of images for both secular and religious verse, and sensitivity to context was and is required in order to determine the sense. To read a sexual meaning into a poem which is more overtly religious than the 'Noche' is to mistake the context and therefore to apply the wrong sense, as though in Donne's 'Holy Sonnets' lines like 'nor ever chast, except you ravish mee' and 'when she'is embrac'd and open to most men' were to be removed from the argument of the poem and treated entirely literally.[14] Or as though poets who use the language of inebriation (as many mystics do) were closet alcoholics whose imagery betrayed their unresolved conflicts. A purely erotic reading of an isolated line like this not only impoverishes the reading of the whole but leads to a failure to follow the argument as it develops through metaphors based on human love. The 'Llama' must be read either as love poem, in which case it will include allusions to vaginal penetration and orgasm, or as a religious poem which consciously uses sexual imagery because the tradition in which it was written does so, in which case all such images form part of a metaphorical whole, as they do in Donne. When San Juan writes, as he does in his commentary on this line, that 'la oración breve penetra los cielos' (1.33), 'the short prayer penetrates the heavens', he is citing Ecclesiasticus 35.21, and the verb does not have the sexual connotations it can have in other contexts.

In any case, as O'Reilly has observed, the more natural human setting of the line is the chivalric joust.[15] San Juan uses the verb 'embestir', 'to thrust', 'to attack', several times in his commentary, here and elsewhere, and jousts were known as 'encuentros'. The 'tela' was the barrier placed between the jousting knights, to prevent them doing injury to one another. To break it implied that the encounter was violent, and might lead to death. San Juan also has a more traditional image in mind, the 'tela' or veil which divides life on earth from heaven, and which can only be passed through death.[16] He explains that there are three 'telas' or barriers between the soul and God. The first two, the creatures and the soul's natural operations, belong to the dark nights, to which he has already referred to in his discussion of the flame which is no longer painful, and to pass through them is a prerequisite for union. The third is the barrier of death, which will free the soul from the limitations of the body and enable her to enter into blessedness; and because the poem has 'tela' in the singular it is this last one to which it refers.[17] It is called 'tela' for three reasons: it is the boundary between flesh and spirit, between the soul and God, and through it divinity shines.

This barrier separating bodily life from death has become 'tan sutil y delgada y espiritualizada' (1.29), 'so subtle and thin and spiritualized' by now that the flame burns sweetly, unlike its earlier and harsher effects. The soul prays for death, since 'precious in the sight of the Lord is the death of his saints' (Psalm 115 [116].15), and for the thread to be torn ('rompe'), rather than cut or removed ('corte', 'acaba'). San Juan gives four reasons for the appropriateness of his chosen verb: whether he is being wise after the event or not, he is careful to argue for the congruence of the word he has selected with the meaning he intends to convey. 'Romper' fits the image of 'encuentro' better than the others, suggesting the forceful and impatient way in which love acts, and love's desire for all to be accomplished in the minimum possible time; tearing, too, is less premeditated and requires less preparation than 'cortar' and 'acabar' (1.33).

He proceeds in a similar way to argue for the appropriateness of 'encuentro', though further use of the verb 'penetra' will also encourage those who prefer an erotic reading:

> Hace él en ella estos embestimientos divinos y gloriosos a manera de encuentros, que, como son a fin de purificarla y sacarla de la carne, verdaderamente son encuentros en que siempre penetra endiosando la sustancia de el alma, haciéndola divina, en lo cual absorbe el alma sobre todo ser a ser de Dios. (1.35)
>
> He [God] makes in her those divine and glorious thrusts like encounters, which, since their purpose is to purify her and take her out of the flesh, truly are encounters by which he penetrates and divinizes the substance of the soul, making her divine, in which he absorbs the soul above every being into the being of God.

These encounters are sweet because they are above all others in preparing the soul for glory. It is not that the language cannot be read as erotic; the chivalric joust itelf might be thought of as a metaphor for the male sexual act. It is that such a reading is inappropriate in the context of a poem which presents serious problems of interpretation as a purely secular lyric. It mistakes the underlying metaphor for the literal sense, instead of asking how the meaning has been transferred from one kind of language to another.

The second stanza of the commentary begins with a statement that the Trinity works this work of union, and just as the divine Persons are one in essence so the 'mano', 'cauterio' and 'toque' of the poem 'en sustancia son una misma cosa' (2.1), 'are in substance the same thing'. This he identifies as a strictly literary trope, the naming of the effects for the cause (metonymy). Language here witnesses to Trinitarian theology, in which both difference and unity are asserted and reconciled, through separate Persons united in a mutual communion of substance. So the images of the poem are distinct but conjoined, located in the same reality: the cautery is the Holy Spirit, the hand is the Father, the touch is the Son.[18] Once again, he is careful to connect his explanation with the conceptual logic implied in his images. The cautery is the work of God, who is a consuming fire, more able to devour a thousand worlds than earthly fire a piece of flax (2.3); yet, having established the scriptural source of the metaphor (Deuteronomy 4.24), San Juan modifies it, in accordance with the poem: the cautery is 'suave', since in the soul it burns as a gentle fire, like the tongues of flame the apostles received at Pentecost.[19] Finally, he makes a natural analogy: this fire is not like fire which turns coal to ash, but one which enlightens and enriches the soul.

Now he turns to the the result of this cauterization, the 'regalada llaga', and again proceeds by likeness and unlikeness. Like the literal cautery, the flame of the Spirit burns away wounds (sins); but unlike it, the wound which is left requires no further treatment and is its own cure:

> Pero en esto hay diferencia de este amoroso cauterio al del fuego material: que éste la llaga que hace no la puede volver a sanar si no se aplican otros medicables, pero la llaga del cauterio de amor no se puede curar con otra medicina, sino que el mismo cauterio que la hace la cura [. . .]; porque cada vez que toca el cauterio de amor en la llaga de amor hace mayor llaga de amor, y así cura y sana más, por cuanto llaga más. Porque el amante, cuanto más llagado, está más sano, y la cura que hace el amor es llagar y herir sobre lo llagado, hasto tanto que la llaga sea tan grande que toda el alma venga a resolverse en llaga de amor; y, de esta manera, ya toda cauterizada y hecha una llaga de amor, está toda sana en amor, porque está transformada en amor. Y en esta manera se entiende la llaga que aquí habla el alma toda llagada y toda sana. (2.7)

> But there is a difference between this loving cautery and the cautery of material fire. In the latter, the wound it causes cannot be healed unless other medicaments are applied, whereas the cautery of love cannot be cured by another medicine: the cautery itself works the cure [. . .]; for each time the cautery of love touches the wound of love it makes that wound greater, and cures and heals the more it wounds. For the lover is the healthier the more wounded he is, and love's cure is to wound and hurt what is already wounded, until the wound is so great that the whole soul becomes a wound of love. Thus, fully cauterized and become a wound of love, it is fully healed in love, because it is transformed in love. That is how this wound is to be understood of which the soul is speaking, altogether wounded and altogether healed.

The intensity of the language and the piling of paradox upon paradox makes this one of the densest passages in the text. The paradox exists partly because of the disjunction between the work of fire in healing physical wounds on the one hand, insufficient of itself, and the wounds brought about by divine love acting on the soul which kindle her desire for union with God on the other; contrary to ordinary medical experience, in such a state the deeper the wound, the more complete the healing. But it also exists because of the likeness San Juan sees between human lovers and the soul's love for God, for both know that the more the lover's desires find satisfaction, the deeper the love which wounds the heart or soul. The wound becomes the cure, as the divine Beloved both increases the desire of the human lover and responds to it. By exploring the paradox in terms of both likeness and unlikeness San Juan is giving content back to an idea emptied of it by repeated conventional use. The presence of the paradox in the poem, in its double form of gentle cauterization and delightful wound, hints at a meaning beneath the surface, one which reflects how like and unlike this is to its human analogue.

The 'soft hand' of the Father is dealt with in a single paragraph (2.16). Whereas the phrase is not paradoxical as it stands in the poem, San Juan draws paradox out of it in his commentary: since divine punishments are light, divine wounds bring healing, and through the touch of death God brings the soul to life. He concentrates into the single image of the hand, so often symbolic of divine action in the Bible, many of the most problematic theological issues: how power and gentleness, judgement and mercy, omnipotence and sweetness can coexist. The 'delicate touch' of the Word, the Son of God, calls forth a passage of exclamatory prose in which San Juan contrasts the 'touch' of the earthquake which shook Mount Horeb with the 'still small voice' in which God finally spoke to Elijah (1 Kings 19.11–12):

> ¡Oh aire delgado y delicado, di, ¿cómo tocas delgada y delicadamente, Verbo, Hijo de Dios, siendo tan terrible y poderoso? ¡Oh, dichosa y mucho dichosa el alma a quien tocares delgada y delicadamente, siendo tan terrible y poderoso! (2.17)

> Oh light and gentle breeze, say, how is it, since you are so awesome and powerful, that your touch is so light and gentle, Word, Son of God? Oh happy and happy again the soul whom you touch so lightly and gently, when you are so awesome and powerful!

San Juan is here reflecting the ancient Patristic belief that the manifestations of God to the patriarchs and prophets were revelations not of the Father (sight of whom caused death) but of the Word, the second Person of the Trinity, before the Word became flesh in Christ. Hence the founder of the Carmelite Order, Elijah himself, encountered the Word in the still, small voice after the wind and earthquake and fire. Once again, he has filled a fairly conventional image with a content quite unlike that of other Golden Age poets, as he turns the touch of lovers into a paradoxical statement of the infinite power and the self-giving love of Christ.

The 'toque' is now further defined as bringing with it a foretaste of eternal life, a phrase which brings explicitly religious language into the poem for the first time ('que a vida eterna sabe'), and alerts the reader to consider the remaining two images of the verse, the cancelling of debts and the changing of death into life. Both could belong to the poetry of human love, which is full of language of indebtedness and of living and dying. If it appears surprising that neither 'y toda deuda paga' nor 'matando, muerte en vida la has trocado' calls forth any explicit reference to the redemptive work of Christ, the commentary makes it plain that these expressions relate to the human side of the journey which this enables. The paradox of death turning into life is interpreted through exegesis of no fewer than five separate texts, forming a summary of Paul's theology of 'putting off the old man' and 'putting on the new' (Ephesians 4.22–4), for that is what he understands the paradox to mean. The exposition, however, turns on the word 'trocado', 'exchanged', from the poem, as he describes in turn how the three faculties, the natural appetites and the natural operations of the soul are all 'exchanged' for the divine, with the result that the soul, though not divine in substance, becomes God by participation (2.34). Hence the payment of the debt is the joy the soul experiences having been purged of her imperfections and sins.

San Juan warns his readers that the third verse may seem 'algo oscura y prolija' (3.1), 'somewhat obscure and wordy' if they have not shared the experience; if they have, it will prove 'clara y gustosa', 'clear and enjoyable'. He bases his exegesis on the grammatical fact that, unlike the five previous apostrophes (and the rest of the poem), this one is addressed to a plural referent. Lamps, he says, have two properties: they give out both light and heat. These lamps are the divine attributes – omnipotence, wisdom, goodness, mercy, justice, love and so on. God in his single Trinitarian being is all of his attributes as it were in their simple, undifferentiated form, so that 'cada uno de estos atributos es una lámpara que luce al alma y da calor de amor [. . .] y así, todas estas lámparas son una lámpara que, según sus virtudes y atributos, luce y arde como muchas lámparas' (3.2–3), 'each of these attributes is a lamp which shines in the soul and warms it with love [. . .] and thus all these lamps are one lamp which, according to its virtues and attributes, shines and burns like many lamps'. The argument is not an easy one, and depends on the double perspective from which the attributes are viewed. Following the traditions of classical positive theology, San Juan believes that the attributes do not exist in separation from each other, since to speak of the goodness of God is also to speak of his love, justice and so on. Therefore to be in union with any one of the divine attributes is to be in union with them all. From the point of view of human experience, however, governed by the limitations both of finitude and language, they can be conceived of separately:

> Por lo cual el alma en un solo acto de la noticia de estas lámparas ama por cada una, y en eso ama por todas juntas [. . .]; porque el resp[l]andecer que le da esta lámpara del ser de Dios en cuanto es omnipotente le da luz y calor de amor de Dios en cuanto es omnipotente, y según esto ya Dios le es al alma lámpara de omnipotencia que le da luz y noticia según este atributo [. . .]. (3.3)

> For this reason in a single act of knowledge of these lamps the soul loves through each one, and in so doing loves through them all [. . .]; because the radiance she receives from this light concerning the being of God in his omnipotence gives her light and heat to love God in his omnipotence, and accordingly God is now a lamp of omnipotence to the soul which gives her light and knowledge according to this attribute.

He connects this with the list of divine attributes mentioned by Moses in Exodus 34.6–7 and with the mysterious vision of Abraham (Genesis 15.17), who sees in a horror of great darkness a vision of a burning lamp passing between the pieces of a sacrifice he has been commanded to make. Between these two references he places the text which inspired him most directly, while remaining focused on the properties of light and heat the lamps of the poem radiate, and the double perspective of multiplicity and unity:

> todas ellas están hechas una luz y y un fuego, y cada una una luz y un fuego; y aquí el alma, inmensamente absorta en delicadas llamas, llagada sutilmente de amor en cada una de ellas, y en todas ellas juntas más llagada y viva en amor de vida de Dios [. . .] conoce bien [. . .] la verdad de aquel dicho de el Esposo en los Cantares, cuando dijo que *las lámparas del amor eran lámparas de fuego y de llamas* (8.6). (3.5)

> they all become one light and one fire, and each of them one light and one fire; and here the soul, absorbed in an immensitude of delicate flames, and subtly wounded by love in each one of them, and in all of them together the more wounded and alive in love of the life of God [. . .] well knows the truth of the Bridegroom's words in the Song: *the lamps of love were lamps of fire and flames* (8.6).[20]

San Juan's insistence on the ideas of separateness and oneness stems from his theology, in which though each divine attribute can be separately enumerated, each contains the rest, because all are found in God, their sum and unity. The passage just quoted is one of many which sum up, represent and take forward the preceding argument by bringing together its separate images: here, the light and heat of the lamps are connected with the earlier images of flames and wounding, and the language imitates the underlying theology, in that each image, though capable of distinct articulation, becomes the other images. This is a theological language which stands at the opposite end of the spectrum from Dionysian negative theology, for it proceeds by affirmation and it attributes to God the fulness of that wisdom, truth, justice (and all the other attributes) which in human experience and language can only ever be its merest shadow. It provides a clear expression of the *via affirmativa* in San Juan's prose, which otherwise we might seek only in his poetry. The God who is darkness, hidden and unknown in the divine *nada*, is now revealed through a series of qualities which can be expressed in human language. But this is only possible once the soul has been completely emptied of the human, and therefore creaturely and finite constructs, by which language normally names them. As long as they are ideas in her mind, creatures of her own limited construction, they must be negated. Once the whole content of the soul derives from a full and free communication with God through his attributes, they can be experienced, and if experienced, described. San Juan seems to be saying that the *via affirmativa* properly belongs to the *via unitiva*, which would square with his affirmation of the delight the soul takes in all the beauty and variety of creation once she has reached this state.

The imagery of fire takes a new and unexpected turn in the next stage of the exposition, in which the mutually exclusive elements of fire and water become images of each other. If divine attributes experienced humanly as discrete cohere in the unity of the Godhead, and if the language which expresses them names them singly but suggests that each participates in the other, this radical antithesis forms a logical illustration of those impossible joinings, the divine and the human, difference and sameness, to which I earlier referred.[21] For the lamps radiating divine attributes now become springs overflowing with divine and living waters, through a series of transformations which culminate in the impossible statement 'aunque es fuego, también es agua':

> Porque, aunque es verdad que esta comunicación [. . .] es luz y fuego de estas lámparas de Dios, pero es este fuego aquí [. . .] tan suave, que, con ser fuego inmenso, es como aguas de vida que hartan la sed del espíritu con el ímpetu que él desea. De manera que estas lámparas de fuego son aguas vivas del espíritu como las que vinieron sobre los Apóstoles (Act 2,3), que, aunque eran lámparas de fuego, también eran aguas puras y limpias; porque así las llamó el profeta Ezequiel cuando profetizó aquella venida del Espíritu Santo, diciendo: *Infundiré [. . .] sobre vosotros aguas y pondré mi espíritu en medio de vosotros* (36,25–6). Y así, aunque es fuego, también es agua [. . .]. (3.8)

> For although it is true that this communication [. . .] is light and fire from these lamps of God, it is here so gentle a fire that although it is an immense fire it is like the waters of life which quench the thirst of the spirit with the force the spirit desires. So these lamps of fire are living waters of the spirit, like those which came upon the Apostles (Acts 2.3), which though lamps of fire were also clean and pure waters. That is what Ezekiel called them when he prophesied the coming of the Holy Spirit in the words: *I will pour out [. . .] waters upon you and I will set my spirit among you* (36.25–6). Therefore, although it is fire, it is also water.

From the opening words of the commentary, the two antithetical elements have been held together: 'Sintiéndose ya el alma toda inflamada en la divina unión y ya su paladar todo bañado en gloria y amor' (1.1), 'The soul, feeling herself now completely inflamed in divine union and her palate now bathed in glory and love'.[22] The example before us is by no means the end of the argument, but it will suffice for our purposes. Beginning with the paradox of the fire which is both a conflagration and yet gentle (the word 'suave' recalls the 'cauterio suave' of the previous verse), San Juan moves to the narrative of the first Christian Pentecost, in which tongues of fire descended upon the Apostles, interpreted through a passage from Ezekiel which has long been taken to prophesy it. The Acts account provides the fire, the prophecy the waters, both images of the Spirit. The phrase 'living waters' is used many times in both Testaments, and the emphasis on their purity recalls their association with baptism, itself the work of the Spirit.

The way in which San Juan combines irreconcilables through argument is once again not far from the correspondences sought (but usually not stated) by English metaphysical and Spanish *conceptista* poets. But it is not, strictly speaking, part of the commentary on the poem, which has no mention of water. The commentary thus introduces further levels of paradox, rather than being content to elucidate those already suggested by the poem. Because it is an exposition, San Juan is able to tease out the correspondences behind the antithesis, which he locates in the Bible's use of different images in different places to express the same reality. In divine language (and hence in God), the paradoxes of human language (a language of creatures, but which have their origin in God) are reconciled. Paradoxes which appear conventional are reborn. Without the *Llama* commentary none of this would be apparent.

So far we have concentrated on the lamps as images of the divine attributes. But the soul 'está hecha Dios de Dios por participación de El y de sus atributos' (3.8), 'becomes God from God by virtue of participation in him and in his attributes'. This is how he understands their 'resplandores' in the poem's next line. In their bright rays further paradoxes are born, this time from the unlikeness of the human and the divine. Human lamps light up what is around them; but these lamps are not external to the soul, for she is glowing within them: San Juan takes the poem's 'en' to mean 'dentro', 'within'. This is a transformative burning, because fire is inflamed air, 'y los movimientos y resplandores que hace aquella llama ni son sólo del aire ni sólo del fuego de que está compuesta, sino junto del aire y de fuego, y el fuego los hace hacer al aire que en sí tiene inflamado' (3.9), 'and the movements and radiance which that flame makes are not caused by the air or fire alone of which it is composed, but of air and fire together, and the fire produces them from the air it has inflamed'. The physics may be Aristotelian, but the association fire–water has been replaced by another elemental joining, fire and air, which are both present (though San Juan only alludes to this) in the Pentecost narrative and therefore both closely associated with the Spirit. The 'resplandores' are a kind of moving of God in the soul and she in him, representing 'los juegos y fiestas alegres' (3.10), 'the joyful games and feasts' of the second verse. He is careful to stress that since God does not move (he is, after all, the Unmoved Mover), the language of movement applies more properly to the soul, and in any case these foretastes of glory are 'establos, perfectos y continuos, con firme serenidad en Dios' (3.11), 'stable, perfect and continuous, with firm calmness in God'. Only beyond death, in glory, will the sensation of movement cease. The introduction of this new symbol – from 'llama' to 'lámparas' and 'resplandores' in the poem, with the addition of water, air and now movement in the commentary – will become important in the final stanza.

Before that, however, the lamps pass through a further antithetical transformation, into the highly unusual word 'obumbración', 'overshadowing' (3.12). The connection is again biblical, and depends on its figurative sense of granting protection and favour: the angel announces to the Virgin Mary that the Holy Spirit will overshadow her when the Christ is conceived (Vg 'obumbrabit'; Luke 1.35). The bright attributes of God cast, as it were, their proper shadow on the soul, but these shadows are as burning and resplendent as the lamps which cast them. Indeed, 'estas sombras serán resplandores' (3.14), 'these shadows will be radiance'. Because the shadows come from the 'resplandores' and these in turn are the work of the 'lámparas de fuego', the divine attributes within the soul, San Juan concludes that they too belong to the attributes, not as these exist in themselves, but as they are communicated within the soul: 'la sombra que hace al alma la lámpara de la hermosura de Dios será otra hermosura al talle y propiedad de aquella hermosura de Dios' (3.14), 'the shadow the lamp of divine beauty casts in the soul will be another beauty with the character and property of that same beauty of God'; and likewise with the power and wisdom of God. The paragraph uses the same enumerative technique as 3.6 in its account of the divine attributes, and concludes by bringing the images of darkness and light back into relationship with the poem's 'lámparas' and the commentary's stress on attributes as both many and one, 'claras y encendidas sombras de aquellas claras y encendidas lámparas, todas en una lámpara de un solo y sencillo ser de Dios, que actualmente resplandece de todas estas maneras' (3.15), 'clear and burning shadows of those clear and burning lamps, all [present] in the one lamp of the one simple being of God, who now shines in all these ways'.

The introduction of the imagery of shadow, providing a fresh antithesis to light and fire, though dependent on them for its existence, is prompted by the poem's only example of the language of darkness, 'las profundas cabernas del sentido/que estava oscuro y ciego', 'the deep caverns of sense/which was dark and blind'. These caverns are the three faculties, now emptied of every creaturely content, even the slightest presence of which is sufficient to prevent the soul from understanding her true nature. Her emptiness of the finite reveals to her her capacity for the infinite; she is now ready for union, whenever God may be pleased to grant it. What in the *Subida-Noche* takes five books to describe is here present in a few lines, as though the long and roundabout journey there could now be contemplated with confidence. As with the 'lámparas', so with the 'cabernas': the plural form permits San Juan a precision of exegesis, as he writes of the understanding's thirst for the waters of divine wisdom, the will's hunger for the perfection of love, and the memory's longing to live in hope of God (3.19–21). He also pinpoints the distinction between this present state of spiritual betrothal, characterized by gifts and visitations, and the union of persons, which is its end (3.24). All that can be achieved by the will and by grace is complete (3.25); the soul must now wait for as long as God knows it to be necessary, until she is ready for union.

The commentary proper resumes at 3.68 after the long digression noted above, with observations on the vast expanses of these caverns and why the faculties are aptly called 'cabernas profundas'. The image well fits San Juan's belief that the inner life is an almost limitless landscape explored only by the very few. In the caverns 'caben las profundas inteligencias y resplandores de las lámparas de fuego' (3.69), 'the deep understandings and glowings of the lamps of fire find space'. Within the purified soul, in other words, is an infinite space where the attributes of God are free to dwell and to become the soul's whole work. 'Que estava oscuro y ciego', naturally enough, refers to the time before this was true, when enslavement to sense-based life experienced the absence of God in darkness. San Juan confidently applies some of the great texts of the Hebrew scriptures to the soul's journey, as well as the more unexpected ones. In 3.38

the soul's progress from meditation to contemplation becomes an inner Exodus, out of captivity in Egypt, which offers at best only the making of bricks from straw, to the promised land of milk and honey, to which her spiritual director is supposed to guide her. She is called into the desert clad in the riches plundered from the Egyptians (the sensitive part), whose armies drown in the sea of contemplation, in which they can find neither foothold nor object to which to cling. Now it is the Genesis creation story which is applied to her, for 'hasta que el Señor dijo: *Fiat lux* (Genesis 1.3), estaban las tinieblas sobre la haz del abismo de la caverna del sentido del alma' (3.71), 'until the Lord said: *Let there be light* (Genesis 1.3), darkness was upon the face of the abyss of the cavern of the senses of the soul'. This is not the darkness of faith or the Dionysian 'rayo de tiniebla' (3.49), but of ignorance. Until God enlightens her,

> esle imposible alzar los ojos a la divina luz ni caer en su pensamiento, porque no sabe cómo es, nunca habiéndola visto; y, por eso, ni la podrá apetecer, antes apetecerá tiniebla, porque sabe cómo es, y irá de una tiniebla en otra, guiado por aquella tiniebla, porque no puede guiar una tiniebla sino a otra tiniebla [. . .]. (3.71)

> it is impossible for her to raise her eyes to the divine light or think about it, because she does not know what it is, never having seen it; and therefore she cannot desire it, but will desire darkness, because she knows what that is, and will go from one darkness to another guided by that darkness, because one darkness cannot lead except to another darkness [. . .].

By locating the soul's journey in the antithesis of darkness and light and the image of the abyss in the Creation narrative and in a reworking of the Gospel saying about the blind leading the blind, San Juan cuts through pages of exposition on the subject in his earlier treatise and enables the reader to form a vivid impression of one essential aspect of his teaching. In the dark nights, it is the soul's dependence on what is familiar to her which must be broken and she must be brought to desire what she does not see or know (i.e. God) by the progressive letting go of what she does. He finds two texts from the Psalms which echo the Genesis imagery (18 [19].3; 41 [42].8): day calls unto day, night teaches night; abyss calls unto abyss. Like must call to like; so the divine grace which illuminates the soul is responding to 'otro abismo de gracia, que es esta transformación divina de el alma en Dios', 'another abyss of grace, which is this divine transformation of the soul in God'.

The line 'que estava oscuro y ciego' distinguishes darkness from blindness, and San Juan turns next to the blindness of human appetites, in terms of a cataract or cloud placed over the eye of the senses, which enables them only to see the obstacle and imagine that it, rather than the beauty which it covers, is the God they seek. For a moment he turns to an imaginary reader who raises an objection, that desire for God is surely to be encouraged. San Juan's response is a brief summary of his teaching in the third book of the *Subida*, since the desire and love of spiritual things can themselves become obstacles: 'entonces cataratas pones en el ojo y animal eres' (3.75), 'you put cataracts in your eye and become an animal'. But he also seems to lose patience with his own invented voice: 'Y si tienes más dudas, no sé qué te diga, sino que lo vuelvas a leer; quizá lo entenderás, que dicha esá la sustancia de la verdad y no se sufre aquí en esto alargarme más', 'And if you have any more doubts, I do not know what to say to you, except that you should read it again; you may understand it, for the substance of the truth has been explained and this is not the place for me to say more about it.' The comment is a bit rich from one who has just concluded a digression which threatens to throw the whole commentary off balance.

The last two lines of the verse take the commentary back to the theology of divine attributes, but associate them with one of San Juan's most characteristic teachings, the 'reentrega de amor', or mutual exchange of love between God and the soul.[23] These deep caverns of sense, once dark and blind, themselves now radiate 'calor y luz', and 'con estraños primores'. The juxtaposition of heat and light takes us back to the exegesis of the lamps of the first line of the verse, in which San Juan defined their properties in these terms (3.2). As befits the state of betrothal, the keynote is mutual giving and receiving: 'estando estas cavernas de las potencias ya tan mirífica y maravillosamente infundidas en los admirables resplandores de aquellas lámparas [. . .], están ellas enviando a Dios en Dios [. . .] esos mismos resplandores de las lámparas divinas, dando al Amado la misma luz y calor de amor que reciben' (3.77), 'since these caverns of the faculties are already so marvellously and wondrously pervaded with the wonderful radiance of those lamps [. . .], they are sending forth to God, in God, [. . .] this very radiance from the divine lamps, returning to the Beloved the very light and heat of love they are receiving'.

Several words in the quotation – 'cavernas', 'resplandores', 'lámparas', 'dando al Amado la misma luz y calor' – relate directly back to the poem. Others – 'mirífica y maravillosamente', 'admirables' – stress the wonder of the experience. But it is the phrase 'enviando a Dios en Dios' which is both puzzling and revealing. Prepositions, as we have seen on a number of occasions, count for San Juan, and, as here, are often not the expected ones. The meaning is this: the purified soul receives by divine infusion into the faculties knowledge and love and remembrance of the divine attributes. In receiving these 'primores', these excellent qualities, the soul becomes one with God, and 'en cierta manera es ella Dios por participación' (3.78), 'in a certain manner she is God by participation', since the faculties have been emptied of all finite obstacles which prevent union, and their whole content is divine. The word 'participation' is important.[24] This is not, and cannot be, a 'substantial' union, a union of substances or beings, because the soul is a creature and God is the Creator. But the soul participates in God because she knows and loves and remembers nothing other than God in his strength, beauty and justice (3.78), the 'primores' of the poem. If not union, it is a transformation of her substance, though she is but yet, to use the earlier image, 'como una sombra de Dios', 'like a shadow of God'. In this state of shadow, 'hace ella en Dios por Dios lo que El hace en ella por sí mismo al modo que [El] lo hace, porque la voluntad de los dos es una, y así la operación de Dios y de ella es una', 'she does in God through God what he does in her through himself, in his own way, because the two wills are one, and hence God's working and hers are one'. God's free and gracious gift is given to her, and she may return it as it is, freely, graciously, forming a

> verdadera y entera dádiva de el alma a Dios. Porque allí ve el alma que verdaderamente Dios es suyo, y que ella le posee con posesión hereditaria, con propiedad de derecho, como hijo de Dios adoptivo y por la gracia que Dios le hizo de dársele a sí mismo [. . .]. (3.78)

> true and entire gift of the soul to God. For there the soul sees that truly God is hers, and that she possesses him by hereditary possession, in her own right, as an adoptive son of God, and through the grace God bestowed on her by giving himself to her [. . .]

There is therefore a constant exchange between the soul and God, ever renewing the love between them and enabling the soul to love God with God's own love, instead of her finite affections. Though no biblical texts are cited, the Pauline language of adoption, sonship and inheritance (Romans 8.15–17; Galatians 4.5–7) marks this passage out in San Juan's mind as based on scriptural authority. This is the essence of the spiritual marriage:

> Y así entre Dios y el alma está actualmente formado un amor recíproco en conformidad de la unión y entrega matrimonial, en que los bienes de entrambos, que son la divina esencia, poseyéndolos cada uno libremente por razón de la entrega voluntaria del uno al otro, los poseen entrambos juntos. (3.79)

> And thus between God and the soul there is formed in actuality a reciprocal love in conformity with the giving and union of marriage, in which the goods of each, which are the divine essence, are both possessed jointly, each freely possessing the other's by dint of each having freely given the self to the other.

The capacity of the soul to give back to God infinitely more than she could ever contain is due entirely to his transforming work. Conscious, perhaps, of the difficulty of such a statement, San Juan draws a metaphor from politics: a ruler of many realms and peoples can bestow them on whomsoever he will, though they are far greater in extent than he is. In other words, even human experience provides analogies of how an individual can make gifts out of all proportion to that individual's physical limitations.

This, then, is the marriage, the highest state attainable in mortal life, a state of reciprocal exchange between God and the soul, in which the soul returns the 'primores' she receives 'junto a su querido', as the poem says, 'porque junta es la comunicación del Padre y del Hijo y del Espíritu Santo en el alma, que son luz y fuego de amor en ella' (3.80), 'because joint is the communication of Father, Son and Holy Spirit in the soul, who are the light and fire of love within her'. San Juan does not lose sight of the controlling image of the 'lámparas de fuego', givers both of light and heat, as he expounds the new phrase. But he has not finished yet with the 'primores'. It is 'cierta imagen de fruición' (3.81), 'a certain image of fruition', a double modification of the second noun, which, like the image of the transformed soul as 'shadow', or the presence of remaining 'veils and curtains' (4.7), makes it clear that San Juan understands even the marriage as only a foretaste of the glory of the eternal enjoyment of God beyond death. This 'fruition' is defined through a series of 'primores', representing the love, joy, praise and thanksgiving which the soul here experiences (3.81–5).

The first three stanzas of the poem were all addressed to different aspects of the fire of love: the flame, the cautery and the lamps. The fourth stanza, though still exclamatory, describes the effects they have. More precisely, it resumes the second person singular address from the end of the second verse. The subject of the three verbs in the last stanza is not altogether clear: it could be the 'llama de amor' or any of the four objects addressed in the second verse, the last of which, and therefore the logical subject, is the 'toque delicado'. What the poem conceals the commentary clarifies: the unexpressed subject is the 'Verbo Esposo', the Word who is the Bridegroom of the soul.

A new image dominates the first part of the exposition, and leads to San Juan's profoundest insights into the relationship between the creatures and God, the material world and the realm of pure Spirit. The poem's verb 'recuerdas' leads him to reflect on the many 'recuerdos' God gives to the soul and in particular to a remarkable description of this 'remembrance' or 'awakening' which God effects in the soul so 'manso y amoroso', 'gently and lovingly'. Whereas the term might lend itself well to an exploration of Platonic anamnesis, it turns out to prompt not the recovery of a lost memory, but the divine vision of a creation renewed:

> este recuerdo es un movimiento que hace el Verbo en la sustancia del alma de tanta grandeza, señorío y gloria, y de tan íntima suavidad, que le parece al alma que todos los bálsamos y especies odoríferas y flores del mundo se trabucan y menean, revolviéndose para dar su suavidad, y que todos los reinos y señoríos del mundo y todas las potestades y virtudes del cielo se mueven; y no sólo eso, sino que también todas las virtudes y sustancias y perfecciones y gracias de todas las cosas criadas relucen y hacen el mismo movimiento, todo a una y en uno. Que, por cuanto, como dice San Juan (1,3–4), *todas las cosas en él son vida; y en él viven y son y se mueven*, como también dice el Apóstol (Act 17,28), de aquí es que, moviéndose este tan grande Emperador en el alma, *cuyo principado*, como dice Isaías, *trae sobre su hombro* (9,6), que son las tres máquinas, celeste, terrestre e infernal, y las cosas que hay en ellas *sustentándolas todas*, como dice San Pablo (Hebr 1,3), con *el Verbo de su virtud*, todas a una parezcan moverse – al modo que al movimiento de la tierra se mueven todas las cosas materiales que hay en ella como si no fuesen nada-, así es cuando se mueve este príncipe que trae sobre sí su corte, y no la corte a él. (4.4)

> This remembrance is a movement made by the Word in the substance of the soul, of such grandeur, majesty and glory, and so intimate and gentle, that it seems to the soul that all the balsams and fragrant spices and flowers of the world are moving and mingling together as they turn and give off their sweet fragrance; that all the kingdoms and realms of the world and all the powers and virtues of the heavens are moving; and not only this, but all the virtues and substances and perfections and graces of every created thing are shining as together they move, each to the other and in each other. For as St John says (1.3), *all things in him are life*; and as the Apostle also says (Acts 17.28), *in him they live and move and have their being*. Hence, when this Emperor *whose government,* as Isaiah says (9.6), *is upon his shoulder* (by which is meant the three created spheres of heaven, earth and hell and everything in them, *upholding all things*, as St Paul says (Hebrews 1.3), *by the Word of his power*) moves within the soul, all seem to move as one. Just as all material things on earth move as the earth moves, as if they were nothing, so it is when this prince moves, whose court is upon himself, not he upon it.

This extraordinary piece of writing is the final theological answer of San Juan to those who see him as negating all forms of earthly beauty, and complements the artistic response given by his poetry. The four biblical texts he paraphrases provide the justification for holding together in an indissoluble unity the realms of sense and spirit, creatures and God, the finite and the infinite – all those 'contrarios' which in the *Subida-Noche* had to be prised apart so that the temptation to give the first the allegiance due only to the second could be resisted and overcome. But now that process is complete. The created order, in all its variety, no longer poses the unintended threat it did when the soul's disordered attachments to it desired to turn it into a possession to be grasped and an object to be worshipped. It resumes its freedom and becomes for the soul what God has always intended it to be – itself, in its beauty and variety, no longer the soul's unwitting servant, which will equally unwittingly enslave her, but her equal, her brother and sister. San Juan evokes the fragile beauty and fragrance of flowers and spices, representing the realm of nature, but also the radiant beauties of every created thing. He then turns to images of power – the political systems human empires construct, and the vastness of the universe itself. No longer are these seen as separate phenomena, but as part of one single movement, in which each conserves its particularity yet shares in all the others:

> Todos descubren las bellezas de su ser, virtud y hermosura y gracias, y la raíz de su duración y vida; porque echa allí de ver el alma cómo todas las criaturas de arriba y abajo tienen su vida y duración y fuerza en él [. . .] Y aunque es verdad que echa allí de ver el alma que estas cosas son distintas de Dios en cuanto tienen ser criado, y las ve en El con fuerza, raíz y vigor, es tanto lo que conoce ser Dios en su ser con infinita inminencia todas estas cosas, que las conoce mejor en su ser que en ellas mismas. Y éste es el deleite

grande de este recuerdo: conocer por Dios las criaturas, y no por las criaturas a Dios; que es conocer los efectos por su causa y no la causa por los efectos, que es conocimiento trasero, y esotro esencial. (4.5)

All reveal the beauties of the being, power, loveliness and graces, and the root of their duration and life. Because the soul sees there how all the creatures, above and below, have their life and duration and strength in him [. . .] And although it is true that the soul sees there that these things are distinct from God in that their being is a created one, and that she sees them in him with their strength, root and vigour, so great is her knowledge of God's being in his infinite immanence in them all that she knows them better in his being than in their own. And this is the great delight of this remembrance: to know the creatures through God, not God through the creatures; which is to to know the effects through their cause and not the cause through the effects, which is knowledge from behind, while this is knowledge of the essence.

When in the fifth stanza of the 'Cántico' the creatures had replied to the Bride's question about her Beloved's whereabouts they had spoken of the 'gracias' and 'hermosura' he had bestowed upon them, as San Juan does now. But their beauty could not satisfy the Bride's quest, because the Beloved had passed through them but gone on. That verse, as we saw, is San Juan's representation of a famous passage in Augustine's *Confessions*, and of the well-worn theme of the creation as a book to be read for knowledge of the Creator. We have also noted how often San Juan returns to the story of Moses' vision of the 'back parts' of God in Exodus 33; in S 2.24.3, for example, it is clearly stated to be a vision of the divine essence or substance. Now San Juan seems to be implying by his contrast between 'conocimiento trasero' and 'esencial' that it was something less. The discrepancy is not important; the distinction between the two kinds of knowledge of God is. The one is indirect, mediated by the world of creatures, the 'efectos' of an unseen cause; the other is direct, unmediated, their cause. To see the whole created order as God sees it is to recognize its source and its goal, and to know its true beauty. That is why San Juan can say that in this vision the creatures are better perceived than when they are seen as a dim reflection of the God who brought them into being.

The relationship of cause to effect is, of course, one deeply rooted in philosophy, and San Juan would have encountered it in his study of Aristotle. But it is also a rhetorical trope, metonymy. The vision is described in terms of a movement of God within the soul, though it should be remembered that in his earlier discussion of divine movement (3.11) the term was qualified. Where he had seen the presence of the Trinity in the poem through the naming of effects to signify causes (in the exegesis of the 'cauterio', 'mano' and 'toque' in 2.1) he now applies the same reasoning to explain the paradox of the unmoved Mover who moves. What appears to be the movement and the remembering of God is in fact the soul being moved and remembered by God:

> Y cómo sea este movimiento en el alma – como quiera que Dios sea inmovible – es cosa maravillosa, porque, aunque entonces Dios no se mueve realmente, al alma le parece que en verdad se mueve; porque, como ella es la innovada y movida por Dios para que vea esta sobrenatural vista, y se le descubre con tanta novedad aquella divina vida y el ser y armonía de toda criatura en ella con sus movimientos en Dios, parécele que Dios es el que se mueve, y que toma la causa el nombre de el efecto que hace. (4.6)
>
> And how this movement in the soul takes place is a wondrous thing, since God is not moved, because although God does not actually move it seems to the soul that he really is moving; because since it is she who is renewed and moved by God so that she can see this supernatural sight, and since his divine life and the harmony of every creature in that life with its movements in God is revealed to her, it seems to her that God is the one who is moving, and so the cause is named from the effect it produces.

San Juan connects this perception with the lowly estate of the human condition, in which we measure others according to ourselves: thieves believe everyone else steals, good people think well of everyone, and when we are neglectful and sleeping before God, we imagine that God is neglectful and sleeping towards us (4.8). So effect is confused for cause; we create God in our image, as we construct people and objects, and because we are not aware of this we misread and misuse them. So too the poetic trope, unless it is recognized for what it is, leads to error; rhetoric betrays the truth when its artfulness is assumed to possess only the meaning apparent on the surface. Though San Juan does not tease out all these implications, they are surely present, since these remarks follow immediately on the distinction he draws between cause and effect in relation to the two kinds of knowledge of God.

Unsurprisingly, perhaps, for those used to mystical literature, the account of this 'recuerdo' is followed by a return to the ineffability topos: 'totalmente es indecible' (4.10), 'it is completely inexpressible', and beyond enumeration: 'suena en el alma una potencia inmensa en voz de multitudes de excelencias de millares de millares de virtudes nunca numerables de Dios', 'there sounds in the soul an immense power through the voice of the multitude of the excellences of thousands upon thousands of virtues of God which can never be counted'. How can the soul bear this? The poem reveals the answer in the adjectives 'manso' and 'amoroso', which in the commentary acquire a paradoxical meaning through their association with this 'recuerdo'. God's power and glory are given in gentleness and love, because in him all the divine attributes are one: 'Y así, tanta mansedumbre y amor siente el alma en él cuanto poder y señorío y grandeza, porque en Dios todo es una misma cosa' (4.12), 'Thus the soul experiences as much gentleness and love in him as she does power and lordship and greatness, because in God all is one and the same thing.' San Juan's biblical warrant comes from the book of Esther, which, like the Song, never mentions God explicitly, but contains nuptial imagery (albeit in a narrative rather than a poetic text) which is easily spiritualized.[25] The soul, like Esther, becomes queen, enthroned with God, in the place where he alone dwells, her inmost substance.

This secret dwelling of God in the soul, from the poem's alliterative 'donde secretamente solo moras', brings the commentary to a close, since the last three lines of the verse are dealt with very briefly and with further emphasis on ineffability. San Juan takes the verb 'moras' and weaves around it a series of statements which define the indwelling of God in different souls. He is present, hidden, in them all, but

> en unas mora solo, y en otras no mora solo; en unos mora agradado, y en otras mora desagradado; en unas mora como en su casa, mandándolo y rigiéndolo todo, y en otras mora como extraño en casa ajena, donde no le dejan mandar nada ni hacer nada. El alma donde menos apetitos y gustos moran propios es donde El más solo y más agradado y más como en casa propia mora, rigiéndola y gobernándola, y tanto más secreto mora cuanto más solo (4.14).

> in some he dwells alone, and in others he does not; in some he dwells well-pleased, and in others ill-pleased; in some he dwells as in his own home, commanding and ruling everything, and in others he dwells as a stranger in an alien house, where he is not allowed to rule or do anything. The soul in which fewest of her own appetites and pleasures dwell is where he dwells more alone and more pleased and more as in his own home, directing and governing it, and the more alone he is the more secretly he dwells.

This dwelling is not secret to the perfected soul, but nor is it experienced continually. It is a kind of rest or sleep. Through this new image San Juan writes words which could well have served as a commentary to the sixth verse of the 'Noche oscura':

En mi pecho florido,	In my flowering breast
que entero para él solo se guardaba,	which wholly for him alone was kept,
allí quedó dormido [. . .]	there he fell asleep [. . .]

> Pero a la misma alma en esta perfección no le está secreto, la cual siente en sí este íntimo abrazo; pero, según estos recuerdos, no siempre, porque, cuando los hace el Amado, le parece al alma que recuerda él en su seno, donde antes estaba como dormido, que, aunque le sentía y gustaba, era como al amado dormido en el sueño; y, cuando uno de los dos está dormido no se comunican las inteligencias y amores de entrambos hasta que ambos están recordados. (4.14)

> But it is not secret to the soul in this perfected state, who feels within herself this intimate embrace; but not always, in these remembrances, because when the Beloved brings them it seems to the soul that he is awakening in her bosom, where before he lay as if asleep; although she

> experienced and enjoyed him, he was like the beloved fast asleep; and when one of the two is asleep their mutual love and knowledge is not communicated, until both are awake.

He is always present, 'como dormido en este abrazo con la esposa' (4.15), 'asleep in this embrace with the Bride', but the remembrances are intermittent for her. Were they continual, she would be in the glory for which she longs.

Finally, this divine 'recuerdo' is the poem's 'aspirar sabroso/de bien y gloria lleno' by which God loves the soul, and is the work of the Holy Spirit, as the image of breath implies. The last paragraph may stand as representative of all San Juan's prose expositions, because it repeats the impossibility of describing so lofty a state and immediately proceeds to define it – the contradiction which is the seed-bed from which all mystical writing springs:

> En la cual *aspiración llena de bien y gloria* y *delicado amor* de Dios para el alma yo no querría hablar, ni aun quiero, porque veo claro que no lo tengo de saber decir [. . .] Porque es una *aspiración* que hace al alma Dios, en que, por aquel *recuerdo* del alto conocimiento de la Deidad, la *aspira* el Espíritu Santo con la misma proporción que fue la inteligencia y noticia de Dios, en que la absorbe profundísimamente en el Espíritu Santo, *enamorándola* con *primor y delicadeza* divina, según aquello que vio en Dios; porque, siendo la aspiración *llena de bien y gloria*, en ella *llenó* el Espíritu Santo al alma *de bien y gloria*, en que la *enamoró* de sí sobre toda lengua y sentido en los profundos de Dios: Al cual sea honra y gloria in saecula saeculorum. Amen. (4.17)

> I would not wish to speak, nor shall I, of *this breath full of good and glory and of the delicate love of God* towards the soul, because I see clearly that I am unable to know what to say [. . .] *Because it is a breath of God* to the soul, in which, by *that remembrance of the lofty* knowledge of the Godhead, *he breathes the Holy Spirit* into her in proportion to the understanding and knowledge received from God, into which she is profoundly *absorbed in the Holy Spirit, who enamours her with divine excellence and delicacy,* according to what she saw in God. *For since this breath is full of good and glory, the Holy Spirit filled the soul through it with good and glory, which made her fall in love with himself* above all language and meaning in the deep things of God: to whom be honour and glory, for ever and ever. Amen.

I have emphasized the words and expressions in the Spanish text which come directly from the poem, to show how closely San Juan follows it in his exposition. Given that his first words express his wish not to speak of this 'aspirar [. . .] de bien y gloria lleno' because he cannot, and that the rest of the paragraph contradicts this, we should note how important the poem is in providing him with a language with which he can begin to do so. The text ends with a traditional ascription of glory to God, and San Juan's words fall silent. But the fact that poetry, prose and the insufficiency of language are all brought together at this climactic point, and are resolved into praise, makes a fitting conclusion to San Juan's endeavours. Each is affirmed because each is allowed a place; yet together they do no more than reveal their own inadequacy.

When we take San Juan's commentaries seriously, and the *Llama* above all, there emerges not only a theory of language and its insufficiency but also a rhetoric of paradoxical discourse without which the paradoxes of the poetry hang detached and might seem superficial. The commentary reproduces the style of the poem in its exclamatory periods and use of direct address, and it pays careful attention to many of the words in the poem and the precise meaning they carry in that context. The biblical references often add a further level of imagery which, when brought alongside the poetic images, creates a stylistic technique in which correspondences are established between apparently unrelated objects through some common point, and work with the intellectual density of *conceptista* writing. But, above all, the commentary is a prolongation of paradox, from beginning to end, in which new patterns of paradox are being continually woven out of poetic, biblical and exegetical material. By this means, San Juan clarifies the nature of the poem's underlying images and metaphors, and nowhere more so than when he proceeds to unwrap the terms of the paradox and finds in it relations both of likeness and unlikeness. The flame, the wound, light and darkness are given a content which without the commentary they could not have.

How many of the images of the 'Llama' poem came attached with a ready-made spiritual interpretation at the moment of composition is impossible to know. It was not written before 1582 (when San Juan met Ana de Peñalosa in Granada for the first time), and the commentary implies that some time elapsed between the writing of the poem and its exposition (Prol. 3). By 1582 he had already written at least parts of his other commentaries, and may well have composed the 'Llama' poem, unlike the others, with the intention of providing it with one. But we do know that he wrote naturally and unaffectedly about divine love in terms of human love. He understood the nature of the metaphor, and he redeemed its tired paradoxes by applying them to a love which language can never capture because language is finite and creaturely, while this love is infinite and its speaking and its acting are one.

The *Llama* commentary represents the most successful fusion of San Juan's poetic and spiritual writing, the nearest San Juan comes to resolving the formal generic contradictions caused by combining poetic exposition and doctrinal treatise. Its prose is highly symbolic and poetic – often, as we have tried to show, creating complex textures through variations on a few fundamental images or ideas. Its rhetoric, like the poem's, is often exclamatory and almost always tightly structured, with frequent use of techniques of repetition. It is not completely successful, because such writing never can be. Its use of the topos of inexpressibility and its digressions both point beyond its confines, in the first case into the abyss of the wordless and imageless, in the second away from the flame of union into the background against which it plays.

Nonetheless, the *Llama* shows that in the end San Juan is not simply a negative theologian. The symbol of the 'llama' is in many ways the positive counterbalance to the 'noche'. The painful detachment required in the dark night is one and the same with the purgation by burning in the flame. Unlike the night, the flame is less the beginning of the journey or the journey itself, but above all its end, the transformation of the soul who has reached the desired goal, life in the Holy Trinity. When the image of the divine 'recuerdo' appears in the final stanza, the *Llama* resolves the earlier negative attitudes towards creation by affirming the beauty and freedom of each created thing, present to the soul but known and loved as God loves it, instead of desired in order to satisfy the unpurged soul's possessiveness, which it can never do. Therefore, however much San Juan has come to be regarded as the theologian of negation and *nada*, he is in the end as much a witness to the fire of love in which the soul is joyfully transformed as of the sufferings of the dark night. Both symbols, one might say, are in the end different ways of speaking about the same inexpressible reality.

NOTES

1 For example, Fernando Lázaro Carreter, 'Poética de San Juan de la Cruz', *Actas*, I, pp. 25–45 (pp. 25–6). The term *lira* was taken to include a number of different forms; see I. Caramuel [Lobkowitz, bishop of Vigevano], *Primus Calamus*, 2 vols. (Rome: 1663–68), II, pp. 345–75, 627–32. San Juan's only 'error' lies in referring to the 'Llama' as 'estas liras', when the model for the verse is the shorter half of a *silva* turned into a six-line *lira*. On this poem, see George Tavard, *Poetry and Contemplation in St John of the Cross* (Athens: Ohio University Press, 1988), pp. 181–96.

2 See above, pp. 199, 224; also L 1.11–12.

3 Luce López-Baralt, *Asedios a lo indecible: San Juan de la Cruz canta al éxtasis transformante (Madrid: Trotta, 1998)*, pp. 191, 230.

4 This process is studied by Luis Miguel Fernández, 'El desdoblamiento en la "Llama de amor viva" (una cala en la canción tercera)', *Actas*, I, pp. 387–98.

5 See above, p. 86.

6 Famously in his 'Vida retirada' ode.

7 See F. Ruiz, H. Hatzfeld, Alberto de la Virgen del Carmen; quoted in Gabriel Castro, '*Llama de amor viva*', in *Introducción a San Juan de la Cruz*, pp. 493–529, 494. For a recent scholarly translation, see *The Living Flame of Love, Versions A and B*, trans. Jane Ackerman (Binghamton, NY: Medieval and Renaissance Texts and Studies, 1995). On the commentary, see Tavard, *Poetry and Contemplation*, pp. 193–216.

8 The authenticity of the second redaction has not been seriously questioned. For a summary of the changes, see Castro, *Introducción a San Juan de la Cruz*, pp. 501–2.

9 For the significance of the inflammation of language, see above, pp. 232–3.

10 Spanish 'vivo' has both the meaning of bright and living.

11 See above, pp. 144–5, 218, for earlier comments about readership.

12 See Alastair Hamilton, *Heresy and Mysticism in Sixteenth-Century Spain: The Alumbrados* (Cambridge: James Clarke, 1992).

13 See Ian Macpherson, '"Rompe la tela de este dulce encuentro": San Juan's *Llama de amor viva* and the Courtly Context', in *Studies in Honor of Bruce W. Wardropper*, ed. Dian Fox, Harry Sieber and Robert Ter Horst (Newark, Delaware: Juan de la Cuesta, 1989), pp. 193–203.

14 'Batter my heart, three-person'd God', and 'Show me deare Christ, thy Spouse', respectively; from *John Donne*, ed. John Hayward (Penguin: Harmondsworth, 1950), pp. 172–3.

15 Terence O'Reilly, 'Courtly Love and Mysticism in Spanish Poetry of the Golden Age', *JHR*, 1 (1992–3), pp. 53–76; especially pp. 68–72.

16 2 Corinthians 3.13–16; Hebrews 6.19, 10.20.

17 The classical and biblical overtones of the 'thread' of life do not seem to fit the third of these explanations, which is more original (though he might have used 2 Corinthians 3.13). He does not make any connection with Matthew 27.51, though it may have been in the back of his mind: 'Et ecce velum templi scissum est in duas partes a summo usque deorsum', 'And lo, the veil of the temple was rent in twain from top to bottom', often interpreted as the death of Christ opening a way of direct access to the Father.

18 The attributions are not as forced as they may seem; Irenaeus interprets the Son and the Spirit as the hands of the Father: 'Per manus enim Patris, id est, per Filium et Spiritum, fit homo secundum similitudinem Dei'; in *Sancti Irenæi Episcopi Lugdunensis: Libri Quinque Adversus Hæreses*, 2 vols (Cambridge: Typis Academicis, 1857), II, p. 333 (note 2).

19 San Juan cites both St Gregory (*Homil. 30 in Evang.; PL* 76, 1220) and the Breviary (Resp. 1 Mat. fer. V oct. Pent.) in support of his argument.

20 Cf. 'the coals thereof are coals of fire, which hath a most vehement flame' (AV).

21 See above, p. 242.

22 For a detailed stylistic analysis of the opening of the commentary, see Gaetano Chiappini, 'El modelo general de la semántica del "deseo" en la primera declaración de la "Llama de amor viva" (Texto B)', in *Actas,* I, pp. 233–44.

23 See Juan de Jesús María, '"Le amará tanto como es amada"', *EphCarm*, 6 (1955), pp. 3–103; above, pp. 179–83.

24 See above, p. 182.

25 There are six references to Esther in the *Llama*, and only two outside it; three of the six, however, come from the deuterocanonical additions, which do name God.

11

Conclusion

I return for the last time to San Juan's poetry. At various points I have raised the question of its nature as a theological statement. I do not mean that a positive assessment in this respect would make it any less of a work of art; but that as such theologians as well as literary critics may properly reflect on what it says and how it says it. Among the former, Hans Urs von Balthasar has claimed that San Juan's poems 'are the decisive statement' in his work compared with the 'unsuccessful, defective commentary' on them.[1] Only one book, as far as I am aware, has taken up the challenge implied in that judgement.[2] Equally, most of all in the *Llama*, I have wondered about the nature of his theology as poetry; that is, as a statement which does not claim to exhaust dogmatic truths, but rather to point always beyond their human formulation to the God who is their source. San Juan's writing comes from the margins; out of the poverty and suffering of his childhood and his final months, and the life of a contemplative friar, far removed from circles of power, influence and wealth. We have noted how different it is from that of his contemporaries, in genesis, motivation and purpose. Sometimes he seems to speak to us from a great distance: his words face us on the page, but they belong to a closed world. At other times a phrase or an image catches fire in the imagination and burns steadily there. His marginality creates the difference, and if his poetry can be said to be a theology, or his theology, poetry, the reasons will lie in that difference.

Can his poetry be understood as part of his theological and spiritual achievement, without destroying its artistic integrity? If it cannot be, there will always be a disjunction between its literal and spiritual meanings and between art and spirituality, rather than a continuity or spectrum; and from this disjunction will naturally arise those interpretations which seek (for example) to reduce San Juan to barest Freudian essentials. I believe San Juan's poetry needs to be seen as a kind of extended metonymy, a naming of effects to signify a cause, through recourse to linguistic techniques, many of which are strange even in the context of sixteenth-century religious poetry. The cause of the poetry is intense mystical experience, which cannot be captured by words but which, if my earlier judgement is correct, is not beyond their power to represent, however inadequately. That experience itself has a cause, or more precisely, Cause, since not only is God in all his inaccessible mystery its agent, God in his self-giving love is the Creator and Redeemer of humanity and all the creatures, including language. The fact that San Juan's *liras* use language so originally can in itself be seen as evidence that what it signifies in them is different from what its particular signifiers might, in another context, suggest. If that is so, the poems as they stand, without need of any commentary, are themselves a witness to the effects brought about by the experience of union with the Cause. The experience they represent disrupts the normal vision of the world and forces the poet to undertake its rewriting. When San Juan describes how the creatures are revalued and affirmed by the divine 'recuerdo' in the soul (L 4.4–7) because they are now seen from God's perspective – unutterably beautiful, but also free for her to enjoy them in a way she could not while she remained attached to them – might not this same vision be predicated of the language of the three great *lira* poems?

I argued that the 'Cántico' represented a reordering of the cosmos, a world made new, in which elements from the familiar world combine in new and unexpected ways, so that as we read the poem we begin to see that world differently and sense something of its beauty and wonder.[3] Nature, art and human love all have their place in it, and though some images represent distractions and disturbances, especially in the earlier part of the Lover's trajectory, even they do not have a purely negative meaning, since they are used at other points of lover and Beloved alike. The negative side, explored so thoroughly in the *Subida-Noche,* is connected with the soul's creatureliness and sinfulness, and with the transcendence and otherness of God. Negation, usually expressed in terms of purgation and detachment, is never an end in itself, but must be undergone for the sake of the greater wonders to come. But the positive side is the first and last witness to union: the poetry, in which San Juan first sought to express his experience, and the *Llama* commentary, his last reflection on it. In terms of his writing, the negative part, therefore, is enclosed between the two literary manifestations of the positive, though each has elements of the other: the 'Noche' is dark, but the darkness is joyful and affirmative; the 'Llama' is ardent, but the flame wounds, and there has been darkness to negotiate before its light and heat can be felt.

With all his emphasis on detachment and 'nada', 'nothing', San Juan is most commonly thought of as a negative theologian. But that is only part of the story, the beginning and the middle, not the end. There are three distinct phases in San Juan's teaching about attitudes towards the created world. The first, which has already taken place before the 'Cántico' begins, requires the detachment of the senses from its beauties, not because they are evil but because they are evanescent, and therefore cannot satisfy her hunger for permanence. The second enables the soul to read the book of creation for signs of the Beloved (C 4–5). If the existence and nature of the Creator can, as was widely believed, be read from the multiplicity and variety of the creatures, who bear the stamp of their origin, it follows that they can become images of God for the divinized soul, or of the 'places' where human lover and divine Beloved are united. The third, only explicitly stated in the *Llama,* allows the soul in union with God to glory in the whole creation because she sees it as he does, not as something to be desired and possessed for its own sake or hers. This surely is the context to which one of San Juan's most celebrated utterances belongs, the so-called 'Oración del alma enamorada'. 'Prayer of the soul in love', his gloss on St Francis of Assissi's exclamation 'Deus meus et omnia', 'My God and all things':

> Míos son los cielos y mía es la tierra. Mías son las gentes. Los justos son míos, y míos los pecadores. Los ángeles son míos, y la Madre de Dios y todas las cosas son mías. Y el mismo Dios es mio y para mí, porque Cristo es mío y todo para mí. Pues, ¿qué pides y buscas, alma mía? Tuyo es todo esto, y todo es para ti. (*Dichos de luz y amor*, 26)[4]
>
> Mine are the heavens and mine the earth. Mine are the nations. The just are mine and mine are the sinners. The angels are mine and the Mother of God and all things are mine. And God himself is mine and for me, because Christ is mine and altogether for me. So what is it you desire and seek, my soul? All this is yours, and everything is for you.

Contrary to conventional linguistic usage, the repeated possessive pronouns and adjectives, which would normally indicate selfishness and greed, represent their antithesis: detachment from the desire to possess anything at all for oneself, so that everything can be freely appreciated for what it is, not for what it might offer one's desires or contribute to one's self-esteem. Language has been undermined, made to say the opposite of what the words appear to mean.

Undeniably, San Juan's poetry posseses a remarkable ability to open the reader's eyes to the world of nature and art so that they may be seen afresh, and their true beauty and wonder be sensed as if for the first time. The effect of creating new and surprising combinations of images taken from a variety of poetic traditions, and even the effect of taking the already mysterious images of the Song and reworking them into patterns which depart from their biblical order, allow the reader to experience the beauty of the familiar and the unfamiliar in constantly changing ways. San Juan is much more radical in this respect than any other poet of the Golden Age, Góngora included. Góngora may twist word order, introduce new words from Latin or Greek, create the most extraordinary metaphors which can only be elucidated by intellectual processes, even if their very density or outlandishness cause the reader to react to commonplace objects with *admiratio.* Through such techniques, simple, everyday objects acquire a sense of mystery and wonder, rather like the cabbages, melons and quinces in the still-life paintings of Sánchez Cotán, displayed with almost geometric proportions against a dark background, so that they are no longer humble objects from the kitchen but infinitely mysterious creations.[5] Yet San Juan's poetry does not generally concentrate on particular things, or shine an unusual spotlight on them (the dark night excepted). In the 'Cántico' it offers a constantly changing world in which the only stable point is the love between the protagonists, as this moves from absence and longing to fulfilment and joy. Circling that point are constellations of images in which now one star and now another shine briefly, disappear, only to appear again, perhaps in a new guise.

One reason San Juan's poetry has found favour in the last 50 years is that in its use of symbols and its impressionistic and sometimes surreal techniques it appears to anticipate the twentieth century's breakdown of traditional patterns of narrative and poetry and to encourage thereby an openness to multiple readings. But whereas twentieth-century artistic experimentation has reflected a widespread breakdown in traditional beliefs, values and cultural continuities, precisely the opposite occurs in the case of San Juan. For him, the language of his poetry represents the breakdown of human certainties and dogmas as humanity is remodelled in the dark nights by divine otherness. Human language and concepts cannot contain God, yet in the fracturing of their norms there is a witness to his presence. The inadequacy of language is on a par with the inadequacy of any finite, created object to bring about union with God. But that does not mean it has no purpose or function. Its frustrations are redemptive. It can point beyond itself and it can move the emotions and the spirit, opening doors of perception which more ordered discourse closes.

Returning to the topos of the universe as a book to be read as proof of the existence of God, one might take the vision in *Llama* 4 as a further example of the way San Juan confounds expectations. He is unhappy with this traditional view, not because the whole structure is breaking down under the impetus of Copernicus, of what would become science in the modern sense, but because it is partial, analogous with language itself. The creatures do not, in C 4–5, exist as a book to be read; even Fray Luis de Granada, the great exponent of this theology, writes of them as 'letras quebradas', 'broken letters'; they can only stammer something and point beyond themselves. San Juan's mystical vision thus finds itself on the side of the modern, as it does in his attitude towards language. But, as there, for radically different reasons: not that there is nothing, no meaning, no God in a world which can be explained in its own terms, but that human beings cannot grasp what their meaning might be until they have undertaken the harder journey within themselves, which is where the unitive path becomes revealed. Only then can the fragments of knowledge displayed so beautifully in the exterior world find their significance in the larger pattern which comes from knowledge of the self, and in that self, of a hidden God who is knowable there.

Von Balthasar's contention about the primacy of San Juan's poetry might also be tested in terms of the theological implications of San Juan's use of sexual language. Western thought has come to separate sexuality and spirituality in a way which tends to cheapen the first and disembody the second. Hence interpreting San Juan's mystical poetry has so often become a matter of choosing between an erotic and a religious reading. But if one looks for conjunctions, not discontinuities, a very different reading emerges, in which both can be affirmed. In terms of the erotic reading, embodied in his poetry and its world of mutual self-giving, tenderness, intimacy and joy, are important insights into the nature of human love: its beauty, sensitivity and mystery, as opposed to possessiveness, abuse and self-gratification. In its own way, therefore, it affirms the highest ideals of Christian teaching on human sexuality. But it is also a metaphor for human spiritual love, and the two are and must be connected because no human being can live a spiritual life without a body, as Santa Teresa seems to understand better than San Juan (or at least she is more direct about it).[6] But San Juan's poetry implies this connection. His too is an incarnational faith, in which the act of creation through the second Person of the Trinity and the Incarnation of that Person in the historical Christ binds together the material and the spiritual, and in which the Christian sacraments constantly represent that union, despite the Church's best attempts to separate them. If one takes the language and imagery of San Juan's poetry seriously as religious metaphor, one discovers that the worlds of matter and spirit are bound together: spiritual truths cannot be articulated apart from physical realities, nor can material realities exclude the spiritual, because God has bound himself to the world and to humanity in the Incarnation.

We have come full circle in our study of San Juan's poetry, back to the ballads on the opening verses of St John's Gospel, where the divine marriage with humanity takes place, the narrative framework and the theological foundation for the intensely lyrical and sensuous world of the 'Cántico', and the fundamental image around which that world is constructed. San Juan wrote in an age commonly associated in the popular imagination with the Inquisition, the imposition of orthodox dogma and the repression of all forms of independent and creative thought. The religion of that age seems based on fear of a God who is angered by human sin and who judges the wicked fit only for the fires of hell, of which the bonfires of an *auto-da-fe* might be a vivid foretaste. San Juan's poetry knows nothing of this, his prose very little. Fire, for example, is one of his great symbols for the purifying and transforming love of God. The only torments of which he writes are those which humans undergo as they make the painful transition from attachment to the realm of the finite, which cannot in the end, for all its beauty, stay their hunger, to the breaking in of infinity into their souls, which, paradoxically, is at the same time their own journeying within. In an age in which images of God seem fearful and tyrannical and people have to be frightened into compliance and controlled by threats and punishments, San Juan's God seeks his children in love, can be hurt by them, but does not cease searching for them. He is beautiful and gracious, and he gives his beauty and grace to the soul. Marriage between the divine and human worlds is his gift. One should not neglect the significance of such an understanding of the nature of God in the second half of sixteenth-century Spain. It should be restored to its rightful place, as part of the history of the Church in that period, and a welcome and refreshing counterbalance to the fear of divergence from an inflexible norm.

NOTES

1 Hans Urs von Balthasar, *The Glory of the Lord: A Theological Aesthetics*, 7 vols (Edinburgh: T. & T. Clark, 1982), III, pp. 120, 171.

2 Teodoro Polo, *San Juan de la Cruz: La fuerza de un decir* (Madrid: Espiritualidad, 1993).

3 Perrin sees this as a process shared by both author and reader: 'Juan, through his poetic world, actually shapes his experience and refigures the world'; David Brian Perrin, *Canciones entre el alma y Espasa of Juan de la Cruz: A Hermeneutical Interpretation* (San Francisco: Catholic Scholars Press, 1996), p. 74.

4 *Obras* (SJ), p. 45.

5 On Sánchez Cotán, see Jonathan Brown, *The Golden Age of Painting in Spain* (New Haven: Yale University Press, 1991), pp. 98–99; William B. Jordan and Peter Cherry, *Spanish Still Life from Velazquez to Goya* (London: National Gallery, 1995), pp. 26–34.

6 For example, her insistence on the value of works and on the need for the active and contemplative lives to be held together; see *Moradas del castillo interior*, 7.4.6, 10, 14. Also, her humorous criticism of San Juan for being too spiritual; *Obras* (ST), p. 1135.

Select Bibliography

Ackerman, Jane (trans.), *The Living Flame of Love, Versions A and B* (Binghamton, NY: Medieval and Renaissance Texts and Studies, 1995)

Agustín, San, *De doctrina christiana,* in *Obras de San Agustín,* edited by Balbino Martín, 2nd edn, 22 vols (Madrid: BAC,1969), XV

Alfonso el Sabio, *Las siete partidas del rey don Alfonso el Sabio,* 3 vols (Madrid: Imprenta Real, 1807)

Alín, José María (ed.), *Cancionero tradicional* (Madrid: Castalia, 1991)

Alonso, Dámaso, *La poesía de San Juan de la Cruz* (Madrid: CSIC, 1942); 4th edn (Madrid: Aguilar, 1966)

Alonso, Dámaso, 'La caza de amor es de altanería', *Obras completas,* 10 vols (Madrid: Gredos, 1972–93), II, pp. 1057–75

Alonso de la Madre de Dios, *Vida, virtudes y milagros del Santo Padre Fray Juan de la Cruz,* edited by Fortunato Antolín (Madrid: Espiritualidad, 1989)

Alvar, Manuel, 'La palabra y las palabras de San Juan de la Cruz', in *Presencia,* pp. 183–215

[anon] *Liber de la Institución* (Ávila: Vda. de Sigirano, 1959)

Anselm, St, *Prayers and Meditations of St Anselm,* translated by Sister Benedicta Ward (Harmondsworth: Penguin, 1973)

Antolín, Fortunato, 'En torno al culto de San Juan de la Cruz en Segovia', *SJC,* 12 (1993), pp. 267–78

Antolín, Fortunato (ed.), Primeras biografías y apologías de San Juan de la Cruz (Valladolid: Junta de Castilla y León, 1991)

Arrizabalaga, Jon, Henderson, John and French, Roger, *The Great Pox: The French Disease in Renaissance Europe* (New Haven: Yale University Press, 1996)

Atwan, Robert and Wieder, Laurance (eds), *Chapters into Verse,* 2 vols (Oxford and New York: Oxford University Press, 1993)

Balthasar, Hans Urs von, *The Glory of the Lord: A Theological Aesthetics,* 7 vols (Edinburgh: T. & T. Clark, 1982), III

Barth, Karl, *Church Dogmatics,* 13 vols (Edinburgh: T. & T. Clark, 1936–77)

Baruzi, Jean, *Saint Jean de la Croix et le problème de l'expérience mystique* (Paris: Alcan, 1924; 2nd edn, 1931)

Bataillon, Marcel, 'La tortolica de *Fontefrida* y del *Cantico espiritual*', *NRFE,* 7 (1953), pp. 291–306

Bayón, Balbino Velasco, 'La villa de Fontiveros a mediados del siglo XVI', in *'Juan de la Cruz, espíritu de llama',* pp. 23–39

Bayón, Balbino Velasco, 'El colegio de Carmelitas de Santa Ana de Medina', in *'Juan de la Cruz, espíritu de llama'*, pp. 111–27

Bayón, Balbino Velasco, 'Fray Juan de Santo Matía en Salamanca', in *'Juan de la Cruz, espíritu de llama'*, pp. 157–73

Bayón, Balbino Velasco, *Historia del Carmelo español*, 2 vols (Rome: Institutum Carmelitanum, 1992)

Bell, Aubrey F. G., *Castilian Literature* (Oxford: Clarendon, 1938)

Beltrán, Gabriel, 'San Juan de la Cruz en Baeza: Textos y notas del Libro de Protocolo del Colegio de San Basilio', *SJC*, 14 (1994), pp. 233–47

Bernard of Clairvaux: On the Song of Songs, translated by Kilian Walsh, 4 vols (Kalamazoo, Michigan: Cistercian Publications, 1979–83)

Blecua, José M., 'Los antecedentes del poema del *Pastorcico* de San Juan de la Cruz', *RFE*, 33 (1949), pp. 378–80

Blecua, José M., *Sobre poesía de la Edad de Oro* (Madrid: Gredos, 1970)

Blecua, José M. (ed.), *Francisco de Quevedo: Poemas escogidos* (Madrid: Castalia, 1972)

Bolado, Alfonso Álvarez, 'En medio y a las afueras de la sociedad secularizada: mística y secularización', *Actas*, III, pp. 249–76

Bouterwek, Friedrich, *History of Spanish and Portuguese Literature*, translated by Miss Thomasina Ross (London: Boosey, 1823)

Boyce, Philip, 'The influence of St John of the Cross in England', *Teresianum*, 42 (1991)

Brändle, Francisco, *Biblia en san Juan de la Cruz* (Madrid: Espiritualidad, 1990)

Brenan, Gerald, *The Literature of the Spanish People* (Harmondsworth: Penguin, 1963 [1951])

Brenan, Gerald, *St. John of the Cross: His Life and Poetry* (Cambridge: Cambridge University Press, 1973)

Brenner, Athalya, *The Song of Songs* (Sheffield: Sheffield Academic Press,1989)

Brown, Jonathan, *The Golden Age of Painting in Spain* (New Haven: Yale University Press, 1991)

Bruun, Bertel (ed.), Håkan Delin, Lars Svensson, *Guía de campo de aves de España y de Europa*, edn revised (Barcelona: Omega), 1990

Buckley, Michael, 'Atheism and Contemplation', *Theological Studies*, 40 (1979), pp. 680–99

Butler, Cuthbert, *Western Mysticism*, 3rd edn (London: Constable, 1967)

Calderón de la Barca, Pedro, *No hay más fortuna que Dios* (Manchester: Manchester University Press, 1949)

Calderón de la Barca, Pedro, *La vida es sueño*, edited by Ciriaco Morón Arroyo, 18th edn (Madrid: Cátedra, 1991)

Campbell, Roy (trans.), *Poems of St John of the Cross* (Glasgow: Collins, 1979 [London: Harvill, 1951])

Cantalapiedra, Fernando, 'Nota semióticas sobre el poema "¡Qué bien sé yo la fonte . . . " ', *Actas*, I, pp. 373–85

Caramuel [Lobkowitz], I., *Primus Calamus*, 2 vols (Roma: 1663–68)

Carreter, Fernando Lázaro, 'Poética de san Juan de la Cruz', *Actas*, I, pp. 25–45

Casado, Juan Delgado, *Diccionario de impresores españoles (siglos XV-XVII)*, 2 vols (Madrid: Arcos, 1996)

Castellano, Jesús, 'La experiencia del misterio litúrgico en San Juan de la Cruz', *Experiencia y pensamiento*, pp. 114–54

Castro, Gabriel, '*Llama de amor viva*', in *Introducción a san Juan de la Cruz*, pp. 493–529

Cervantes, Miguel de, *Novelas ejemplares*, edited by Harry Sieber, 2 vols (Madrid: Cátedra, 1986)

Cervantes, Miguel de, *Los trabajos de Persiles y Sigismunda*, edited by Juan Bautista Avalle-Arce (Madrid: Castalia, 1969)

Chaide, Malón de, *La conversión de la Magdalena*, edited by Félix García, 3 vols Clásicos castellanos, 3rd edn (Madrid: Espasa-Calpe, 1957–59)

Chiappini, Gaetano, 'El modelo general de la semántica del "deseo" en la primera declaración de la 'Llama de amor viva' (Texto B)', *Actas*, I, pp. 233–44

Cohen, J. M., *The Penguin Book of Spanish Verse* (Harmondsworth: Penguin, 1956)

Collinson, Patrick, 'Separation In and Out of the Church: The Consistency of Barrow and Greenwood', *The Journal of the United Reformed Church History Society*, 5 (1994), pp. 239–58

Córdoba, Sebastián de, *Las obras de Boscán y Garcilasso trasladadas en materias Christianas y religiosas* (Zaragoza: Juan Soler, 1577)

Covarrubias, Sebastián de, *Tesoro de la lengua castellana* (1611), facsimile edn (Barcelona: Horta, 1943)

Creel, Bryant L., *The Religious Poetry of Jorge de Montemayor* (London: Tamesis, 1981)

Crisógono de Jesús, *Vida y obras completas de San Juan de la Cruz*, 5th edn (Madrid: BAC, 1964)

Cross, F. L. and Livingstone, E. A. (eds), *The Oxford Dictionary of the Christian Church*, 3rd edn (Oxford: Oxford University Press, 1997)

Cuadro, Fernando Moreno, 'El arte de las fiestas sanjuanistas', *SJC*, 15–16 (1995), pp. 9–104

Cueto, Ronald, 'A Quest for Order in a Poet-Saint's Choice of Order', in *Essays and Poems Presented to Daniel Huws* (Aberystwyth: National University of Wales, 1994), pp. 329–50

Cuevas, Cristóbal, 'El bestiario simbólico en el "Cántico" de San Juan de la Cruz', in *Simposio sobre San Juan de la Cruz* (Ávila: Miján, 1986), pp. 181–203

Cuevas, Cristóbal, 'La literatura como signo de lo inefable: el género literario de los libros de San Juan de la Cruz', in *La literatura como signo*, edited by José Castillo Romera *et al.* (Madrid: Playor, 1981), pp. 98–106

Cuevas, Cristóbal, 'Estudio literario', *Introducción a San Juan de la Cruz*, pp. 125–201

Cuevas, Cristóbal (ed.), *'Cántico espiritual' de San Juan de la Cruz* (Mexico: Alhambra, 1985)

Cugno, Alain, *Saint John of the Cross: The Life and Thought of a Christian Mystic* (London: Burns & Oates, 1982)

Cummins, Norbert, *Freedom to Rejoice: Understanding St John of the Cross* (London: HarperCollins, 1991)

Dearmer, Percy and others (eds), *The Oxford Book of Carols*, (London: Oxford University Press, 1928)

Delgado, Vicente Muñoz, 'Filosofía, teología y humanidades en la Universidad de Salamanca durante los estudios de San Juan de la Cruz (1564–1568)', in *'Juan de la Cruz, espíritu de llama'*, pp. 175–211

Diccionario de Autoridades, 3 vols (Madrid: Gredos, 1984)

Dios, Efrén de la Madre de and Steggink, Otger (eds), *Obras completas de Santa Teresa de Jesús*, 2nd edn (Madrid: BAC, 1967)

Dombrowski, Daniel A. *St John of the Cross: An Appreciation* (New York: State University of New York Press, 1992)

Edmée, Sister, SLG, 'The Song of Songs and the Cutting of Roots', *Anglican Theological Review*, 80 (1998), pp. 547–61

Egido, Teófanes, 'Contexto histórico de San Juan de la Cruz', *Experiencia y pensamiento*, pp. 335–77

Egido, Teófanes, 'El hermano de San Juan de la Cruz: reliquias y testamento', *Actas*, II, pp. 483–92

Egido, Teófanes, 'Los Yepes, una familia de pobres', *Aspectos históricos*, pp. 39–41

Eire, Carlos M. N., *From Madrid to Purgatory: The Art and Craft of Dying in Sixteenth-Century Spain* (Cambridge: Cambridge University Press, 1995)

Estrada, Francisco López, 'Volando en las alturas: Persecución de una imagen poética en San Juan de la Cruz', *Presencia*, pp. 265–89

Falk, Marcia, *The Song of Songs: A New Translation and Interpretation* (San Francisco: HarperSanFrancisco, 1990)

Fernández, Luis Miguel, 'El desdoblamiento en la "Llama de amor viva" (una cala en la canción tercera)', *Actas*, I, pp. 387–98

Forcione, Alban K., *Cervantes and the Humanist Vision: A Study of Four 'Exemplary Novels'* (Princeton: Princeton University Press, 1982)

Frenk, Margit (ed.), *Lírica española de tipo popular*, (Madrid: Cátedra, 1994)

Fuentes, F. Gómez Menor, *El linaje familiar de Santa Teresa y de San Juan de la Cruz* (Toledo: Gráficas Cervantes, 1970)

Fumagalli, María Cristina, 'The Eternal Fountain of Poetic Imagination: Seamus Heaney's Translation of Juan de la Cruz's "Cantar de la alma que se huelga de conoscer a Dios por fee"', *Agenda*, 35 (no. 2), pp. 162–73

Gaitán, José Damián, '*Subida del monte Carmelo*', in *Introducción a la lectura de San Juan de la Cruz*, pp. 361–99

Gale, Glen R. (ed.), *Sebastián de Córdoba: Garcilaso a lo divino*, (Ann Arbor: University of Michigan, 1971)

Garnica, Manuel Muñoz, *San Juan de la Cruz: Ensayo histórico* (Jaén: Rubio, 1875)

Garrido, Pablo María, 'Francisco de Yepes, hermano de San Juan de la Cruz: Un juglar "a lo divino"', *'Juan de la Cruz, espíritu de llama'*, pp. 63–83

Garrido, Pablo María, 'El solar carmelitano de San Juan de la Cruz', in *'Juan de la Cruz, espíritu de llama'*, pp. 85–109

Garrido, Pablo María, 'El convento carmelita de Santa Ana de Medina del Campo: Presencia e irradiación sanjuanistas', *SJC*, 9 (1993), pp. 9–26

Garrido, Pablo María, 'La biografía de San Juan de la Cruz: Nuevas precisiones y correcciones', *SJC*, 13 (1994), pp. 33–71

Gil y Zárate, Antonio, *Manual de literatura*, 10th edn (Madrid: Gaspar y Roig, 1862)

Goudreau, Marie M. *Mysticism and Image in St John of the Cross* (Frankfurt: Peter Lang, 1976)

Goytisolo, Juan, 'Palmera y mandrágora (Notas sobre la poética de José Ángel Valente)', in *El sol a medianoche*, pp. 205–11

Goytisolo, Juan, *Las virtudes del pájaro solitario* (Barcelona: Seix Barral, 1988)

Granada, Fray Luis de, *Introducción del Símbolo de la Fe*, ed. José María Balcells (Madrid: Cátedra, 1989)

Grierson, H. J. C. and Bullough, G. (eds), *The Oxford Book of Seventeenth-Century Verse* (Oxford: Clarendon, 1934)

Guerra, Augusto, 'Para la integración existencial de la *Noche oscura*', in *Experiencia y pensamiento*, pp. 225–50

Guillén, Jorge, *Lenguaje y poesía* (Cambridge, Mass.: Harvard University Press, 1961)

Hamilton, Alastair, *Heresy and Mysticism in Sixteenth-Century Spain: The Alumbrados* (Cambridge: James Clarke, 1992)

Hamilton, Walter (trans.), *Plato: Phaedrus & Letters VII and VIII* (Harmondsworth: Penguin, 1973)

Handley, Paul (ed.), *The English Spirit* (London: Darton, Longman and Todd, 1988)

Hardman, Sister Anne, *Life of the Venerable Anne of Jesus* (London: Sands, 1932)

Hart, Henry, *The Poetry of Geoffrey Hill* (Carbondale: Southern Illinois, 1986)

Hatzfeld, Helmut, *Estudios literarios sobre mística española*, 2nd edn, Biblioteca románica hispánica (Madrid: Gredos, 1968)

Hayward, John (ed.), *John Donne* (Harmondsworth: Penguin, 1950)

Heaney, Seamus, *Station Island* (London: Faber and Faber, 1984)

Hepper, F. Nigel, *Illustrated Encyclopedia of Bible Plants* (London: InterVarsity Press, 1992)

Hermida, Jacobo Sanz, 'El *passer solitarius* sanjuanista, algunos aspectos', *Actas* I, pp. 309–23

Hill, Christopher, *The English Bible and the Seventeenth Century* (London: Allen Lane, 1993)

Hill, Geoffrey, *Collected Poems* (Harmondsworth: Penguin, 1985)

Howe, Elizabeth Teresa, *Mystical Imagery: Santa Teresa de Jesús and San Juan de la Cruz* (New York: Peter Lang, 1988)

Hudleston, Dom Roger (ed.), *The Spiritual Letters of Dom John Chapman*, 2nd edn (London: Sheed and Ward, 1941)

Huerga, Álvaro, *Los alumbrados de Baeza* (Jaén: Diputación Provincial, 1978)

Irenaeus, St, *Sancti Irenæi Episcopi Lugdunensis: Libri Quinque Adversus Hæreses*, 2 vols (Cambridge: Typis Academicis, 1857)

James, William, *The Varieties of Religious Experience* (London: Collins, 1960 [1902])

Javierre, José María, *Juan de la Cruz: Un caso límite* (Salamanca: Sígueme, 1992)

Jennings, Elizabeth, *A Sense of the World* (London: André Deutsch, 1958)

Jennings, Elizabeth, *Every Changing Shape* (London: André Deutsch, 1961; [repr.] Manchester: Carcanet, 1996)

Jennings, Elizabeth, *Collected Poems, 1967* (London: Macmillan, 1967)

Jennings, Elizabeth, *Song for a Birth or a Death*, (London: André Deutsch, 1981)

Jesús, Crisógono de, *Vida de San Juan de la Cruz* (Madrid: BAC, 1946)

Jesús María, José de (Quiroga), *Historia de la vida y virtudes del Venerable Padre Fr. Juan de la Cruz* (Brussels: Jean Meerbeeck, 1628)

Jesús María, Juan de, '"Le amará tanto como es amada"', *EphCarm*, 6 (1955), pp. 3–103

Jésus-Marie, Bruno de, *Saint Jean de la Croix* (Paris: Plon, 1929)

Jones, R. O., *The Golden Age: Prose and Poetry* in *A Literary History of Spain* (London: Ernest Benn, 1971)

Jordan, William B. and Cherry, Peter, *Spanish Still Life from Velázquez to Goya* (London: National Gallery, 1995)

Josipovici, Gabriel, *The World and the Book*, 2nd edn (London: Macmillan, 1979)

Julian, John (ed.), *A Dictionary of Hymnology* (London: John Murray, 1892)

Kagan, Richard L., *Students and Society in Early Modern Spain* (Baltimore: Johns Hopkins, 1974)

Katz, Steven T. (ed.) *Mysticism and Philosophical Analysis* (London: Sheldon, 1978)

Katz, Steven T. (ed.) *Mysticism and Language* (New York: Oxford University Press, 1992)

Kavanaugh, Kieran and Rodríguez, Otilio (trans.), *The Collected Works of St. John of the Cross*, revised edn (Washington, DC: ICS, 1991)

Keenan, Brian, *An Evil Cradling* (London: Arrow, 1993)

Knowles, Dom David, *The English Mystical Tradition* (London: Burns & Oates, 1961)

Laredo, Bernardino de, *La subida del monte Sión*, in *Místicos franciscanos españoles*, 3 vols (Madrid: BAC, 1948–49)

Leclercq, Jean, *The Love of Learning and the Desire for God* (London: SPCK, 1978 [New York: Fordham University Press, 1961])

Lee, Desmond (trans.), *Plato: The Republic*, Penguin Classics, 2nd edn (Harmondsworth: Penguin, 1974)

León, Fray Luis de, *Obras completas castellanas*, edited by Félix García, 2 vols, 4th edn (Madrid: BAC, 1957)

López-Baralt, Luce, *San Juan de la Cruz y el Islam* (Mexico: El Colegio de Mexico, 1985)

López-Baralt, Luce, *Huellas del Islam en la literatura española: De Juan Ruiz a Juan Goytisolo* (Madrid: Hiperión, 1985)

López-Baralt, Luce, *Asedios a lo indecible: San Juan de la Cruz canta al éxtasis transformante* (Madrid: Trotta, 1998)

Lora, José Luis Sánchez, *San Juan de la Cruz en la revolución copernicana* (Madrid: Espiritualidad, 1992)

Lorca, Francisco García, *La escondida senda: de fray Luis a San Juan* (Madrid: Castalia, 1972)

Louth, Andrew, *The Origins of the Christian Mystical Tradition* (Oxford: Oxford University Press, 1981)

Louth, Andrew, *Denys the Areopagite* (London: Geoffrey Chapman, 1989)

Lozano, J. Jiménez, *San Juan de la Cruz: Poesía completa* (Madrid: Taurus, 1983)

Maccise, Camilo, 'Lectura latinoamericana de San Juan de la Cruz desde una perspectiva liberadora', in *Experiencia y pensamiento*, pp. 271–95

McCarthy, John and Morrell, Jill, *Some Other Rainbow*, Corgi Books (London: Transworld, 1993)

McGinn, Bernard, *The Foundations of Mysticism* (London: SCM Press, 1992)

McKenrick, Melveena, *Theatre in Spain: 1490–1700* (Cambridge: Cambridge University Press, 1989)

Mackenzie, Ann L., 'Upon Two "Dark Nights": Allison Peers' Translations of "En una noche oscura"', *BHS*, 62 (1985), pp. 270–9

McNeill, John T. (ed.), *Calvin: Institutes of the Christian Religion*, 2 vols (Philadelphia: Westminster, 1960)

Macpherson, Ian, '"Rompe la tela de este dulce encuentro": San Juan's *Llama de amor viva* and the Courtly Context', in *Studies in Honor of Bruce W. Wardropper*, edited by Dian Fox, Harry Sieber and Robert Ter Horst (Newark, Delaware : Juan de la Cuesta, 1989)

Mancho, María Jesús and Pascual, José Antonio, 'La recepción inicial del 'Cántico espiritual' a través de las variantes manuscritas del texto', *Actas*, I, pp. 107–22

Marín, Francisco María Martínez, *Compendio histórico de la vida [. . .] del Doctor San Juan de la Cruz* (Cuenca: Gómez, 1875)

Martín, Alberto Marcos, 'San Juan de la Cruz y su ambiente de pobreza', *Actas*, II, pp. 143–84

Martin, L. C. (ed.), *The Poems of Richard Crashaw*, 2nd edn (Oxford: Clarendon Press, 1957)

Martín, Luis Fernández, 'El colegio de los jesuitas en Medina del Campo', in *'Juan de la Cruz, espíritu de llama'*, pp. 41–61

Martz, Louis L. (ed.), *George Herbert and Henry Vaughan*, The Oxford Authors (Oxford: Oxford University Press, 1986)

Martz, Louis L. (ed.) *George Herbert and Henry Vaughan*, The Oxford Authors (Oxford: Oxford University Press, 1986)

Matthew, Iain, 'The Knowledge and Consciousness of Christ in the Light of the Writings of St John of the Cross' (unpublished D. Phil. thesis, University of Oxford, 1991)

Mendoza, J. Carlos Vizuete, 'La prisión de San Juan de la Cruz: El convento del Carmen de Toledo en 1577 y 1578', *Actas*, II, pp. 427–36

Menéndez y Pelayo, Marcelino, *San Isidoro, Cervantes y otros estudios*, 3a edn (Madrid: Espasa-Calpe, 1947)

Molina, Francisco Contreras, 'El Cantar de los Cantares y el Cántico espiritual', *SJC*, 11 (1993), pp. 27–73

Morel-Fatio, Alfred, 'Les lectures de Sainte Thérèse', *BH*, 10 (1908), pp. 17–67

Moriones, Ildefonso, *Ana de Jésus y la herencia teresiana: ¿humanismo cristiano o rigor primitivo?* (Rome: Teresianum, 1968)

Morros, Bienvenido (ed.) *Garcilaso de la Vega: Obra poética y textos en prosa* (Barcelona: Crítica, 1995)

Nalle, Sara T., 'Literacy and Culture in Early Modern Castile', *Past and Present*, 125 (1989), pp. 65–96

Neruda, Pablo, *Veinte poemas de amor y una canción desesperada* (Buenos Aires: Losada, 1944 [1924])

New Sunday Missal, The (London: Geoffrey Chapman, 1982)

Nieto, José C., 'Mystical theology and "salvation-history" in John of the Cross: two conflicting methods of biblical interpretation', *BHR*, 36 (1974), pp. 17–32

Nieto, José C., *San Juan de la Cruz: Poeta del amor profano* (San Lorenzo de El Escorial: Swan, 1988)

O'Connor, J. Murphy, *The Holy Land* (Oxford: Oxford University Press, 1986)

O'Connor, J. (trans.), *The Song of the Soul* (Capel-y-ffin, Abergavenny, 1927)

Olmedo, F., *Juan Bonifacio (1538–1606) y la cultura literaria del Siglo de Oro* (Santander: Sociedad de Menéndez Pelayo, 1939)

O'Malley, John W., *The First Jesuits* (Cambridge, Mass: Harvard University Press, 1993)

O'Reilly, Terence, 'The literary and devotional context of the *Pastorcico*', *FMLS*, 18 (1982), pp. 363–70

O'Reilly, Terence, 'San Juan de la Cruz y la lectura de la Biblia: el *romance* "Encima de las corrientes"', *Actas*, I, pp. 221–31

O'Reilly, Terence, 'St John of the Cross and the Traditions of Monastic Exegesis', *Leeds Papers on Saint John of the Cross*, edited by Margaret A. Rees (Leeds: Trinity and All Saints College, 1991), pp. 105–26

O'Reilly, Terence, 'Courtly Love and Mysticism in Spanish Poetry of the Golden Age', *JHR*, 1 (1992–3), pp. 53–76

O'Reilly, Terence, *From Ignatius Loyola to John of the Cross* (Aldershot and Brookfield, VT: Variorum, 1995)

Oro, José García, *La reforma de los religiosos españoles en tiempo de los Reyes Católicos* (Valladolid: Instituto 'Isabel la Católica', 1969)

Oro, José García, 'Observantes, recoletos, descalzos: La monarquía católica y el reformismo religioso del siglo XVI', *Actas*, II, pp. 53–97

Orozco, Emilio, *Poesía y mística* (Madrid: Guadarrama, 1959)

Ortega y Gasset, José, *Obras completas*, 12 vols (Madrid, Revista de Occidente, Alianza: 1946–83)

Ovid, *Metamorphoses*, trans. Frank Justus Miller, Loeb Classical Library, 3rd edn (Cambridge, Mass: Harvard University Press, 1977)

Pacho, Eulogio, *San Juan de la Cruz y sus escritos* (Madrid: Cristiandad, 1969)

Pacho, Eulogio, *San Juan de la Cruz: Obras completas* (Burgos: Monte Carmelo, 1982)

Pacho, Eulogio, *Reto a la crítica: Debate histórico sobre el Cántico espiritual de s. Juan de la Cruz* (Burgos: Monte Carmelo, 1988)

Pacho, Eulogio, 'Nuevo manuscrito del "Cántico espiritual"', *El Monte Carmelo,* 99 (1991), pp. 243–71

Pacho, Eulogio, 'Hagiografías y biografías de San Juan de la Cruz', *Actas*, II, pp. 119–42

Pacho, Eulogio, 'Cántico espiritual', in *Introducción a la lectura de San Juan de la Cruz*, pp. 443–91

Parker, A. A., *Luis de Góngora: Polyphemus and Galatea* (Edinburgh: Edinburgh University Press, 1977)

Payne, Steven, 'The Christian Character of Christian Mystical Experience', *Religious Studies*, 20 (1984), pp. 417–27

Payne, Steven, *John of the Cross and the Cognitive Value of Mysticism* (Dordrecht: Klouwer, 1990)

Payne, Steven, 'The Relationship between Public Revelation and Private Revelation in the Theology of Saint John of the Cross', *Teresianum*, 43 (1992), pp. 175–215

Peers, E. Allison, *Spirit of Flame: A Study of St. John of the Cross* (London: SCM Press, 1943)

Peers, E. Allison (trans.), *The Complete Works of Saint John of the Cross*, 3 vols (London: Burns, Oates & Washbourne, 1934–35); [repr. 1 vol] (Wheathampstead: Anthony Clarke, 1974)

Peers, E. Allison (trans.), *The Poems of St John of the Cross* (London: Burns & Oates, 1947)

Pérez, Serafín Puerta, 'Manifestaciones literarias en las fiestas sanjuanistas', *SJC*, 15–16 (1995), pp. 109–60

Perrin, David Brian, *Canciones entre el alma y el Esposo of Juan de la Cruz: A Hermeneutical Interpretation* (San Francisco: Catholic Scholars Press, 1996)

Pikaza, Xavier, 'Amor de Dios y contemplación cristiana: Introducción a San Juan de la Cruz', *Actas*, III, pp. 51–96

Polo, Gaspar Gil, *Diana enamorada*, edited by Rafael Ferreres, Clásicos castellanos (Madrid: Espasa-Calpe, 1953)

Polo, Teodoro, *San Juan de la Cruz: La fuerza de un decir* (Madrid: Espiritualidad,1993)

[pseudo-Aquinas] *S. Thomae Aquinatis: Opera omnia*, edited by Roberto Busa, S.I., 7 vols (Stuttgart-Bad Cannstadt: Fromann-Holzboog, 1980)

[pseudo-Augustine] *Liber soliloquiorum animae ad Deum* (PL 40, 863–98)
[pseudo-Augustine] *The Soliloquies of St. Augustine*, translated by L.M.F.G. (Edinburgh: Sands & Co, 1912)

Rejoice and Sing (Oxford: Oxford University Press, 1991)
Ricard, Robert, '"La Fonte" de Saint Jean de la Croix et un chapitre de Laredo', *BH*, 58 (1956), pp. 265–74
Rizzuto, Ana María, 'Reflexiones psicoanalíticas acerca de la experiencia mística', en *El sol a medianoche*, pp. 61–75
Rodríguez, José Vicente, 'Demonios y exorcismos, duendes y otras presencias diabólicas en la vida de San Juan de la Cruz', *Actas*, II, pp. 295–346
Rodríguez, José Vicente, 'Historiografía sanjuanista', *Aspectos históricos*, pp. 7–24
Rodríguez, Luis Enrique-San Pedro Bezares, *La formación universitaria de Juan de la Cruz* (Valladolid: Junta de Castilla y León, 1992)
Ruiz, Federico (ed.), *Dios habla en la noche* (Madrid: Espiritualidad, 1990)
Ruiz, Federico, 'Vida y experiencia carmelitana en los escritos de San Juan de la Cruz', in '*Juan de la Cruz, espíritu de llama*', pp. 673–86
Russell, P. E. (ed.), *Spain: A Companion to Spanish Studies* (London: Methuen, 1973)

San José, Jerónimo de, *Historia del Venerable Padre Fr. Juan de la Cruz* (Madrid: Diego Díaz de la Carrera, 1641)
San Juan de la Cruz, *San Juan de la Cruz: Manuscrito de Jaén*, 2 vols (Junta de Andalucía, Madrid: Turner, 1991)
San Juan de la Cruz, *San Juan de la Cruz: Manuscrito de Sanlúcar de Barrameda*, 2 vols (Junta de Andalucía, Madrid: Turner 1991)
San Román, Juan Bosco, 'El tercer centenario de la muerte de San Juan de la Cruz (1891) en España', *Teresianum*, 42 (1991), pp. 185–226
Sánchez, Manuel Diego, *San Juan de la Cruz: Bibliografía del IV Centenario de su muerte (1989–1993)* (Rome: Teresianum, 1993)
Sánchez, Patrocinio Ríos, 'Un protestante ante dos místicos: San Juan de la Cruz y fray Luis de León', *Revista agustiniana*, 32 (1991), pp. 1067–93
Santa Salomé, Gregorio de, *Vida del extático Padre San Juan de la Cruz* (Madrid: Asilo de Huérfanos del S.C. de Jesús, 1884)
Santa Teresa, Silverio de (ed.), *Obras de San Juan de la Cruz*, Biblioteca Mística Carmelitana, X–XIV (Burgos: El Monte Carmelo, 1929–31)
Sarmiento, Edward, *Three Translations from St. John of the Cross* (Ware: Carmel, 1976)
Saura, Carlos, *La noche oscura* (Murcia: Mundografic, 1993) [videorecording]
Senabre, Ricardo, 'Sobre la composición del Cántico espiritual', *Actas*, I, pp. 95–106
Sesé, Bernard, 'Estructura dramática de la *Noche oscura* (tres aspectos del poema)', *Actas*, I, pp. 245–56
Sismondi, J. C. L., *De la littérature du midi de l'Europe* (Paris: Treuttel et Würtz, 1813)
Smart, Elizabeth, *By Grand Central Station I Sat Down and Wept* (London: HarperCollins, 1991 [1945])
Smet, Joachim, *The Carmelites: A History of the Brothers of Our Lady of Mount Carmel*, 5 vols (Darien, IL: The Carmelite Press, 1988)
Stace, W. T., *Mysticism and Philosophy* (London: Macmillan, 1961)

Staring, Adrianus (ed.) 'Nicholas of France, *Sagitta ignea*', *Carmelus*, 9 (1962), pp. 237–307

Steggink, Otger, 'Arraigo de fray Juan de la Cruz en la Orden del Carmen', in '*Juan de la Cruz, espíritu de llama*', pp. 129–55

Steggink, Otger, 'Fray Juan de la Cruz, carmelita contemplativo: vida y magisterio', *Actas*, II, pp. 251–69

Steggink, Otger, 'Dos corrientes de reforma en el Carmelo español del siglo XVI: La observancia y la descalcez, frente a la "Reforma del rey"', *Aspectos históricos*, pp. 117–42

Stewart, Stanley, *The Enclosed Garden: The Tradition and the Image in Seventeenth-Century Poetry* (Madison: University of Wisconsin, 1966)

Sullivan, J., 'Night and Light: the Poet John of the Cross and the *Exultet* of the Easter Liturgy', *EphCarm*, 30 (1979), pp. 52–68

Sullivan, Lawrence, 'The *Moralia* of Pope St Gregory the Great and its Influence on St John of the Cross (A General Approach)', *EphCarm*, 27 (1976), pp. 453–88; 28 (1977) pp. 59–103

Symons, Arthur, 'The Poetry of Santa Teresa and San Juan de la Cruz', *The Contemporary Review*, 75 (1899), pp. 542–51

Tapia, Serafín de, 'El entorno morisco de San Juan de la Cruz', *Aspectos históricos*, pp. 43–76

Tapia, Serafín de, 'Las primeras letras y el analfabetismo en Castilla. Siglo XVI', *Actas*, II, pp. 185–220

Tarn, Nathaniel (trans.), *Selected Poems. Pablo Neruda* (London: Jonathan Cape, 1970)

Tavard, George, *Poetry and Contemplation in St John of the Cross* (Athens: Ohio University Press, 1988)

Terry, Arthur, 'Reading Valente: A Preface to *Tres lecciones de tinieblas*', in *Hispanic Studies in Honour of Geoffrey Ribbans*, *BHS* (1992), pp. 325–34

Thompson, C. P., *The Poet and the Mystic* (Oxford: Oxford University Press, 1977)

Thompson, C. P., *El poeta y el místico* (El Escorial: Swan, 1985)

Thompson, C. P., *The Strife of Tongues* (Cambridge: Cambridge University Press, 1988)

Thompson, C. P., *La lucha de las lenguas* (Valladolid: Junta de Castilla y León, 1995)

Thompson, C. P., 'The Many Paradoxes of the Mystics', in *Homenaje a Eugenio Asensio*, edited by Luisa López Grigera y Augustin Redondo (Madrid: Gredos, 1988), pp. 471–85

Thompson, C. P., 'San Juan de la Cruz, Freud and the human soul', in *Conflicts of Discourse*, edited by Peter W. Evans (Manchester: Manchester University Press, 1990), pp. 166–83

Thompson, C. P., '"Aminadab tampoco parecía": presencia y ausencia en el "Cántico" y en el "Cantar"', *Ínsula*, 537 (septiembre 1991), pp. 10–11

Thompson, C. P., 'La tradición mística occidental: dos corrientes distintas en la poesía de San Juan de la Cruz y fray Luis de León', *Edad de Oro*, 11 (1992), pp. 187–94

Thompson, C. P., 'El mundo metafórico de San Juan', *Actas*, I, pp. 75–93

Thompson, C. P., '"The Resonances of Words": Lope de Vega and Geoffrey Hill', *MLR*, 90 (1995), pp. 55–70

Thompson, C. P., 'La presencia de san Juan de la Cruz en la literatura del siglo XX: España e Inglaterra', in *El sol a medianoche*, pp. 189–203

Thompson, C. P., 'Translation and the Art of Poetry: *Cancionero* Poetry and Geoffrey Hill's "The Pentecost Castle" (1979)', *BHS*, 85 (1998), pp. 31–54

Thornton, Martin, *English Spirituality* (London: SPCK, 1963)

Ticknor, George, *History of Spanish Literature*, 3 vols (London: John Murray, 1849)

Tillmans, W. G., *De aanwezigheid van het bijbels in het "Cántico espiritual" van San Juan de la Cruz* (Brussels: Paleis der Academiën, 1967)
Torres Sánchez, Concha, *Ana de Jesús (1545–1621)* (Madrid: Orto, 1999)
Trueman Dicken, E. W., *The Crucible of Love* (London: Darton, Longman and Todd, 1963)
Turner, Denys, *The Darkness of God* (Cambridge: Cambridge University Press, 1995)
Tuve, Rosamund, *A Reading of George Herbert* (London: Faber & Faber, 1952)

Unamuno, Miguel de, *En torno al casticismo*, 6th edn (Madrid: Espasa-Calpe, 1964)

Valente, José Angel, 'Una nota sobre relaciones literarias hispano-inglesas en el siglo XVII', in *La piedra y el centro* (Madrid: Taurus, 1982), pp. 113–21
Vassberg, David E., *Land and Society in Golden Age Castile*, Cambridge Iberian and Latin American Studies (Cambridge: Cambridge University Press, 1984)
Vaughan, Robert Alfred, *Hours with the Mystics*, 2 vols (London: John W. Parker & Son, 1856)
Vázquez Núñez, Guillermo, 'Fray Gaspar de Torres', *Mercedarios ilustres* (Madrid: Revista Estudios, 1966), pp. 281–9
Velasco, José de, *Vida y virtudes del Venerable Varón Francisco de Yepes* (Valladolid: Godínez de Milles, 1616; Jerónimo Murillo, 1617)
Velasco, Juan Martín, 'Experiencia de Dios desde la situación y la conciencia de la ausencia', *Actas*, III, pp. 213–47
Vilnet, Jean, *Bible et mystique chez saint Jean de la Croix* (Desclée de Brouwer: Paris, 1949)

Whinnom, Keith, *A Glossary of Spanish Bird-Names* (London: Tamesis, 1966)
White, T. H., *The Book of Beasts* (Gloucester: Alan Sutton, 1984 [Jonathan Cape, 1954])
Williams, George H., *Wilderness and Paradise in Christian Thought* (New York: Harper, 1962)
Williams, Rowan, *The Wound of Knowledge* (London: Darton, Longman and Todd, 1979)
Wilmart, A., *Auteurs spirituels et textes dévots du Moyen Age latin* (Paris: Études Augustiniennes, 1971 [1932])
Wilson, Margaret, *San Juan de la Cruz: Poems* (London: Grant and Cutler, 1975)
Wind, Edgar, *Pagan Mysteries in the Renaissance*, revised edn (Oxford: Oxford University Press, 1980)
Wolters, Clifton (trans.), *Julian of Norwich: Revelations of Divine Love*, Penguin Classics (Harmondsworth: Penguin, 1966)
Wolters, Clifton (trans.), *The Cloud of Unknowing*, Penguin Classics (Harmondsworth: Penguin, 1961)
Wolters, Clifton (trans.), *Rolle: The Fire of Love*, Penguin Classics (Harmondsworth: Penguin, 1972)Woodward, L. J., 'Verb Tense and Sequential Time in the *Cántico espiritual* of San Juan de la Cruz', *FMLS*, 27 (1991), pp. 148–58
Woodward, L. J., 'Verb Tense and Sequential Time in the *Cántico espiritual* of San Juan de la Cruz', *FMLS*, 27 (1991), pp. 148–58.

Ynduráin, Domingo (ed.), *San Juan de la Cruz: Poesía* (Madrid: Cátedra, 1989)
Ynduráin, Domingo, *Humanismo y Renacimiento en España* (Madrid: Cátedra, 1994)
Ynduráin, Domingo, 'El pájaro solitario', *Actas* I, pp. 143–61

Zaehner, R. C., *Mysticism Sacred and Profane* (Oxford: Clarendon Press, 1957)
Zambrano, María, *Filosofía y poesía* (México: Fondo de Cultura Económica, 1987 [1939])

Index of Biblical Citations from the Vulgate [Authorized Version]

Index of Names and Subjects